W9-BCK-352

The Negro in American History

I.   BLACK AMERICANS 1928-1971

II. A TASTE OF FREEDOM 1854-1927

III. SLAVES AND MASTERS 1567-1854

Mortimer J. Adler *General Editor*

Charles Van Doren *Editor*

George Ducas *Executive Editor*

E185
N 4
v. 1

The Negro in American History

I. BLACK AMERICANS 1928-1971

With an introduction by Saunders Redding

ENCYCLOPAEDIA BRITANNICA EDUCATIONAL CORPORATION

William Benton *Publisher*

JAN 2 9 1975

186069

Copyright © 1969, 1972 by Encyclopaedia Britannica Educational Corporation

ALL RIGHTS RESERVED

Library of Congress Catalog Number: 68-56369
International Standard Book Number: 0-87827-007-8

Printed in the United States of America

This work may not be transmitted by television or other devices or processes nor copied, recast, transformed or adapted, in whole or in part, without permission in writing from the publisher.

The editors wish to express their gratitude for permission to reprint material from the following sources:

Kenneth Allsop for the selection on pp. 290-297, from *Encounter*, April 1960. Amsco Music Publishing Company for the lyric on pp. 376-377, from *This Singing Land*, compiled and ed. by Irwin Silber, © 1965 Amsco Music Publishing Co. *Army* Magazine for the selection on pp. 129-135, by Robert B. Rigg, Copyright © 1968 by Association of the United States Army. *Atlanta Magazine* for the selection on pp. 39-48, © 1969 *Atlanta Magazine*, reprinted by permission. Bantam Books for the selection on pp. 35-39 from *Soledad Brother: the Prison Letters of George Jackson*, copyright © 1970 by World Enterprises Limited, published by Coward, McCann, and Geoghegan, Inc. and Bantam Books, Inc. Basic Books, Inc. for the selection on pp. 55-65, from *Black Rage*, by William H. Grier and Price M. Cobbs, © 1968 by William H. Grier and Price M. Cobbs, Basic Books, Inc., Publishers, New York. Brandt & Brandt for the selection on pp. 406-416, from *A Southerner Discovers the South*, by Jonathan Daniels, The Macmillan Company, Copyright 1938 by Jonathan Daniels. The Chicago Tribune for the selection by Jesse Jackson on pp. 16-21.

The Christian Century for the selection on pp.239-247, by Martin Luther King, Jr., Copyright © 1963 by the Christian Century Foundation. Columbia University Press for the lyric on p. 392, from *Negro Folk Music, U.S.A.*, ed. by Harold Courlander. The Crisis Publishing Company for the selection on pp. 164-167, by Roy Wilkins, from *The Crisis*, September 1966. Joan Daves for the selection on pp. 65-75, by Martin Luther King, Jr., from *Look*, Copyright © 1968 by Cowles Communications, Inc. Also for the selection on pp. 224-228, by Martin Luther King, Jr., from *The SCLC Story in Words and Pictures*, Copyright © 1963 by Martin Luther King, Jr. The Devin-Adair Company for the selection on pp. 277-289, from *The Case for the South*, by William D. Workman, Jr., Copyright © 1960 by William D. Workman, Jr. The Dial Press, Inc. for the selection on pp. 234-238, from *The Fire Next Time*, by James Baldwin, Copyright © 1963, 1962 by James Baldwin.

Harper & Row, Publishers, for the selection on pp. 254-259, abridged from *The Negro Revolt*, by Louis E. Lomax, Copyright © 1962 by Louis E. Lomax. Also for the selection on pp. 377-387, from *An American Dilemma*, Vol. II, by Gunnar Myrdal, Copyright 1944 by Harper & Row, Publishers, Incorporated. Also for the selection on pp. 416-437, from *Black Boy*, by Richard Wright, Copyright 1937, 1942, 1944, 1945 by Richard Wright. Hill and Wang, Inc. for the selection on pp. 361-363, from *The Best of Simple*, by Langston Hughes, © 1961 by Langston Hughes. Houghton Mifflin Company for the selection on pp. 297-306, from *Black Like Me*, by John Howard Griffin, Copyright © 1960, 1961 by John Howard Griffin.

Grace Nail Johnson for the selection on pp. 451-462, by James Weldon Johnson, Copyright © 1928 by Harper's Magazine, Inc. Reprinted from the November 1928 issue of *Harper's Magazine* by special permission.

The Macmillan Company for the selection on pp. 260-268, from *The Other America*, by Michael Harrington, © Michael Harrington 1962. Also for the selection on pp. 306-318, from *Black Bourgeoisie: The Rise of a New Middle Class in the United States*, by E. Franklin Frazier, Copyright 1957 by The Free Press, a Corporation, Copyright © 1962 by The Free Press, a division of The Macmillan Company. Also for the selection on pp. 397-405, from *Father of the Blues*, by W. C. Handy, Copyright 1941 by W. C. Handy. Merit Publishers and Betty Shabazz for the selection on pp. 216-224, from *Malcolm X Speaks: Selected Speeches and Statements*, ed. by George Breitman, Copyright © 1965 by Merit Publishers and Betty Shabazz. *Muhammad Speaks* (newspaper) for the material on pp. 76-81, by Elijah Muhammad *et al.*, from the Aug. 16, 1968 issue.

National Review, 150 East 35th Street, New York, N.Y. 10016, for the selection on pp. 121-128, by Mark Edelson, © National Review, Inc., 1968. *The New York Review of Books* for the selection on pp. 135-153, Copyright © 1967 by Tom Hayden. *The New York Times* for the selection on pp. 87-93, by Thomas A. Johnson, © 1968 by The New York Times Company. Oak Publications for the lyrics of: "Oh Freedom," "We Shall Not Be Moved," "Keep Your Eyes on the Prize," "Woke Up This Morning with My Mind Stayed on Freedom," "Ain't Gonna Let Nobody Turn Me Round," "This Little Light of Mine," on pp. 248-252, from *We Shall Overcome!* Songs of the Southern Freedom Movement, compiled by Guy and Candie Carawan for the Student Nonviolent Coordinating Committee. The Organization of American Historians for the selection on pp. 48-52 by C. Vann Woodward, reprinted from "Clio with Soul," the *Journal of American History*, pp. 5-20, June 1969. *Playboy* Magazine for the interview with Ray Charles on pp. 27-34, copyright 1970 by Playboy.

The Progressive for the selection on pp. 269-274, by James Farmer, Copyright 1968 The Progressive magazine, Madison, Wisconsin. Marion H. Sass for the selection on pp. 323-331, by Herbert Ravenel Sass, from *The Atlantic Monthly*, November 1956, Copyright © 1956 by the Atlantic Monthly Company, Boston, Mass. Student Nonviolent Coordinating Committee for the selection on pp. 154-164, by Stokely Carmichael, from *The New York Review of Books*, September 22, 1966.

Contents

Editors' Preface

This set of books contains 186 selections by 134 different authors, ranging over almost exactly 400 years of American history. Each selection is prefaced by a short contextual headnote describing the historical circumstances that gave rise to it, and suggesting its relation to events of the time in which it first appeared. The selections are reprinted in reverse chronological order, beginning (in Vol. 1) with the present and extending (in Vol. 3) back to the middle of the sixteenth century. A short biographical sketch of every author in the set appears at the end of the volume in which a selection by him is reprinted. Some of the authors are black and some are white, but their subject is always the role of the black man in the life of this continent or – in a few cases – of this hemisphere.

In certain respects the set bears a close resemblance to another collection that Encyclopaedia Britannica is bringing out at the same time. *The Annals of America* is a 20-volume set of books containing over 2,200 different selections, by 1,100 authors, and including a two-volume Conspectus, or topical index of Great Issues in American life. The selections in the *Annals* are also prefaced by short contextual headnotes. In fact, 165 of the selections in the present set are reprinted (some with minor editorial changes) from the parent set; the headnotes are in most cases the same; and many of the biographical sketches are carried over verbatim from the larger collection.

Indeed, *The Negro in American History* is but the first in a series of books that will be drawn from the *Annals*. The parent set, produced under the general editorship of Mortimer J. Adler, contains the makings of many collections of source materials on specialized subjects and themes. In the present instance, the subject chosen was of great importance for contemporary Americans. On other occasions and in other times it will be found desirable to produce collections on other subjects, as well.

However, although this set has many similarities to the *Annals*, it also differs from it in significant respects. Some 21 of the selections that appear in these pages are new – that is, they do not appear in the *Annals* – and they altogether account for somewhat less than one-fifth of the whole, since many of the new additions are relatively long. Furthermore, the ordering of the selections is wholly different. But it is the fact that all of the selections in these volumes bear on the same subject that gives the collection its real novelty. To some extent, at least, the appearance of the very same material in the *Annals*, intermixed, as it there is, with a much greater amount of material on other subjects and themes, tends to divert the reader's or student's attention from the problem, or complex of problems, with which this set deals. The effect of reprinting over 400,000 words of writing by Americans all on the same subject serves to isolate that subject, to illuminate it, and to identify those aspects of it that require either thought or action at the present time.

The teaching of American history in U.S. schools and colleges is undergoing radical change at the present time. A generation ago, teachers everywhere, on all educational levels but the highest (and even in some universities), were largely dependent on textbooks for the substance of their courses, and this was particularly true, of course, in high schools. This was partly because many teachers were themselves not very well acquainted with American history, partly because their own training had been accomplished primarily with the help of textbooks, and partly because students, on the whole, reacted more predictably to the careful mental pigeon-holing that a textbook can produce. Readings were easy to assign, and tests were easy to draw up on the readings. The textbook insured that the subject matter would be "covered," and the textbook's dullness and superficiality were made up for by its apparent comprehensiveness and comprehensibility.

Most of these things are no longer true. Teachers are better prepared than ever before in our history, and students, by and large, are better too—more curious, less inclined to accept easy or pat answers, more interested in knowing about the problems of their world. (For this reason, perhaps, they may be harder to teach than they used to be!)

The problems that textbook authors face are difficult ones. The writer of such a book must try to be true to the facts at the same time that he is fair to everyone in all sections of the country. He must try to "cover" the whole of his subject at the same time that he emphasizes those aspects of it that seem most important to him. He must try to mask any personal eccentricities—of style or approach—at the same time that he writes—or attempts to write—an interesting or even compelling account. Taken all together, these are almost impossible demands. It is no wonder that most history textbooks do not succeed.

Collections of source materials, on the contrary, avoid most of these problems from the outset. They are inherently controversial, as a textbook can seldom afford to be—but the controversy they contain is the responsibility of the separate and distinct authors of the various selections, not of the supposedly impartial author or editor. They are better reading, too, because they are anthologies of the best writing available—the strongest statements, the most eloquent expressions of views that, though often conflicting, always reflect the feelings and beliefs of some readers, if not all. Last but not least, they are the very stuff of living history, not history as seen through the eyes of someone who may be very far removed from it. Thus, whatever source materials may lose in "coverage," they gain —doubly—in interest and authenticity.

Collections of original materials like the present set have other benefits as well, if less dramatic ones. Scientists often emphasize the importance of heuristic theories, methods, or procedures. Heuristic theories are ones that, although incapable of proof, are suggestive and productive of further lines of research. Heuristic methods are empirical and often promote fruitful though unexpected results. The heuristic is open-ended; there is never any telling where it will lead.

The use of source materials, as opposed to the use of a textbook, is heuristic in this sense. Fundamentally, it is an empirical approach to history. For this reason, it is more likely to turn teachers into scholars, and pupils into students. A teacher who is also a scholar — even if only temporarily — is always a better teacher. And a pupil who is also a student — curious, anxious to proceed farther than he is asked to, willing to devote extra time and effort — is always more rewarding to teach.

It seems likely, indeed, that the study of history, and particularly of American history, cannot survive as an independent discipline without the application of an heuristic approach, at least to some problems, at least some of the time. History has changed much from the gentleman's hobby that, in all but a few isolated instances, it used to be. It is now a profession — or aspires to be. For most intellectual disciplines to be professions nowadays, it is necessary that they involve experiment and research, and that they allow for, and take account of, emergent insights and discoveries. History, in short, cannot change and progress unless it deals with the real. Textbooks are images, and original sources are the real thing.

These remarks, of course, are more true of the study of certain kinds of historical subject matters than of others. They are especially true of the study of Negro history — more precisely, the study of the role of Negroes in American history. This is one area in which textbooks are likely to be not only inadequate but also dangerous. Who is to write such a textbook — a white or a black? In either case, there may be bias, perhaps concealed but nevertheless there. Even given an ideally unbiased author, from what point of view is such a book to be written? It is hard to think of any that would be totally satisfactory. Finally, any such narrative account must inevitably seem out of date within a very few years. American Negroes are making history at the present day. Next year, or the year after, we may all — white and black alike — have very different opinions and feelings about what this history means, and whither it is tending.

There are many reasons, then, to make use of source materials in the teaching of this subject, either alone or in conjunction with a good textbook. At the same time, it is important that any such collection be well edited, that it be both fair and authentic.

The selections reprinted here, although often excerpts from longer works, have all been edited with meticulous care. The great majority — indeed, all but a very few — are reprinted from originals that have been found, sometimes after great effort, in the libraries of the country; editorial cuts are always indicated by ellipses. Every attempt has been made to write contextual headnotes that describe neither more nor less than the facts. Each headnote indicates a bibliographical source; these source lines, altogether, add up to an extensive bibliography of the subject. The biographical notes on authors have been prepared with equal attention to detail. This is a set of books on which one can depend.

The claim of impartial coverage is harder to substantiate, while at the same time it is even more necessary to do so. Let it be said, at least, that *The Negro in American History* differs sharply from many other collections dealing with this subject matter that have recently appeared. Many of these are one-sided; they provide the pro, as it may be called, with the con. But the American Negro has been a subject of controversy for generations. His history cannot be understood without listening to every shade of opinion. Nor is it sufficient merely to hear his own words, in his own behalf. A history of the Irish in America could not make use only of writings by Irishmen. The history of American Jewry is partly the reactions of non-Jews, in various times and places. So with the Negro. He has been talked about, as well as having done much of the talking. And all of it is here.

Ignorance of history has many consequences, one of them being the impression that the present is newer than it really is. The naive see novelties in everything that happens. The sophisticated know that many of these things have happened before.

History does not repeat itself, but human beings stay much the same and therefore the forms of change — in the institutions and arrangements of our life — remain remarkably constant. In particular, we say the same things, though in different words, even when we think we are expressing new insights and making new discoveries.

Our awareness of change, however, is itself subject to change. That is perhaps the most important conclusion to be drawn from this collection of readings.

The very form of this set suggests it. The blacks are a problem, to themselves and to everyone else. The fact is, *they have always been a problem*. The reason is simple: injustice is wrong and makes men unhappy, whether they are unjust themselves or are subjected to unjust treatment. And few living men would deny the injustice, in both past and present.

But we have not always known this. It took Americans 300 years—roughly, the 300 years covered by the third volume of this set—to learn it (although some knew very early, and said so). Having learned it, and having paid the cost of their ignorance in a terrible war, Americans took the first hesitant steps to right the wrongs they had taken so long to see. But a century had to pass (very roughly, the period covered by the second volume) before they learned that those first steps were too hesitant, that they did not go far enough. It is only in the last generation (the period, roughly, that is covered by the first volume of the set) that they have begun to learn the whole lesson. They must go all the way. In a country that is dedicated to the proposition that all men are created equal, there must be no bars to equality for anyone.

These remarks apply to blacks as well as to whites. Only in recent years have American Negroes discovered that, in right, there are and can be no limits, short of full equality, on their demands. Inhabitants of this land for longer than most of us and the producers, in past and present, of much of its wealth, they have a fair and undeniable claim to the rights and perquisites that citizenship confers. They should and they will participate fully in the political process, they should and they will enjoy equal educational opportunities, they should and they will share the economic advantages that accrue to citizens of the United States.

Between "should" and "will," however, there is still a great gap; it is this gap that is the problem. It is a lacuna in progress, an emptiness in the otherwise eventful history of our nation and time. It is all very well for white men to urge patience. With patience, all will be achieved. But why should blacks be patient? Why should they, and they alone, have to be?

Time, it has been said, is the essence of tragedy. If Oedipus had had time to investigate, he would have enjoyed a happier fate. If Hamlet had been patient he would, in due time, have inherited the kingdom of Denmark and lived happily ever after, with Ophelia as his bride. But men do not have time. Time is our enemy; and a man's own time is not the same as that of his children.

Martin Luther King, Jr., spoke of these things in his great and impassioned "Letter from Birmingham Jail." The time, for us, is *now*, he said; waiting, for us, means never. This was an accurate assessment, and it means, what is quite true, that the problem of the Negro is a tragic one for all of us.

The *problem* is tragic; the *dénouement* may not have to be. We will have to wait and see. And work as hard as we can to make it a happy ending.

At the same time, anyone concerned with justice must express his deep gratitude to the blacks of America and of the world. Throughout all of history it has been the movement of the oppressed that has produced progress toward justice. The oppressor has never moved the world forward; he has not only not helped, but also hindered. This was true in classical times, it was true in the seventeenth and eighteenth centuries, it is true now. The cry of the downtrodden, of the wronged, is the cry of justice itself. It is not heard unless men speak out. The blacks have spoken out in recent years, and by doing so they have put us in their debt.

The reason is simple. It has often seemed to the oppressors that it was in their interest to maintain the *status quo*. This was always a misjudgment on their part. Justice is the interest of every man. Plato said this more than twenty centuries ago, and we know in our hearts that it is true. In so far as our society is unjust it is a bad society, and in consequence all of us suffer. It does not really matter that the actions and the words of blacks have sometimes gone to the extreme. For human institutions are such that sometimes two wrongs *do* make a right—ultimately, at least.

It is against the law in the United States to advocate a violent revolution. This is as it should be; as Abraham Lincoln said in his First Inaugural Address, "no government proper ever had a provision in its organic law for its own termination." He also said, in this speech delivered only weeks before the onset of the Civil War: "If by the mere force of numbers a majority should deprive a minority of any clearly written constitutional right, it might, in any moral point of view, justify revolution." In fact, violence almost always frustrates the aims it hopes to achieve. A peaceful revolution is another matter. Every man should advocate that, since it means change toward a better world. Without the help of the blacks, without their words and their actions, we could not even hope, much less expect, to achieve it.

Change can be too rapid, which is another way of saying that violence is usually self-defeating. We do not know, of course, whether the equalitarian revolution in this country (a revolution, as the selections in these volumes indicate, that has been going on for 200 years) will erupt into violence in the near future. As white men, we hope not; and we believe that many black men feel the same. But change must occur, rapid change, perhaps breathtaking change. We look forward to it. Despite our troubles, these are good times to be alive, as William Wordsworth said of the period of the French Revolution.

We probably should not forget that he added that to be young, in those exciting days, was "very heaven."

A collection of this size and scope must necessarily depend on the efforts of many people and institutions. The aid of the various libraries and other institutions to which we are indebted for original texts is acknowledged in *The Annals of America*, and that acknowledgment cannot be repeated in this place. Our gratitude to the proprietors of copyright materials reprinted in this set is acknowledged at the appropriate places throughout the volumes. But the work of a few individuals needs to be mentioned here.

We are grateful to Marlys A. Buswell, Celia Wittenber, and Helen K. Hanson for the patience and skill with which they prepared copy for the press and performed other essential editorial tasks. We are indebted to Wayne Moquin for helpful suggestions about material to include, and to Arthur L. H. Rubin for advice about the general form of the set. We are particularly grateful to Dr. Saunders Redding, Director of the Division of Research and Publication of the National Endowment for the Humanities; to Professor Earl E. Thorpe, Chairman of the Department of History at North

Carolina College (Durham); and to Dr. Charles H. Wesley, Director of the Association for the Study of Negro Life and History, in Washington, D.C., for the introductions they have supplied, respectively, for Vols, 1, 2, and 3. The short historical essays they have written are illuminating and add an important quality to the set. It goes without saying, of course, that none of them is responsible for any defects the set may contain.

We cannot close without mentioning our very special debt to Geoffrey Ward, who procured many of the illustrations, wrote drafts of the commentaries for the picture stories, and, with the help of Joseph Szwarek, designed most of the picture pages. The twelve picture stories, comprising in all 138 pages of illustration, which they prepared for this set of books provide both the student and the general reader with an additional resource, and a highly attractive one, for further understanding of the problems with which the volumes deal. The illustrations also touch on some historical incidents and events that the selections themselves do not discuss.

September 1968

This revised edition of *The Negro in American History* contains nine new selections covering the period from 1969 to 1971. The new selections appear at the beginning of Volume 1 and are listed in its table of contents. Short biographies of their authors are included in the index at the back of the volume.

Publication of a new edition has provided the opportunity to prepare a subject index of the entire collection. It will be found at the end of Volume 3.

Despite the fact that many events have occurred since the introductions to the three volumes, by Messrs. Redding, Thorpe, and Wesley, were written in 1968, it was deemed desirable to leave them as they originally stood. They reflect the views of three distinguished scholars of black American history as of the date of writing, and therefore can be considered to be documents of the same general kind as the other selections in the set.

Chicago
March 1972

Introduction

When Alfred E. Smith stood for the presidential election in 1928, thousands of Negroes in the North voted the Democratic ticket for the first time. Republican assurances were petering out for them; Republican promises remained unfulfilled. The notable era of the Negro Harlem renaissance, corrupted into a fad, was disappearing in a haze of commercial exploitation. The academic interest in Negro life was not being translated, as hoped, into policies and programs designed to generate the good will of the body politic and to better the social and economic status of the black community. Jobs that industry had been compelled to open to Negroes because of the manpower shortage of the war years, and to keep open in an effort to meet the postwar demands for consumer goods, were closing down. But even at the height of the boom, Negroes were little more than ciphers in the statistical data and the qualitative analysis of the economy. There was no "full employment" for them, and the "unprecedented prosperity" touched only those Negro musicians and entertainers who had made it to Broadway and the night club circuit. It was clear, too, that Negroes did not figure in the current plans of the Republican Party, which campaigned vigorously in the South and was completely silent on the "Negro question."

On the other hand, as they had done in 1924, though with little success, the Democrats went after the Negro vote with ringing declarations against racial discrimination and with promises of black representation in Democratic political councils. And what the Democrats did during the four years of the Hoover administration further weakened the Negroes' traditional ties to the Republican Party. In New York, for instance, the Democrats converted the United Colored Democracy from an in-name-only constituent of the party into a functioning machine and a clearing house for political patronage in Harlem. In 1930, powerful Democrats joined with Negroes in opposing the confirmation of John J. Parker, a reactionary anti-Negro, anti-labor North Carolinian, to the Supreme Court. Meantime, the great Depression set in and Negroes, in common with millions of whites, blamed it on the Republicans, who could not stem the tide that swept Franklin D. Roosevelt into the White House. In the congressional contests of 1934, a black Democrat, Arthur W. Mitchell, was elected to Congress from Illinois, and other Negro Democrats went into state legislatures in Maryland, West Virginia, Illinois, Pennsylvania, and New York. By 1936, the allegiance of the blacks to the Republican Party was almost completely eroded.

If, as the *New York Times* said, the Negroes' defection to the Democrats was a "splendid revolt," President Roosevelt's New Deal was a quickening reformation. It challenged the old laissez faire concept of the less government the better, and the old notion of the triumph of rugged individualism. "One third of the nation," the President declared, "is ill-housed, ill-clad, ill-nourished." This was just barely an exaggeration. Three million Negroes (of a total of roughly ten million) and fifteen million whites were unemployed or underemployed and on public relief. A quarter of the country's housing was sub-standard, and ever-widening sections of the nation's cities could be classified only as slums. Physical and spiritual decay was evident everywhere.

To combat this, the New Deal created programs of relief, recovery, and reform. The National Industrial Recovery Act, the Home Owners Loan Corporation, the Civilian Conservation Corps, the National Youth Administration, and other agencies were designed to improve the lot of workers and the poor. Directed by men of liberal inclination and high purpose, these agencies brought in Negro sub-administrators and "race relations" officers, whose duty it was to see to it that blacks, too, were benefited by federal programs. William Hastie, later to be the first Negro judge in the Federal District Court system, Robert Weaver, now (in 1968) a member of President Johnson's Cabinet, Ralph Bunche, currently Undersecretary of the UN, and Mary McLeod Bethune helped to establish agency policies. They came to be called the Black Brain Trust. During the course of their activities in various government departments – Interior, Justice, Commerce, Labor – from 1935 to the start of World War II – 200,000 Negro youths were employed in conservation and reclamation projects; 50,000 Negro farmers received government loans; and the average income of Negro farm families nearly doubled between 1936 and 1939. Thanks to the National Youth Administration, hundreds of young black men and women were able to continue their education. The Works Progress Administration, which conducted a variety of programs, employed skilled Negro artisans, artists, actors, and writers. In some Northern cities, the Federal Housing Administration constructed projects for racially integrated occupancy.

The millennium had not come, however. It was still necessary to give direct relief in food, clothing, and other commodities to 2,-000,000 black people. All too often the authority delegated to local officials under the National Industrial Recovery Act and the Agricultural Adjustment Act was exercised to discriminate against Negroes. Paid by the government to reduce crop acreage, Southern landowners evicted tenants and dismissed farm hands. Wage differentials in industry kept Negroes at the bottom of the scale. The abuses suffered by the landless poor led, in 1935, to the founding of the biracial Southern Tenant Farmers Union. In that year, too, the Committee for Industrial Organization (later renamed the Congress of Industrial Organizations, or CIO) was established, and by 1940 included more than 200,000 Negroes among its members. And in 1938, congressional approval of the Wages and Hours Bill gave promise of bettering the Negro worker's economic situation.

Meantime certain events tended to forge the unity of American black people. A. Philip Randolph, head of the Brotherhood of Sleeping Car Porters, had preached for years on the "organization of a people" for equality, justice, and power. The directors of the National

Association for the Advancement of Colored People, moving on another level, had worked toward the same end. But as broad-gauged and sincere as many of these efforts were, they did not really reach the mass of blacks, who felt that leaders like W. E. Burghardt Du Bois, Lester Granger, Charles S. Johnson, Walter White, and even Philip Randolph were concerned principally with the problems of the very small Negro middle class—the educated, the relatively affluent, the "dicty Negroes."

Then in 1931, in the town of Scottsboro, Alabama, nine Negro boys were arrested on a charge of raping two hoboing white girls. The conflicting stories that the girls told left scarcely a doubt that the boys were innocent; but their speedy conviction in the first trial, which inspired critical headlines around the world, solidified Negroes to a degree hitherto believed impossible. They held mass meetings, and prayer meetings, and parades in city after Northern city, and, poor though they were, raised nearly a million dollars for the legal defense of the Scottsboro boys.

Before the case ended five years later, Italy had overrun Ethiopia, Hitler had risen to power in Germany, and the German prize-fighter, Max Schmeling, had defeated the hero of all American Negroes, Joe Louis. Black Americans, who thought of Ethiopia as a Negro nation, saw the Italian conquest as a symbol of the universal victory of whites over blacks; the rise of Hitler as the malevolent flowering of the Nazi theory of the "master race," which they were the first Americans to condemn; and the defeat of Joe Louis as a personal humiliation. Black Americans were united in a bond of misery and bitterness.

But shortly there were events to rejoice them, too, as when Louis knocked out Schmeling in the first round of the return match in 1938, and—a quite different matter—when in that same year a Negro's admission suit against the University of Missouri resulted in a Supreme Court ruling that a state's failure to provide an equal education to Negroes within the borders of the state violated the U.S. Constitution.

The increasing unity of Negroes was voiced in 350 weekly newspapers, most of which used the services of the Associated Negro press, and some of which—the *Baltimore Afro-American*, the *Norfolk Journal and Guide*, the *Pittsburgh Courier*, the *Chicago De-*

fender, and the *Los Angeles Eagle*—circulated nationally. Negro magazines and scholarly journals, such as *The Crisis, Opportunity, Phylon*, and the *Journal of Negro History*, also carried the message.

Nor was activist expression of black unity missing. In 1931, the St. Louis branch of the Urban League organized a Jobs-for-Negroes campaign, the major aspect of which was a boycott of chain stores that, though located in Negro neighborhoods, employed no Negroes. Catching on in St. Louis, the campaign moved to cities east and south, and a few Negroes were given employment. A chain store in Atlanta, rather than yield to such demands, moved out of the Negro neighborhood. In Harlem, in March 1935, racial discrimination in employment set off a riot. Embittered Negroes looted stores along 125th Street of several hundred thousand dollars of goods and did more than two million dollars of damage. Three Negroes were killed by the police.

But perhaps the most striking evidence of black unity in the years just prior to World War II was the founding of the National Negro Congress in 1936, and of the Southern Negro Youth Congress a year later. The former brought together 500 Negro organizations—political, religious, fraternal, social—representing all classes of Negroes. The Southern Negro Youth Congress encompassed high school and college students, and, later, was the model for the Student Nonviolent Coordinating Committee (SNCC). Both organizations worked against segregation and proscriptive discrimination, while at the same time they fostered black pride and tried to make black power an effective working component in the life of the general society. Both, however, were infiltrated by Communists, whose ideas and purposes were something else again. In both organizations dissension arose and disintegration set in. By the early 1940s, their dissolution was complete.

If the unity of the Negro people was unknown, or incomprehensible, or generally ignored by the white public, it came to full notice within a month of America's declaration of war against Japan. All through 1940, as war plants increased production to make good the country's commitment as the "arsenal of democracy," there was no appreciable change in the Negroes' employment status. Indeed, because of increased automation, there were fewer jobs for the unskilled than formerly. Also the opportunities for Negroes to acquire skills remained closed in spite of the open door policy of the federal Defense Training Program and the Office of Production Management's special branch for the training and employment of blacks. Lower level officials ignored the policy and neglected the practice. It was not enough for government to lay down the principle. Negro leaders knew from experience that government at the highest level must act to implement it.

At a meeting in January 1941, Philip Randolph, Walter White of the NAACP, Lester Granger of the Urban League, Rayford Logan, and other Negro leaders and intellectuals drew up a list of grievances and presented them to Washington. If their demands were ignored, they were prepared, they warned, to organize 100,000 Negroes to march on the nation's capital. This was no idle threat; plans were already made. When President Roosevelt, other high government officials, and public figures including Mrs. Eleanor Roosevelt were unable to persuade the Negro petitioners, the President issued Executive Order 8802, on June 25, 1941. "There shall be no discrimination in the employment of workers in defense industries and Government," it said, "because of race, creed, color, or national origin."

The order established a Committee on Fair Employment Practices (FEPC), which went at the job of investigating complaints and correcting abuses with such commendable vigor that the doors to the training and employment of Negroes opened, though often reluctantly, especially in the South. Within months, nearly 60,000 Negroes were enrolled in industrial pre-employment training programs. Before the war ended, 100,000 Negroes held skilled and semi-skilled jobs in aircraft plants, and more than 300,000 went into other industries, and a few of them rose to supervisory positions. By 1946, the number of Negro federal civil service employees increased to approximately 200,000 from 47,000 in 1933. Though the great majority of these were in the lowest grades, there were enough in the middle and upper-middle echelons to make a good showing.

The cohesiveness of black people, combining with their increasing visibility in urban centers south, north, east, and west, and with widening public attention, had its effect in other areas. The majority of Americans had simply never thought of Negroes as being deliberately excluded from the rights, opportunities, and responsibilities that devolve on citizens in a democracy. When they thought of Negroes at all, they thought of them as a socially and intellectually inferior people, a few of whom had the talent—chiefly as entertainers, musicians, and singers—to rise above the servant, common-labor status to which most of them belonged. The white majority's knowledge of the Negro's history ended with slavery. Its acquaintance with the Negro character was based on the stereotypes of Sambo, Black Mammy, Stepin Fetchit, the chicken thief, and the rapist. The white majority did not read books by Negroes, and books about Negroes by such authors as Octavus Roy Cohen, Irwin S. Cobb, Sherwood Anderson, and Margaret Mitchell amused, romanticized, and perpetuated the racial stereotypes and myths. Scholarly works on race and race relations—Gunnar Myrdal's *The American Dilemma;* St. Clair Drake and Horace R. Cayton's *Black Metropolis*—did not interest them at all. William Faulkner's fiction was too difficult, and all they got from Erskine Caldwell were the "dirty" passages. *Native Son* (1940), by the Negro author Richard Wright, which many did read, shocked them for the wrong reasons. Most other Negro writers were not worth reading at all.

But in the 1940s, as the war raged, the unity, the visibility, and the publicity provoked questions that stirred the conscience and gradually awakened many to the realization that the ideals of self-determination, freedom, and equality, for which the war was being fought, could not be won by blood alone. At least the federal government, well-seeded with liberals and humanitarians, moved toward this realization in cautious steps. It moved, for instance, to reduce bit by bit discrimination in the armed services. The War Department began a program of training for black fighter pilots in 1940. Restricted to messmen ratings—stewards, waiters, cooks—in the Navy prior to 1942, and completely excluded from the Marine Corps, Negroes were enlisted in general ratings and as "Leathernecks." In most branches of the armed forces, they were trained as officers in integrated units. Negro women were enlisted in the WAC and the WAVE. Near the end of the war, in which nearly a million black men and women served in every theatre and in all the military establishments at home and abroad, black platoons were integrated with white platoons in the fighting in Germany. This was called an experiment, and army officials testified that it went very well. Integration in the armed services, however, was not fully accomplished until the Korean conflict.

Negroes also served as civilians in war-connected offices and activities. They joined the Merchant Marine, and four commanded integrated crews on cargo ships. Negroes worked in the Office of Civilian Defense, the Office of War Information, the Office of Price Administration, and on the War Manpower Commission. A few were highly trained economists, lawyers, psychologists, and journalists, and when the ad hoc agencies were abolished in 1945-46, some of these transferred to permanent government departments, where, they were told, no bars to professional advancement existed.

Although the progressive policies of the federal government under President Roosevelt and, later, under Harry S. Truman accounted for these advances and certainly influenced the liberalization of attitudes in some state and local governments and in some private sectors of the social and economic structure, problems remained. They were not all "Negro" problems. Urbanization was not. The war had swollen the tide of migration from rural areas and small towns to industrial cities in Pennsylvania, New Jersey, New York, Connecticut, and Massachusetts. Beginning in the first year of the war and continuing beyond its duration, nearly a thousand people a day streamed into Los Angeles. White and black, skilled and unskilled, ignorant and educated, they came from everywhere. The population of metropolitan San Francisco grew to two and two-thirds million, including more than 250,000 blacks, by 1960. Denver, Portland, and Seattle were flooded, too. Jobs were plentiful, especially for the skilled. Housing, schools, and social services were not plentiful for anybody. The machinery of local governments was not designed to meet the extraordinary demands put upon it. Ghettoes proliferated and grew denser. Tensions heightened. Crime rates soared in ghettoes and slums. In Los Angeles, in 1942, rioting broke out between whites and Negroes, between whites and Mexican-Americans. The next year, the President had to send troops to restore order and keep the peace in Detroit. The Negro was widely quoted as saying, "If I've got to die, I might as well die right here fighting for myself as to go abroad and die fighting for somebody else."

Dr. Kenneth B. Clark, a distinguished professor of psychology at the City College of New York, expressed the opinion that Negro morale after the Second World War was more "reality-bound"; that it tended to express the realities of the Negro's status in American life.

Several things created the illusive impression that that status was high, when in reality it was only scarcely a noticeable degree higher than it had been before. Because of the war, the Negro was in a somewhat stronger moral, political, and economic position. The FEPC had got him some jobs, and the War Labor Board had equalized his wages in some occupations. John L. Lewis' CIO had brought him into the active ranks of organized labor. The Supreme Court had outlawed lily-white primaries. The armed services, as we have seen, were moving against discrimination. And even Southern liberals, heretofore frightened of public pronouncements, had met in Durham, N.C., and given assurance of their "sincere good will" and desire to cooperate with Negroes in all of their "legitimate" demands.

Still progress was slow and in some areas nonexistent. White people were settling back into their old attitudes, their old ways of thinking. In public life and public institutions — schools and hospitals, parks and playgrounds, orphanages and prisons — segregation and discrimination prevailed, and would not yield to such pressure as Negro leaders could bring to bear. Faced with this reality, Negro leaders turned to the United Nations. It seemed to be the embodiment of their hopes and of the hopes and ambitions of nonwhite peoples throughout the world. The Charter of the UN spoke their language. "We the Peoples of the United Nations . . . reaffirm faith in fundamental human rights, in the dignity and worth of the human person, in the equal rights of men and women and of nations large and small . . . and respect for human rights and for fundamental freedoms for all without distinction as to race, sex, language, or religion."

On the basis of this declaration, the NAACP, acting on behalf of every black civil rights group in the country, presented to the UN in 1946 an "Appeal to the World, a Statement on the Denial of Human Rights to Minorities in the Case of Citizens of Negro Descent in the United States and an Appeal to the United Nations for Redress."

The Attorney General of the United States expressed dismay that "any American citizens should feel compelled to go over the heads of their government in seeking redress of grievances." But other officers of the government, including President Truman, were impressed. The President spoke out for "the integrity of the individual human being, sustained by the moral consensus of the whole nation, protected by a government based on equal freedom under just laws."

Progress that had stopped in the relaxed period after the war resumed — some thought with headlong speed. Though the pace was less than rash, and the progress was a good deal less than inclusive, it was steady and obvious, and it continued through the 1940s and early 1950s. Moreover, active opposition to it was not very effective. The Dixiecrat rebellion of 1948 had relatively little solid support. When the President's Committee on Civil Rights recommended an end to segregation in every area of American life and the establishment of a permanent Fair Employment Practices Commission, Southern congressmen and plain Southern citizens did react as was the wont of the Solid South. Nevertheless, President Truman made the precedent-shattering appointment of a Negro as governor of the Virgin Islands, and another as an assistant secretary of labor, and a third as a member of the Federal Trade Commission. Though Negroes generally had opposed his election, only a few months after taking office President Eisenhower brought about the desegregation of places of public accommodation in the nation's capital.

Meantime, too, the Supreme Court was moving toward a more liberal interpretation of the Constitution. In 1943, it declared the exclusion of Negroes from juries unconstitutional. Three years later it ruled that state laws requiring segregation in public carriers were invalid in interstate transportation. In 1948, the Court declared that the private covenants prohibiting Negroes from owning and occupying real estate had no legal force. And in 1950, in a decision that was to have far-reaching consequences, it ruled that Negroes must be granted educational equality with whites.

The 1950 ruling did not disturb the doctrine of "separate but equal." But Southern and border states had rigidly applied the "separate" and altogether ignored the "equal" for more than fifty years. Negro schools, libraries, and other publicly supported educational facilities and services were obviously woefully inferior. Constantly urged by the black masses to press harder and with more speed for equal rights, and encouraged by the 1950 ruling, the NAACP now determined to challenge the separate but equal doctrine itself with the sociological theory that segregated education is inherently inferior. It was a bold, new concept with implications of social morality touching upon the whole pattern of segregation.

After months of painstaking legal staff work and the careful preparation of testimony by distinguished sociologists, psychologists, and educators, and following, too, the prosecution of five separate suits in four states and the District of Columbia, the NAACP legal staff, led by Thurgood Marshall, was ready to appeal to the Supreme Court. The case was presented in 1952. Two years and several supporting briefs later, the Court held that separate schools are inherently inferior and that enforced segregation in education violates the Fourteenth Amendment to the Constitution. In 1955, the Court ruled that the states must proceed to desegregate their schools "with all deliberate speed."

The Court's decrees aroused bitter opposition throughout the South. The states resisted the new law "by all legal means." Virginia organized "massive resistance" and devised administrative and legal stratagems. It permitted some schools to close rather than integrate. The state legislature authorized the expenditure of public funds for tuition grants and the hasty organization of "private" schools for students who did not want to mix with Negroes. Whites in the deeper South, where White Citizens Councils were quickly brought into being and the Ku Klux Klan was reactivated, were less moderate. They resorted to harassment, terror, and violence. Negroes were driven from jobs, lost their credit, had their mortgages foreclosed, their insurance canceled. Their homes, churches, and places of business were set afire. Murder was committed in the name of preserving the "Southern way of life" and "preserving the purity of the white race." In Birmingham, Alabama, white terrorists bombed a church during a religious service, killing four young Negro girls and injuring a score of others. Claiming a constitutional right to interpose the authority of the state between the federal law and the federal power to enforce it, the governor of Arkansas called out the state militia to prevent nine black children from entering a white high school. President Eisenhower promptly federalized the militia and ordered it to uphold the federal law. But the President had no power over the local school system, and Governor Faubus ordered all high schools closed. They remained closed for a year. But in 1959, they reopened on a desegregated basis.

These events made ugly headlines in Europe, Asia, and Africa, and millions of enlightened Americans were sensitive to the image they created in a world where more than three-quarters of the population was non-white, was black, brown, and yellow. The President and other high government officials were particularly sensitive to Communist criticism, for they thought of the American system as competing with Communism for leadership in the world. What America did about her black citizens was a test of her claim and of her moral capacity to lead the world.

The best leadership in the South was influenced by this point of view, as well as by other factors in the complex social and political equation of race relations. It deplored the violence and extremism, which horrified the rest of the country and the world. It tended to respect the moral authority of the President, and under President Eisenhower that moral authority was exerted at least on the side of moderation and compromise. Finally, the best leadership in the South could not ignore the Negroes themselves.

The behavior of Negroes was exemplary, but their determination to secure their rights was undiminished as the 1950s reached mid-point. The determination was expressed in their response to the emergence of new black nations and the end of the white man's rule in West Africa. It was verbalized in their newspapers and magazines, and in books—*White Man, Listen*; *Black Power*; *Simple Speaks His Mind*; *Notes of a Native Son*—which white people in growing numbers were beginning to read for the first time. The Negroes' impatient determination was signalized in the stepped-up activity of their traditional organizations such as the NAACP, the Urban League, the Congress of Racial Equality, and the Southern Regional Council; in the resurgence of the Black Muslims; and in the formation of new groups, such as the Montgomery Improvement Association and, later, the Student Nonviolent Coordinating Committee, with young leaders dedicated to a new kind of militancy.

Though the activities of these organizations differed, the tone of all, save the Black Muslims, was the same. And anyway, the Black Muslims—the Nation of Islam—could hardly be called a civil rights organization. Under Elijah Muhammad it was—and remains—a kind of sham hagiarchy, which renounced Christianity, advocated complete segregation, excoriated all whites, and awaited the day when the white race would be utterly destroyed. Strike and the Black Muslims strike back. But with equal vigor, the old-line organizations pursued their long-established policies and programs. Roy Wilkins, Thurgood Marshall, and the NAACP continued the legal struggle against segregation and discrimination. Whitney Young and the Urban League did battle, usually in private in the board rooms of industrial corporations, for greater Negro participation in the economy, and continued quietly to educate, explain, show reasons why. James Farmer's CORE perfected techniques of protest, demonstrated at banks, stores, theatres. But well into the 1960s, the tone of all these organizations and activities was non violent militancy. It was frequently miscalled communistic and revolutionary, but the leaders of these organizations did not want to overthrow the political, social, or economic structure. They did not want out. They wanted in. They wanted some of the action.

That ultimate goal and the drum-beat by which they struggled toward it was set by Martin Luther King, Jr. "In the process of gaining our rightful place," King told his people and the world, ". . . we must rise to the majestic heights of meeting physical force with soul force. The marvelous new militancy which has engulfed the Negro community must not lead us to distrust all white people, for many of our white brothers . . . have come to realize that their destiny is tied up with our destiny."

This was the substance of King's earliest declarations, when he was simply the pastor of the Montgomery (Alabama) Dexter Avenue Baptist Church. These words summed up his personal philosophy. They explained, too, the rationale of the Southern Christian Leadership Conference (SCLC), which he helped to found in 1957. He had tested that rationale the year before in the Montgomery bus boycott, which brought him international renown, and which resulted in a series of nonviolent crusades joined by thousands of whites across the nation. There were sit-ins, kneel-ins, wade-ins, prayer meetings, freedom rides. They were not all successful. The rationale did not always meet the test of practice in Southern states.

In May 1963, a massive civil rights demonstration in Birmingham, Alabama, was savagely put down by police using fire hoses, clubs, electric cattle prods, and dogs. Revolted like most of the rest of the nation and the world, President John F. Kennedy addressed his countrymen. He spoke of a "moral crisis," which could not be resolved by police action, by force. "It is a time," he said, "to act in the Congress, in your state, and local legislative body and, above all, in all of our daily lives."

Later that night, Medgar Evers, a representative of the NAACP in Mississippi, was killed from ambush.

But in spite of such instances of brutal suppression and, indeed, perhaps because of them, a consensus seemed to be developing behind the civil rights bill that President Kennedy submitted to Congress on June 19, 1963, one week after the assassination of Evers. The bill prohibited discrimination in all programs and agencies and on all projects assisted or financed by federal funds. It penalized the interference with citizens in pursuit of their civil rights. It empowered the Attorney General to bring suit to eliminate segregation in public educational institutions. It banned discrimination on account of race in stores, hotels, restaurants, and places of amusement. It set up a federal agency to help communities eliminate discrimination and the attitudes that promote it.

To rally public opinion behind this bill, as well as to protest the treatment of Negroes, on August 28, SCLC, the NAACP, the Urban League, CORE—all the civil rights organizations, joined by white religious groups, labor groups, college youths, politicians of both major parties, fraternal clubs, the whole spectrum of American society—converged on Washington to march from the Washington Monument to the Lincoln Memorial. The gathering was organized by a Negro named Bayard Rustin, who had done such work before for causes he believed in, like peace, brotherhood, and one world. It was led by A. Philip Randolph, Roy Wilkins, Whitney Young, and Martin Luther King, Jr. By the lowest estimate, 200,000 Americans, a quarter of them white, marched that day. There were Senators and Congressmen, governors of states and mayors of cities, notable and famous people from all walks of life. It was the greatest gathering of Americans united in a common cause that the nation had ever seen. Black and white together, they linked arms, they carried banners, they prayed, they sang the hymns of the black protest movement, they shouted slogans: "Freedom Now!" "Equality Now!" Finally, they listened to the speech of Dr. King, a speech that was both a prophecy and a warning. "There will be neither rest nor tranquillity in America until the Negro is granted his citizenship rights. The whirlwinds of revolt will continue to shake the foundations of our nation until the bright day of justice emerges. . . . I have a dream that one day this nation will rise up and live out the true meaning of its creed."

Following months of debate, conferences, filibusters, following compromises and changes, and following the assassination of President Kennedy, who had been its principal architect, the Civil Rights Act passed the Senate on June 19, 1964, exactly one year after it was presented to Congress.

Though there was gratifying compliance with the new law in many places even in the deep South, the die-hard segregationists were quick to find loopholes, cause delays, set up obstructions. They brought suits to contest some of its provisions. In many places Negroes found it impossible to exercise their new-won right to register to vote. Registration officials disqualified them on the flimsiest excuses, or they changed the time and place of registration without notice. In Georgia, Alabama, and Mississippi Negroes were intimidated and terrorized. In Plaquemine Parish, La., white toughs attacked Negro children while the police of the town looked on.

Meantime civil rights organizations had anticipated the passage of the bill and had made plans to take especial advantage of its voting rights provisions. The Council of Federated Organizations (COFO) was the administrative agency for a loose consortium of CORE, SNCC, SCLC, the NAACP, the Urban League, and the National Council of Churches. Dominated by SNCC, COFO sent 700 student volunteers of both races, 200 clergymen and lawyers, and a small corps of professional civil rights workers into Mississippi in the summer of 1964. The idea was to conduct a voter education campaign. The job of the volunteers was to teach Negroes what their voting rights were and how to exercise them. The apprehension that this plan generated in some parts of the country was justified. Though the project could count some small gains—a thousand new Negro registrants; the formation of the Mississippi Freedom Democratic Party—many of the volunteers were beaten by gangs of white private citizens and police. Many, many more—a thousand all told—were arrested. Sixty-five churches and homes where volunteers gathered were burned or bombed. At least six people were murdered. Three of these were professional civil rights workers, two of them white. After an intensive search of several weeks, the FBI discovered their bodies buried in a dam.

Many Negroes were beginning to be disillusioned with nonviolence, but their adherence to it held up pretty well, despite the charisma and the oratorical appeal of the Black Muslim leader, Malcolm X. Thrown out of Elijah Muhammad's movement in 1963, Malcolm X continued to preach hatred of the white man, complete segregation, and retaliatory violence. Under his influence, small groups of Negroes here and there formed secret paramilitary clubs pledged to violent reprisal. Then, late in 1964, Malcolm X made a "pilgrimage to Mecca." When he returned he began to test the temperature of the moderate mainstream of the civil rights movement, moving toward compliance with the movement's more realistic policy of black-white cooperation. Suddenly, and more effectively than anyone else, he was articulating the grievances and the aspirations of Negroes in northern ghettoes. Unemployment, poverty, and squalor were grievances, and jobs and cleanliness were aspirations. De facto school segregation and ignorance were grievances, and quality education was an aspiration. Police brutality and the white man's concept of justice for the Negro were grievances, and a police force trained in humane methods and courts where true justice prevailed were aspirations.

Malcolm X, a man in his mid-thirties, was the herald of a new stage in the black protest movement.

Temporarily balked especially in the South by well-meant admonitions to go slow, by token compliance with civil rights legislation, by the animosity of local courts, by state governors like Ross Barnett, Paul Johnson, and George Wallace, and by violence against which they refused to retaliate, and their sense of being thus neutralized somewhat mollified by the obvious sincerity of President Johnson and many members of the Congress, and by the programs of certain federal agencies such as the Civil Rights

Commission, the office of the Attorney General, and OEO, the leaders of the first stage of the black protest movement were fading into the wings. The first act was drawing to its close. Though neither moribund nor silent, and still united in the common purpose of bringing black and white together in a national community, the early leaders were of an older generation. Not time, but circumstances made them old.

And a new generation was moving in and up. It saw Malcolm X's murder (in 1965) as sainted martyrdom. It saw history as beginning just yesterday. It counted even Martin Luther King, Whitney Young, and Bayard Rustin as "Uncle Toms." Perhaps what rang the curtain down on the first stage was President Johnson's speech to the 1965 graduating class at predominantly Negro Howard University. Reduced to its substance, that speech dealt with the problems of the urban ghetto Negro—with, quite simply, the race problems in the cities of both South and North. And there to confront them was another generation, urban ghetto-bred—Stokely Carmichael and H. Rap Brown, Ron Katanga and Nathan Wright, James Forman and Jesse Gray—backed by a nameless host of the despairing, the frustrated, the deprived and despised.

Differences in public attitudes, techniques, and law quite aside, racism—the Presidential Advisory Committee on Civil Disorders reports—operates with the same deadly force in Negro life in the North as in the South. Educational inequality, poverty, social instability are hidden by a facade of political liberalism, but the power structure's exclusion of the Negro in Los Angeles, Philadelphia, New York, Chicago, Detroit, and Newark is not only symbolically but openly expressed in the exercise of the police power that controls the city ghettoes. The Kerner Report tried to make this clear to millions of whites. But the new, young, black protesters were born with this knowledge. It does not matter to them that the basic problems of poverty, ignorance, and crime-drift, of sickness and old age are not exclusively racial. It does not matter that in absolute terms there are more poor, deprived, and exploited whites than blacks. What does matter is that whites—all whites—have their whiteness going for them, and that blacks—all blacks—have their blackness going against them. What matters is that poor whites with gumption can claw a way into the power structure, can have a say, can choose, can cry yea or nay, while blacks with no matter how much gumption remain outside and in the final showdown have their lives controlled by the white man's whim.

So, black power now! the new protesters cried.

Black power meant different things to different people. To some it meant Black Muslim separatism; that integration cannot work. To some it meant an assertion of pride, a corollary to "black is beautiful." To many black intellectuals it meant the competitive development of black institutions—political, educational, and social—so strong, viable, and effective that whites will have to reckon with them, cooperate with them, and, in the millennium of integration, join them. To some—and the evidence seems to be that these include a great number of whites—it meant crime and lawlessness, riot and looting. It meant what happened in Watts in 1965—though not, for whites, the cumulative causes; and what happened in Newark in 1967, and in Detroit the same summer of the same year; and in Washington in 1968; and in a dozen other cities from time to time. It meant: Burn, baby, burn!

Between 1965 and the mid-point of 1968, 147 people were killed and 800 million dollars of damage was done in 103 riots. The last of these was touched off by the murder of probably the greatest civil rights leader of modern times. Martin Luther King, Jr., was a devoutly religious man who believed in the redemptive power of charity and knowledge. He inspired a mobilization of national purpose and commitment that generated, among other things, a concert of national programs that are designed to reach down into the masses, black and white, who cannot cope intellectually with the abstract concept of civil rights, but who will benefit from the practical application of civil rights. Perhaps the national purpose and commitment will recede again and again, but, hopefully, it will endure. "I've seen the promised land," King said the night before he was murdered.

The promised land is the America that will be.

Saunders Redding
Washington, September 1968

1. The Diffusion of Black Power

1969-1971

VERNON JORDAN
Black People and the Unions

*Black membership in the large industrial unions has steadily increased since
the years of labor strife in the 1930s. Urban industrial areas such as New York,
New Jersey, Pittsburgh, Detroit, the cities of northern Ohio, and Chicago-Gary
have thousands of unionized black workers. But in the craft unions —
electricians, masons, carpenters, iron workers, etc. — blacks have been much
underrepresented. These are high salaried trades, and through the
apprenticeship system of training they have been able to become selective,
even blatantly discriminatory, in their "hiring" practices. In the late 1960s
urban blacks made strident attempts, notably in Philadelphia and Chicago, to
gain entrance into these unions. Some openings were made, and a few training
programs begun; but by the end of 1971 the gains had not been spectacular.
This failure of unionism among blacks was the subject of an address, reprinted
in part here, given by Vernon Jordan to the national AFL-CIO convention at
Miami on November 22, 1971. Jordan had been appointed executive director
of the National Urban League in June, to replace the late Whitney Young, Jr.
[Source: Vital Speeches, January 1, 1972.]*

In the sixties, we were fighting for our rights, which we tore from a
reluctant nation. In the sixties, the burning issue was whether
blacks would be allowed to ride the busses and where they would sit.
In the seventies, the issues have shifted. Now the issues are whether black people will be allowed to drive that bus, whether the masses of black people will have the money to pay the fare, whether
blacks have their rightful place as executives and directors of the
bus company and the unions it deals with, and whether the bus
routes will link the black ghetto to where the jobs are.

The issue of the day is, then, the economic empowerment of
black people. This is the task to which we of the Urban League have
committed ourselves, and it is the task which the labor movement,
of all the partners in the coalition for justice in America, should find
the most congenial to its special talents and interests.

I would like to discuss with you today the goals of black Americans, the nature of the coalition strategy, and the specific role I see
for the labor movement, in joint action with black people, in bring-

ing an end to poverty, joblessness and hardship in this nation of unprecedented wealth and power.

It goes without saying that the goal of black Americans is for total, unconditional and complete equality. For too long have we been excluded from parity with white Americans. For too long have we been victims of racism and discrimination.

We want a share of the America we've fought and died for. We want our fair share of the jobs, the income, the opportunities and the political representation our numbers call for. The media has thrown a sharp spotlight on the blacks running for major offices around the country, but did you know that black people, who make up 12 per cent of the population, hold only three-tenths of one per cent of all the elective offices at local, state and federal levels of government?

The Black Caucus has received considerable press attention because of its forthright uncompromising position in favor of black people and working people. But are you aware that the Congressional Black Caucus comprises only three per cent of the House of Representatives?

Much — too much — has been made of the economic gains blacks have made in the past decade. Somehow, we are supposed to be overjoyed that we've finally achieved 61 per cent of white income or that the numbers of black families making over $10,000 have tripled or that the numbers of blacks attending college or holding professional and managerial jobs has increased.

But did you know that the dollar gap between whites and blacks has actually grown? In 1960 $2,600 separated the median black family income from white; in 1970, the dollar gap grew to $3,800. Did you know that the percentage of white families making over $10,000 is double the percentage of black families in that bracket? Are you aware that it takes three workers in a black family to make as much as one worker in the average white family? Or that black college graduates still average lower incomes than whites who never attended college? Or that blacks still have far less than our fair share of the top-dollar, top-status jobs while we continue to be disproportionately concentrated in lower-paying occupations?

About the only area where we have more than our fair share of the opportunities is poverty and unemployment. We are not eleven per cent of the nation's poor; we are thirty per cent. We are not eleven percent of the unemployed, we are twenty per cent.

Through our goal of economic empowerment of black people, we seek to turn those figures around and achieve parity with other citizens of this nation whose skin is white, whose opportunities have not been withheld, and whose progress has been steady.

And we seek to do this through active alliances and coalitions with those elements of our society whose actions and ideals are consistent with ours, whose interests are similar and who share our commitment to a society that is just, a society that is fair, and a society that is decent.

One of the prerequisites of such coalitions is honesty. The partners must deal with each other from positions of equality and mutual respect. At times, they will say things that hurt, but it is far better for such feelings to be out in the open, freely discussed and dealt with, than to be festering beneath the surface, only to explode later.

It is in this spirit of mutual respect and the honesty our coalition demands, that I must call to your attention the deep frustration and suspicions some black people have of the labor movement. These feelings are entirely due to the racially restrictive practices of a handful of unions.

I refuse to magnify the wrongdoings of a few unions and thus join those who are the real enemies of black people, poor people, and working people. I recognize that the AFL-CIO and the labor movement in general is the home of some of the most progressive elements in American life, and is the beneficiary of the loyalty of black workers.

Black workers do not question the value of the union card; it is universally acknowledged to be a passport to economic freedom. In fact, a higher proportion of black workers than white are unionized. Blacks are 13 per cent of all union members. But because of restrictive practices, proportionately twice as many white construction craftsmen as blacks are organized. Where blacks are permitted to enter construction unions—primarily in the lower-skilled categories—a higher percentage of blacks are union members than are white. The payoff is in the paycheck. Wages of black construction craftsmen who have managed to enter unions average forty per cent higher than the wages of those who have not.

The existence of large numbers of unorganized black construction tradesmen can ultimately work to the disadvantage of the unions, in that they represent a temptation to throw more business to non-union contractors, they represent a constant threat of dual unionism, and their continued exclusion serves as a ripe excuse for anti-union forces within our society. Finally, the public image of the entire labor movement is unfairly harmed because of the continued practices of a small part of it. . . .

I know that your leadership is working hard on this problem. I know that the Urban League and other groups are cooperating with many unions in the joint efforts to increase the numbers of black craftsmen and apprentices. And I am pleased that the Urban League has made progress with some construction unions. But in all candor I must say it is too little and too slow, in the face of what remains to be done. In the fraternal spirit of our mutual interests in economic justice, in the recognition that change must come from within, and in the conviction that deeds, not resolutions are called for, I ask this convention to intensify the pressures upon your backward brothers and raise them to the moral and pragmatic standards the rest of the labor movement follows. . . .

First, we must organize the unorganized. The AFL-CIO has already done great work in helping farm workers, hospital workers, and sanitation workers win the right of union recognition. But in some instances it was the workers themselves who first organized unions, and then received assistance from the labor movement. I ask you to reverse that process; to place an even greater emphasis and impetus on bringing the benefits of unionism to the underpaid, exploited and poverty-stricken laboring men and women of America.

To an alarming degree, blacks and minorities are disproportionately represented among the unorganized poor. We read much about the shift to a service economy and the lack of growth in manufacturing. But what does this service economy mean to the labor movement? It is more than growth in the numbers of doctors, lawyers, and other professional service occupations. It means growing numbers of laundry workers, sanitation men, day care center workers, paraprofessional aides, domestics, and many other categories of workers whose wages are low, employment uncertain, and pros-

6

pects dim. In the South especially, black and white workers outside the union umbrella are vulnerable to the pressures of local land barons and repressive petty dictators.

The labor movement has demonstrated that it can deliver, and now it is charged to deliver its benefits to the masses of the unorganized. The need cannot be taken lightly. There is hunger in this land. There is abject poverty in our country. There is deep suffering in the urban ghettos and in the rural shacks of America. There is every bit as much of an emergency now as in the Depression, when unions organized similarly disadvantaged industrial workers. You got the Wagner Act to breathe life into your claims for justice; I now ask you to formulate an "AFL-CIO Act" to breathe life into the crying need for justice of today's unorganized laboring masses. Only you have the energy, the resources, and the expertise to do it.

Second: there is a need for greater numbers of blacks in union leadership roles. This is something that the Urban League with your cooperation and backing has encouraged. There are thousands of young budding Phil Randolphs all across the country, men and women who have been steeled in the struggle for civil rights to recognize the need for social justice and the benefits of unionism. A movement-wide campaign to identify, train and place this cadre of energetic unionists in positions of leadership within the labor movement will pay off in an internal strengthening of the movement and in the recognition among all black people that the union movement is indeed a progressive joining together of black and white workers for the benefit of all.

Third: I would urge you to expand your very valuable political education programs to make an even greater impact upon the black community. Here too, the Urban League stands ready and willing to join with you. In the coming months, we will be announcing a new program of voter registration and education in northern and western cities. Black people and poor people are underregistered. They are still kept from the ballot box by restrictive practices and by an unwritten desire to keep power from the hands of the powerless. This is going to be a major Urban League priority in the coming years, and I would like to see the AFL-CIO support our efforts and redouble its own.

Finally, I believe the labor movement can break the zoning restrictions that are primarily responsible for the creation of the white suburban noose around the necks of increasingly black cities. The suburbs are where the new factories and offices are being built. The jobs are going to be at the end of the highway and not in the center of town. But because of zoning restrictions and a refusal to build homes that low and moderate income people can afford, white and black workers will be kept from those jobs. It is in your interest for your members to have access to suburban jobs; and it is in the interests of black people and all Americans to have access to the homes and jobs of suburbia.

KENNETH A. GIBSON
Economic Crisis in the Cities

The rising number of blacks elected to public office in the late 1960s and early 70s gave evidence that perhaps black Americans were finally entering into full participation in American life. But for the black mayors of several large cities the gain was largely offset by the severe plight in which most urban centers found themselves. Increased welfare rolls, decayed housing, a diminished tax base, impoverished school systems, chronic minority unemployment, rising crime rates, and insufficient public transportation plagued most city administrations. Mayor Carl Stokes of Cleveland exclaimed: "I never dreamed — I just never dreamed — of the day to day crisis environment in which a mayor lives." As is often the case with elected officials, the mayors often received much of the blame for conditions they had not been responsible for; and there was very likely some muted hope on the part of white constituents that they would make a poor showing against overwhelming odds. There was little willingness to admit that the problems had accumulated through decades of negligence, short-sightedness, and corruption at the hands of the white power structure. More and more the cities found it necessary to turn to the states and to the federal government for aid, which when forthcoming was rarely more than enough to meet current crises. The following selections, both by Mayor Kenneth A. Gibson of Newark, New Jersey, suggest the depth of the urban distress with which he has had to deal. Gibson, a civil engineer, defeated incumbent Hugh Addonizio in the mayoralty contest of June 1970. The first

8

*selection below is a letter to President Nixon, dated August 17, 1971, three
days after the announcement of a new federal economic policy. The second
article is a statement on welfare reform delivered to the U.S. Conference of
Mayors at Boston on September 23, 1971. [Source: Congressional Record, 92
Cong., 1 Sess., October 6, 1971.]*

A. LETTER TO THE PRESIDENT

Dear Mr. President:

The recent announcement of your new economic policy, which
clearly points up the power and authority of the Chief Executive,
has rightfully generated much immediate public response. The
prospects of a generation of peace and prosperity must be the number one priority of all Americans.

I applaud the new direction you have taken in attempting to slow
down inflation and increase employment. Decisive action against
these two enormous problems could no longer be delayed.

I do question, however, some of the steps you have taken towards
our common goal of economic stability. For, in a certain sense, the
cities of America seem destined to bear the heaviest burdens of your
new economic policy.

The high prices and unemployment which now afflict all Americans have existed chronically and with greater severity in our cities
for the past decade. Any postponement of immediate and massive
Federal action can only serve to insure these conditions in our urban centers for years to come.

Mr. President, the unemployment rate in Newark is now approximately 16%; while another 30% of our people are under-employed.
Our property tax is among the highest in the nation with the result
that buildings are being abandoned at the rate of one a day. The
poor who remain in Newark, approximately half the population of
the city, are paying more and more for inferior goods.

In short, Newark is a ravaged economy.

It appears to me that none of the measures you have just taken
will effectively cure this condition. In fact, some of your actions will
definitely aggravate the already desperate problems of Newark and
other troubled American cities.

Postponing revenue-sharing and welfare reform legislation further puts off the long delayed fundamental assistance that our cities

9

must have in order to survive. Every delay makes survival an even more tenuous question.

In light of your desire "to reorder our budget priorities," I would hope that the $4.7 billion cut in Federal spending will not come at the expense of the people who need assistance most. I hope the needs of the poor will not be postponed as those of the cities have been by your new economic policy. Our most precious national resource is the people, and any major decrease in Federal programs aimed at total human development will cause far greater damage to this country than the past decade of unemployment. The cutbacks should only be made in those areas which are of secondary importance to the survival of this nation such as space exploration and wasteful military projects.

In short, Mr. President, I would hope that this price freeze and the other aspects of your new program could be aimed more at the battle to end the enduring problems of this economy and not so much at "freezing" the misery of the poor so that big business and the middle-class can regain their lost prosperity.

Unfortunately it seems that your policy will do no more than simply maintain the disparity of wealth which pervades the Newarks of America. The citizens of Newark willingly stand ready to share the responsibility of stabilizing the economy but we must not become victims in the process.

B. STATEMENT TO THE MAYORS' CONFERENCE

After months of delay by the U.S. Senate in acting on welfare reform, we were dismayed at the President's request for a one-year delay of welfare reform legislation. In light of the President's desire "to reorder budget priorities," I hope that the projected $4.7 billion cut in federal spending will not come at the expense of the people who need assistance most. The long-delayed promise of national welfare reform is more urgently needed today than ever before.

While several years of debate have produced no major changes in the Federal welfare program, States have begun to act in negative and restrictive ways. Recent legislation in New Jersey and other States is aimed at reducing eligibility levels and benefits for already hard-pressed welfare recipients. These State actions increase the welfare burden which must be carried at the local level.

The deficiencies in the welfare system are clear:

(1) Benefit levels are too low to support individuals and families. Inadequate welfare payments almost guarantee a continuation of the present welfare syndrome.

(2) Welfare benefits, requirements, and financing in the 50 States vary widely. We treat a national problem as if it were 50 separate local problems.

(3) There are inadequate incentives for the family unit to remain together.

(4) There are inadequate incentives for able-bodied persons to seek employment.

These deficiencies will not be corrected without a federally administered and financed national welfare system—a system which must be designed to provide adequate maintenance support levels for all Americans in need. If our welfare system continues to be shaped by individual State actions in response to local tax and fiscal pressures, the result will be disaster for millions of poor Americans and for the cities in which they live.

The responsibility to reform the present inadequate welfare system rests at this moment with the Congress and particularly the Senate, where welfare reform legislation now is bogged down in Committee. We urge the Administration and the Congress to recognize that our most precious national resource is our people. Postponement of national reform of our welfare system, at the same time that we allocate hundreds of millions of dollars for subsidies of ailing corporations and idle farmlands, would be a cruel and deceitful hoax for the Newarks of America.

Urban Americans stand ready to share the responsibility of stabilizing the economy, but we must not become victims in the process. We must not "freeze" the misery of the poor, in the process of returning big business and the middle-class to their lost prosperity.

SHIRLEY CHISHOLM

Of Course Women Dare

Shirley Chisholm was elected to Congress in 1968, from the 12th District in Brooklyn, after four years in the New York Assembly. From the moment of her arrival in the 91st Congress she has not ceased to be a vocal and articulate advocate of women's rights and black rights as well as a spokesman for her constituency. Re-elected to the 92nd Congress, she announced in 1971 that she would seek the Democratic Party's presidential nomination in 1972. This news disconcerted some black leaders because they were uncertain whether she was running as a black people's candidate or as a proponent of women's liberation. In the address printed below she demonstrates her devotion to both causes. The speech was delivered at the National Women's Political Caucus in Washington, D.C., early in July 1971. [Source: Congressional Record, 92 Cong., 1 Sess., July 12, 1971.]

Do women dare take an active part in society and in particular do they dare take a part in the present social revolution? I find the question as much of an insult as I would the question, "Are you, as a black person, willing to fight for your rights?"

America has been sufficiently sensitized to the answer whether or not black people are willing to both fight and die for their rights to make the question itself asinine and superfluous. America is not yet sufficiently aware that such a question applied to women is equally asinine and superfluous.

I am, as is obvious, both black and a woman. That is a good vantage point from which to view at least two elements of what is becoming a social revolution; the American black revolution and the women's liberation movement. But it is also a horrible disadvantage. It is a disadvantage because America, as a nation, is both racist and anti-feminist. Racism and anti-feminism are two of the prime traditions of this country.

For any individual, challenging social traditions is a giant step: a giant step because there are no social traditions which do not have corresponding social sanctions, the sole purpose of which is to protect the sanctity of the traditions.

Thus when we ask the question "Do women dare?" we are not asking are women capable of a break with tradition so much as we are asking: "Are they capable of bearing with the sanction that will be placed upon them?"

Coupling this with the hypothesis presented by social thinkers and philosophers that in any given society, the most active groups are those that are nearest to the particular freedom that they desire, it does not surprise me that those women most active and vocal on the issue of freedom for women are those who are young, white, and middle-class, nor is it too surprising that there are not more from that group involved in the women's liberation movement.

There certainly are reasons why more women are not involved. This country, as I said, is both racist and anti-feminist. Few, if any, Americans are free of the psychological wounds imposed by racism and anti-feminism.

A few months ago while testifying before the office of federal contract compliance, I noted that anti-feminism, like every form of discrimination, is destructive both to those who perpetrate it and to their victims: that males, with their anti-feminism, maim both themselves and their women. . . .

In 1966 the median earnings of women who worked full-time for the whole year was less than the median income of males who worked full-time for the whole year. In fact, white women workers made less than black male workers and, of course, black women workers made the least of all.

Whether it is intentional or not women are paid less than men for the same work, no matter what their chosen field of work. Whether it is intentional or not, employment for women is regulated still more in terms of the jobs that are available to them. This is almost as true for white women as it is for black women.

Whether it is intentional or not, when it becomes time for a young high school girl to think about preparing for her career, her counselors, whether they be male or female, will think first of her so called "natural" career—housewife and mother—and begin to program her for a field with which marriage and children will not unduly interfere.

That is exactly the same as the situation of the young black or Puerto Rican who the racist counselor advises to prepare for service-oriented occupations because he does not even think of them entering the professions.

The response of the average young lady is precisely the same as the response of the average young black or Puerto Rican—tacit agreement—because the odds do seem to be stacked against them.

This is not happening as much as it once did—to young minority-group people. It is not happening because they have been radicalized and the country is becoming sensitized to its racist attitudes and the damage that it does.

Women must rebel—they must react to the traditional stereo-typed education mapped out for them by the society. Their education and training is programmed and planned for them from the moment the doctor says, "Mr. Jones, it's a beautiful baby girl!" and Mr. Jones begins deleting mentally the things that she might have been and adds the things that society says that she must be.

That young woman (for society begins to see her as a stereotype the moment that her sex is determined) will be wrapped in a pink blanket (pink because that is the color of her caste) and the unequal segregation of the sexes will have begun.

Small wonder that the young girl sitting across the desk from her counselor will not be able to say "no" to educational, economic, and social slavery. Small wonder because she has been a psychological slave and programmed as such since the moment of her birth!

On May 20th of last year I introduced legislation concerning the equal employment opportunities of women. At that time I pointed out that there were three and one-half million more women than men in America but women held only two percent of the managerial positions; that no women sit on the AFL-CIO Council or the Supreme Court; that only two women had ever held cabinet rank and that there were at that time only two women of ambassadorial rank in the diplomatic corps. I stated then as I do now that this situation is outrageous. . . .

A few short years ago if you called most Negroes black it was tantamount to calling them niggers. But now black is beautiful and black is proud. There are relatively few people, white or black, who do not recognize what has happened.

Black people have freed themselves from the dead weight of the albatross of blackness that once hung around their neck. They have done it by picking it up in their arms and holding it out with pride for all the world to see. They have done it by embracing it—not in the dark of the moon but in the searing light of the white sun . . . They have said "yes" to it and found that the skin that was once seen as symbolizing their shame is in reality their badge of honor.

Women must come to realize that the superficial symbolisms that surround us are negative. We must begin to replace the old

14

negative thoughts about our femininity with positive thoughts and positive actions affirming it and more.

But we must also remember that that will be breaking with tradition and we must prepare ourselves—educationally, economically and psychologically—in order that we will be able to accept and bear with the sanctions that society will immediately impose upon us. . . .

We are challenged now as we never were before. The past twenty years, with its decline for women in employment and government; with the status quo in preparation of young women for certain professions, it is clear that evolution is not necessarily always a process of positive forward motion. Susan B. Anthony, Carrie Nation and Sojourner Truth were not evolutionaries. They were revolutionaries, as are many of the young women of today. More women and more men must join their ranks.

New goals and new priorities, not only for this country, but for all mankind, must be set. Formal education will not help us do that, we must therefore depend on informal learning.

We can do that by confronting people with their own humanity and their own inhumanity. Confronting them wherever we meet them—in the church, in the classroom, on the floor of Congress and the State Legislatures, in bars and on the streets. We must reject not only the stereotypes that others hold of us but also the stereotypes that we hold of ourselves and others.

In a speech made a few weeks ago to an audience that was predominantly white and all female I suggested the following if they wanted to create change: "You must start in your own homes, your own schools and your own churches . . . I don't want you to go home and talk about integrated schools, churches or marriages when the kind of integration you are talking about is black with white.

"I want you to go home and work for—fight for—the integration of male and female—human and human. Franz Fanon pointed out in *Black Skins—White Masks* that the anti-Semite was eventually the anti-feminist. And even further, I want to indicate that all discrimination is eventually the same thing—anti-humanism."

JESSE JACKSON
What Urban Blacks Want

When Martin Luther King, Jr., brought his civil rights crusade to Chicago in 1966, a branch of his national Southern Christian Leadership Conference was opened there under the name Operation Breadbasket with the Reverend Jesse Jackson as its chairman. Operation Breadbasket's activities have been directed primarily at economic problems plaguing urban blacks: housing, jobs, and consumer fraud. After King's death, Jackson came to be recognized as one of the abler national spokesmen for blacks, and his efforts have broadened to include most of the issues with which urbanites are concerned. In the fall of 1971, because of a disagreement with SCLC's national officers over SCLC-sponsored Black Expo in Chicago, Jackson was relieved of his position as director of Operation Breadbasket. He immediately formed his own organization, People United to Save Humanity, or PUSH. In the summer of 1970, while still with SCLC, Mr. Jackson wrote the article from which the following selection is taken. [Source: Chicago Tribune, July 19, 1970. "What Blacks of Chicago Want."]

What does the black man in Chicago want?

He wants to share responsibility in the reshaping of this city. He wants to participate in the reshaping of this state and the nation. The black man wants—and is demanding—power. He seeks to be able to make decisions on the direction that his community should move. He wants and intends to stop white usurpation of such significant black duties as deciding who runs black politics, what police policies are going to be, and what educational practices will be in the ghetto.

The black man wants empowerment, the power to determine his own destiny. He wants power to make freedom and justice—indeed democracy—prevail thruout America and the world.

By justice, I refer to that condition of which Aristotle spoke wherein every man gets his due, an equitable portion, a fair and equal share of whatever is being distributed. Justice demands among other things in this day and age, a job or an income for every man, white, black, or any color, since a man must be able to satisfy his basic needs and those of persons dependent upon him.

16

By freedom, I mean the unhampered capacity to choose between alternatives and, then, to be able to act on one's choices. The black man aspires to more than just freedom *from* discrimination where race is the basis for blacks being shunted aside regarding decent housing, quality education, and a good job. The black man looks forward to freedom *to*, as in the freedom to reconstruct or build anew his community and to control the policies and procedural workings of such community institutions as educational and police services.

Blacks seek the freedom to be judges, jurors, and policemen in proportionate numbers to their population ratio so we will be able to control systematically the conduct in our community. For example, things are out of hand with the black juvenile in terms of delinquent conduct—especially growing out of the youth gang situation—in large part because of the policies and practices of white prosecutors, white lawyers, white juries, white judges, all who make up what I often refer to as the "white felony" which produces and/or abets "black misdemeanor."

If a black person is caught for delinquency in the white community, the white community tries him. But, if a white person commits a crime in the black community and by some chance is charged, whites do the trying and judging, not blacks. So white slumlords, white grocers who sell blacks bad meat in the black community, and even the white policeman who shoots the black suspect [or some black innocent] in the back, can do their white thing with practical immunity from authentic prosecution and fair judgment by those whom they victimized or by those who are truly impartial.

Blacks need the freedom, the unhampered opportunity not only to be parents with power in their own communities, participants in the judicial order. They also need the freedom to become scientists, workers in the media—radio, television, newspapers, movies, the building trades, and other fields.

The black man must be empowered if freedom and justice are to cease being cherry-pie American ideals hanging high up somewhere in snow-white clouds. The black man must have power if the nation's vaunted ideals are to become down-to-earth realities. If Chicago, if Illinois, if America are going to be changed from what they have been and are to become what they ought to be, the black man must secure power.

17

Furthermore, blacks must empower themselves thru group unity and not thru uniformity with white standards or white wishes. Blacks can align themselves with whites of conscience and vision who see justice and democracy as indivisible and impossible of attainment without the intelligence, integrity, and involvement of all citizens. Such whites would realize, of course, that the country's present aristocratic democracy is a contradiction from the "get-go," which allows the white upper-classes to reign virtually unchecked over the poor black and white masses. . . .

We didn't come to Chicago from the South seeking more ample welfare grants. We came to Chicago prepared to and seeking work, drawn by the lure of Northern industry. We have always worked hard, harder than any other minority group in American history. We worked at the nastiest jobs and for the lowest pay. Our labor made cotton king. We hoed out Tobacco Road, hollowed out mountains, nursed, cooked for and raised white folks' children often to the neglect of our own.

What America needs is a redefinition of work in this age of automation and the declining need for unskilled labor. Whites must come to view black would-be laborers as valuable products and manifestations of an advanced stage of technological development rather than as mere trapped, useless, unemployable prisoners. Such attitudinal liberalism would facilitate thinking which could result in establishing federal and state programs such as the guaranteed annual wage, the negative income tax, and family subsidy grants.

What is needed in White America is more of that all-American virtue of tolerance and white acceptance and appreciation of the black assertions that will surely come.

Among the fronts on which whites can expect black assertions are those involving:

Procedural justice.
Law enforcement.
Politics.
Housing.
Education.
Health care.
Eradication of hunger.

Regarding procedural justice, we expect to have accused blacks judged by juries of their peers, not lilywhite Caucasian jurors, not a salt and token-pepper scene of 11 white jurors and one "white-minded Negro" juror.

In law enforcement, we seek either the lowering or limiting of the number of white policemen in the ghetto to a proportionate ratio with black policemen to suburbia. We are calling for blacks in a third of all top ranking jobs in the police department from chiefs, commanders, and captains on down.

In Chicago politics, we demand the liberation of voting registration procedures to open up the polls to the poor locked up blacks and other disenfranchised so that voting eligibility is as easy as draft eligibility or eligibility for paying taxes. There are more unregistered black voters in Chicago than in the entire state of Mississippi.

Blacks constitute upwards of 40 per cent of the city's population, yet we have only one-ninth or so of the city's aldermanic and committeeman slots. We should have 22 aldermen and 22 ward committeemen based on our population ratio instead of the 11 aldermen and 9 committeemen which we have.

In housing, blacks are going to press for a breaking open of the tight residential noose choking us off from healthy housing dispersal. Ashland Avenue still constitutes a symbolic and a concrete "iron curtain," or Berlin Wall, just as it did four years ago when the late Dr. Martin Luther King Jr. led thousands across this local Rubicon of racism trying to open up housing opportunities in this city, and in Cicero, which could accommodate a notorious felon, Al Capone, and yet would offer no room in its many inns for a world-renowned son of peace and justice like Dr. King.

The racist manipulations of the city's real estate moguls, their underling agents and slumlord co-conspirators have led to such a deplorable situation as 74,000 blacks currently being sardine-packed into Kenwood-Oakland community where only 10,000 white people lived 20 years ago.

As a result of the conditions spawned from such density, Kenwood-Oakland has an infant mortality rate and tubercular rate that is 20 times worse than the national average, worse than anything in Mississippi, worse than most parts of the world, and compares only with the rates of death and disease in Calcutta, India.

The recent hassle between the [black] Contract Buyers League

19

and the [white] Universal Builders group over the discriminatory and exorbitantly high purchase price the black buyers paid on contracts—when the blacks weren't allowed to buy on mortgage arrangements like whites—shows that all blacks, regardless of income level and level of responsibility and respectability, including doctors, lawyers, postmen, school teachers, and policemen, still have to pay a disastrously steep and unfair "black tax" on common goods and services. Yes, the so-called black bourgeois, too, is trapped in the binds of white racism just like its poorer black brothers and sisters.

We want the establishment of an "in fact" unitary public school system, ending the double-dealing, "de-facto" setup. The present dualistic, two separate races educational system provides a decent educational program for the city's white children and an indecent educational program for the city's black pupils.

We demand the virtual doubling of per capita moneys allocated for the education of black children in Chicago's public schools to equalize the "per capita" allocations made to educate white children in the city.

We demand an equalizing of teacher-pupil ratios in black schools, lowering the number of pupils per teacher, so as to compare with the more favorable situation of white pupils per teacher in Chicago.

We believe that additional moneys should be spent on enriching educational preparedness and qualifications of black and other minority group administrators and teachers. Public school and anti-poverty funds which, too often, go now to shore up a rotten political machine or go to naive, dilettante, "do-gooder" type whites who mess up more than they help in attempting to deal with the poverty problems of Chicago blacks, poor whites, and Spanish-speaking persons.

The health care and hunger eradication problems will require substantial moneys, but no more than is reasonable. The projected costs of such programs are certainly well within the range of the city's budgetary programming.

The hunger feeding ordinance which Operation Breadbasket set before the City Council would cost only 5 per cent of the city's budget and is much sounder and a much more beneficial program than scores of programs in which the city is already involved — at 3 and 4 and 10 and 20 times the cost.

What can and should Chicagoland whites do in the face of that which Chicago blacks want and demand?

Whites in government immediately must deal with the question of whether they intend to see democracy extended to all Americans. If they can countenance — as they should be able to — the spread of democracy, they should do their part right now, right in the corner where they work, at their desks, and over their phones.

They should begin to see to the mobilization of white political conscience in Chicago, just as was developed in Cleveland, Gary, and Newark. Such white concern and effort became a valuable part of a broadly-based coalition led by concerted black endeavor which sparked a new dawning in urban politics and government operations in communities which were politically thread-bare and in despair.

Whites in businesses such as the mass media — in newspapers, television, magazines, radio, and movies — have a tremendous responsibility since the media can do so much to dispel the dark clouds of ignorance abroad in the land on question of race. It is such ignorance which precipitates fear which leads to things such as real estate panicking, George Wallace-like reactionary band-wagons and political repression.

The media has the awesome responsibility to help the right wing decide to be "right," and, thereby truly all-American. The right wing must come to see that there is no more red-blooded an American group than the nation's black citizenry.

WHITNEY YOUNG, JR.

A Strategy for the Seventies

As executive director of the National Urban League until his untimely death on March 11, 1971, while touring Africa, Whitney Young, Jr., was one of the most articulate and respected black spokesmen in the United States. Not given to sloganeering, he was a proponent neither of separatism nor of integration as such, but was an uncompromising advocate of equality of rights and opportunities for all Americans. He worked to achieve his goals through the painstaking and often patience-shredding tasks of devising the mechanics whereby economic and social injustices could be overcome. On the occasion of the 60th anniversary celebration of the Urban League, Young examined the current ills of society and made wide-ranging suggestions for future action in dealing with them. His address was delivered in New York City on July 19, 1970. [Source: Vital Speeches, September 15, 1970.]

Our task at this Conference will be to devise the strategies that will ensure that the cause of equality, for which so much blood and tears have been shed, will triumph in this land. In our sessions and work-shops we will question the prevailing myths that entangle current thinking on economic and political problems afflicting blacks and other minorities, and we will continue to move beyond the narrow limits of debate to get at the roots of the problem of bringing power to the powerless. . . .

The past year also saw the Urban League initiate a broad coalition of groups to influence what we tried to make the first accurate Census count of non-white peoples in the history of the nation. The "Make Black Count" campaign was founded on the realization that by undercounting the actual numbers of blacks and browns in America, the government, in effect, was withholding from them the federal aid distributed on a per capita basis. Black communities across the land were not getting their fair share of hospital and school monies, or even proper representation in Congress and State Legislatures. The figures are not all in yet, but the "Make Black Count" staff will be "riding herd" on the Census Bureau to insure that blacks—blacks—for a welcome change—get a fair count.

But equal to the importance of the count itself was the way the campaign was able to bring black people together, making it possible to deal with the Census Bureau from a position of strength.

The "Make Black Count" campaign has been a unified effort of the black community. It has been a coalition of all representative groups—organized welfare mothers, street gangs, church members, sororities, civil rights organizations, and others. The Urban League was the catalyst, the enabler, the provider of resources and techni-

22

cal assistance. We were content to take a back seat in this. Our intent was not to hog headlines or be pictured on television. All literature, posters, publicity, etc., highlighted the coalition, not the Urban League. Our goal was to bring the community together on a vital issue, and to set in motion the national and local coalitions that will become the basis for further cooperation and unity. Our experience in this campaign convinces me that our purpose has been successful, and we shall build upon it in the coming months.

We joined, also, with others to mount campaigns to protest the willful murders of Black Panthers and black college students by our home-grown version of the SS, and to successfully protest the nomination of insensitive judges to the Supreme Court that protects our liberties from the very system of racism they represent.

The Urban League is active on a broad series of fronts:

. . . At the request of key Congressional leaders we are submitting to the Congress a detailed agenda for an updated Domestic Marshall Plan which we first proposed in 1964 to do for the victims of American racism and the poor of all colors what America so willingly did for the European victims of World War II.

. . . We have started the National Urban League Housing Foundation to expand the supply of low and moderate income housing and to give the black people a share in the building and control of their own housing.

. . . We took a giant step toward strengthening black colleges through the Black Executive Exchange Program that brings blacks who have made it in the competitive give-and-take of the professions and business to lecture and advise students and faculty at black institutions of higher education.

. . . And we have served the needs of ghetto youth in a variety of ways, including consultation and assistance for Youth Organizations United, the national federation of over 200 city street gangs that is helping to channel the energies of these youngsters into constructive action on behalf of their communities.

And, further serving youth, our summer student program brought 100 college student leaders again into the ghettos of America in a constructive program to help organize the black community, and to place the talent and spirits of campus youth at the service of their brothers and sisters.

. . . We moved to fill the nationwide vacuum in child care through a Day Care Center Corporation that promises to fill a crying need for neighborhood day care centers operated and controlled by the community.

. . . Our new Consumer Protection Program is designed at organizing the exploited minority community to a new awareness of making the most effective use of their scarce dollars and ending the callous preying upon the poor that typifies so much of the economic life of the ghetto.

. . . The Urban League's pioneering Street Academies will come to many more communities through the establishment of an Urban Education Institute that will provide the framework for planning and consulting with other institutions and the community in order to duplicate many times over our successes in helping deprived youngsters to recover from the failures of the heartless educational bureaucracies, and go on to higher educational goals.

. . . Our Labor Education Advancement Program (LEAP) is responsible for the greatest breakthrough of black apprentices into the building trades in history, while at the same time creating and supporting black contractors.

. . . Our On-the-Job Training programs are the most efficient in the country, with the highest retention rate at the lowest cost per trainee.

Other Urban League programs are helping to develop black businessmen, bring new opportunities to returning veterans, and family planning and mental retardation services to the black community under its own control for the first time. And our various job placement and training programs pumped $400 million of cool, green cash into the black community in new and added wages and salaries.

But we cannot be complacent about our successes, accomplished with limited resources. They represent a challenge for still greater efforts in the future; a base from which we must build the coalitions and unity without which racism will remain supreme, and poverty will possess the souls of the real forgotten Americans—the blacks, the browns, and the reds of the rural and urban ghettos.

This new decade could bring promise of a new era in the relations between the races. Just as the nation as a whole is at a crossroads, so, too, black people face a new turning point, a decisive strategic moment that may put us on a new path to freedom. Just as there is some doubt whether the nation will choose the right path to greatness there must be doubts, especially in the light of this historic racism of America, that the seventies will bring true equality for black people. But while we may question the future, it becomes our duty to mobilize and steel ourselves for a new phase of struggle.

Black Americans first pursued a *strategy of conciliation*. Fresh from the prison of slavery, the Freedmen and their sons tried to work with whites and convince them to act with decency. Whites remained in basic control of all matters affecting blacks, and the strategy of conciliation became, above all, a strategy of survival, a strategy to squeeze short-term gains under adversity.

Then there came a *strategy of organization*. Blacks created the institutions without which there can be no community and no progress in a hostile society. These were the years that saw the birth of the NAACP, the Urban League, and educational, civil, religious and business associations. The institutional structure of the black community took shape, and, abandoned by white society, blacks came together to build strength for the inevitable future confrontation with unbridled white power.

The next phase was the *strategy of confrontation*, in which the institutions of the black community staged a frontal assault on the pillars of racism. This was the era of the boycott, the sit-in, ride-ins, wade-ins, lie-ins and all the other disruptive tactics that confronted Americans not with the pliant, silent oppressed blacks they wanted, but with the proud, determined black men and women who insisted on equality.

We will be forever grateful for the dedicated, fearless warriors of CORE, SNCC, SCLC, the NAACP and the Urban League who fought the evils of racism on its home grounds—in the Southern Black Belt, and in the rigged courts and bigoted cities of the North.

And, basically, this strategy worked. To it we owe the destruction of the formal, legal structure of racism in America To it we owe the passage of laws and the legal decisions that provide a framework from which we can pursue the goals of complete equality. To it we owe the world-wide realization that America is plagued by racism, and our country has won not the respect, not even the envy, of the

25

world's peoples, but their pity that so great a nation can be so incapable of morality and action to end poverty and bigotry. . . .

I propose that the just and the powerful deal with each other as equals in a *strategy of negotiation.*

White society has the trappings of power—its police, its army, its law. But blacks have demonstrated effectively that unless our just demands are dealt with, these trappings of power only make a society muscle-bound; only drive it into displays of raw, naked power, displays that solve nothing and tear apart everything. . . .

A strategy of negotiation demands from black America the power to negotiate from a position of strength. I believe we have demonstrated that power. In one sense, we have amply demonstrated a power to disrupt. In another sense, we have demonstrated, through the election of black mayors and legislators, political strength, and through the relentless accomplishment of our people against great odds, a changing economic and educational strength. We have made the most of the limited opportunities available to the point where we have the pride, the strength, and the accomplishments which should compel white leadership to sit down with us as equals.

A strategy of negotiation demands of black leadership a sense of unity and purpose, without which we will be subject to the old divide-and-conquer tactics oppressors have always used. It will demand of us a discipline and a willingness to rise above differences of doctrine and personality for the greater good of all black people. We must, more than ever, impose upon ourselves and our organizations a community of spirit and a fraternal bond that will enable us to better negotiate from a base of strength and unity. . . .

The economic and power dimensions of the problems facing us can be met through alliances with others in this twisted society who are hurting, too.

The problems of poverty are not black alone. There is hunger in the tenements and shacks of whites and browns and reds as well. There is misery in Appalachian ghost-towns, in the barrios of the West, in migrant labor camps, and in Indian reservations. And there is misery here in New York's Harlem, South Bronx, and Bedford Stuyvesant.

America has grown fat and heavy with the sweat and labor of all minorities; now she must grow proud and strong through an alliance based on our realism and sense of purpose. There is at hand the raw material for building the strong alliance for social justice that is essential if America is to be saved—and we must save her if we are not *all* to go down the drain. While it is an historic fact that we came here on different ships, it is imperative that we realize that we're in the same boat now.

An Interview with Ray Charles

In two decades entertainer Ray Charles has evolved from a nationally known talent into an international musical institution. Beginning as a blues singer, he has artfully combined jazz, country-western, and rock to give them a universal appeal through his own distinctive style. Born in September 1930, in Albany, Georgia, Charles overcame the drawbacks of being poor and black in the rural South, compounded with the blindness that set in at age seven due to glaucoma, to get what musical education he could at a school for the blind in St. Augustine, Florida. His first big selling record, "I Got A Woman," was released in 1954. He followed that success with a string of hits that included "Georgia on My Mind," "Born to Lose," and the enormously popular "I Can't Stop Lovin' You." In an interview with Playboy *magazine, reprinted in part below, Charles answered questions dealing with his career, personal life, other black artists, and a variety of national issues.* [*Source:* Playboy, *March 1970.*]

PLAYBOY: You were one of the first singers in what music critic Barbara Gardner once called the "natural Negro idiom" to gain wide acceptance among black and white audiences alike. How do you explain this broad appeal?

CHARLES: For the real answer to that question, you'd have to ask the people who buy my records and come to my shows—the black people and the white people. All I can say is that I'm sincere in my work; I give it all I've got. But I'm not saying that's the answer, either, because lots of performers are just as earnest as I am, maybe more so, and luck has it that they've never made it. Who knows why? I guess my emotions have a lot to do with the way my songs

27

come out. Some nights I sing the blues and I'm under control. Other nights I sing the same songs and I can hardly keep the tears from rolling down my face. I just try never to be mechanical about what I'm doing and I try not to shortchange my audiences – whether I'm playing to 100 people or 100,000.

PLAYBOY: Your fans obviously go for that approach, because to many of them, you're known as "The Genius." Frank Sinatra even went as far as to call you the "only genius in the business."

CHARLES: Yeah, Frank did say that. Although I really appreciate the nice names people call me – especially since, in this business, I'm bound to get called a few dirty ones, too – I'm kind of scared of that label. Genius means the top of the heap, which, if a guy doesn't watch himself, can also mean in a rut.

PLAYBOY: You're also known as "the genius of soul." Since the word soul has so many interpretations, what's yours?

CHARLES: It's got different strokes for different folks. To me, when you're talking about people with soul, you're talking about warm, understanding, down-to-earth people that do things from the heart. If you're talking about a soulful relationship with a member of the opposite sex, that means one that's genuine, for real. It's when nobody's faking nothing – when you're truly communicating with your partner. If you're talking about soul food, you're talking about the kind of food I love: neck bones, knuckles, collard greens, black-eyed peas and chitterlings. They're mostly foods that became popular during slavery and the Depression, when black people had to make a little bit go a long way. Many of us still have to do that, but nowadays, people all over have found out how good it is; even Lyndon Johnson eats some of it. I don't know if he's soulful enough for chitterlings yet, but he knows all about ham hocks and collards.

PLAYBOY: You're often quoted as saying that you "want people to *feel* my soul." Why this great urge to open your innermost self to your audiences – people who are strangers?

CHARLES: I love this business I'm in; it's like a hobby that I happen to get paid for. Besides, my mother always told me to be as sincere as I can at whatever I'm doing in life – whether it's shining other folks' shoes, emptying other folks' garbage or singing other folks' troubles away. After all, the other name of this game is the communications business. I've got to be able to reach the pub-

28

lic – to make them feel that the girl I'm singing about really did take all my money and run off with my best friend last night – or I won't be around long as a performer. The way I seem to communicate best is through sad songs, because when people are sad – which is most of the time – they want to hear something that compounds that sadness, something that makes 'em cry that much more. Then, when they've got it all out of their systems, they can go through the rest of the day fine. That's why so many people have leaned on the blues over all these years. The blues won't go out of style until people stop hurting each other. But certain blues singers go out of style quick if the public doesn't believe they really know what pain is all about.

PLAYBOY: Today, in what might be called the post-Beatle era, many white groups have gone in for full-blooded adaptations of blues styles – the Muddy Waters-B. B. King-Howlin' Wolf approach – coupled with an abundance of electronic amplification. What about that blend?

CHARLES: White kids will never feel about Muddy or B. B. the way they feel about the Rolling Stones or Blood, Sweat & Tears. They've got to have entertainers from their own race to idolize, it seems. Negroes have been singing rhythm-and-blues, or soul music, as it's called now, more or less as you hear it today, since before I was born. But white mothers weren't going to let their daughters swoon over those black cats, so they never got widely known. Then along came Elvis Presley and the white kids had a hero. All that talk about rock 'n' roll began then, but black musicians started to get a little play, too. When the English boys came on the scene, they admitted where they got their inspiration and that caused even more interest in the real blues. I'm glad to see these youngsters doing our music. It enhances the guys who originated it, the same as one of those symphony orchestras enhances Beethoven.

PLAYBOY: Then you view the current interest in soul among whites as a healthy phenomenon, instead of a case of cultural robbery, as some black and white critics have claimed?

CHARLES: Just because Bell invented the telephone is no reason to say Ray Charles can't use it. It's ridiculous to have certain music for certain races. I've heard some people say that the big production

29

about soul is just another one of the white man's second-story jobs, but there certainly are many more black artists being heard on white stations today who weren't there a few years ago—and their music is being played just the way *they* play it. I mean that these white stations—some of them are top-40 and some are called underground stations—are playing the real blues, with no water in the whiskey. This makes for understanding, and the more of it we can get . . .—I don't care if it's through music, sports or what, as long as people can get together and realize that so-and-so is not such a bastard after all—the better off we'll all be. . . .

PLAYBOY: Do you think that the musical forms now identified with blacks, as well as those of country-and-western and such exotic influences as the Greek and East Indian, will eventually merge to produce a single American sound?

CHARLES: They might, but there'll still be differences—according to who's singing. You're not going to find a whole lot of whites who can sing like Muddy Waters. You may find one or two who come close—come to think of it, I've heard one or two lately—but, generally speaking, there'll always be that little difference.

PLAYBOY: Are you saying that whites can't really sing the blues?

CHARLES: I didn't say that; they tell me that *anything's* possible. I only say that I've never heard a white singer who can sing the blues effectively—the way, say, that Aretha Franklin sings them. But who knows—tomorrow, maybe somebody will come along. After all, the blues is mainly music about people's troubles, and everybody's entitled to a few of those; it's the degree of trouble that makes the difference. If the blues ever really gets sung by a white person, it'll be the Jew that does it. I think they've had a history very similar to the black man's: They've been persecuted all over the world and they've known what it is to be somebody else's footstool.

PLAYBOY: Accepting your argument that environment and personal experiences determine one's artistic validity, how do you justify yourself—a black man—as a country-and-western singer?

CHARLES: What I did was take country-and-western songs and sing them *my* way. In other words, I didn't try to imitate Hank Snow or Grandpa Jones. I did the same thing with songs like *Geor-*

gia, which has been around for over 30 years. I think there's a vast difference between putting your thing on a song and trying to be a certain kind of singer. Whatever the song, jazz or country-and-western, it's got to sound like I did it or I'm not going to release it.

PLAYBOY: Were you aware at the time you cut your country-and-western albums that a number of purists among your fans objected to your venturing into that area?

CHARLES: I've been listening to *Grand Ole Opry* since I was eight or nine years old, and I happen to dig it. But the main reason I did these hillbilly tunes was that there are millions of everyday people who listen to this music – not just in the States but in Europe and Asia, too. Country-and-western, to my mind, is a very sincere form of music, just like the blues. It's the kind of music that you don't go to school to learn to play; you've either got it in your soul or you haven't – just like the blues. It's not prettied up or glossed over, and it's about poor people and dirt farmers and all the little folks who are having a tough time of it just staying alive – exactly like the blues. . . .

PLAYBOY: But there is a difference in cultural environment between the groups.

CHARLES: Of course there is. Just looking at a white guy living in the hills of Kentucky, you might say: "He lives in a tar-paper shack, not enough to eat and raggedy clothes on his back, just like the black man; he's in poverty, just like the black man." But if you come to that conclusion, I must say to you that the hillbilly man can go anywhere he wants to; he can do anything he wants to; he doesn't have any restrictions against him whatsoever; he can even live in a black ghetto if he wants to. But it takes ten housing laws and 30 tanks for a black man to get into some of these white suburbs. Americans love to say they hate communism, but a Russian can come over here and get better treatment than a black American citizen. And, Christ, don't let me forget the real American: the red man. Yeah, it'll be Jews, or maybe Indians, who sing the blues first after us, because that poor hillbilly either likes the way he lives – and that's perfectly all right with me – or he's just too damn lazy to make something of himself. The blues isn't about *choosing* to be in poverty. . . .

PLAYBOY: A moment ago, you observed a parallel between Jews

and blacks. That seems ironic, in view of the reported upsurge of anti-Semitism in the black areas of America's cities.

CHARLES: Yes, I know that some black people are saying the Jew has been in our communities, sapping us of this and stealing that. But, hell, I know some black people in those same communities who have been sapping and stealing from black folks as fast as that Jew. One of the white man's faults has been that he's been too quick to condemn my whole race. Now, if black people turn right around and say that all Jews are thieves and crooks, we're just as wrong as the white man, and it might as well be dog eat dog. I say this: If black folks find a Jew in their community who's not giving them a fair shake, they should throw his ass out. While they're at it, they might also kick out those Negroes who're overcharging and short-weighting them. This can be done by just not patronizing them; they'll soon have to close up. Frankly, I must say that Jews have been some of the black man's biggest supporters in this country, so I can't see spitting on a helping hand. Besides that, the black man could stand to take a page or two out of the Jews' book by sticking together and helping one's own. . . .

PLAYBOY: Could we persuade you to talk a little more on the subject of racism?

CHARLES: That's a different story.

PLAYBOY: All right. How old were you when you first became aware of race prejudice?

CHARLES: The impact wasn't strong until I was about ten years old. Before that, all us kids – black and white – used to play together, and it never occurred to me that anybody was different from anybody else. Sometime after I was in the blind school, I started asking myself why they had a white side and a colored side to the campus. Of course, that's not the case anymore; but back then, all the facilities on the white side were better than the ones on the colored side. There was only one hospital at the school and, of course, it was on the white side. If we had to be separated like that, I wondered why the damn hospital wasn't in the middle. The whole thing about having different sides seemed stupid to me, because, hell, we were all blind.

PLAYBOY: Of course, you are both black and blind. Which one have you found to be the bigger obstacle?

32

CHARLES: As I've said, I learned how to handle my blindness pretty early in life, thanks to my mother and a little hard work. I'm a lot better equipped to handle things than a lot of blind people I know; I do what I want and I go where I want. But because I'm a black man, whatever affects my people affects me. This means that the greatest handicap I've had — and still have — is my color. Until every man in America can get any job that he's qualified for or any house he's got the money to buy, regardless of his color, I'll always be handicapped.

PLAYBOY: The voter-registration campaigners of the early Sixties felt that casting ballots was the best method of attaining the kind of black power you're talking about. But a smaller percentage of the registered black voters utilized their franchise in the last national election than in 1964. Do you think this indicates that blacks are beginning to regard the electoral process as a futile exercise?

CHARLES: I don't know why many of us didn't vote in the last election, but it was a bad thing. When I consider that men like Martin Luther King and a lot of other black and white people — the Kennedys included — got themselves beaten into the ground, stomped, spit on and killed so that black people could have the ballot, I hate to think that they went through all of that hell for nothing. I believe more in the power of the vote than in getting a gun and trying to kill off the whole white race. I think that's absolutely stupid. There aren't enough of us, to begin with. If the white man wanted to, all he'd have to say is that every dollar in the United States is void. Then he could issue new currency — to whites only — and we'd be up shit's creek. One of the only sensible weapons the black man's got is the ballot. If neither Humphrey nor Nixon looks good to me, I'll still have to go with the lesser of two evils. I hear a lot of black people saying they're sorry that Nixon's in now. I ask 'em if they voted for Humphrey or anybody else. "No," they say. "Well, then," I tell them, "you don't have the right to be sorry now."

PLAYBOY: During the Johnson Administration, Congress passed a record number of measures supporting civil rights, and the Warren Court drew cries from the right for the impeachment of its Chief Justice because of the liberality with which he led that body. Nevertheless, all this did little, if anything, to reduce the level of animosity

33

among black and whites. Furthermore, to the delight of white seg-regationists, a growing number of blacks have now rejected inte-gration as a goal. How do you feel about a geographically and racially divided U.S.A.?

CHARLES: I am 100 percent for the country being united. Right now, Vietnam is divided and at war. It's practically the same in Korea. Then there's Nationalist China and mainland China, Nigeria and Biafra, black America and white America. Too many people have been burned, lynched and nailed to the cross fighting for equal rights to separate this country now. We've got all the laws on the books that the books can hold, but we find that's still not enough, because you can't legislate a person's loves or his hates. What we've got to do now is start learning how to communicate with each other. Without that, we'll never achieve anything. I'm not for going around hating people; I just don't go for that, and I don't go for living apart from all other races in this country. A black man can have his own thing, just like the Italians, the Irish and the Jews have here, without detaching himself from America. After all, no matter how small it's been made to look, the black man's stake is awfully big in this country.

Besides, until we get our own A.T.&T. or General Motors, I don't think the majority of black people will be interested in separating from white America and leaving behind all we helped build up here. Are all the black mothers who gave up their sons in World War Two and Korea and Vietnam just going to say, "OK, take this country, I'm leaving"? Hell, no. Personally, I've paid too many dues for me and my wife and family to give up everything and split. And no-body's going to *make* me give it up, either—white or black.

GEORGE JACKSON
Letter to Angela Davis

Chicago-born and raised, George Jackson's run-ins with the police began when he was in his early teens, living in the West Side ghetto; but it was after his family's move to the Watts area of Los Angeles that his troubles with the law *became serious. From then on it was for him a life in and out of jail on a number of offenses, most frequently robbery, until 1960 when he was caught stealing $70 from a gas station. In hopes of leniency he made a full confession, but was sentenced to from one year to life. Even in prison his trouble was not over, for in 1970 he was again on trial, along with two other inmates of Soledad Prison at Salinas, for killing a prison guard. But his years "inside" gave him time for education and reading that he had never had before. The reading he did, largely in the works of revolutionaries such as Marx, Lenin, Engels, Trotsky, and Mao, gave him a rationale for his attitude toward white society and produced a deep concern with the problems of "third-world" peoples and the movements for social change everywhere. Jackson's own propensity for violence as an agent of change was certainly increased by the treatment accorded non-white inmates of California's prisons. On August 21, 1971, Jackson, along with another inmate and three guards, was killed in an apparent prison-break attempt at San Quentin. The circumstances surrounding his death have been so obscured by contradictory charges and statements that it is difficult to determine what actually did happen that day. But by the time of his death he was regarded as one of the more eloquent champions of militant black power, as this letter to Angela Davis, written in the spring of 1970, testifies. Within a year Miss Davis herself was under indictment as an accessory to murder and kidnapping following a violent confrontation at San Rafael courthouse, where Jackson's younger brother, Jonathan, was killed in an attempted escape. [Source: Soledad Brother: The Prison Letters of George Jackson, N.Y., 1970.]*

They hate us, don't they? I like it that way, that is the way it's supposed to be. If they didn't hate me I would be doing something very wrong, and then I would have to hate myself. I prefer it this way. I get little hate notes in the folds of my newspaper almost every day now. You know, the racist stuff, traditional "Dear nigger" stuff, and how dead I am going to be one day. They think they're mad at me now, but it's nothing compared to how it will be when I really get mad myself. . . .

Pigs are punks Angela. We've made a terrible mistake in overestimating these people. It reflects on us badly that we have allowed them to do the things they have done to us. Since they are idiots, what does that make us. I just read Bobby Seale's account of that scene in Chicago (*Ramparts*, June '70). It started in San Francisco with that flight to evade charge. One of the pigs commented that "this was so easy." But it shouldn't have been. Brothers like that are the best of us. It shouldn't have gone down like that. We should never make it easy for them—by relaxing—at this stage of the educational process. Examples are crucially important. Well that's the name of the game right now.

I have ideas, ten years' worth of them, I'd like all those brothers on Fiftieth Street to be aware of them. Tell Fay Stender to give you a copy of my thoughts on Huey Newton and politics. . . . At the end of these writings, titled "Letter to Huey Newton," there should be a note on revolutionary culture and the form it should take in the black American colonies. That was the best section. Without that section the power would be lost. Fay and I don't agree altogether on political method. But that is only because we are viewing things from very different levels of slavery. Mine is an abject slavery.

I think of you all the time. I've been thinking about women a lot lately. Is there anything sentimental or otherwise wrong with that? There couldn't be. It's never bothered me too much before, the sex thing. I would do my exercise and the hundreds of katas, stay busy with something . . . this ten years really has gone pretty quickly. It has destroyed me as a person, a human being that is, but it was sudden, it was a sudden death, it seems like ten days rather than ten years.

Would you like to know a subhuman? I certainly hope you have time. I'm not a very nice person. I'll confess out front, I've been forced to adopt a set of responses, reflexes, attitudes that have made me more kin to the cat than anything else, the big black one. For all of that I am not a selfish person. I don't think so anyway, but I do have myself in mind when I talk about us relating. You would be the generous one, I the recipient of that generosity.

They're killing niggers again down the tier, all day, every day. They are killing niggers and "them protesters" with small workings of mouth. One of them told a pig today that he was going to be awful disappointed with the pig if the pig didn't shoot some niggers or protesters this evening when he got off work. The pig found it very amusing. They went off on a twenty-minute political discussion, pig and his convict supporter. There is something very primitive about these people. Something very fearful. In all the time I've been down here on Maximum Row, no brother has ever spoken to one of these people. We never speak about them, you know, across the cells. Every brother down here is under the influence of the party line, and racist terms like "honky" have never been uttered. All of these are beautiful brothers, ones who have stepped across the line into the position from which there can be no retreat. All are fully committed. They are the most desperate and dauntless of our kind. I love them. They are men and they do not fight with their mouths. They've brought them here from prisons all over the state to be warehoused or murdered. Whichever is more expedient. That Brother Edwards who was murdered in that week in January told his lawyer that he would never get out of prison alive. He was at the time of that statement on Maximum Row, Death Row, Soledad, California. He was twenty-one years old. We have made it a point to never exchange words with these people. But they never relent. Angela, there are some people who will never learn new responses. They will carry what they incorporated into their characters at early youth to the grave. Some can never be educated. As an historian you know how long and how fervently we've appealed to these people to take some of the murder out of their system, their economics, their propaganda. And as an intelligent observer you must see how our appeals were received. We've wasted many generations and oceans of blood trying to civilize these elements over here. It cannot be done in the manner we have attempted it in the past. Dialectics, understanding, love, passive resistance, they won't work on an activistic, maniacal, gory pig. It's going to grow much worse for the black male than it already is, much, much worse. We are going to have to be the vanguard, the catalyst, in any meaningful change. . . .

There is so much that could be done, right now. . . . But I won't talk about those things right here. I will say that it should never be easy for them to destroy us. If you start with Malcolm X and count *all* of the brothers who have died or been captured since, you will find that not even one of them was really *prepared* for a fight. No imagination or fighting style was evident in any one of the incidents. But each one that died professed to know the nature of our enemies. It should never be so easy for them. Do you understand what I'm saying? Edward V. Hanrahan, Illinois State Attorney General, sent fifteen pigs to raid the Panther headquarters and murder

Hampton and Clark. Do you have any idea what would have happened to those fifteen pigs if they had run into as many Viet Cong as there were Panthers in that building. The VC are all little people with less general education than we have. The argument that they have been doing it longer has no validity at all, because they were doing it just as well when they started as they are now. It's very contradictory for a man to teach about the murder in corporate capitalism, to isolate and expose the murderers behind it, to instruct that these madmen are completely without stops, are licentious – totally depraved – and then not make adequate preparations to defend himself from the madman's attack. Either they don't really believe their own spiel or they harbor some sort of subconscious death wish.

None of this should have happened as it did. I don't know if we'll learn in time or not. I am not well here. I pretend that all is well for the benefit of my family's peace of mind. But I'm going to cry to you, so you can let the people of Fiftieth Street know not to let this happen to them, and that they must resist that cat with *all* of their strength when he starts that jail talk.

When the menu reads steak we get a piece of rotten steer (I hope) the size of a quarter. When it reads cake we get something like cornbread. Those are the best things served. When two guys fight, the darker guy will get shot. To supplement their incomes the pigs will bring anything into the prison and sell it to the convict who smuggles money in from his visits. Now black people don't visit their kin in the joint much and those that do can't afford to give up any money. So we have less of everything that could make life more comfortable – and safe (weapons are brought in too). Pigs are fascist right out front, the white prisoner who is con-wise joins the Hitlerian party right here in the joint. He doesn't have to worry about the rules, he stays high. When he decides to attack us, he has the best of weapons (seldom will a pig give a con a gun, though. It has happened, however, in San Quentin three times to my knowledge. But they will provide cutlery and zip guns). The old convict code died years ago. These cons work right with the police against us. The only reason that I am still alive is because I take everything to the extreme, and they know it. I never let any of them get within arm's reach, and their hands must be in full view. When on the yard I would stay close to something to get under. Nothing, absolutely nothing comes as a surprise to me. There is much to be said about these places but I must let this go right now or I won't be able to post it until tomorrow. In the event that you missed it (my writing is terrible, I know), I think a great deal of you. This is one slave that knows how to love. It comes natural and runs deep. Accepting it will never hurt you. Free, open, honest love, that's me.

JULIAN BOND AND ROY V. HARRIS
Dialogue on Integration

Early in 1969 a meeting took place at the Commerce Club of Atlanta, Georgia, between Julian Bond, nationally known black member of the state legislature, and Roy V. Harris, one of Georgia's avowed segregationists. Harris, at 73, had long been active in Georgia politics and had served as speaker of the state's House of Representatives. During the 1968 presidential campaign he was state manager for George C. Wallace. Bond had first risen to national prominence when, elected to the state legislature in 1965 from a predominantly black district, he was refused a seat because of his strong criticism of the Vietnam War. In special elections in February and November 1966, he was again re-elected, and again refused a seat. After the U.S. Supreme Court declared the legislature's action unconstitutional, he was finally admitted in January 1967. At the 1968 national Democratic Convention in Chicago, Bond led a delegation of insurgent Georgia Loyal National Democrats that had won half the state's representation; and at the same convention he became the first black man of a major party ever to have his name placed in nomination for the vice-presidency. He was forced to withdraw, however, because, at age 28, he was several years under the constitutional age requirement for the office. [Source: Atlanta, April 1969.]

HARRIS: I think we do have a problem, and I think that one of these days it's got to be worked out, the sooner the better. It's a question of which way we're going and how we're going to solve this problem, whether there will be a fusion of the races, or whether we will work out some pattern by which we can live side by side and work together in a state of peace and harmony.

BOND: It seems to be likely—over a period of hundreds and hundreds of thousands of years that there may be a one-race society, but I don't think it's likely to happen any time soon, in either of our lifetimes . . . I don't think there should be a prohibition against it, neither social nor legal. It ought not to be a goal to be worked for because it's probably not from either of our points of view a desirable goal. You can solve the race problem without that kind of fusion. You can solve it by having an equitable division of power in this country. As power begins to be divided more equitably, *then* you're going to see a lessening of what you call the racial problem. I don't think it's going to happen quickly either.

HARRIS: I think you're right. I don't think it can be done quickly. Now understand this. I believe in black power. I believe in black economy. I believe Negroes are entitled to representation. In Augusta, we used to have the City Council elect two from each ward. Each ward elected its own members. Now you run from each ward but you run citywide.

BOND: That's the way they do it here.

HARRIS: And, of course, it was done to keep Negroes out of city council.

BOND: You're the only politician who will say that.

HARRIS: How's that?

BOND: You're the only white politician who will say that.

HARRIS: Is that right?

BOND: (Former Mayor Bill) Hartsfield said it was done to keep corruption down.

HARRIS: But, of course, that's the reason. I tell you they're damn hypocrites.

BOND: That's where you're absolutely right. You need to come down and talk to the Fulton County House delegation, Mr. Harris, and get them straightened out. Why don't you write them each a letter?

HARRIS: Nooo. I've got enough troubles of my own. I'll tell you, though, when a majority of Augusta or Atlanta becomes black, they can have it and they're entitled to it.

REPORTER: *Does it make any difference who's in the Governor's office as far as Negroes are concerned?*

40

BOND: Before I got put out of the legislature, I went with all the other Negro legislators to see Governor (Carl) Sanders. We mentioned a lot of problems to him. One thing was there were no Negroes on any draft boards in the state of Georgia except in Atlanta. He said, "I'll have to study it." A year later, I finally got in the legislature and I went to see Lester Maddox, and you know what Governor Maddox said? "Y'all fight in the Army, don't you?" He said, "You ought to be on the draft boards." He did it just like that. He didn't have to study it or anything. He saw some things are right and some things are wrong. I think that's the difference between the two men. I think Carl Sanders is an equivocator, and he's the kind of man who may talk a good game, but will privately complain about his son having to go to an integrated school.

HARRIS: Yep.

BOND: One thing that strikes me about Lester Maddox is that he comes from a very poor family. He knows what it means to be poor, and he has a lot of sympathy, I think, for poor people. He doesn't care if the poor people are black or white, but if he thinks he can do something for poor people I think he'll try to do it. There are some things he's just more decent about than *any* other politician I've seen.

HARRIS: He's like me. He believes in segregation, but, from a practical standpoint, a fellow like Lester Maddox can do more for the Negro people and get by with it than Carl Sanders because Carl is so suspect. . . .

REPORTER: *How widespread do you think hypocrisy is among white politicians?*

HARRIS: Unfortunately, our leaders amongst the white people have been hypocrites. Like last Monday morning I went into my office and a very prominent man in Augusta called me to complain that his children had to attend an integrated school. Where's he been the last fifteen years? He's been calling *me* a radical and an extremist because he didn't think this thing would ever touch him. I don't know what we are—I'll let somebody else name it, but I think we've at least been honest about it. . . . I was reading in the Atlanta paper one Sunday a write-up of the racial situation in Augusta. The Reverend C. S. Hamilton

41

(a Negro leader) was quoted as saying that the good relations in Augusta were due to eight or ten people and he named me as one of them, which shocked the hell out of me. I think they all have confidence in me, and I think they know I never have mistreated any of them. . . .

REPORTER: *Do you just assume that any white person who favors integration is a hypocrite?*

HARRIS: No, no. Ralph McGill's a fellow that changed and I think Ralph was sincere. I don't think Ralph was a hypocrite. I knew McGill very closely. . . . He and I used to drink liquor and just argue. . . .

REPORTER: *How do you feel about that, Mr. Bond?*

BOND: The word "liberal" means two things. It's used in Georgia as a curse word, and when it's used in another sense I think it refers to someone like Mr. Sanders, who may say one thing and mean another. He's the bad liberal. Then, I think there is a good liberal. I think [Atlanta Mayor Ivan] Allen—or McGill—are good liberals. McGill—I think you're right about that—said one thing and meant it. . . .

REPORTER: *You've said Negro and white leaders should sit down and devise a plan by which the two races can live harmoniously, Mr. Harris. What do you suggest?*

HARRIS: You can't draw an inflexible, exact-to-the-rule line that's as invariable as the law of the Medes and the Persians, see? It's a little bit more delicate . . . I've eaten with several of them (Negroes); that's the reason I say you can't draw an exact line. But, I do think as a general rule you ought to have separate schools and separate churches.

REPORTER: *Separate restaurants?*

HARRIS: No, that's a public institution.

BOND: I remember that, many years ago, it used to be possible, before they integrated the University of Georgia, to get the state to pay me to go to Meharry [Medical College, Nashville, Tenn.] if I wanted to go to medical school. That's really wasteful. It increases your taxes and mine, don't you think?

HARRIS: Yeah, well, of course, understand this, Julian, a lot of things we do are wasteful. But here's the thing. You could not have put it over. You could not have gotten a Negro into the Medical College in those days to save your neck. That was better than nothing. That was one of the steps in the transition that had to come and we're *still* sending some to Meharry. . . .

I don't think you can find anywhere in the country where over the years—of course it hasn't been ideal—where you've had the relationship that you've had here in Atlanta and I think it's come nearer to being a model than anything you can find anywhere.

BOND: Atlanta has been unique. What bothers me is that other cities haven't had these advantages. They haven't had an educated class of Negroes. They haven't had the kind of Negroes that went into commerce, into banking, insurance. But, even with all those advantages, as you say, there are an awful lot of poor white people here, and there are tremendous numbers of poor Negroes here. What is to become of those people? No one, I don't think, cares much about either group—the poor whites or the poor Negroes. Those are the ones, it seems to me, who are completely cut off in this city and in most of the American cities. . . .

REPORTER: *Getting back to the solutions, Mr. Harris.*

HARRIS: I think we've got to acknowledge this. Instead of having a fusion of the races we ought to have two races. Then, you've got to figure out how these two races are going to work together, live together. They've (Negroes) got a lot more power now. . . .

If it was left to the ghettos of New York, Chicago and Philadelphia, you would probably have a black and white race war. But you've got a different condition when you get to Atlanta and Augusta. You've got enough wealthy and educated Negro people. They've got a vested interest, just the same as the rest of the people have. You take the week after Martin Luther King's death, you had riots in 125 cities, but there wasn't one in Georgia. Negro people in Georgia, like white people, they've got roots. They've been here a long time. But, you take Harlem, you've got those people who come in there from all over the world. They've got no deep roots and they never had a decent way of making a living. It's been tough here, but the thing is it hasn't required as much money. As long as we were rural people, we raised a lot of our food. We're living in a period of time that is a little different than it was at the turn of the century when you could open up—these boys here don't know anything about it. Julian, you know what a potato hill is?

BOND: Oh yes, it's a big hill with all the potatoes inside. These (pointing to the reporters in the room) are all big city boys.

HARRIS: All year 'round you could go to the potato hill and get a potato, or you could pull up a turnip right out of the garden. Now, when those folks get in there (a ghetto), they can't get along on a maid or cook's salary, and there isn't a potato hill. When you create a ghetto like that, you create an artificial situation that requires a helluva lot more than money and. . . .

BOND: I'm going to agree with Mr. Harris and disagree at the same time. I think there *is* a difference in the South, and the difference I think is this: that if you're black and you live *anyplace* in this whole region of the Southeast . . . that you can see over the past ten years of your life, no matter how old you are, who you are, what your job is, if you're black, you can see a change. If you live in Atlanta, you can say five years ago, or ten years ago rather, I couldn't eat at Rich's, except in the basement, and now, today, I can, so my life has improved X points. If you live in Harlem, on the other hand, you can say to yourself, I've lived in Harlem twenty-five or thirty years. When I came here, I could eat at Woolworth's. Ten years ago, I could eat at Woolworth's, five years ago, I could eat at Woolworth's, and I ate at Woolworth's this morning, but my life is *exactly* the same now as it was. I still have the same sorry job, I still work in the garment district, say, pushing a truck. Things have not changed for me. Things are just like they were when I first came up here from South Carolina or Georgia. . . .

REPORTER: *How do you account for the disillusionment of the Negro in the North?*

HARRIS: You take Harlem. They never get out of Harlem. They live there all the time. Negroes in the South aren't tied in. They're tied up there. Some of those people have never been a mile or two from where they were born. The easiest way of life for them is prostitution, peddling dope, or selling numbers tickets.

BOND: If you're black and you come from Mississippi to Chicago by Greyhound bus, you get off at that bus terminal—I forget where it is—and somebody from the local Democratic party meets you at the bus. He tells you he works for Congressman Dawson. He tells you where there's an apartment to be found. He gives you a phone number. It's the phone number of the local (Democratic) precinct captain, and your whole life is laid out before you. If you're white, you have to live in a certain section of Chicago where all white people from Appalachia come to live, but the same kind of machinery doesn't meet them. A lot of them come up there, spend five years and go back. But the black people who come up there are really sucked into a kind of machinery.

HARRIS: That's right.

BOND: It just pulls them in.

HARRIS: That's right.

BOND: Chicago is the worst example. It's worse than New York. They're put on welfare. The precinct captain says "You've got three kids, your husband's not here, you're on welfare. Just remember to pull the Democratic lever at election time." And they're just pulled into machinery they cannot escape from. That's why nobody can beat Dawson. . . . The only escape from it is the gangs. But the older people are just in it, and can't get out. I've got an uncle who used to work for the city of Chicago and his job was to see what the water level was in Lake Michigan every day. He'd go down and look at a pile with the numbers on it and if it was ten feet he'd write down ten feet and he'd go turn it in and he's retired now on a pension. Why should he fight against anything? . . . Chicago strikes me as the most hostile city of any I've ever been in. I always get the feeling as I'm walking down the street in Chicago that anybody, white or black, at any moment is going to hit me for no reason whatsoever . . . I felt that same way when I moved to Atlanta. . . . The only thing I knew about the South was what I read about in The Pittsburgh Courier and my mother wanted me to go to Rich's to buy a new suit so I could go to college in the fall. I wouldn't go because I thought that white people in Rich's would beat me up. That's funny now, but I believed that. I let her go instead. I let my mother go.

REPORTER: *What is the answer to the plight of these trapped people, Mr. Bond?*

BOND: You have to find some mechanism to raise people's income. Whether simply by dole, which I think would be least desirable, or by guaranteed job—some kind of WPA project—I don't know. We've got to find some way to put money in people's hands. The easiest would be the dole. Just increase welfare benefits and, say, if you make under a certain amount of money, you qualify for it. This is probably the least expensive in the short run. The best thing to do is to find some way to get people jobs. Look at all the things that need to be done in a state like this—highway construction or beautification. People could be put to work at those kinds of things at government expense.

HARRIS: He's right. The easy way always is the dole. It's simpler and you just get rid of it (the problem), just kind of brush it under the rug. Now the old WPA served a good purpose back in its day, and it did a lot of good all over the state. Of course they talked about seeing them hanging on their shovels, standing up resting on the handles of the shovels. But, look what they've done with these damn poverty funds like in Chicago. I think the most flagrant example occurred with one of those gangs. They just hired them to be good. They didn't burn up any houses and they didn't riot. Now, I guess that's better than nothing but it doesn't solve anything. It would have been a lot better if they had gone in there and organized those folks into a work force. During the old depression, England had a corps similar to ours for middle-aged people. They took them and the first thing they did was give them a set of teeth. Then they fixed their hernias up. Then they started training them on something they could make a living on. When you do that you put a man into shape where he can get out and earn three meals a day.

REPORTER: *Mr. Bond, you introduced your first piece of legislation this year. What is it about?*

BOND: It's a local bill just applying to the city of Atlanta. If you have a home that's declared unfit for human habitation, you don't pay rent to the landlord but for six months you pay rent to an escrow account in the bank. At the end of six months if the landlord hasn't brought it up to code standard then you can withdraw the money from the bank account. . . .

HARRIS: Well, let me tell you something: That's one I would have joined you in.

REPORTER: *That's what?*

HARRIS: That's one I would have joined you in. Among my pet peeves in life are these damn loan sharks and the next thing is these folks who take these houses out there and don't ever do a thing to them, just keep renting them year in and year out. They don't give a damn what shape they're in and that's the kind of property that won't get in an urban renewal project.

BOND: That's right.

HARRIS: Now, of course, what these damn landlords say is that they've got tenants that won't take care of them. But I'll tell you what: You know that Hornsby subdivision (Negro homes) we started in Augusta? You go down there and you don't find any nicer neighborhood or houses any better kept. They're still that way today. Who in the hell gives a damn about an old broken down shack? Who *wants* to take care of it?

BOND: Especially if you don't own it.

HARRIS: Yeah, and the other fellow is making you pay twice what it's worth. . . .

REPORTER: *Have you followed Mr. Bond's career, Mr. Harris?*

HARRIS: Well, as far as the newspapers are concerned.

BOND: You know you can't believe all that, Mr. Harris. . . .

HARRIS: I think that statement he made back there about the draft card burning was right unfortunate. . . .

BOND: Well, I'll tell you something I feel about that draft card burning thing is that people didn't really understand what had been said, and I think part of the fault is due to the Atlanta papers, which ran these scare headlines and never printed the original statement until three days after the statement on Sunday. I thought it was a legitimate statement. What I said was, I wouldn't burn my card but I understood why people did burn theirs, and I admired their courage because I thought they did it with full knowledge of what the penalty was.

And, any reasonable man can agree with that, can't he?

HARRIS: Yeah, I don't think I would object to that, as big an extremist as I am.

BOND: I wish you'd been in the legislature.

C. VANN WOODWARD
Black History and White History

The many contributions of numerous ethnic groups to the building of American society have not been totally ignored in the teaching of the nation's history, but it would be fair to say that they have been relegated to a status of marginal importance. Blacks, Indians, Mexican Americans, Orientals, and others have made what amounted to cameo appearances in the textbooks, while the whole sweep of our national history has been exhibited as the progress of a white populace (mostly Anglo-Saxon-Teutonic) from East to West, fighting, conquering, building, planning, and managing what the country has become. In the past few years, owing mainly to the civil rights and black power advances, many Americans have been made aware that the traditional content of American history has been selective and one-sided, often to the point of being propagandistic. In the spring of 1969 Professor C. Vann Woodward of Yale University spoke to the Organization of American Historians on the issue of revamping the study of history by a balanced reassessment of black contributions to our national heritage. A portion of his presidential address is reprinted here. [Source: The Journal of American History, June 1969.]

Moral preoccupations and problems shape the character of much that is written about the Negro and race relations by modern white historians, but they are predominantly the preoccupations and moral problems of the white man. His conscience burdened with guilt over his own people's record of injustice and brutality toward the black man, the white historian often writes in a mood of contrition and remorse as if in expiation of racial guilt or flagellation of the guilty. . . .

This is not to deny to the historian the role of moral critic or to dismiss what has been written out of deep concern for moral values. The history of the Negro people and race relations has profited more from the insights and challenges of this type of writing in the last two decades than from the scholarship of the preceding and much longer era of moral neutrality and obtuseness. . . .

Granting the value of the part white historians have played in this field, the Negro still has understandable causes for dissatisfaction. For however sympathetic they may be, white historians with few exceptions are primarily concerned with the moral, social, political and economic problems of white men and their past. They are prone to present to the Negro as *his* history the record of what the white man believed, thought, legislated, did and did not do *about* the Negro. The Negro is a passive element, the man to whom things happen. He is the object rather than the subject of this kind of history. It is filled with the infamies and the philanthropies, the brutalities and the charities, the laws, customs, prejudices, policies, politics, crusades, and wars of whites *about* blacks.

"Racial attitudes" or "American attitudes" in a title mean white attitudes. "The Negro image" means the image in white minds. In this type of history, abolitionists, radical Republicans, and carpetbaggers are all of the same pale pigmentation. . . . Not until the civil rights workers of the 1960s do the prime movers and shakers of Negro history take on a darker hue in the history books, and not in all of them at that.

Negro history in this tradition—and many Negro historians themselves followed the tradition, virtually the only one available in university seminars—was an enclave, a cause or a result, a commentary on or an elaboration of white history. Black history *was* white history. Denied a past of his own, the Negro was given to understand that whatever history and culture he possessed was supplied by his association with the dominant race in the New World and its European background. Thoroughly Europo-centric in outlook, American whites subscribed completely to the myth that European culture, *their* culture, was so overwhelmingly superior that no other could survive under exposure to it. They also shared the European stereotypes, built up by three centuries of slave traders and elaborated by nineteenth- and twentieth-century European imperialists, of an Africa of darkness, savagery, bestiality, and degrada-

49

tion. Not only was the African stripped of this degrading heritage on American shores and left cultureless, a Black Adam in a new garden, but also he was viewed as doubly fortunate in being rescued from naked barbarism and simultaneously clothed with a superior culture. The "myth of the Negro past" was that he had no past. . . .

Like their American kin, the Africans had also been denied a past of their own, for European historians of the imperialist countries held that the continent, at least the sub-Saharan part, had no history before the coming of the white man. Historians of the new African states have not been backward in laying counterclaims and asserting the antiquity of their history and its importance, even its centrality in the human adventure.

Inevitably some black patriots have been carried away by their theme. One Ghanaian historian, for example, goes so far as to assert that Moses and Buddha were Egyptian Negroes, that Christianity sprang from Sudanic tribes, and that Nietzsche, Bergson, Marx, and the Existentialists were all reflections of Bantu philosophy. How much of this overwrought nationalism of the emergent African states will take root in American soil remains to be seen. Already something like it has found expression in cults of black nationalism and is seeking lodgement in the academies.

It seems possible that the new pride in Africa's achievements, identification with its people and their history, and the discovery of ancestral roots in its culture could contribute richly to the self-discovery and positive group identity of a great American minority. What had been suppressed or regarded with shame in this American subculture could now be openly expressed with confidence and pride. . . .

There are, unhappily, less desirable consequences conceivable for the preoccupation with Africa as a clue to racial identity. For in the hands of nationalist cults it can readily become a *mystique* of skin color and exclusiveness, of alienation and withdrawal. It can foster a new separatism, an inverted segregation, a black apartheid. It can seek group solidarity and identity by the rejection of the White Devil and all his works simply because of white association. This is part of what Erik Erikson meant by "negative identity," the affirmation of identity by what one is not. With reference to that concept, he remarked on "the unpleasant fact that our god-given identities often live off the degradation of others." . . . It would be one of the most appalling ironies of American history if the victims of this system of human debasement should in their own quest for identity become its imitators.

One manifestation of black nationalism in academic life is the cry that only blacks are truly qualified to write or to interpret or to teach the black experience. In the special sense that, other things being equal, those who have undergone an experience are best qualified to understand it, there is some truth in this claim. . . .

American history, the white man's version, could profit from an infusion of "soul." It could be an essential corrective in line with the tradition of countervailing forces in American historiography. It was in that tradition that new immigrant historians revised first-family and old-stock history, that Jewish scholars challenged WASP interpretations, that Western challengers confronted New England complacencies, Yankee heretics upset Southern orthodoxies, Southern skeptics attacked Yankee myths, and the younger generation, since the beginning, assaulted the authority of the old. Negro historians have an opportunity and a duty in the same tradition.

An obligation to be a corrective influence is one thing, but a mandate for the exclusive preemption of a subject by reason of racial qualification is quite another. They cannot have it both ways. Either black history is an essential part of American history and must be included by all American historians, or it is unessential and can be segregated and left to black historians.

But Negro history is too important to be left entirely to Negro historians. . . .

The fact is that there are few countries left in the New World that are not multiracial in population. In many of them racial intermixture and intermarriage are prevalent. To impose the rule of racial qualification for historians of such multiracial societies as those of Trinidad, Cuba, Jamaica, Brazil, or Hawaii would be to leave them without a history. What passes for racial history is often the history of the relations between races—master and slave, imperialist and colonist, exploiter and exploited, and all the political, economic, sexual, and cultural relations, and their infinitely varied intermixtures.

To leave all the history of these relations in the hands of the mas-

51

ters, the imperialists, or the exploiters would result in biased history. But to segregate historical subjects along racial lines and pair them with racially qualified historians would result in fantastically abstract history. This is all the more true since it is the relations, attitudes, and interactions between races that are the most controversial and perhaps the most significant aspects of racial history. . . .

Whether the revision of Negro history is undertaken by black historians or white historians, or preferably by both, they will be mindful of the need for correcting ancient indignities, ethnocentric slights, and paternalistic patronizing, not to mention calculated insults, callous indifference, and blind ignorance. They will want to see full justice done at long last to Negro achievements and contributions, to black leaders and heroes, black slaves and freedmen, black poets and preachers. . . .

It is to be hoped that white as well as black historians will reserve some place for irony as well as for humor. If so they will risk the charge of heresy by pointing out in passing that Haiti, the first Negro republic of modern history, though born of a slave rebellion, promptly established and for a long time maintained an oppressive system of forced labor remarkably similar to state slavery; that Liberia, the second Negro republic, named for liberty, dedicated to freedom, and ruled by former slaves from the United States, established a flourishing African slave trade; and that Kwame Nkrumah, dictator of Ghana, with a misguided instinct for symbolism, selected as his official residence at Accra the Christiansborg Castle, one time barracoon from which his ancestors had sold their kinsmen into slavery.

These instances are not adduced to alleviate the guilt of the white man, who rightfully bears the greater burden. . . . In all the annals of Africa there could scarcely be a more ironic myth of history than that of the New World republic which reconciled human slavery with natural rights and equality, and on the backs of black slaves set up the New Jerusalem, the world's best hope for freedom. The mythic African counterparts look pale beside the American example. They do serve, however, as reminders that the victims as well as the victors of the historical process are caught in the human predicament.

52

2. Showdown for Nonviolence

1966-1968

WILLIAM H. GRIER and PRICE M. COBBS
Black Rage

It is no easy thing to be black in the land of the free. Much has changed since twenty Negro indentured servants were landed at Jamestown in 1619, yet the heritage of slavery is still alive in the silent war between whites and blacks even when there is no open violence. Over two hundred years of the "peculiar institution" and another hundred of struggle for equality have left their mark on the nation. Hatred of the blacks, according to Negro psychiatrists Grier and Cobbs, has become so much a part of the fabric of the nation that the principle of white supremacy has become the unspoken assumption even of blacks against themselves — a final irony and almost an insuperable burden in the struggle for equality between the races. The amount of aggression and potential violence that is born of this black grief is the subject of the final chapter of Black Rage *(1968), reprinted here.*

History may well show that of all the men who lived during our fateful century none illustrated the breadth or the grand potential of man so magnificently as did Malcolm X. If, in future chronicles, America is regarded as the major nation of our day, and the rise of darker people from bondage as the major event, then no figure has appeared thus far who captures the spirit of our times as does Malcolm.

Malcolm is an authentic hero, indeed the only universal black hero. In his unrelenting opposition to the viciousness in America, he fired the imagination of black men all over the world.

If this black nobleman is a hero to black people in the United States and if his life reflects their aspirations, there can be no doubt of the universality of black rage.

Malcolm responded to his position in his world and to his blackness in the manner of so many black boys. He turned to crime. He was saved by a religious sect given to a strange, unhistorical explanation of the origin of black people and even stranger solutions to their problems. He rose to power in that group and outgrew it.

Feeding on his own strength, growing in response to his own commands, limited by no creed, he became a citizen of the world and an advocate of all oppressed people no matter their color or belief. Anticipating his death by an assassin, he distilled, in a book, the essence of his genius, his life. His autobiography thus is a legacy and, together with his speeches, illustrates the thrusting growth of the man — his evolution, rapid, propulsive, toward the man he might have been had he lived.

The essence of Malcolm X was growth, change, and a seeking after truth.

Alarmed white people saw him first as an eccentric and later as a dangerous radical — a revolutionary without troops who threatened to stir black people to riot and civil disobedience. Publicly, they treated him as a joke; privately, they were afraid of him.

After his death he was recognized by black people as the "black shining prince" and recordings of his speeches became treasured things. His autobiography was studied, his life marveled at. Out of this belated admiration came the philosophical basis for black activism and indeed the thrust of Black Power itself, away from integration and civil rights and into the "black bag."

Unlike Malcolm, however, the philosophical underpinnings of the new black militancy were static. They remained encased within the ideas of revolution and black nationhood, ideas Malcolm had outgrown by the time of his death. His stature has made even his earliest statements gospel and men now find themselves willing to die for words which in retrospect are only milestones in the growth of a fantastic man.

Many black men who today preach blackness seem headed blindly toward self-destruction, uncritical of anything "black" and damning the white man for diabolical wickedness. For a philosophical base they have turned to the words of Malcolm's youth.

This perversion of Malcolm's intellectual position will not, we submit, be held against him by history.

Malcolm's meaning for us lies in his fearless demand for truth and his evolution from a petty criminal to an international statesman — accomplished by a black man against odds of terrible magnitude — in America. His message was his life, not his words, and Malcolm knew it.

Black Power activism — thrust by default temporarily at the head of a powerful movement — is a conception that contributes in a significant way to the strength and unity of that movement but is unable to provide the mature vision for the mighty works ahead. It will pass and leave black people in this country prouder, stronger, more determined, but in need of grander princes with clearer vision.

We believe that the black masses will rise with a simple and eloquent demand to which new leaders must give tongue. They will say to America simply:

"GET OFF OUR BACKS!"

The problem will be so simply defined.

What is the problem?

The white man has crushed all but the life from blacks from the time they came to these shores to this very day.

What is the solution?

Get off their backs.

How?

By simply doing it — now.

This is no oversimplification. Greater changes than this in the relations of peoples have taken place before. The nation would benefit tremendously. Such a change might bring about a closer examination of our relations with foreign countries, a reconsideration of economic policies, and a re-examination if not a redefinition of nationhood. It might in fact be the only change which can prevent a degenerative decline from a powerful nation to a feeble, third-class, ex-colonialist country existing at the indulgence of stronger powers.

In spite of the profound shifts in power throughout the world in the past thirty years, the United States seems to have a domestic objective of "business as usual," with no change needed or in fact wanted.

All the nasty problems are overseas. At home the search is for bigger profits and smaller costs, better education and lower taxes, more vacation and less work, more for me and less for you. Problems at home are to be talked away, reasoned into nonexistence, and put to one side while we continue the great American game of greed.

There is, however, an inevitability built into the natural order of things. Cause and effect are in fact joined, and if you build a sufficient cause then not all the talk or all the tears in God's creation can prevent the effect from presenting itself one morning as the now ripened fruit of your labors.

America began building a cause when black men were first sold into bondage. When the first black mother killed her newborn rather than have him grow into a slave. When the first black man slew himself rather than submit to an organized system of man's feeding upon another's flesh. America had well begun a cause when all the rebels were either slain or broken and the nation set to the task of refining the system of slavery so that the maximum labor might be extracted from it.

The system achieved such refinement that the capital loss involved when a slave woman aborted could be set against the gain to be expected from forcing her into brutish labor while she was with child.

America began building a potent cause in its infancy as a nation.

It developed a way of life, an American ethos, a national life style which included the assumption that blacks are inferior and were born to hew wood and draw water. Newcomers to this land (if white) were immediately made to feel welcome and, among the bounty available, were given blacks to feel superior to. They were required to despise and depreciate them, abuse and exploit them, and one can only imagine how munificent this land must have seemed to the European — a land with built-in scapegoats.

The hatred of blacks has been so deeply bound up with being an American that it has been one of the first things new Americans learn and one of the last things old Americans forget. Such feelings have been elevated to a position of national character, so that individuals now no longer feel personal guilt or responsibility for the oppression of black people. The nation has incorporated this oppression into itself in the form of folkways and storied traditions, leaving the individual free to shrug his shoulders and say only: "That's our way of life."

This way of life is a heavy debt indeed, and one trembles for the debtor when payment comes due.

America has waxed rich and powerful in large measure on the backs of black laborers. It has become a violent, pitiless nation, hard and calculating, whose moments of generosity are only brief intervals in a ferocious narrative of life, bearing a ferocity and an aggression so strange in this tiny world where men die if they do not live together.

With the passing of the need for black laborers, black people have become useless; they are a drug on the market. There are not enough menial jobs. They live in a nation which has evolved a work force of skilled and semi-skilled workmen. A nation which chooses simultaneously to exclude all black men from this favored labor force and to deny them the one thing America has offered every other group—unlimited growth with a ceiling set only by one's native gifts.

The facts, however obfuscated, are simple. Since the demise of slavery black people have been expendable in a cruel and impatient land. The damage done to black people has been beyond reckoning. Only now are we beginning to sense the bridle placed on black children by a nation which does not want them to grow into mature human beings.

The most idealistic social reformer of our time, Martin Luther King, was not slain by one man; his murder grew out of that large body of violent bigotry America has always nurtured—that body of thinking which screams for the blood of the radical, or the conservative, or the villain, or the saint. To the extent that he stood in the way of bigotry, his life was in jeopardy, his saintly persuasion notwithstanding. To the extent that he was black and was calling America to account, his days were numbered by the nation he sought to save.

Men and women, even children, have been slain for no other earthly reason than their blackness. Property and goods have been stolen and the victims then harried and punished for their poverty. But such viciousness can at least be measured or counted.

Black men, however, have been so hurt in their manhood that they are now unsure and uneasy as they teach their sons to be men. Women have been so humiliated and used that they may regard womanhood as a curse and flee from it. Such pain, so deep, and such real jeopardy, that the fundamental protective function of the family has been denied. These injuries we have no way to measure.

Black men have stood so long in such peculiar jeopardy in America that a *black norm* has developed—a suspiciousness of one's environment which is necessary for survival. Black people, to a degree that approaches paranoia, must be ever alert to danger from their white fellow citizens. It is a cultural phenomenon peculiar to black Americans. And it is a posture so close to paranoid thinking that the mental disorder into which black people most frequently fall is paranoid psychosis.

Can we say that white men have driven black men mad?

An educated black woman had worked in an integrated setting for fifteen years. Compliant and deferential, she had earned promotions and pay increases by hard work and excellence. At no time had she been involved in black activism, and her only participation in the movement had been a yearly contribution to the N.A.A.C.P.

During a lull in the racial turmoil she sought psychiatric treatment. She explained that she had lately become alarmed at waves of rage that swept over her as she talked to white people or at times even as she looked at them. In view of her past history of compliance and passivity, she felt that something was wrong with her. If her controls slipped she might embarrass herself or lose her job.

A black man, a professional, had been a "nice guy" all his life. He was a hard-working non-militant who avoided discussions of race with his white colleagues. He smiled if their comments were harsh and remained unresponsive to racist statements. Lately he has experienced almost uncontrollable anger toward his white co-workers, and although he still manages to keep his feelings to himself, he confides that blacks and whites have been lying to each other. There is hatred and violence between them and he feels trapped. He too fears for himself if his controls should slip.

If these educated recipients of the white man's bounty find it hard to control their rage, what of their less fortunate kinsman who has less to protect, less to lose, and more scars to show for his journey in this land?

The tone of the preceding . . . has been mournful, painful, desolate, as we have described the psychological consequences of white oppression of blacks. The centuries of senseless cruelty and the permeation of the black man's character with the conviction of his own hatefulness and inferiority tell a sorry tale.

This dismal tone has been deliberate. It has been an attempt to evoke a certain quality of depression and hopelessness in the reader and to stir these feelings. These are the most common feelings tasted by black people in America.

The horror carries the endorsement of centuries and the entire lifespan of a nation. It is a way of life which reaches back to the beginnings of recorded time. And all the bestiality, wherever it occurs and however long it has been happening, is narrowed, focused, and refined to shine into a black child's eyes when first he views his world. All that has ever happened to black men and women he sees in the victims closest to him, his parents.

A life is an eternity and throughout all that eternity a black child has breathed the foul air of cruelty. He has grown up to find that his spirit was crushed before he knew there was need of it. His ambitions, even in their forming, showed him to have set his hand against his own. This is the desolation of black life in America.

Depression and grief are hatred turned on the self. It is instructive to pursue the relevance of this truth to the condition of black Americans.

Black people have shown a genius for surviving under the most deadly circumstances. They have survived because of their close attention to reality. A black dreamer would have a short life in Mississippi. They are of necessity bound to reality, chained to the facts of the times; historically the penalty for misjudging a situation involving white men has been death. The preoccupation with religion has been a willing adoption of fantasy to prod an otherwise reluctant mind to face another day.

We will even play tricks on ourselves if it helps us stay alive.

The psychological devices used to survive are reminiscent of the years of slavery, and it is no coincidence. The same devices are used because black men face the same danger now as then.

The grief and depression caused by the condition of black men in America is an unpopular reality to the sufferers. They would rather see themselves in a more heroic posture and chide a disconsolate brother. They would like to point to their achievements (which in fact have been staggering); they would rather point to virtue (which has been shown in magnificent form by some blacks); they would point to bravery, fidelity, prudence, brilliance, creativity, all of which dark men have shown in abundance. But the overriding experience of the black American has been grief and sorrow and no man can change that fact.

His grief has been realistic and appropriate. What people have so earned a period of mourning?

We want to emphasize yet again the depth of the grief for slain sons and ravished daughters, how deep and lingering it is.

If the depth of this sorrow is felt, we can then consider what can be made of this emotion.

As grief lifts and the sufferer moves toward health, the hatred he had turned on himself is redirected toward his tormentors, and the fury of his attack on the one who caused him pain is in direct proportion to the depth of his grief. When the mourner lashes out in anger, it is a relief to those who love him, for they know he has now returned to health.

Observe that the amount of rage the oppressed turns on his tormentor is a direct function of the depth of his grief, and consider the intensity of black men's grief.

Slip for a moment into the soul of a black girl whose womanhood is blighted, not because she is ugly, but because she is black and by definition all blacks are ugly.

Become for a moment a black citizen of Birmingham, Alabama, and try to understand his grief and dismay when innocent children are slain while they worship, for no other reason than that they are black.

Imagine how an impoverished mother feels as she watches the light of creativity snuffed out in her children by schools which dull the mind and environs which rot the soul.

For a moment make yourself the black father whose son went innocently to war and there was slain – for whom, for what?

For a moment be any black person, anywhere, and you will feel the waves of hopelessness that engulfed black men and women when Martin Luther King was murdered. All black people understood the tide of anarchy that followed his death.

It is the transformation of *this* quantum of grief into aggression of which we now speak. As a sapling bent low stores energy for a violent backswing, blacks bent double by oppression have stored energy which will be released in the form of rage—black rage, apocalyptic and final.

White Americans have developed a high skill in the art of misunderstanding black people. It must have seemed to slaveholders that slavery would last through all eternity, for surely their misunderstanding of black bondsmen suggested it. If the slaves were eventually to be released from bondage, what could be the purpose of creating the fiction of their subhumanity?

It must have seemed to white men during the period 1865 to 1945 that black men would always be a passive, compliant lot. If not, why would they have stoked the flames of hatred with such deliberately barbarous treatment?

White Americans today deal with "racial incidents" from summer to summer as if such minor turbulence will always remain minor and one need only keep the blacks busy till fall to have made it through another troubled season.

Today it is the young men who are fighting the battles, and, for now, their elders, though they have given their approval, have not joined in. The time seems near, however, for the full range of the black masses to put down the broom and buckle on the sword. And it grows nearer day by day. Now we see skirmishes, sputtering erratically, evidence if you will that the young men are in a warlike mood. But evidence as well that the elders are watching closely and may soon join the battle.

Even these minor flurries have alarmed the country and have resulted in a spate of generally senseless programs designed to give *temporary summer jobs!!* More interesting in its long-range prospects has been the apparent eagerness to draft black men for military service. If in fact this is a deliberate design to place black men in uniform in order to get them off the street, it may be the most curious "instant cure" for a serious disease this nation has yet attempted. Young black men are learning the most modern techniques for killing—techniques which may be used against *any* enemy.

But it is all speculation. The issue finally rests with the black masses. When the servile men and women stand up, we had all better duck.

We should ask what is likely to galvanize the masses into aggression against the whites.

> Will it be some grotesque atrocity against black people which at last causes one-tenth of the nation to rise up in indignation and crush the monstrosity?
>
> Will it be the example of black people outside the United States who have gained dignity through their own liberation movement?
>
> Will it be by the heroic action of a small group of blacks which by its wisdom and courage commands action in a way that cannot be denied?
>
> Or will it be by blacks, finally and in an unpredictable way, simply getting fed up with the bumbling stupid racism of this country? Fired not so much by any one incident as by the gradual accretion of stupidity into fixtures of national policy.

All are possible, or any one, or something yet unthought. It seems certain only that on the course the nation now is headed it will happen.

One might consider the possibility that, if the national direction remains unchanged, such a conflagration simply might *not* come about. Might not black people remain where they are, as they did for a hundred years during slavery?

Such seems truly inconceivable. Not because blacks are so naturally warlike or rebellious, but because they are filled with such grief, such sorrow, such bitterness, and such hatred. It seems now delicately poised, not yet risen to the flash point, but rising rapidly nonetheless. No matter what repressive measures are invoked against the blacks, they will never swallow their rage and go back to blind hopelessness.

If existing oppressions and humiliating disenfranchisements are to be lifted, they will have to be lifted most speedily, or catastrophe will follow.

For there are no more psychological tricks blacks can play upon themselves to make it possible to exist in dreadful circumstances. No more lies can they tell themselves. No more dreams to fix on. No more opiates to dull the pain. No more patience. No more thought. No more reason. Only a welling tide risen out of all those terrible years of grief, now a tidal wave of fury and rage, and all black, black as night.

MARTIN LUTHER KING, JR.

Showdown for Nonviolence

Early in 1968 Memphis garbage collectors struck against the city government, charging prejudicial treatment of Negroes in municipal hiring practices. Memphis' newly elected mayor was adamant, and the strike dragged on. The Reverend Martin Luther King, Jr., the foremost American apostle of nonviolence, the leading Negro moderate, and a Nobel Peace Prize winner, went to Memphis to lead a protest in behalf of the strikers. There, on Thursday, April 4, he was shot and killed while standing on a motel balcony. The irony of his death, as well as genuine grief at the passing of a greatly distinguished man, convulsed the country for a week. Riots in a number of Northern cities occurred, his funeral monopolized the air waves, and the Congress passed a watered down version of an open housing bill that it had been long considering. The eulogists at the funeral said he had not died in vain. But Mike Royko, Chicago columnist, wrote that King had been "executed by a firing squad that numbered in the millions" — the white racists who, he charged, had hated King from the beginning and were unmoved by his death. "We have pointed a gun at our own head," he concluded, "and we are squeezing the trigger. And nobody we elect is going to help us. It is our head and our finger." Reprinted here is an article by King that appeared shortly after he died. [Source: Look, April 16, 1968.]

The policy of the federal government is to play Russian roulette with riots; it is prepared to gamble with another summer of disaster. Despite two consecutive summers of violence, not a single basic cause of riots has been corrected. All of the misery that stoked the flames of rage and rebellion remains undiminished. With unemployment, intolerable housing, and discriminatory education a scourge in Negro ghettos, Congress and the administration still tinker with trivial, halfhearted measures.

65

Yet only a few years ago, there was discernible, if limited, progress through nonviolence. Each year, a wholesome, vibrant Negro self-confidence was taking shape. The fact is inescapable that the tactic of nonviolence, which had then dominated the thinking of the civil rights movement, has in the last two years not been playing its transforming role. Nonviolence was a creative doctrine in the South because it checkmated the rabid segregationists who were thirsting for an opportunity to physically crush Negroes. Nonviolent direct action enabled the Negro to take to the streets in active protest, but it muzzled the guns of the oppressor because even he could not shoot down in daylight unarmed men, women, and children. This is the reason there was less loss of life in ten years of Southern protest than in ten days of Northern riots.

Today, the Northern cities have taken on the conditions we faced in the South. Police, National Guard, and other armed bodies are feverishly preparing for repression. They can be curbed, not by unorganized resort to force by desperate Negroes but only by a massive wave of militant nonviolence. Nonviolence was never more relevant as an effective tactic than today for the North. It also may be the instrument of our national salvation.

I agree with the President's National Advisory Commission on Civil Disorders that our nation is splitting into two hostile societies and that the chief destructive cutting edge is white racism. We need, above all, effective means to force Congress to act resolutely — but means that do not involve the use of violence. For us in the Southern Christian Leadership Conference, violence is not only morally repugnant, it is pragmatically barren. We feel there is an alternative both to violence and to useless timid supplications for justice. We cannot condone either riots or the equivalent evil of passivity. And we know that nonviolent militant action in Selma and Birmingham awakened the conscience of white America and brought a moribund, insensitive Congress to life.

The time has come for a return to mass nonviolent protest. Accordingly, we are planning a series of such demonstrations this spring and summer, to begin in Washington, D.C. They will have Negro and white participation, and they will seek to benefit the poor of both races.

We will call on the government to adopt the measures recommended by its own commission. To avoid, in the Commission's words, the tragedy of "continued polarization of the American community and ultimately the destruction of basic democratic values," we must have "national action—compassionate, massive, and sustained, backed by the resources of the most powerful and the richest nation on earth."

The demonstrations we have planned are of deep concern to me, and I want to spell out at length what we will do, try to do, and believe in. My staff and I have worked three months on the planning. We believe that if this campaign succeeds, nonviolence will once again be the dominant instrument for social change—and jobs and income will be put in the hands of the tormented poor. If it fails, nonviolence will be discredited and the country may be plunged into holocaust—a tragedy deepened by the awareness that it was avoidable.

We are taking action after sober reflection. We have learned from bitter experience that our government does not correct a race problem until it is confronted directly and dramatically. We also know, as official Washington may not, that the flash point of Negro rage is close at hand.

Our Washington demonstration will resemble Birmingham and Selma in duration. It will be more than a one day protest—it can persist for two or three months. In the earlier Alabama actions, we set no time limits. We simply said we were going to struggle there until we got a response from the nation on the issues involved. We are saying the same thing about Washington. This will be an attempt to bring a kind of Selma-like movement, Birmingham-like movement, into being, substantially around the economic issues. Just as we dealt with the social problem of segregation through massive demonstrations and we dealt with the political problem—the denial of the right to vote—through massive demonstrations, we are now trying to deal with the economic problems—the right to live, to have a job and income—through massive protest. It will be a Selma-like movement on economic issues.

We remember that when we began direct action in Birmingham and Selma, there was a thunderous chorus that sought to discourage us. Yet, today, our achievements in these cities and the reforms that radiated from them are hailed with pride by all.

We've selected fifteen areas — ten cities and five rural districts — from which we have recruited our initial cadre. We will have 200 poor people from each area. That would be about 3,000 to get the protests going and set the pattern. They are important, particularly in terms of maintaining nonviolence. They are being trained in this discipline now.

In areas where we are recruiting, we are also stimulating activities in conjunction with the Washington protest. We are planning to have some of these people march to Washington. We may have half the group from Mississippi, for example, go to Washington and begin the protest there, while the other half begins walking. They would flow across the South, joining the Alabama group, the Georgia group, right on up through South and North Carolina and Virginia. We hope that the sound and sight of a growing mass of poor people walking slowly toward Washington will have a positive, dramatic effect on Congress.

Once demonstrations start, we feel, there will be spontaneous supporting activity taking place across the country. This has usually happened in campaigns like this, and I think it will again. I think people will start moving. The reasons we didn't choose California and other areas out West are distance and the problem of transporting marchers that far. But part of our strategy is to have spontaneous demonstrations take place on the West Coast.

A nationwide nonviolent movement is very important. We know from past experience that Congress and the President won't do anything until you develop a movement around which people of goodwill can find a way to put pressure on them, because it really means breaking that coalition in Congress. It's still a coalition-dominated, rural-dominated, basically Southern Congress. There are Southerners there with committee chairmanships, and they are going to stand in the way of progress as long as they can. They get enough right-wing Midwestern or Northern Republicans to go along with them.

This really means making the movement powerful enough, dramatic enough, morally appealing enough, so that people of goodwill, the churches, labor, liberals, intellectuals, students, poor people themselves begin to put pressure on congressmen to the point that they can no longer elude our demands.

Our idea is to dramatize the whole economic problem of the poor. We feel there's a great deal that we need to do to appeal to Congress itself. The early demonstrations will be more geared toward educational purposes—to educate the nation on the nature of the problem and the crucial aspects of it, the tragic conditions that we confront in the ghettos.

After that, if we haven't gotten a response from Congress, we will branch out. And we are honest enough to feel that we aren't going to get any instantaneous results from Congress, knowing its recalcitrant nature on this issue, and knowing that so many resources and energies are being used in Vietnam rather than on the domestic situation. So we don't have any illusions about moving Congress in two or three weeks. But we do feel that, by starting in Washington, centering on Congress and departments of the government, we will be able to do a real educational job.

We call our demonstration a campaign for jobs and income because we feel that the economic question is the most crucial that black people, and poor people generally, are confronting. There is a literal depression in the Negro community. When you have mass unemployment in the Negro community, it's called a social problem; when you have mass unemployment in the white community, it's called a depression. The fact is, there is a major depression in the Negro community. The unemployment rate is extremely high, and among Negro youth, it goes up as high as 40 percent in some cities.

We need an Economic Bill of Rights. This would guarantee a job to all people who want to work and are able to work. It would also guarantee an income for all who are not able to work. Some people are too young, some are too old, some are physically disabled, and yet, in order to live, they need income. It would mean creating certain public-service jobs, but that could be done in a few weeks. A program that would really deal with jobs could minimize—I don't say stop—the number of riots that could take place this summer.

Our whole campaign, therefore, will center on the job question, with other demands like housing, that are closely tied to it. We feel that much more building of housing for low-income people should be done. On the educational front, the ghetto schools are in bad shape in terms of quality, and we feel that a program should be developed to spend at least a thousand dollars per pupil. Often, they are so far behind that they need more and special attention, the best quality education that can be given.

These problems, of course, are overshadowed by the Vietnam war. We'll focus on the domestic problems, but it's inevitable that we've got to bring out the question of the tragic mix-up in priorities. We are spending all of this money for death and destruction and not nearly enough money for life and constructive development. It's inevitable that the question of the war will come up in this campaign. We hear all this talk about our ability to afford guns and butter, but we have come to see that this is a myth, that when a nation becomes involved in this kind of war, when the guns of war become a national obsession, social needs inevitably suffer. And we hope that as a result of our trying to dramatize this and getting thousands and thousands of people moving around this issue, that our government will be forced to reevaluate its policy abroad in order to deal with the domestic situation.

The American people are more sensitive than Congress. A Louis Harris poll has revealed that 56 percent of the people feel that some kind of program should come into being to provide jobs to all who want to work. We had the WPA when the nation was on the verge of bankruptcy; we should be able to do something when we're sick with wealth. That poll also showed that 57 percent of the people felt the slums should be eradicated and the communities rebuilt by those who live in them, which would be a massive job program.

We need to put pressure on Congress to get things done. We will do this with First Amendment activity. If Congress is unresponsive, we'll have to escalate in order to keep the issue alive and before it. This action may take on disruptive dimensions, but not violent in the sense of destroying life or property: it will be militant non-violence.

We really feel that riots tend to intensify the fears of the white majority while relieving its guilt, and so open the door to greater repression. We've seen no changes in Watts, no structural changes have taken place as the result of riots. We are trying to find an alternative that will force people to confront issues without destroying life or property. We plan to build a shantytown in Washington, patterned after the bonus marches of the Thirties, to dramatize how many people have to live in slums in our nation. But essentially, this will be just like our other nonviolent demonstrations. We are not going to tolerate violence. And we are making it very clear that the demonstrators who are not prepared to be nonviolent should not participate in this. For the past six weeks, we've had workshops on nonviolence with the people who will be going to Washington. These people will form a core of the demonstration and will later be the marshals in the protests. They will be participating themselves in the early stages, but after two or three weeks, when we will begin to call larger numbers in, they will be the marshals, the ones who will control and discipline all of the demonstrations.

We plan to have a march for those who can spend only a day or two in Washington, and that will be toward the culminating point of the campaign. I hope this will be a time when white people will rejoin the ranks of the movement.

Demonstrations have served as unifying forces in the movement; they have brought blacks and whites together in very practical situations, where philosophically they may have been arguing about Black Power. It's a strange thing how demonstrations tend to solve problems. The other thing is that it's little known that crime rates go down in almost every community where you have demonstrations. In Montgomery, Ala., when we had a bus boycott, the crime rate in the Negro community went down 65 percent for a whole year. Anytime we've had demonstrations in a community, people have found a way to slough off their self-hatred, and they have had a channel to express their longings and a way to fight nonviolently—to get at the power structure, to know you're doing something, so you don't have to be violent to do it.

We need this movement. We need it to bring about a new kind of togetherness between blacks and whites. We need it to bring allies together and to bring the coalition of conscience together.

A good number of white people have given up on integration too. There are a lot of "White Power" advocates, and I find that people do tend to despair and engage in debates when nothing is going on. But when action is taking place, when there are demonstrations, they have a quality about them that leads to a unity you don't achieve at other times.

I think we have come to the point where there is no longer a choice now between nonviolence and riots. It must be militant, massive nonviolence, or riots. The discontent is so deep, the anger so ingrained, the despair, the restlessness so wide, that something has to be brought into being to serve as a channel through which these deep emotional feelings, these deep angry feelings, can be funneled. There has to be an outlet, and I see this campaign as a way to transmute the inchoate rage of the ghetto into a constructive and creative channel. It becomes an outlet for anger.

Even if I didn't deal with the moral dimensions and questions of violence versus nonviolence, from a practical point of view, I don't see riots working. But I am convinced that if rioting continues, it will strengthen the right wing of the country, and we'll end up with a kind of right-wing take-over in the cities and a Fascist development, which will be terribly injurious to the whole nation. I don't think America can stand another summer of Detroit-like riots without a development that could destroy the soul of the nation, and even the democratic possibilities of the nation.

I'm committed to nonviolence absolutely. I'm just not going to kill anybody, whether it's in Vietnam or here. I'm not going to burn down any building. If nonviolent protest fails this summer, I will continue to preach it and teach it, and we at the Southern Christian Leadership Conference will still do this. I plan to stand by nonviolence because I have found it to be a philosophy of life that regulates not only my dealings in the struggle for racial justice but also my dealings with people, with my own self. I will still be faithful to nonviolence.

But I'm frank enough to admit that if our nonviolent campaign doesn't generate some progress, people are just going to engage in more violent activity, and the discussion of guerrilla warfare will be more extensive.

In any event, we will not have been the ones who will have failed. We will place the problems of the poor at the seat of government of the wealthiest nation in the history of mankind. If that power refuses to acknowledge its debt to the poor, it will have failed to live up to its promise to insure "life, liberty, and the pursuit of happiness" to its citizens.

If this society fails, I fear that we will learn very shortly that racism is a sickness unto death.

We welcome help from all civil rights organizations. There must be a diversified approach to the problem, and I think both the NAACP and the Urban League play a significant role. I also feel that CORE and SNCC have played very significant roles. I think SNCC's recent conclusions are unfortunate. We have not given up on integration. We still believe in black and white together. Some of the Black Power groups have temporarily given up on integration. We have not. So maybe we are the bridge, in the middle, reaching across and connecting both sides.

The fact is, we have not had any insurrection in the United States because an insurrection is planned, organized, violent rebellion. What we have had is a kind of spontaneous explosion of anger. The fact is, people who riot don't want to riot. A study was made recently by some professors at Wayne State University. They interviewed several hundred people who participated in the riot last summer in Detroit, and a majority of these people said they felt that my approach to the problem — nonviolence — was the best and most effective.

I don't believe there has been a massive turn to violence. Even the riots have had an element of nonviolence to persons. But for a rare exception, they haven't killed any white people, and Negroes could, if they wished, kill by the hundreds. That would be insurrection. But the amazing thing is that the Negro has vented his anger on property, not persons, even in the emotional turbulence of riots.

But I'm convinced that if something isn't done to deal with the very harsh and real economic problems of the ghetto, the talk of guerrilla warfare is going to become much more real. The nation has not yet recognized the seriousness of it. Congress hasn't been willing to do anything about it, and this is what we're trying to face this spring. As committed as I am to nonviolence, I have to face this fact: if we do not get a positive response in Washington, many more Negroes will begin to think and act in violent terms.

I hope, instead, that what comes out of these nonviolent demonstrations will be an Economic Bill of Rights for the Disadvantaged, requiring about ten or twelve billion dollars. I hope that a specific number of jobs is set forth, that a program will emerge to abolish unemployment, and that there will be another program to supplement the income of those whose earnings are below the poverty level. These would be measures of success in our campaign.

It may well be that all we'll get out of Washington is to keep Congress from getting worse. The problem is to stop it from moving backward. We started out with a poverty bill at $2.4 billion, and now it's back to $1.8 billion. We have a welfare program that's dehumanizing, and then Congress adds a Social Security amendment that will bar literally thousands of children from any welfare. Model cities started out; it's been cut back. Rent subsidy, an excellent program for the poor, cut down to nothing. It may be that because of these demonstrations, we will at least be able to hold on to some of the things we have.

There is an Old Testament prophecy of the "sins of the fathers being visited upon the third and fourth generations." Nothing could be more applicable to our situation. America is reaping the harvest of hate and shame planted through generations of educational denial, political disfranchisement, and economic exploition of its black population. Now, almost a century removed from slavery, we find the heritage of oppression and racism erupting in our cities, with volcanic lava of bitterness and frustration pouring down our avenues.

Black Americans have been patient people and perhaps they could continue patient with but a modicum of hope; but everywhere, "time is winding up," in the words of one of our spirituals, "corruption in the land, people take your stand; time is winding up." In spite of years of national progress, the plight of the poor is worsening. Jobs are on the decline as a result of technological change, schools North and South are proving themselves more and more inadequate to the task of providing adequate education and thereby entrance into the mainstream of the society. Medical care is virtually out of reach of millions of black and white poor. They are aware of the great advances of medical science—heart transplants, miracle drugs—but their children still die of preventable diseases and even suffer brain damage due to protein deficiency.

In Mississippi, children are actually starving, while large landowners have placed their land in the soil bank and receive millions of dollars annually not to plant food and cotton. No provision is made for the life and survival of the hundreds of thousands of sharecroppers who now have no work and no food. Driven off the land, they are forced into tent cities and ghettos of the North, for our Congress is determined not to stifle the initiative of the poor (though they clamor for jobs) through welfare handouts. Handouts to the rich are given more sophisticated nomenclature such as parity, subsidies, and incentives to industry.

White America has allowed itself to be indifferent to race prejudice and economic denial. It has treated them as superficial blemishes, but now awakes to the horrifying reality of a potentially fatal disease. The urban outbreaks are "a fire bell in the night," clamorously warning that the seams of our entire social order are weakening under strains of neglect.

The American people are infected with racism — that is the peril. Paradoxically, they are also infected with democratic ideals — that is the hope. While doing wrong, they have the potential to do right. But they do not have a millennium to make changes. Nor have they a choice of continuing in the old way. The future they are asked to inaugurate is not so unpalatable that it justifies the evils that beset the nation. To end poverty, to extirpate prejudice, to free a tormented conscience, to make a tomorrow of justice, fair play, and creativity — all these are worthy of the American ideal.

We have, through massive nonviolent action, an opportunity to avoid a national disaster and create a new spirit of class and racial harmony. We can write another luminous moral chapter in American history. All of us are on trial in this troubled hour, but time still permits us to meet the future with a clear conscience.

The Muslim Program

The Black Muslim (Nation of Islam) movement was founded by Wali Farad, believed to have been an orthodox Muslim born in Mecca around 1877, who migrated to the United States in 1930 and established his first mosque in Detroit a year later; a second was founded shortly thereafter in Chicago. Farad promised his followers, who believed him to be an incarnation of Allah, that if they would give heed to his teachings they would overcome their white "slavemasters" and be restored to a position of dignity among the peoples of the world. In 1934 Farad mysteriously disappeared and was succeeded by Elijah Muhammad (born Elijah Poole in Georgia), under whom the movement spread slowly at first. By the end of World War II, however, American Negroes had caught the spirit of protest and black nationalism that was sweeping Africa, and the movement spread to all large cities with sizable Negro populations. [Source: Muhammad Speaks, August 16, 1968.]

ELIJAH MUHAMMAD
The Black Man Must Know the Truth

No. 1 – TO KNOW THE TRUTH of the Presence of the God of Truth and that His Presence is the Salvation of the Lost and Found people of America is to know your life and its happiness.

No. 2 – TRUTH is in favor of you and me, for the truth of our enemies that we have been serving here in the U.S.A. for over 400 years who we did not know to be our enemies by nature, is the truth that the Black Man must have knowledge of to be able to keep from falling into the deceiving traps that are being laid by our enemies, to catch us to go their way which is opposed to the right way of the righteous, of whom we are members.

No. 3 – THE ARCH DECEIVER. We are warned throughout the Bible and Holy Quran to shun this deceiver if we are members of the Black Nation (the righteous). There is nothing that is left of the truth of these people that God has not made manifest. And I am teaching you daily of this people. There are some Black Americans who will, after knowledge, sympathize with the arch deceiver (the devil) for the sake of advantage. Even some of our highly educated people will accept speaking in defense of this arch enemy of ours, for the sake of trying to gain their respect and sympathy so they can gain higher places with this arch deceiver. And some of them will tell me and the Believers of Islam that they do not believe in any religion and in no God of religion. The Bible foretold that this kind of talk against the truth would come in the last days; that the fool will say in his heart "there is no God." This prophecy is now being fulfilled among even our most educated class of people.

You cannot see the Hereafter unless you believe in righteousness and unless you are a submissive one to the God and Author of righteousness, because righteousness is the type of world that we will have to live under, after the destruction of this evil and deceitful world.

No. 4—THE CHRISTIAN CHURCH. There are "die hards" in the Christian church. Slowly but surely the Spirit of Allah is making manifest to the Black Man that the church and its religion called Christianity is the chain that binds the Black Man in mental slavery (seeking salvation where there is none), and thinking that they must die first to get to heaven. This is really a misunderstanding, because heaven is a condition of life and not a special place. Heaven is enjoying peace of mind and contentment with the God of the righteous and the Nation of the righteous. It can be here in America, in the isles of the Pacific, or on the continents of Asia and Africa, but it is only a condition of life.

Black Christian believers are warned in the Bible in the 18th Chapter of Revelation (last book) to come out of her ("her" means the way and belief of the white race and the so-called Christian religion), that you be not partakers with them in their Divine plagues of God upon her (U.S.A.). This is the religion that the prophets prophesied to you that the enemy will deceive you with. Christianity was not the teachings of Jesus. Their theologians and religious scientists will agree with us, in a show-down, that it was not the religion of Jesus, for the religion of Jesus was Islam as it was the religion of Moses and all the prophets of God. The Holy Quran teaches us that the prophets' religion was none other than Islam, the religion of Truth, Freedom, Justice, and Equality. This, the Christians preach with their mouths, but they do not practice Truth, Freedom, Justice, and Equality with us, the Black people. Since knowledge of them, we do not want to follow them in any religion, because they are not by nature made to lead people into righteousness.

No. 5—REVOLUTION between white and Black is due to the work of Allah and His Truth among the Black people of America. Never before in all your life have you seen the white man so anxious to keep the Black Man near to him in his society and especially in Christianity, the great false, deceiving religion. He even offers to bribe any Black people of note and for accepting his invitation and high places, they are reduced by a sudden fall to the level of disgrace and shame.

No. 6—LEADERS. We, the Black Nation, today with the knowledge of the truth cannot accept leaders made and offered to us for our guidance. I warn each of you to no more accept the white man's made or chosen leaders for you. This is what has kept us bound in the mental chains of slavery since the days of slavery. Our leaders are by their choice. These kind of leaders are Uncle Toms, who are licking the boots of the white man for his pleasure and wealth, regardless to what happens to you and me for they care not.

No. 7—ABRAHAM'S PROPHECY. But, I ask you to remember this: In the parable in the Bible of the rich man and Lazarus— which means none other than the white and Black people of America, the rich man died (deprived of authority and wealth). In the anguish of the torment of his loss of wealth and power, the parable refers to the rich man as being in hell. And, in this condition, the beggar (Lazarus) saw no hope to beg any longer, that once rich man for some of his sumptuous table of food. Then, he turned to go for self (Abraham's bosom).

The prophecy which Abraham was the recipient of only means that after 400 years of our enslavement, all these things are coming to pass. I ask you to be in time and accept the truth and do not mix up the truth with falsehood while you know it, for the sake of untrue friendship.

What the Muslims Want

This is the question asked most frequently by both the whites and the blacks. The answers to this question I shall state as simply as possible.

1. We want freedom. We want a full and complete freedom.

2. We want justice. Equal justice under the law. We want justice applied equally to all, regardless of creed or class or color.

3. We want equality of opportunity. We want equal membership in society with the best in civilized society.

4. We want our people in America whose parents or grandparents were descendants from slaves, to be allowed to establish a separate state or territory of their own—either on this continent or elsewhere. We believe that our former slave masters are obligated to provide such land and that the area must be fertile and minerally rich. We believe that our former slave masters are obligated to maintain and

supply our needs in this separate territory for the next 20 to 25 years – until we are able to produce and supply our own needs.

Since we cannot get along with them in peace and equality, after giving them 400 years of our sweat and blood and receiving in return some of the worst treatment human beings have ever experienced, we believe our contributions to this land and the suffering forced upon us by white America, justifies our demand for complete separation in a state or territory of our own.

5. We want freedom for all Believers of Islam now held in federal prisons. We want freedom for all black men and women now under death sentence in innumerable prisons in the North as well as the South.

We want every black man and woman to have the freedom to accept or reject being separated from the slave master's children and establish a land of their own.

We know that the above plan for the solution of the black and white conflict is the best and only answer to the problem between two people.

6. We want an immediate end to the police brutality and mob attacks against the so-called Negro throughout the United States.

We believe that the Federal government should intercede to see that black men and women tried in white courts receive justice in accordance with the laws of the land – or allow us to build a new nation for ourselves, dedicated to justice, freedom and liberty.

7. As long as we are not allowed to establish a state or territory of our own, we demand not only equal justice under the laws of the United States, but equal employment opportunities – NOW!

We do not believe that after 400 years of free or nearly free labor, sweat and blood, which has helped America become rich and powerful, that so many thousands of black people should have to subsist on relief, charity or live in poor houses.

8. We want the government of the United States to exempt our people from ALL taxation as long as we are deprived of equal justice under the laws of the land.

9. We want equal education – but separate schools up to 16 for boys and 18 for girls on the condition that the girls be sent to women's colleges and universities. We want all black children educated, taught and trained by their own teachers.

Under such schooling system we believe we will make a better nation of people. The United States government should provide, free, all necessary text books and equipment, schools and college buildings. The Muslim teachers shall be left free to teach and train their people in the way of righteousness, decency and self-respect.

10. We believe that intermarriage or race mixing should be prohibited. We want the religion of Islam taught without hinderance or suppression.

These are some of the things that we, the Muslims, want for our people in North America.

What the Muslims Believe

1. WE BELIEVE in the One God Whose proper Name is Allah.

2. WE BELIEVE in the Holy Quran and in the Scriptures of all the Prophets of God.

3. WE BELIEVE in the truth of the Bible, but we believe that it has been tampered with and must be reinterpreted so that mankind will not be snared by the falsehoods that have been added to it.

4. WE BELIEVE in Allah's Prophets and the Scriptures they brought to the people.

5. WE BELIEVE in the resurrection of the dead — not in physical resurrection — but in mental resurrection. We believe that the so-called Negroes are most in need of mental resurrection; therefore, they will be resurrected first.

Furthermore, we believe we are the people of God's choice, as it has been written, that God would choose the rejected and the despised. We can find no other persons fitting this description in these last days more than the so-called Negroes in America. We believe in the resurrection of the righteous.

6. WE BELIEVE in the judgement; we believe this first judgement will take place as God revealed, in America . . .

7. WE BELIEVE this is the time in history for the separation of the so-called Negroes and the so-called white Americans. We believe the black man should be freed in name as well as in fact. By this we mean that he should be freed from the names imposed upon him by his former slave masters. Names which identified him as being the slave master's slave. We believe that if we are free indeed,

we should go in our own people's names—the black peoples of the earth.

8. WE BELIEVE in justice for all, whether in God or not; we believe as others, that we are due equal justice as human beings. We believe in equality—as a nation—of equals. We do not believe that we are equal with our slave masters in the status of "freed slaves."

We recognize and respect American citizens as independent peoples and we respect their laws which govern this nation.

9. WE BELIEVE that the offer of integration is hypocritical and is made by those who are trying to deceive the black peoples into believing that their 400-year-old open enemies of freedom, justice and equality are, all of a sudden, their "friends." Furthermore, we believe that such deception is intended to prevent black people from realizing that the time in history has arrived for the separation from the whites of this nation.

If the white people are truthful about their professed friendship toward the so-called Negro, they can prove it by dividing up America with their slaves.

We do not believe that America will ever be able to furnish enough jobs for her own millions of unemployed, in addition to jobs for the 20,000,000 black people as well.

10. WE BELIEVE that we who declared ourselves to be righteous Muslims, should not participate in wars which take the lives of humans. We do not believe this nation should force us to take part in such wars, for we have nothing to gain from it unless America agrees to give us the necessary territory wherein we may have something to fight for.

11. WE BELIEVE our women should be respected and protected as the women of other nationalities are respected and protected.

12. WE BELIEVE that Allah (God) appeared in the Person of Master W. Fard Muhammad, July, 1930; the long-awaited "Messiah" of the Christians and the "Mahdi" of the Muslims.

We believe further and lastly that Allah is God and besides HIM there is no God and He will bring about a universal government of peace wherein we all can live in peace together.

Hunger in the United States

In July 1967 the Citizens' Crusade Against Poverty in Washington, D.C., established a Citizens' Board of Inquiry into Hunger and Malnutrition in the United States, with Benjamin Mays and Leslie Dunbar as cochairmen. Hearings were conducted in nearly all parts of the country, and data were collected bearing on the pervasiveness of hunger among the population. The report of the board, published in April 1968, showed that very few states did not have counties with serious hunger problems. National, state, and local welfare programs were found to be almost wholly inadequate to cope with the situation. The following selection includes portions of the Foreword and of the Introduction to the report. [Source: Hunger, U.S.A., Washington, 1968, pp. 4-5, 8-9.]

If you will go look, you will find America a shocking place.

No other Western country permits such a large proportion of its people to endure the lives we press on our poor. To make four-fifths of a nation more affluent than any people in history, we have degraded one-fifth mercilessly. . . . Wherever we have gone we have seen the multitudinous castoffs of an economic system which, bewilderingly, can build up ever greater national achievements without affecting the immense and economically useless pockets of the impoverished. Curiously, the desolate poor are heavily weighted on the side of old inhabitants: Indians, Negroes, Appalachian whites, Spanish-speaking residents of the Southwest. . . .

We feel fairly confident that most Americans must believe – if they think of it at all – that the federal food programs (including the school lunch program) are designed to serve the interests and needs of beneficiaries. This is not true. They are designed and administered within the context of the national agricultural policy. That policy, as led by the Department of Agriculture and congressional committees and subcommittees of agriculture and agricultural appropriation, is dominated by a concern for maximizing agricultural income, especially within the big production categories.

Other objectives always yield to this one. Those other objectives include farm production, soil conservation, the welfare of individual farmers, and farm employment. Our agricultural policy can be and often is attentive to those other objectives, but *only when they do not conflict with the dominant objectives of maximizing income.* But almost never does our agricultural policy take a direct concern with the interests of consumers and, certainly, not of poor consumers.

Rather than criticize this we think it preferable (*a*) to recognize that the Department of Agriculture and the committees of Congress that it is responsive to have this dominant concern; and (*b*) to remove from their care the administration of the food programs which are and have always been extraneous to this primary concern.

The second main direction that our recommendations follow is toward freeing the poor, as far as we can see possible, from the special and often oppressively undignified guardianship of any bureaucracies. We think those who are poor can be safely assumed to have a concern for their own and their children's best interests and can, therefore, be trusted to look after themselves. The principal recommendation of this Board is, therefore, a free food stamp program keyed to need and to the objective of a completely adequate diet, and one which would be administered with minimum controls. . . .

In issuing this report, we find ourselves somewhat startled by our own findings, for we too had been lulled into the comforting belief that at least the extremes of privation had been eliminated in the process of becoming the world's wealthiest nation. Even the most concerned, aware, and informed of us were not prepared to take issue with the presumption stated by Michael Harrington on the opening page of his classic *The Other America:*

> To be sure, the other America is not impoverished in the same sense as those poor nations where millions cling to hunger as a defense against starvation. This country has escaped such extremes.

But starting from this premise, we found ourselves compelled to conclude that America has not escaped such extremes. For it became increasingly difficult, and eventually impossible, to reconcile our preconceptions with statements we heard everywhere we went:

—that substantial numbers of newborn, who survive the hazards of birth and live through the first month, die between the second month and their second birthday from causes which can be traced directly and primarily to malnutrition.

—that protein deprivation between the ages of six months and a year and one-half causes permanent and irreversible brain damage to some young infants.

—that nutritional anemia, stemming primarily from protein deficiency and iron deficiency, was commonly found in percentages ranging from 30 to 70 percent among children from poverty backgrounds.

—that teachers report children who come to school without breakfast, who are too hungry to learn, and in such pain that they must be taken home or sent to the school nurse.

—that mother after mother in region after region reported that the cupboard was bare, sometimes at the beginning and throughout the month, sometimes only the last week of the month.

—that doctors personally testified to seeing case after case of premature death, infant deaths, and vulnerability to secondary infection, all of which were attributable to or indicative of malnutrition.

—that in some communities people band together to share the little food they have, living from hand to mouth.

—that the aged living alone subsist on liquid foods that provide inadequate sustenance.

We also found ourselves surrounded by myths which were all too easy to believe because they are so comforting. We number among these:

Myth: The really poor and needy have access to adequate surplus commodities and food stamps if they are in danger of starving.

Fact: Only 5.4 million of the more than 29 million poor participate in these two government food programs, and the majority of those participating are not the poorest of the poor.

Myth: Progress is being made as a result of massive federal efforts in which multimillion-dollar food programs take care of more people now than ever before.

Fact: Participation in government food programs has dropped 1.4 million in the last six years. Malnutrition among the poor has risen sharply over the past decade.

Myth: Hunger and starvation must be restricted to terrible places of need, such as Mississippi, which will not institute programs to take adequate care of its people.

Fact: Mississippi makes more extensive use of the two federal food programs than any state in the United States.

In addition to the hearings, the site visits, the personal interviews, the anecdotal stories, we learned from government officials, statistics, studies, and reports that where, by accident or otherwise, someone looked for malnutrition, he found it—to an extent and degree of severity previously unsuspected. If this report is marred by any single element, it is the anomaly of asserting that a phenomenon exists, and that it is widespread, without being able to ascertain its exact magnitude or severity because no one ever believed it existed.

To the best of our knowledge, we have collected the studies and information compiled by all who have gone before us and have supplemented it with the best evidence that our own direct efforts could uncover. At best, we can make an educated guess as to the order of magnitude of the problem. But the chief contribution we can make does not rest with engaging in a numbers game.

It lies elsewhere—with the reversal of presumption. Prior to our efforts, the presumption was against hunger, against malnutrition; now the presumption has shifted. The burden of proof has shifted. It rests with those who would deny the following words of one of our members, "There is sufficient evidence to indict" on the following charges:

1. Hunger and malnutrition exist in this country, affecting millions of our fellow Americans and increasing in severity and extent from year to year.

2. Hunger and malnutrition take their toll in this country in the form of infant deaths, organic brain damage, retarded growth and learning rates, increased vulnerability to disease, withdrawal, apathy, alienation, frustration, and violence.

3. There is a shocking absence of knowledge in this country about the extent and severity of malnutrition—a lack of information and action which stands in marked contrast to our recorded knowledge in other countries.

85

4. Federal efforts aimed at securing adequate nutrition for the needy have failed to reach a significant portion of the poor and to help those it did reach in any substantial and satisfactory degree.

5. The failure of federal efforts to feed the poor cannot be divorced from our nation's agricultural policy, the congressional committees that dictate that policy, and the Department of Agriculture that implements it; for hunger and malnutrition in a country of abundance must be seen as consequences of a political and economic system that spends billions to remove food from the market, to limit productions, to retire land from production, to guarantee and sustain profits for the producer.

Perhaps more surprising and shocking is the extent to which it now rests within our power substantially to alleviate hunger and malnutrition. While new programs are needed, and new legislation is desired and urged, there are now reserves of power, of money, of discretionary authority, and of technical know-how which could make substantial inroads on the worst of the conditions we have uncovered — and this could be commenced not next year or next month — but today.

THOMAS A. JOHNSON
The Negro in Vietnam

Negroes constituted about 20 percent of the U.S. combat troops in Vietnam during 1967-1968, a fact that led some critics to charge the government with prejudicial treatment. There were good reasons for the disproportionately high numbers of Negroes who saw action: both the Negro primary enlistment rate and the Negro reenlistment rate were higher than those for whites, and a higher proportion of Negroes were drafted. There were thus more Negroes in the Army and available for duty. But there were reasons for the criticism, too, for all of these factors reflected the unequal economic and social status of the Negro at home, which tended to keep him from acquiring a deferred status in the draft, and which also made a combat career relatively attractive. The problems thus created for an orderly transition back to civilian life were treated in three articles written by Thomas A. Johnson for the New York Times. *Portions of the first and third articles are reprinted here.* [*Source:* New York Times, *April 29, May 1, 1968.*]

Saigon, South Vietnam—The Army sergeant with the coal-black face muttered: "What in the hell am I doing here? Tell me that—what in the hell am I doing here?" But there was a smile on his face.

At the moment, he and the men of his understrength platoon—about half of them Negroes—were crouching on a jungle trail as artillery shells pounded the brush 100 yards away.

At the same time, some 50,000 other Negroes in Vietnam were unloading ships and commanding battalions, walking mountain ranges and flying warplanes, cowering in bunkers and relaxing in Saigon villas. They were planning battles, moving supplies, baking bread, advising the South Vietnamese Army, practising international law, patrolling Mekong Delta canals, repairing jets on carriers in the Tonkin Gulf, guarding the United States Embassy, drinking in sleazy bars and dining in the best French restaurants in Saigon, running press centers, burning latrines, driving trucks and serving on the staff of Gen. William C. Westmoreland, the American commander.

They were doing everything and they were everywhere. In this highly controversial and exhaustively documented war, the Negro, and particularly the Negro fighting man, has attained a sudden visibility—a visibility his forefathers never realized while fighting in past American wars.

Fourteen weeks of interviews with black and white Americans serving here reveal that Vietnam is like a speed-up film of recent racial progress at home. But Vietnam also demonstrates that the United States has not yet come close to solving its volatile racial problem.

Why was the sergeant—a thirty-four-year-old career soldier—in Vietnam?

He talked with good humor of the "good Regular Army" to a Negro correspondent, he shuddered with anger recalling that his hometown paper in the Deep South called his parents "Mr. and Mrs." only when referring to their hero son, and he pointed out that he had stayed in the Army because his hometown offered only

87

"colored" jobs in a clothing factory where whites did the same work for higher pay.

Most often, Negro and white civilians and career soldiers see Vietnam as a boon to their careers and as a source of greater income than at home. It was not unusual to hear civilians and career soldiers – Negro and white – express such views as, "Hell, Vietnam's the only war we've got."

For the Negro there is the additional inducement that Southeast Asia offers an environment almost free of discrimination.

One civilian remarked, "Bread and freedom, man, bread and freedom."

"The big question is whether the black cat can walk like a dragon here in South Vietnam and like a fairy back in the Land of the Big PX. Also, can America expect him to?"

The speaker, who said he had observed "America's wars both at home and abroad," was at a Negro civilian's villa on Cong Ly Street, near Independence Palace.

The year 1968 was just a few hours old, and a "soul session" was in full swing at the villa.

The answers to the questions about Negroes in the war zone and Negroes back home in a bountiful America were, for the most part, that "the black cat" could not accept a double standard and should not, but that "while America could not honestly expect him to, she would – in that undying hypocrisy for which she is so justly famous."

The session was a gathering of "soul brothers" – Negro military men and civilians, including a correspondent. Earlier, several had made their appearances at the American community's most "in" New Year's party, on Phan Thanh Gian Street (the invitation had read: "The flower people of Saigon invite you to see the light at the end of the tunnel"), and now they had got down to "the problem."

Saigon's 11 P.M. curfew was not strictly enforced that night, and the first dawn of 1968 found the soul-session participants in general agreement that the presence of the Negro in Vietnam raised more questions than it answered.

With his sudden visibility on the battlefield, the Negro has achieved the most genuine integration and the fullest participation in policies that America has yet granted. "And," it was pointed out during the soul session, "the brother is dying in order to partici-pate—again."

The Negro is 9.8 percent of all United States military forces here, close to 20 percent of the combat forces, about 25 percent of the front-line combat leaders, and currently 14.1 percent of those killed in action.

Front-line commanders are partial to whoever will volunteer to fight, white or black. And the prime requirement, when a GI, black or white, looks for a bunker companion, is a man who will stick with him when the shooting starts.

But the Negro here has achieved his blood-spattered "equality" in America's most unpopular war. While some Americans praise him as a hero, others condemn him as a mercenary.

While he battles the Viet Cong and the North Vietnamese, he reads of racial outbreaks at home, and of authorities putting down these outbreaks with varying degrees of force and counterviolence. He hears predictions of more to come.

Discharged from the service, he is approached by black ultra-militants eager to capitalize on his battle skills and on his resent-ment—a resentment that the militants are certain will follow when a former serviceman realizes that at-home America has not reached the state of racial integration that Vietnam-America has.

Those who stay in the service—especially in the elite units—can expect to be used to help put down any racial outbreaks.

The Negro in Vietnam has achieved this war-zone integration 10,000 miles from home and at a time when the loudest black voices—if not the most representative—clamor for racial separa-tion. And there is an undeniable truth in the most effective argu-ment of these voices: The degree of equality that has been struggled into here is not available in some places in the United States and is not yet a hope in many places at home.

This is the first time in the history of American wars that national Negro figures are not urging black youths to take up arms in sup-port of American policy to improve the lot of the black man in the United States. . . .

The Rev. Dr. Martin Luther King, Jr., who was perhaps the most charismatic of contemporary Negro spokesmen, directly opposed the war.

Also opposed to the war are H. Rap Brown and Stokely Car-michael, the present and former chairmen of the Student Non-violent Coordinating Committee, who are believed to have significant influence among young Negro militants in the ghettos. Floyd B. McKissick, head of the Congress of Racial Equality, which seeks to carry its economic, social, and political concept of black power into Negro population centers, is also opposed to the war.

The national board of the largest civil rights organization, the 450,000-member NAACP, has refused to take a public stand on the war, stating that peace efforts and civil rights should not be mixed. But the New York State Conference of the association, the largest state unit, voted last autumn, after a stormy session in Albany, to oppose the war.

Whitney M. Young, Jr., executive director of the Urban League, a civil rights group that enjoys good cooperation with government and industry, takes an after-the-fact position: "since" the Negro performs well in Vietnam, he should not suffer discrimination in America.

The most hawkish statements from blacks on the war in Vietnam have come from Negro military men. A Negro field-grade officer commented:

"You won't find many public doves—if any at all—among Negro or white career military men, no more than you'd find ambitious executives in a Ford plant urging company workers to buy Chevrolets. An executive is product-conscious."

The war's lack of popularity at home seems to have had little effect on the Negro soldier's willingness to fight it. The job, the mission, takes precedence. . . .

Most Negro servicemen interviewed in Vietnam over three and a half months felt that their uniforms kept them from participating in traditional civil rights activities, but many career men contended that their staying in the service was in itself a civil rights battle.

"We were working our show the same as Negroes back home," said Sgt. George Terry of the Army. "We brought democracy to the service by sticking it out."

"Many people called us Uncle Toms, but we were actually holding the line," said Lieut. Col. Felix L. Goodwin, a twenty-seven-year veteran who is information officer for the First Logistical Command.

Another Negro lieutenant colonel recalled that when he was graduated from Infantry Officer Candidate School at Fort Benning, Ga., in the late 1940s, a party was given in the back room of a Negro beauty parlor in "colored town" for the few Negro graduates. "A Negro chaplain told us 'not to make trouble' by insisting on attending the main graduation party on the base," he said. "We should have 'made trouble,' but we did not. I simply can't conceive of anything happening like that nowadays. Anyway, I went back to Benning a few years ago and I lived on Colonels' Row." . . .

Should recent trends continue, about two-thirds of the first-term Negro servicemen will reenlist. Some 41,000 Negroes will be discharged this year, and about 5,000 of these will have served in Vietnam.

While some Negro militants predict that the returning Vietnam veteran will supply the cadre for a black-vs.-white civil war, some government spokesmen say he will be a leader for integration.

There is evidence to support both predictions.

Some groups that are considered extremist have added returning veterans to their number. One such recruit in New York remarked to a Negro correspondent: "I saved two white boys' lives in Vietnam. I must have been out of my Goddamn mind."

"You were," said the militant who had recruited him, "but you're on Straight Street now."

On the other hand, some returning veterans have ignored the pleas of ultramilitants.

Melvin Murrel Smith, a Negro from Syracuse who served as a Marine sergeant, maintains that "the friendships formed between whites and Negroes in Vietnam will never die because of what we went through together." Mr. Smith, whose organization of self-defense units in the Vietnamese village of Tuyloan caused the Viet Cong to place a $1,700 price on his head, said that he and several white buddies from Vietnam now often telephoned and visited one another. "Civilians can't see this because they've never been through what we went through together," Mr. Smith said.

The big question is still what will happen to the Negro grunt whose skills with the M-16 rifle and the M-79 grenade launcher are hardly marketable and who, if historical patterns prevail, will find employers much less interested in him than front-line commanders were.

There are programs trying to reverse the historic patterns. The Urban League and the American Legion are seeking jobs for the returning veteran. And an armed forces training program—Project Transition, set up on 86 military posts—gives courses in civilian skills for the serviceman who is to be discharged.

Although relatively new, these programs are being attacked by Negro militants as hypocritical. Much effort, they say, is being made to keep the Negro veteran from becoming disillusioned with the American system while "the war on poverty is being scrapped."

Militants are also quick to point out that Project Transition is helping city police forces to recruit Negro veterans—to pit blacks against blacks, in the view of these critics, should violence flare.

And the speculation continues over whether the Negro veteran will integrate or disintegrate: Will he riot?

A young Negro naval officer at Camranh Bay called this "a white question, since whites like to convince themselves that people start riots intentionally." "I say yes," the officer added. "He will riot—if white people make him."

S. Sgt. Hector Robertin, a Puerto Rican born in Spanish Harlem who supervises an Army photography team, said it was hard for most people to "realize just why people do riot."

"Take a middle-class white of nineteen from Oregon," he said. "You could never make him understand the resentment of a cop pushing you off a street corner just because you're there, the credit gyps and landlord leeches and the feeling you come to have that if you ever get anything, you're going to have to take it."

"People talk about burning down their own neighborhood. Hell, the people there don't own a damn thing, and the government should've burned down those rat traps years ago to give people a chance for a better life. But how do you make people understand that who've never seen it, lived it?"

A Negro field-grade officer took a related view, if more gently. "There is no doubt about it," he said. "You'll have a new Negro coming out of Vietnam who has seen that America will allow him to die without discrimination, and he'll want to live without discrimination.

"You've also got a new Negro on the streets back home demanding only what white people take for granted every day.

92

"But what will happen? That's a question for America—for white people, not me.

"I think we stumbled into this war in Vietnam. God, I hope we don't stumble into another one back home."

Then the question was asked: "And what about you? What about you when and if we 'stumble' into a civil war back home?"

"I honestly don't know," the officer said. "I'm a soldier, yes, and I believe in America, yes, and I'm certain that it is the only country capable of bringing about a true democracy and a good standard of living for all people—but I really don't know.

"Those kids on the street—they are angry, they are inarticulate and nobody can talk to them, but do you realize they are saying no less than what Patrick Henry said?"

On Civil Disorders

During the summer of 1967 nearly 150 cities in the United States experienced civil disorders, of which the most severe were the July riots in Newark and Detroit. In their wake President Johnson established a National Advisory Commission on Civil Disorders, with Governor Otto Kerner of Illinois as chairman, to investigate the origins of the disturbances, the means by which they could be controlled, and the role of the local, state, and federal governments in dealing with them. The Commission's report, portions of which appear below, was issued on March 1, 1968, and immediately gained a large audience. Reactions to the findings were mixed, ranging from strong disapproval to warm praise. The President himself did not endorse the report, and elected officials generally showed themselves unwilling to embrace the vast programs for social renewal recommended by the Commission. [Source: Report of the National Advisory Commission on Civil Disorders, Washington, 1968, pp. 5-16, 63-74, 91-93, 147, 218-231.]

PREFACE

Last summer over 150 cities reported disorders in Negro—and in some instances, Puerto Rican—neighborhoods. These ranged from minor disturbances to major outbursts involving sustained and widespread looting and destruction of property. The worst came during a 2-week period in July when large-scale disorders erupted first in Newark and then in Detroit, each setting off a chain reaction in neighboring communities.

It was in this troubled and turbulent setting that the President of the United States established this Commission. He called upon it "to guide the country through a thicket of tension, conflicting evidence and extreme opinions." . . .

Much of our report is directed to the condition of those Americans who are also Negroes and to the social and economic environment in which they live—many in the black ghettos of our cities. But this Nation is confronted with the issue of justice for all its people—white as well as black, rural as well as urban. In particular, we are concerned for those who have continued to keep faith with society in the preservation of public order—the people of Spanish surname, the American Indian and other minority groups to whom this country owes so much.

We wish it to be clear that in focusing on the Negro, we do not mean to imply any priority of need. It will not do to fight misery in the black ghetto and leave untouched the reality of injustice and deprivation elsewhere in our society. The first priority is order and justice for all Americans.

In speaking of the Negro, we do not speak of "them." We speak of us—for the freedoms and opportunities of all Americans are diminished and imperiled when they are denied to some Americans. The tragic waste of human spirit and resources, the unrecoverable loss to the Nation which this denial has already caused—and continues to produce—no longer can be ignored or afforded.

Two premises underlie the work of the Commission:

That this Nation cannot abide violence and disorder if it is to ensure the safety of its people and their progress in a free society.

That this Nation will deserve neither safety nor progress unless it can demonstrate the wisdom and the will to undertake decisive action against the root causes of racial disorder.

This report is addressed to the institutions of government and to the conscience of the Nation, but even more urgently, to the mind and heart of each citizen. The responsibility for decisive action,

94

never more clearly demanded in the history of our country, rests on all of us.

We do not know whether the tide of racial disorder has begun to recede. We recognize as we must that the conditions underlying the disorders will not be obliterated before the end of this year or the end of the next and that so long as these conditions exist a potential for disorder remains. But we believe that the likelihood of disorder can be markedly lessened by an American commitment to confront those conditions and eliminate them—a commitment so clear that Negro citizens will know its truth and accept its goal. The most important step toward domestic peace is an act of will; this country can do for its people what it chooses to do. . . .

PATTERNS OF DISORDER

Disorders are often discussed as if there were a single type. The "typical" riot of recent years is sometimes seen as a massive uprising against white people, involving widespread burning, looting, and sniping, either by all ghetto Negroes or by an uneducated, Southern-born Negro underclass of habitual criminals or "riffraff." An agitator at a protest demonstration, the coverage of events by the news media, or an isolated "triggering" or "precipitating" incident, is often identified as the primary spark of violence. A uniform set of stages is sometimes posited, with a succession of confrontations and withdrawals by two cohesive groups, the police on one side and a riotous mob on the other. Often it is assumed that there was no effort within the Negro community to reduce the violence. Sometimes the only remedy prescribed is application of the largest possible police or control force, as early as possible.

What we have found does not validate these conceptions. We have been unable to identify constant patterns in all aspects of civil disorders. We have found that they are unusual, irregular, complex, and, in the present state of knowledge, unpredictable social processes. Like many human events, they do not unfold in orderly sequences. . . .

Based upon information derived from our surveys, we offer the following generalizations:

1. No civil disorder was "typical" in all respects. Viewed in a

national framework, the disorders of 1967 varied greatly in terms of violence and damage: while a relatively small number were major under our criteria and a somewhat larger number were serious, most of the disorders would have received little or no national attention as "riots" had the Nation not been sensitized by the more serious outbreaks.

2. While the civil disorders of 1967 were racial in character, they were not *inter*racial. The 1967 disorders, as well as earlier disorders of the recent period, involved action within Negro neighborhoods against symbols of white American society—authority and property—rather than against white persons.

3. Despite extremist rhetoric, there was no attempt to subvert the social order of the United States. Instead, most of those who attacked white authority and property seemed to be demanding fuller participation in the social order and the material benefits enjoyed by the vast majority of American citizens.

4. Disorder did not typically erupt without preexisting causes as a result of a single "triggering" or "precipitating" incident. Instead, it developed out of an increasingly disturbed social atmosphere, in which typically a series of tension-heightening incidents over a period of weeks or months became linked in the minds of many in the Negro community with a shared reservoir of underlying grievances.

5. There was, typically, a complex relationship between the series of incidents and the underlying grievances. For example, grievances about allegedly abusive police practices, unemployment and underemployment, housing, and other conditions in the ghetto, were often aggravated in the minds of many Negroes by incidents involving the police, or the inaction of municipal authorities on Negro complaints about police action, unemployment, inadequate housing, or other conditions. When grievance-related incidents recurred and rising tensions were not satisfactorily resolved, a cumulative process took place in which prior incidents were readily recalled and grievances reinforced. At some point in the mounting tension, a further incident—in itself often routine or even trivial—became the breaking point, and the tension spilled over into violence.

6. Many grievances in the Negro community result from the

discrimination, prejudice, and powerlessness which Negroes often experience. They also result from the severely disadvantaged social and economic conditions of many Negroes as compared with those of whites in the same city and, more particularly, in the predominantly white suburbs.

7. Characteristically, the typical rioter was not a hoodlum, habitual criminal, or riffraff; nor was he a recent migrant, a member of an uneducated underclass, or a person lacking broad social and political concerns. Instead, he was a teenager or young adult, a lifelong resident of the city in which he rioted, a high school dropout—but somewhat better educated than his Negro neighbor—and almost invariably underemployed or employed in a menial job. He was proud of his race, extremely hostile to both whites and middle-class Negroes and, though informed about politics, highly distrustful of the political system and of political leaders.

8. Numerous Negro counterrioters walked the streets urging rioters to "cool it." The typical counterrioter resembled in many respects the majority of Negroes, who neither rioted nor took action against the rioters, that is, the noninvolved. But certain differences are crucial: the counterrioter was better educated and had higher income than either the rioter or the noninvolved.

9. Negotiations between Negroes and white officials occurred during virtually all the disorders surveyed. The negotiations often involved young, militant Negroes as well as older, established leaders. Despite a setting of chaos and disorder, negotiations in many cases involved discussion of underlying grievances as well as the handling of the disorder by control authorities.

10. The chain we have identified—discrimination, prejudice, disadvantaged conditions, intense and pervasive grievances, a series of tension-heightening incidents, all culminating in the eruption of disorder at the hands of youthful, politically-aware activists—must be understood as describing the central trend in the disorders, not as an explanation of all aspects of the riots or of all rioters. Some rioters, for example, may have shared neither the conditions nor the grievances of their Negro neighbors; some may have coolly and deliberately exploited the chaos created by others; some may have been drawn into the melee merely because they identified with, or wished to emulate, others. Nor do we intend to

97

suggest that the majority of the rioters, who shared the adverse conditions and grievances, necessarily articulated in their own minds the connection between that background and their actions.

11. The background of disorder in the riot cities was typically characterized by severely disadvantaged conditions for Negroes, especially as compared with those for whites; a local government often unresponsive to these conditions; Federal programs which had not yet reached a significantly large proportion of those in need; and the resulting reservoir of pervasive and deep grievance and frustration in the ghetto.

12. In the immediate aftermath of disorder, the status quo of daily life before the disorder generally was quickly restored. Yet, despite some notable public and private efforts, little basic change took place in the conditions underlying the disorder. In some cases, the result was increased distrust between blacks and whites, diminished interracial communication, and growth of Negro and white extremist groups.

THE PATTERN OF VIOLENCE AND DAMAGE

Levels of Violence and Damage. Because definitions of civil disorder vary widely, between 51 and 217 disorders were recorded by various agencies as having occurred during the first 9 months of 1967. From these sources we have developed a list of 164 disorders which occurred during that period. We have ranked them in three categories of violence and damage, utilizing such criteria as the degree and duration of violence, the number of active participants, and the level of law enforcement response:

Major Disorders. Eight disorders, 5 percent of the total, were major. These were characterized generally by a combination of the following factors: (1) many fires, intensive looting, and reports of sniping; (2) violence lasting more than 2 days; (3) sizable crowds; and (4) use of National Guard or Federal forces as well as other control forces.

Serious Disorders. Thirty-three disorders, 20 percent of the total, were serious but not major. These were characterized generally by: (1) isolated looting, some fires, and some rock throwing; (2) violence lasting between 1 and 2 days; (3) only one sizable crowd or many

The Search for Identity

HENRI CARTIER-BRESSON—MAGNUM

Ever since the first indentured servants landed at Jamestown in 1619, black
people in America have faced almost insuperable obstacles in the struggle that
every man must make to find his soul. Through three and a half centuries of
conscious and unconscious white oppression, many blacks came to believe that
they were, in fact, the strange and contradictory beings that white fantasy
believed them to be. Now, in the final third of the 20th century, young
Negroes are discarding the old stereotypes and making demands for a more
accurate understanding of their place in American history. The pictures in this
and the following volumes offer some clues to the black man's experience
in America.

Here, in one crowded print, is the traditional image of American society. It was made in 1876 to advertise the ''Uncle Sam'' woodburning stove and celebrates the 100th anniversary of the Declaration of Independence. Seated at the table are Uncle Sam, twin boys representing the South and West, a fair-haired girl symbolizing New England, and a jolly globe examining an exotic bill of fare. Over Uncle Sam's shoulder stands Miss Liberty. And at the stove, smiling as he works, is a young Negro about to serve the guests. The implicit attitude of those who designed and distributed

LIBRARY OF CONGRESS

this poster (with its assumption that Negro Americans should wait table rather than participate equally in the American feast) has been characteristic of much white society since 1776. It was assumed that this unjust system was the right order of things and, perhaps even worse, that Negroes themselves were content with their position. It is unlikely that Negroes were ever content with this state of affairs, even if it is only in recent times that increasing numbers of blacks have given vent to their anger and impatience.

ROGER MALLOCH FROM BLACK STAR (RIGHT)
LIBRARY OF CONGRESS

FUN.—May 13, 1865.

EMANCIPATION.

Columbia:—"TAKE THY FREEDOM, AND BE THANKFUL; FOR IT HAS COST ME MUCH."

White society has traditionally decreed what Negroes were to learn in school and, whether by accident or design, black history has rarely been included. This post-Civil War cartoon shows the Negro as he has most often appeared in American textbooks. He crouches while Miss Liberty entreats him to "Take thy freedom, and be thankful, for it has cost me much." Since whites took away his freedom in the first place, it is difficult for the modern black reader to see why he should be grateful for its return. Young blacks are now demanding that new curricula include full accounts of the black man's role in the nation's history. In temporary schoolrooms like the storefront "Freedom Day School," at right, they are attempting to make up for lost time with cram courses in black history.

If the psychologists are right, the belief that "white is right" when entertained by black men is the source of much of the self-hatred as well as the feelings of inferiority that are all too common among blacks. Daily exposure to white television, white advertising, and white teachers tends to make even the youngest black children feel inadequate because of their color.

BRUCE DAVIDSON—MAGNUM

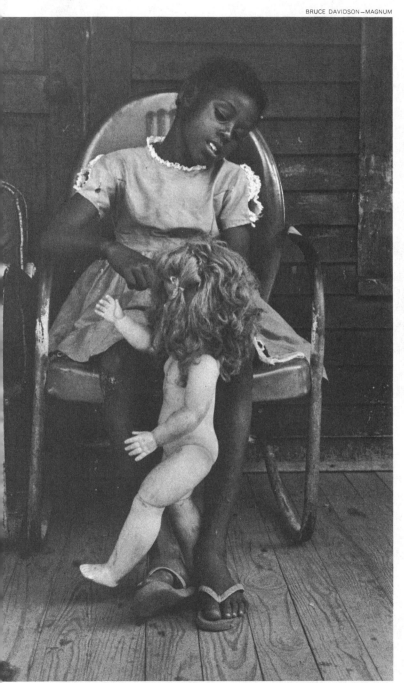

Today many young Negroes have found a new source of pride in their blackness. At a black cultural center in Harlem, above, African-inspired fashions are designed and made by blacks.

CULVER PICTURES

DENNIS STOCK—MAGNUM

Negro culture—from "soul food" to "soul music"—has become a new source of Negro pride. Black culture no longer has to be diluted or made "dignified" (white-like) to be enjoyed. The Fisk Jubilee Singers, above, who did much to familiarize white America with the Negro spiritual at the turn of the century, felt they had to "improve" their raw material with elaborate arrangements and solemn presentation. Such modern Negro artists as the late gospel singer Mahalia Jackson, left, now feel no compunctions about presenting their music pure and unadulterated.

small groups; and (4) use of state police though generally not National Guard or Federal forces.

Minor Disorders. One hundred and twenty-three disorders, 75 percent of the total, were minor. These would not have been classified as "riots" or received wide press attention without national conditioning to a "riot" climate. They were characterized generally by: (1) a few fires or broken windows; (2) violence lasting generally less than 1 day; (3) participation by only small numbers of people; and (4) use, in most cases, only of local police or police from a neighboring community.

The 164 disorders which we have categorized occurred in 128 cities. Twenty-five (20 percent) of the cities had two or more disturbances. New York had five separate disorders, Chicago had four, six cities had three and 17 cities had two. Two cities which experienced a major disorder—Cincinnati and Tampa—had subsequent disorders; Cincinnati had two more. However, in these two cities the later disorders were less serious than the earlier ones. In only two cities were later disorders more severe.

Three conclusions emerge from the data:

The significance of the 1967 disorders cannot be minimized. The level of disorder was major or serious, in terms of our criteria, on 41 occasions in 39 cities.

The level of disorder, however, has been exaggerated. Three-fourths of the disorders were relatively minor and would not have been regarded as nationally-newsworthy "riots" in prior years.

The fact that a city had experienced disorder earlier in 1967 did not immunize it from further violence. . . .

THE RIOT PROCESS

The Commission has found no "typical" disorder in 1967 in terms of intensity of violence and extensiveness of damage. To determine whether, as is sometimes suggested, there was a typical "riot process," we examined 24 disorders which occurred during 1967 in 20 cities and three university settings. We have concentrated on four aspects of that process:

The accumulating reservoir of grievances in the Negro community;

"Precipitating" incidents and their relationship to the reservoir of grievances;

The development of violence after its initial outbreak;

The control effort, including official force, negotiation, and persuasion.

We found a common social process operating in all 24 disorders in certain critical respects. These events developed similarly, over a period of time and out of an accumulation of grievances and increasing tension in the Negro community. Almost invariably, they exploded in ways related to the local community and its particular problems and conflicts. But once violence erupted, there began a complex interaction of many elements—rioters, official control forces, counterrioters—in which the differences between various disorders were more pronounced than the similarities.

The Reservoir of Grievances in the Negro Community. Our examination of the background of the surveyed disorders revealed a typical pattern of deeply held grievances which were widely shared by many members of the Negro community. The specific content of the expressed grievances varied somewhat from city to city. But in general, grievances among Negroes in all the cities related to prejudice, discrimination, severely disadvantaged living conditions, and a general sense of frustration about their inability to change those conditions.

Specific events or incidents exemplified and reinforced the shared sense of grievance. News of such incidents spread quickly throughout the community and added to the reservoir. Grievances about police practices, unemployment and underemployment, housing, and other objective conditions in the ghetto were aggravated in the minds of many Negroes by the inaction of municipal authorities.

Out of this reservoir of grievance and frustration, the riot process began in the cities which we surveyed.

Precipitating Incidents. In virtually every case a single "triggering" or "precipitating" incident can be identified as having immediately preceded—within a few hours and in generally the same location—the outbreak of disorder. But this incident was usually a relatively minor, even trivial one, by itself substantially disproportionate to the scale of violence that followed. Often it was an incident of a type which had occurred frequently in the same community in the past without provoking violence.

We found that violence was generated by an increasingly disturbed social atmosphere, in which typically not one, but a series of incidents occurred over a period of weeks or months prior to the outbreak of disorder. Most cities had three or more such incidents; Houston had 10 over a 5-month period. These earlier or prior incidents were linked in the minds of many Negroes to the preexisting reservoir of underlying grievances. With each such incident, frustration and tension grew until at some point a final incident, often similar to the incidents preceding it, occurred and was followed almost immediately by violence.

As we see it, the prior incidents and the reservoir of underlying grievances contributed to a cumulative process of mounting tension that spilled over into violence when the final incident occurred. In this sense the entire chain — the grievances, the series of prior tension-heightening incidents, and the final incident — was the "precipitant" of disorder.

This chain describes the central trend in the disorders we surveyed and not necessarily all aspects of the riots or of all rioters. For example, incidents have not always increased tension; and tension has not always resulted in violence. We conclude only that both processes did occur in the disorders we examined.

Similarly, we do not suggest that all rioters shared the conditions or the grievances of their Negro neighbors: some may deliberately have exploited the chaos created out of the frustration of others; some may have been drawn into the melee merely because they identified with, or wished to emulate, others. Some who shared the adverse conditions and grievances did not riot.

We found that the majority of the rioters did share the adverse conditions and grievances, although they did not necessarily articulate in their own minds the connection between that background and their actions. . . .

The Development of Violence. Once the series of precipitating incidents culminated in violence, the riot process did not follow a uniform pattern in the 24 disorders surveyed. However, some similarities emerge.

The final incident before the outbreak of disorder, and the initial violence itself, generally occurred at a time and place in which it was normal for many people to be on the streets. In most of the 24 disorders, groups generally estimated at 50 or more persons were on the street at the time and place of the first outbreak.

In all 24 disturbances, including the three university-related disorders, the initial disturbance area consisted of streets with relatively high concentrations of pedestrian and automobile traffic at the time. In all but two cases – Detroit and Milwaukee – violence started between 7 p.m. and 12:30 a.m., when the largest numbers of pedestrians could be expected. Ten of the 24 disorders erupted on Friday night, Saturday, or Sunday.

In most instances, the temperature during the day on which violence first erupted was quite high. This contributed to the size of the crowds on the street, particularly in areas of congested housing.

Major violence occurred in all 24 disorders during the evening and night hours, between 6 p.m. and 6 a.m., and in most cases between 9 p.m. and 3 a.m. In only a few disorders, including Detroit and Newark, did substantial violence occur or continue during the daytime. Generally, the night-day cycles continued in daily succession through the early period of the disorder.

At the beginning of disorder, violence generally flared almost immediately after the final precipitating incident. It then escalated quickly to its peak level, in the case of 1-night disorders, and to the first night peak in the case of continuing disorders. In Detroit and Newark, the first outbreaks began within two hours and reached severe, although not the highest, levels within 3 hours.

In almost all of the subsequent night-day cycles, the change from relative order to a state of disorder by a number of people typically occurred extremely rapidly – within 1 or 2 hours at the most.

Nineteen of the surveyed disorders lasted more than 1 night. In 10 of these, violence peaked on the first night, and the level of activity on subsequent nights was the same or less. In the other nine disorders, however, the peak was reached on a subsequent night.

Disorder generally began with less serious violence against property, such as rock- and bottle-throwing and window-breaking. These were usually the materials and the targets closest to hand at the place of the initial outbreak.

Once store windows were broken, looting usually followed. Whether fires were set only after looting occurred is unclear. Reported instances of fire-bombing and Molotov cocktails in the 24 disorders appeared to occur as frequently during one cycle of violence as during another in disorders which continued through more than one cycle. However, fires seemed to break out more frequently during the middle cycles of riots lasting several days. Gunfire and sniping were also reported more frequently during the middle cycles. . . .

THE RIOT PARTICIPANT

The Profile of a Rioter. The typical rioter in the summer of 1967 was a Negro, unmarried male between the ages of 15 and 24. He was in many ways very different from the stereotype. He was not a migrant. He was born in the state and was a lifelong resident of the city in which the riot took place. Economically his position was about the same as his Negro neighbors who did not actively participate in the riot.

Although he had not, usually, graduated from high school, he was somewhat better educated than the average inner-city Negro, having at least attended high school for a time.

Nevertheless, he was more likely to be working in a menial or low status job as an unskilled laborer. If he was employed, he was not working full time and his employment was frequently interrupted by periods of unemployment.

He feels strongly that he deserves a better job and that he is barred from achieving it, not because of lack of training, ability, or ambition, but because of discrimination by employers.

He rejects the white bigots' stereotype of the Negro as ignorant and shiftless. He takes great pride in his race and believes that in some respects Negroes are superior to whites. He is extremely hostile to whites, but his hostility is more apt to be a product of social and economic class than of race; he is almost equally hostile toward middle class Negroes.

He is substantially better informed about politics than Negroes who were not involved in the riots. He is more likely to be actively engaged in civil rights efforts, but is extremely distrustful of the political system and of political leaders.

The Profile of the Counterrioter. The typical counterrioter, who risked injury and arrest to walk the streets urging rioters to "cool it," was an active supporter of existing social institutions. He was, for example, far more likely than either the rioter or the noninvolved to feel that this country is worth defending in a major war. His actions and his attitudes reflected his substantially greater stake in the social system; he was considerably better educated and more affluent than either the rioter or the noninvolved. He was somewhat more likely than the rioter, but less likely than the noninvolved, to have been a migrant. In all other respects he was identical to the noninvolved. . . .

THE BASIC CAUSES

The record before this Commission reveals that the causes of recent racial disorders are imbedded in a massive tangle of issues and circumstances — social, economic, political, and psychological — which arise out of the historical pattern of Negro-white relations in America.

These factors are both complex and interacting; they vary significantly in their effect from city to city and from year to year; and the consequences of one disorder, generating new grievances and new demands, become the causes of the next. It is this which creates the "thicket of tension, conflicting evidence, and extreme opinions" cited by the President.

Despite these complexities, certain fundamental matters are clear. Of these, the most fundamental is the racial attitude and behavior of white Americans toward black Americans. Race prejudice has shaped our history decisively in the past; it now threatens to do so again. White racism is essentially responsible for the explosive mixture which has been accumulating in our cities since the end of World War II. At the base of this mixture are three of the most bitter fruits of white racial attitudes:

Pervasive discrimination and segregation. The first is surely the continuing exclusion of great numbers of Negroes from the benefits of economic progress through discrimination in employment and education and their enforced confinement in segregated housing and schools. The corrosive and degrading effects of this condition and the attitudes that underlie it are the source of the deepest bitterness and lie at the center of the problem of racial disorder.

Black migration and white exodus. The second is the massive and growing concentration of impoverished Negroes in our major cities resulting from Negro migration from the rural South, rapid population growth, and the continuing movement of the white middle class to the suburbs. The consequence is a greatly increased burden on the already depleted resources of cities, creating a growing crisis of deteriorating facilities and services and unmet human needs.

Black ghettos. Third, in the teeming racial ghettos, segregation and poverty have intersected to destroy opportunity and hope and to enforce failure. The ghettos too often mean men and women without jobs, families without men, and schools where children are processed instead of educated, until they return to the street—to crime, to narcotics, to dependency on welfare, and to bitterness and resentment against society in general and white society in particular.

These three forces have converged on the inner city in recent years and on the people who inhabit it. At the same time, most whites and many Negroes outside the ghettos have prospered to a degree unparalleled in the history of civilization. Through television—the universal appliance in the ghetto—and the other media of mass communications, this affluence has been endlessly flaunted before the eyes of the Negro poor and the jobless ghetto youth.

As Americans, most Negro citizens carry within themselves two basic aspirations of our society. They seek to share in both the material resources of our system and its intangible benefits—dignity, respect, and acceptance. Outside the ghetto, many have succeeded in achieving a decent standard of life and in developing the inner resources which give life meaning and direction. Within the ghetto, however, it is rare that either aspiration is achieved.

Yet these facts alone—fundamental as they are—cannot be said to have caused the disorders. Other and more immediate factors help explain why these events happened now.

Recently, three powerful ingredients have begun to catalyze the mixture.

Frustrated hopes. The expectations aroused by the great judicial and legislative victories of the civil rights movement have led to frustration, hostility, and cynicism in the face of the persistent gap between promise and fulfillment. The dramatic struggle for equal rights in the South has sensitized northern Negroes to the economic inequalities reflected in the deprivations of ghetto life.

Legitimation of violence. A climate that tends toward the approval and encouragement of violence as a form of protest has been created by white terrorism directed against nonviolent protest, including instances of abuse and even murder of some civil rights workers in the South, by the open defiance of law and Federal authority by state and local officials resisting desegregation, and by some protest groups engaging in civil disobedience who turn their backs on nonviolence, go beyond the constitutionally-protected rights of petition and free assembly and resort to violence to attempt to compel alteration of laws and policies with which they disagree. This condition has been reinforced by a general erosion of respect for authority in American society and the reduced effectiveness of social standards and community restraints on violence and crime. This in turn has largely resulted from rapid urbanization and the dramatic reduction in the average age of the total population.

Powerlessness. Finally, many Negroes have come to believe that they are being exploited politically and economically by the white "power structure." Negroes, like people in poverty everywhere, in fact lack the channels of communication, influence, and appeal that traditionally have been available to ethnic minorities within the city and which enabled them – unburdened by color – to scale the walls of the white ghettos in an earlier era. The frustrations of powerlessness have led some to the conviction that there is no effective alternative to violence as a means of expression and redress, as a way of "moving the system." More generally, the result is alienation and hostility toward the institutions of law and government and the white society which controls them. This is reflected in the reach toward racial consciousness and solidarity reflected in the slogan "Black Power."

These facts have combined to inspire a new mood among Negroes, particularly among the young. Self-esteem and enhanced racial pride are replacing apathy and submission to "the system." Moreover, Negro youth, who make up over half of the ghetto population, share the growing sense of alienation felt by many white youth in our country. Thus, their role in recent civil disorders reflects not only a shared sense of deprivation and victimization by white society but also the rising incidence of disruptive conduct by a segment of American youth throughout the society.

Incitement and encouragement of violence. These conditions have created a volatile mixture of attitudes and beliefs which needs only a spark to ignite mass violence. Strident appeals to violence, first heard from white racists, were echoed and reinforced last summer in the inflammatory rhetoric of black racists and militants. Throughout the year, extremists crisscrossed the country preaching a doctrine of violence. Their rhetoric was widely reported in the mass media; it was echoed by local "militants" and organizations; it became the ugly background noise of the violent summer.

We cannot measure with any precision the influence of these organizations and individuals in the ghetto, but we think it clear that the intolerable and unconscionable encouragement of violence heightened tensions, created a mood of acceptance and an expectation of violence and thus contributed to the eruption of the disorders last summer.

The police. It is the convergence of all these factors that makes the role of the police so difficult and so significant. Almost invariably the incident that ignites disorder arises from police action. Harlem, Watts, Newark, and Detroit—all the major outbursts of recent years were precipitated by arrests of Negroes by white police for minor offenses.

But the police are not merely the spark. In discharge of their obligation to maintain order and insure public safety in the disruptive conditions of ghetto life, they are inevitably involved in sharper and more frequent conflicts with ghetto residents than with the residents of other areas. Thus, to many Negroes, police have come to symbolize white power, white racism, and white repression. And the fact is that many police do reflect and express these white attitudes. The atmosphere of hostility and cynicism is reinforced by a widespread perception among Negroes of the existence of police brutality and corruption and of a "double standard" of justice and protection—one for Negroes and one for whites. . . .

THE COMMUNITY RESPONSE

The racial disorders of last summer in part reflect the failure of all levels of government – Federal and state as well as local – to come to grips with the problems of our cities. The ghetto symbolizes the dilemma: a widening gap between human needs and public resources and a growing cynicism regarding the commitment of community institutions and leadership to meet these needs.

The problem has many dimensions – financial, political, and institutional. Almost all cities – and particularly the central cities of the largest metropolitan regions – are simply unable to meet the growing need for public services and facilities with traditional sources of municipal revenue. Many cities are structured politically so that great numbers of citizens – particularly minority groups – have little or no representation in the processes of government. Finally, some cities lack either the will or the capacity to use effectively the resources that are available to them.

Instrumentalities of Federal and state government often compound the problems. National policy expressed through a very large number of grant programs and institutions rarely exhibits a coherent and consistent perspective when viewed at the local level. State efforts, traditionally focused on rural areas, often fail to tie in effectively with either local or Federal programs in urban areas.

Meanwhile, the decay of the central city continues – its revenue base eroded by the retreat of industry and white middle-class families to the suburbs, its budget and tax rate inflated by rising costs and increasing numbers of dependent citizens and its public plant – schools, hospitals, and correctional institutions deteriorated by age and long-deferred maintenance.

Yet to most citizens, the decay remains largely invisible. Only their tax bills and the headlines about crime or "riots" suggest that something may be seriously wrong in the city. . . .

THE FUTURE OF THE CITIES

Choices for the Future. The complexity of American society offers many choices for the future of relations between central cities and suburbs and patterns of white and Negro settlement in metropolitan areas. For practical purposes, however, we see two fundamental questions:

Should future Negro population growth be concentrated in central cities, as in the past 20 years, thereby forcing Negro and

116

white populations to become even more residentially segregated?

Should society provide greatly increased special assistance to Negroes and other relatively disadvantaged population groups?

For purposes of analysis, the Commission has defined three basic choices for the future embodying specific answers to these questions:

The Present Policies Choice. Under this course, the Nation would maintain approximately the share of resources now being allocated to programs of assistance for the poor, unemployed, and disadvantaged. These programs are likely to grow, given continuing economic growth and rising Federal revenues, but they will not grow fast enough to stop, let alone reverse, the already deteriorating quality of life in central-city ghettos.

This choice carries the highest ultimate price, as we will point out.

The Enrichment Choice. Under this course, the Nation would seek to offset the effects of continued Negro segregation and deprivation in large city ghettos. The enrichment choice would aim at creating dramatic improvements in the quality of life in disadvantaged central-city neighborhoods—both white and Negro. It would require marked increases in Federal spending for education, housing, employment, job training, and social services.

The enrichment choice would seek to lift poor Negroes and whites above poverty status and thereby give them the capacity to enter the mainstream of American life. But it would not, at least for many years, appreciably affect either the increasing concentration of Negroes in the ghetto or racial segregation in residential areas outside the ghetto.

The Integration Choice. This choice would be aimed at reversing the movement of the country toward two societies, separate and unequal.

The integration choice—like the enrichment choice—would call for large-scale improvement in the quality of ghetto life. But it would also involve both creating strong incentives for Negro movement out of central-city ghettos and enlarging freedom of choice concerning housing, employment, and schools.

The result would fall considerably short of full integration. The experience of other ethnic groups indicates that some Negro households would be scattered in largely white residential areas. Others – probably a larger number – would voluntarily cluster together in largely Negro neighborhoods. The integration choice would thus produce both integration and segregation. But the segregation would be voluntary.

Articulating these three choices plainly oversimplifies the possibilities open to the country. We believe, however, that they encompass the basic issues – issues which the American public must face if it is serious in its concern not only about civil disorder, but the future of our democratic society. . . .

CONCLUSIONS

The future of our cities is neither something which will just happen nor something which will be imposed upon us by an inevitable destiny. That future will be shaped to an important degree by choices we make now. We have attempted to set forth the major choices because we believe it is vital for Americans to understand the consequences of our present drift.

Three critical conclusions emerge from this analysis:

1. The nation is rapidly moving toward two increasingly separate Americas.

Within two decades, this division could be so deep that it would be almost impossible to unite:

a white society principally located in suburbs, in smaller central cities, and in the peripheral parts of large central cities; and

a Negro society largely concentrated within large central cities.

The Negro society will be permanently relegated to its current status, possibly even if we expend great amounts of money and effort in trying to "gild" the ghetto.

2. In the long run, continuation and expansion of such a permanent division threatens us with two perils.

The first is the danger of sustained violence in our cities. The timing, scale, nature, and repercussions of such violence cannot be foreseen. But if it occurred, it would further destroy our ability to achieve the basic American promises of liberty, justice, and equality.

The second is the danger of a conclusive repudiation of the traditional American ideals of individual dignity, freedom, and equality of opportunity. We will not be able to espouse these ideals meaningfully to the rest of the world, to ourselves, to our children. They may still recite the Pledge of Allegiance and say "one nation . . . indivisible." But they will be learning cynicism, not patriotism.

3. We cannot escape responsibility for choosing the future of our metropolitan areas and the human relations which develop within them. It is a responsibility so critical that even an unconscious choice to continue present policies has the gravest implications.

That we have delayed in choosing or, by delaying, may be making the wrong choice, does not sentence us either to separatism or despair. But we must choose. We will choose. Indeed, we are now choosing. . . .

RECOMMENDATIONS FOR NATIONAL ACTION

The disorders are not simply a problem of the racial ghetto or the city. As we have seen, they are symptoms of social ills that have become endemic in our society and now affect every American — black or white, businessman or factory worker, suburban commuter or slum-dweller:

None of us can escape the consequences of the continuing economic and social decay of the central city and the closely related problem of rural poverty. The convergence of these conditions in the racial ghetto and the resulting discontent and disruption threaten democratic values fundamental to our progress as a free society.

The essential fact is that neither existing conditions nor the garrison state offers acceptable alternatives for the future of this country. Only a greatly enlarged commitment to national action — compassionate, massive, and sustained, backed by the will and resources of the most powerful and the richest nation on this earth — can shape a future that is compatible with the historic ideals of American society. . . .

Objectives for National Action. Just as Lincoln, a century ago, put preservation of the Union above all else, so should we put creation of a true union — a single society and a single American identity — as our major goal. Toward that goal, we propose the following objectives for national action:

119

Opening up all opportunities to those who are restricted by racial segregation and discrimination, and eliminating all barriers to their choice of jobs, education, and housing.

Removing the frustration of powerlessness among the disadvantaged by providing the means to deal with the problems that affect their own lives and by increasing the capacity of our public and private institutions to respond to those problems.

Increasing communication across racial lines to destroy stereotypes, halt polarization, end distrust and hostility and create common ground for efforts toward common goals of public order and social justice.

There are those who oppose these aims as "rewarding the rioters." They are wrong. A great nation is not so easily intimidated. We propose these aims to fulfill our pledge of equality and to meet the fundamental needs of a democratic and civilized society—domestic peace, social justice, and urban centers that are citadels of the human spirit.

There are others who say that violence is necessary—that fear alone can prod the Nation to act decisively on behalf of racial minorities. They too are wrong. Violence and disorder compound injustice; they must be ended and they will be ended.

Our strategy is neither blind repression nor capitulation to lawlessness. Rather it is the affirmation of common possibilities, for all, within a single society.

MARK EDELSON
Genesis of a Riot

After the Kerner Commission report openly charged that white racism was the main cause of the widespread rioting in Northern cities during 1967 and 1968, popular discussion about the rioting crystallized in two opposing positions. According to one view, repressive measures by the police and military intensified the disturbances, and the danger of loss of life would be minimized by merely surrounding the riot area with troops but otherwise letting the disturbance run its course. According to the other view, it was the passivity of government officials, including police, that posed the greatest danger in the handling of rioters. The latter position is reflected in this article from the National Review of July 30, 1968.

There has been an official interpretation for riots ever since they began in the summer of 1964 in central Harlem; one which has never wavered in its recriminations against the general society, and in its implied exculpation of the rioters. Since "studies" of these affairs all come out the same way (like a fixed fight) and since the deeper the study, the more general the self-recrimination, I felt this time I should see the seminal event "live" and not on tape a few hours old. A prejudice is a prejudice, I thought, and some are old and some are new. And these new ones against the society, which must be really, unusually evil to cause so many cities to burn, sound thinner and more mindless than the old ones, which produced the obscene English of "nigger" and "spic." And I understood that this oppressive, disparaged society had to be me. The indictment was not against the burners, but against those who did not burn, not against the looters, but against those who would not loot. Here, right at hand, lay an opportunity for a study truly in depth.

It was Monday night, July 24, 1967. I entered East Harlem a little after 7:00 P.M., from 125th Street and Lexington Avenue, and found it under occupation. Moving south down Lexington, and then switching over to Madison, I saw police on all four corners of every intersection, usually in pairs, sometimes bunched up in threes and fours. Besides the heavy foot-force there was the cavalry of patrol cars and scooters. The force appeared to be almost 90 per cent white, a fact which has been grist to the mill of some anti-police writers, but which I found viscerally reassuring — an example, alas, of prejudice, but a very comforting one.

The occupiers, however, were not from another country, but merely another area, or areas, of the same city. If you want to postulate East Harlem as a different country in our midst (as do those white ideologues who follow the chic of calling it "El Barrio"), then it means that you are willing to concede a polyglot America, beginning in New York . . . a country which is not willing even to enforce a linguistic homogeneity, and is ready to overseer, or at least oversee, its own cultural fragmentation. If we no longer have an East Harlem, or even a "Spanish Harlem," but instead "El Barrio," then the city is giving itself away in pieces. Chinatown or Little Italy, after all, are linguistic indications of Americanization. "El Barrio" describes, not an oppressive but a tired society, one no longer willing to maintain even its most basic substructure. Then, America would really be Rome or Carthage – though just in the beginning stages.

The blue occupiers were notable for numbers, but even more for passivity. And this was to be their character and role all evening. They were a saturation, but a very quiet and inoffensive one. Unless the presence of an American peace force in an American city (East Harlem) is to be regarded in itself as offensive. The police, even the tactical force (who were off the streets filling the luncheonetts and pizza parlors), looked warm under all their equipment, and some were obviously tired, but I saw no pugnacity or quarrelsomeness on any of their faces. They are, of course, part of that oppressive enclosing society which the automatic partisans of all minorities recriminate in the wake of all rioting, but according to my experience (or prejudice, or both), if there was any easily definable group of good guys in that night's interaction, it could only have been these armed men.

As I moved downtown, switching every couple of blocks, westward toward Park and Madison or east to Third, I saw knots of adolescents and post-adolescents, just off the avenues and on the side streets, which themselves were generally unpoliced. In East Harlem, and Central Harlem also, this is not an unusual sight, particularly in season – the warm months. In the rapidly shrinking enclaves of white New York the people come out in summertime also, but the cluttered and pulsating street is a specific characteristic of the Negro and Puerto Rican areas. This time, however, there was a difference. Hostility was seen and felt on those side streets, just off the avenues. Whether this youth or that young man had undergone brutality at the hands of these other youths and men I do not know – that is a matter for real and careful proof, not easy apologetics for the underdog – but there could be no mistaking their sullen faces and mood to quarrel. It does not take two necessarily to make a quarrel. One can do it if he tries hard enough.

122

Of course, most of the people in the streets were not so predis-posed. They were as pacific and unconcerned as the police. They were living out their early evening as casually as they had just lived out their day. Whether they, too, were the victims of a society which deserves to be recriminated by its own intellectuals, I cannot say — but the thought occurred to me that if it is so, then the Caribbean must breed a masochistic race — did not all these people come here as volunteers and write back signaling their relatives and friends to make the trip, too?

It was now past eight o'clock, and I was on Lexington Avenue below 116th Street, where the clutter of East Harlem is broken, as it so often is, by one of the landscaped and airy city housing projects. I had intended to get a container of coffee and drink it outside, in one of those unofficial little parks between the project buildings, when I noticed a movement of people. It was eastward toward Third, which I had left for Lexington at 116th Street. This was the first sight of something definite, so, giving up my plans, I became part of the movement, and came out on Third at 111th Street.

Almost a block away, I could already see it was the focal point of the argument. But you heard more than you saw. You heard the speaker, a hoarse, abrasive voice (in Spanish), and without knowing Spanish you knew it was not an address, but at the very least a harangue. You also heard the crowd, or parts of it, as animated as the speaker, already an organism, exhilarated by a preliminary victory.

The victory: control of the intersection of 111th Street and Third Avenue. The speaker was standing on what looked like an inverted city litter basket, not on the sidewalk, but where the four roads crossed. The crowd of two or three hundred was itself mostly in the intersection, and it knew as much as the speaker did that the inter-section had been taken from the city and that the city had not reacted. It was a type of minor annexation — for New York, the govern-ment, had retreated a block and a half away. A block and a half north and a block and a half south on Third was again the charac-teristic governmental presence, large numbers of police, but passive and non-reactive. More than that, they were cooperative. Barriers had been placed across Third, and the normally busy traffic was police-directed away. That meant cars, trucks and the important

Third Avenue bus route were all interrupted so that activists against the police could harangue a crowd. To emphasize the tone of the speeches, two people stood beside the platform and held up a large Puerto Rican flag—but there was no American flag, here at Third Avenue and 111th Street, to keep it company, and no one in the crowd seemed to mind.

The speakers continued in English and in Spanish—someone in the crowd next to me translated the Spanish. There was a familiar, almost formula list of complaints about housing, police and the schools, but the tone was not one of petition but one of truculence and, climactically, of ultimatum. Mayor Lindsay was told to come uptown and negotiate by ten o'clock (about an hour away) or the area would explode. It seemed reasonable, I thought, to be truculent. They had already annexed the street. They had cut off traffic. They had seen the city withdraw its authority a block and a half away. They had seen an allegiance to Puerto Rico (but not the United States) placed next to the speakers—and, there was no reaction.

Shortly after nine o'clock a police observer was spotted on one of the roofs overlooking the meeting, and the crowd, by now *itself* truculent and visibly exhilarated, shouted and shrieked to have him brought down on the obvious premise that this area belonged to them, and not to the government of New York City. The roof-observer did come down—he was ordered to do so by a police captain, who came into the insurgent area from his position a block and a half away. Then, both he and the roof-observer retreated to government territory. In one other incident, a patrol car coming into the intersection along 111th Street tried to drive carefully around the crowd, but it massed and rushed on the car, ordering it back out of the area; and it did go back, without contesting the intersection.

These capitulations did not relax or quiet the crowd, they visibly enlivened it—the concessions fed, not tranquility, but aggression. The police were becoming, obviously, not good guys, but small guys. The speeches had heated up the crowd, but I believe it was these small capitulations which pushed it over the line into riot.

It was shortly after the rooftop incident that the first bottle was thrown. It broke in the street without hurting anyone—but it made everyone turn his eyes, not toward the area from which it came but toward the police, just beyond the insurgency. The police, government itself, was being tested again. And, following the pattern, there was no reaction. Within a minute or two, the first bottle was followed by small barrages, not thrown at any person or group, but at the emptied street—the crowd had retreated from the avenue itself and were now along both sidewalks, a great part of it up against the building line. It was now possible to see that a knot of people had emerged from 112th Street, on the east side of the avenue, and that they had made the attack. At first it was a quick sally onto the avenue to throw, and then back into the darkness. But there was no police reaction. Having apparently collected every no-deposit bottle in East Harlem, they came out into the avenue itself. Then, standing in the light, they began throwing the bottles boldly at the buildings and store-fronts, and then at the quiescent policemen themselves.

There were no more speeches—and whether the bottle- and rock-throwers had once been in the audience was something I could not tell; but the violence began just after the harangues, and almost at the same point. Also, the audience which had so protested the police did not, as far as I could hear, protest the obvious brutality of the flying bottles. There were police now among the crowd, and then between it and what was now the start of the riot. They were still, the police, a quiet presence, not active against anyone. They were, in their new position, merely a new and easier target for the rioters. This made us targets, too. The crowd dissolved into doorways, store entrances, flattened against buildings, and moved off the avenue into the side streets. It was a victim of its own work.

The police had now infiltrated the area in strength, still avoiding large movements, always emphasizing presence instead of action. They were now targets, both for the rioters' bottles and the non-rioters' ridicule. Those who had listened to and applauded the repetitious statements of police brutality now taunted the inactive police. (I thought, "That was an awful lot for eight thousand dollars a year.") There was no retort from the police, now helmeted, but they were no longer relaxed. I saw many sullen faces. They were like cats ready to move, but they did not move. When the bottles came at them, now generally in clusters, they flattened as far as they could, against the building line, turning away their heads, taking the fire

125

with their shoulders. It occurred to me: the preponderance of weapons is with the rioters. Because, though the police all have guns they don't use them. And the rounds of ammunition here were glass. It was becoming, as a matter of fact, a contest between armed and unarmed men.

At this point the looting began. All evening, law and government had been probed, defined and repudiated, in measured steps. The key always seemed to be the nonreaction of authority. It seemed to occur this way now. The street and sidewalks were mainly broken glass. There had been no move against the people who had done this, and now they made their own greater move. The rioters moved from their point on the corner of the avenue and 112th Street, and pushing down the avenue itself a few feet, stalled in front of a supermarket boarded up along its whole length. It took almost ten minutes of heavy work to pry open the wooden slats – ten minutes of present but absent government. When the boards finally came off, the rioters stopped to cheer their work, and then began to smash in the plate glass. This, finally, was the point of contact. Squads of police, from several directions, moved in on the rioters – but did not rush them. Apparently they were being given time to get away. This particular store wasn't looted. The rioters broke very quickly and fled before the police, foiled but not captured.

It was now a little past ten o'clock, and for the next two hours I walked Third and Lexington Avenues, between 111th and 102nd Streets, part of the shapeless lump of anarchy that moved from block to block, reproduced itself, and proliferated in many directions. The shape of police, and thus of governmental action, beginning at the captured intersection of 111th and Third, was repeated many times and solidified into the pattern of government for that night. The first duty of government is not to dispense justice but to rule. And in that section of the United States that night, there was no rule, only the shapeless lump of anarchy, moving up and down the avenues and streets, often dispersed by the police, never suppressed.

The mob did not appear brave to me. It was an example of bluster, not of *machismo* – the bully, not the man. The mob always broke before the essentially unarmed police. In the cross-section of riot I saw, I never observed one clubbing, and, though many shots were fired, often in volleys, it was always done for effect, harmlessly into the air.* The rioting never stopped or diminished because the rioters were never apprehended but merely dispersed, moment to moment, to continuously re-form, on other blocks, with the increasing awareness that they had achieved a supra-equality before the law — they were now more equal than others.

The apologists for rioters who from a distance conclude our sympathies should be more with the lawless than the law, should be air-dropped into the middle of the next disturbance to find out from experience whether the flint of anarchy is deprivation or truculence. I saw no hollow cheeks, patched clothes or tragic eyes among the stone-throwers — but I did see continuously the liquor of power in all their faces — and I had the apprehension, as well as they did, of a declining, and even vanishing government. By midnight, when I left the zone, there was only a pinpoint of government left (though it was a heavily occupied area), not because a government was now despised — but because, through its own inactions, it was *properly* despised.

When an organism becomes unable to react, then we know it is dying. A government had become so obsessed with minority complaint that it had forgotten how to rule. There was so much intellectual self-reproach and quibble in its mind that it was unable anymore to express its own right to live. This erosion of power, though internal, has a telepathy which is apprehended as quickly as fear. And it is appetite to truculence. Whatever the quantum of social inequity there may be in New York — after decades of welfare-oriented administrations — still the major phenomenon of this city is not injustice but the decline of government. Self-recrimination and

*Bullets fired "harmlessly" into the air by a police force under lethal attack from glass and stone represent the optimum of restraint, caution and self-risk. But a city block is a confined place and can give a bullet, no matter how harmlessly intended, two or three lives, and the first ricochet can bring a casualty, the result neither of intent nor recklessness. Two died that night of gunshot wounds, traced to police weapons. Both victims were apparently in the "audience" of the riot, which drew many, for many reasons. Though disturbing and repelling (at least to one member of the audience), it was a good show but it was a dangerous attraction. The tragedy of these affairs is that the innocent always get hurt. If the police ever aimed their shots specifically to kill, or even to wound, it was an anomaly of that evening, and not a characteristic. And, in the fairly comprehensive crosscut of the evening I observed, there was not even that anomaly.

127

self-doubt, both cults now, have subtracted from the desire to live. The aftermaths of these riots are more damaging than the period of anarchy itself. If looting and arson are defined as a form of protest or petition, as the curious apologetics always run, then the society which supports and even subsidizes these apologetics is inviting itself to be dissolved, is yearning for its own death.

More dangerous than the exceptional periods of riot are the quieter interludes. For some time now, government has not existed in East Harlem (or Central Harlem) as it exists in Jackson Heights or Flatbush. The real constant in the Negro or Puerto Rican areas is not the police excess, and certainly not the police atrocity, but instead the great difficulty of making normal arrests. The real news is the number of minor mob actions against the police which are never news. The main problem in the various slums is the problem of restoring government itself to these areas. The withering away of the state has progressed further in parts of New York City than any Marxist covenant yet applied.

Someone must have been sacrificing to the rain gods during that night of suspended government, because a little after 2:00 A.M. a heavy downpour fell on the city, both the governed and the ungoverned parts, and a deteriorating situation was cured by weather. The next day, through a process of redefinition, what was palpably a riot to those who had been there was reduced to a "disturbance" by those who had not—part of the new alchemy of government. But a government (or quasi-government) that shuffles definitions to make things come out even must be more interested in theory than in fact. It may not always rain in time.

ROBERT B. RIGG
Military Occupation of the Cities

The issue of the use of force to control and combat civil disorder received much attention following the disturbances in American cities during 1967. Because such widespread disorder was unprecedented in this century, police

*and National Guard officials were frequently unsure of precisely what
measure of force to use. The Kerner Commission Report cited the danger of
overreacting by the police, and this conclusion of the report seemed borne
out by the April 1968 disturbances, when police and military action was more
restrained than 1967 and the loss of life also much less. The threat of future
disorders led many police departments and National Guard units to undertake
programs of riot control. In the following article, reprinted here in part, a
professional soldier who specializes in long-range military strategy told what
steps would be taken by both National Guard and Army units to deal with
urban violence in the United States. [Source: Army, January 1968:
"Made in USA."]*

During the next few years organized urban insurrection could
explode to the extent that portions of large American cities could
become scenes of destruction approaching those of Stalingrad in
World War II. This could result from two main causes:

Man has constructed out of steel and concrete a much better
"jungle" than nature has created in Vietnam.

There is the danger and the promise that urban guerrillas of
the future can be organized to such a degree that their defeat would
require the direct application of military power by the National
Guard and the active Army.

This degree of destruction can easily come about because of
these two circumstances. After all, we have seen many square
blocks totally ruined in Watts, Detroit, and elsewhere, where there
was no organized resistance. Were organized insurrection to break
out and military power needed to suppress it, destruction in city
square miles could mount tremendously over what we have seen.

However, while application of pure military firepower would be a
poor solution, political efforts might prove not much better. There
are measures that offer a better solution if we are to keep our cities
from becoming battlegrounds: penetration by police intelligence,
application of military intelligence, and reliance on traditional FBI
methods. Such efforts must begin now so as to prevent organized
urban guerrilla violence from gaining momentum.

To prevent and to curb urban violence of any order we must
establish an effective system of intelligence in the ghettos of urban
America. If penetration were professionally effective, such a system

129

could warn of any plans for organized violence by subversive elements. Further, should organized violence break out, such an espionage system would be able to keep riot control and counterviolence forces informed during a disturbance.

The real prevention of urban violence and insurrection begins with social, economic, and political efforts. But alongside these measures and efforts there must be the "peripheral insurance policy" of an inside intelligence system that can warn of serious outbreaks and help curb them.

Furthermore, there will also be needed among the well-established political-tactical-military informants those who can help guide troops and police through the maze of buildings, stairwells, streets, alleyways, tunnels, and sewers that may be the key to tactical success. In the countryside we would call this elementary or "grass roots" intelligence; in the city there will be a similar need.

Just as China was plagued with rural guerrilla warfare from the 1920s to the late 1940s, so, too, if present trends persist, could the United States experience similar strife and violence. The singular difference is that the fighting would be urban in nature. Furthermore, it is likely to be of such a special brand that can bear only the unique label, "Made in the U.S.A." Thus, the United States may inadvertently provide the world with a new brand of internal warfare that could haunt and harass large metropolitan areas for decades to come.

This possibility is alarming in light of the population explosion and the urban growth which by the 1980s may result in strip cities extending from Miami to Boston, from Chicago to Detroit, from San Francisco to San Diego—not to mention similar areas abroad. Of further import for the near future is the fact that the older "core cities"—such as Chicago, New York, Detroit, Newark, Oakland, Los Angeles, and others—could become concrete jungles where poverty could spread with their growth. Additionally, such cement-and-brick "jungles" can offer better security to snipers and city guerrillas than the Viet Cong enjoy in their jungles, elephant grass, and marshes. This suggests protracted warfare of a very new kind if city guerrilla forces become well organized by dissident and determined leaders.

City warfare is not new. What would make this type of conflict new, different, and more terrifying would be two elements. One would be the very geographical extent of the concrete jungles that are now simply called ghettos; such slum areas can expand rapidly as suburbia grows and absorbs the more affluent. The other would be lawless forces intoxicated by the ease and security with which they might successfully defy police, National Guardsmen, and Army regulars. The concrete blocks of our great ghettos have vertical acreage and horizontal mileage that offer such tactical protection and vantage points as to make future snipers much "braver" and city guerrillas much bolder than unorganized rioting mobs have been so far.

These are only a few of the trends in the United States which flash warning that our nation could be in for such violent street disorders that to suppress them would ultimately require the civil use of military power on a scale never heretofore visualized.

Racial issues, poverty, political unrest among minorities, the population explosion, and the rapid growth of strip cities that absorb the decaying old core cities—all these represent a combination of future factors and trends that could plague metropolitan areas and breed more violent and better-organized disorder. That urban violence has spread significantly makes the outlook grim, because street violence has found acceptance among minorities.

Today's riots bring more than temporary disorder. They instill a new frame of mind among minorities—an outlook that visualizes rebellion against society and authority as a successful venture for the future. So far the unruly elements, with no real organization, have demonstrated that they can do unusual damage wantonly and indiscriminately. But the sick seed can grow into a menacing weed if in the future the potentials of organization are exploited.

So far the causes of urban violence have been emotional and social. Organization, however, can translate these grievances into political ones of serious potential and result in violence, or even prolonged warfare. Thus, we may find that the danger to a free America is greater from within than from without.

If present trends persist, it is possible that in the next decade at least one major metropolitan area in the United States could be faced with guerrilla warfare of such intensity as to require sizable U.S. Army elements in action and National Guard units on active duty for years. No doubt such an urban conflict could be contained, subdued and defeated, but the effort could possibly require years of concerted military action before even effective social improvements could have impact. This is what the war in South Vietnam has demonstrated. Further, if organized guerrilla resistance spreads to several cities and requires the use of many military units, a national paralysis of very serious proportions might ensue. . . .

Urban riot has been established as an instrument of racial rebellion. But the riots have not been strictly one of Negroes clashing with whites; often the rioters were relieving their frustrations at their ghetto surroundings and relative poverty, and upon authorities. It is important to remember this, especially where it pertains to slums. Violence in the future may even be by whites protesting against poverty and their environment. White or black, here is where the political aspect looms large because Communist elements can penetrate urban America and foment serious trouble.

The future brand of trouble may not necessarily be Communist-inspired. Activists of the left who now expend their energies in protesting against the Vietnam war could become a growing source of urban unrest and trouble. The future problem of city violence bears no particular political label at the moment but it does indicate that trouble can arise from the left or right, or from black or white. Poverty and social problems exist in rural areas, but they can reach explosive and serious proportions only in our cities.

The personal right to own firearms is being seriously debated in Washington today. The argument will linger, and probably with no conclusive results, for a long time. The stark fact remains that from Chicago to the Congo, anyone who wants to shoot can buy small arms and even mortars. World War II, the many limited wars since, and all the military-aid programs have flooded the world with arms and ammunition. If a subversive force or organization wants arms, they are available. If their leaders want them on a wholesale scale, arms for the urban guerrillas of the United States will not be hard to obtain.

Today, one trend is self-evident: metropolitan police cannot cope with even disorganized violence where it reaches high proportions. Tomorrow, police and National Guard units may not be able to cope with urban violence that is well organized. . . .

While the patterns of future urban insurrection may vary, there will be certain problems to confront, if the violence is organized.

Problem No. 1 would be organization itself. To combat this would require political and intelligence penetration of high order and expertise. Here, penetration must be deep enough so as to warn of secret subversive plans, to pinpoint leaders, and to disrupt organization itself.

Problem No. 2 would concern the identification of hideouts, areas where weapons are stored, sources of arms, guerrilla means of transportation, access and escape routes, and probably resistance spots. In other words, we must have intimate and accurate information on the facilities used by urban guerrillas before and during trouble.

Problem No. 3 relates to tactical military action against organized resistance once conflict begins. Hopefully, this assumes that at least fair intelligence and espionage would continue to meet the problems mentioned. But no intelligence report has ever been prepared that included complete information on the enemy *after* the fighting started. Tactical action has always had to rely on what little was known and what could be learned through intelligence gathered by scouting and combat. Imagine a building, or a block of buildings, that houses innocent people but is used at night by snipers and insurrectionists with fire bombs. Tactical action here would take on the proportions of search-and-plant operations by day and retaliation, maneuver, and fighting by night. Night fighting will call for a very delicate decision as to which darkened window to shoot at and which rooftop to blast by mortar fire or to assault by helicopter. A whole new manual of military operations, tactics, and techniques needs to be written in respect to urban warfare of this nature. There are none on the subject today.

Problem No. 4 includes police-Guard-Army and local authority (particularly political) coordination, communications, and control. Here also is a very big problem that can be greatly aggravated by chaos and street fighting. For every city, for every emergency, this one requires much planning in depth. Planning is vital, particularly in terms of political and military control and coordination of all efforts. Once chaos and conflict ensue, command and coordination become even more crucial and necessary. Communications in terms of standing operating procedure, integrated radio networks, liaison, procedures, and the like are big problems that must be solved before conflict and modified to meet the demands of the situation.

Problem No. 5 can be termed "Mixture X." It includes everything from control and safety of a few dozen (or hundreds) of refugees fleeing from buildings to hostages being held by seasoned guerrillas or being used by them as escape shields. It includes the sick and wounded among the innocent. It includes the supply of food and medicine – and medical treatment – to trapped people. It includes evacuation by helicopters and by fire fighters of people trapped in burning buildings. It includes the protection of firemen from sniper fire, the need of which last summer's Detroit riot demonstrated in very grim and dramatic fashion. Plainly, firemen need the Red Cross badge of safety to protect them in their valor and work. They didn't have even this in Detroit. They may suffer heavy casualties during organized urban insurrection of the future unless they are somehow more respected by some agreement or other measure.

Success in coping with organized urban warfare will not rest on agreements but rather depend on tactics and techniques yet to be formulated. The overall problem, and success in meeting it, depend heavily on a new measure of organization, coordination, and study among officials of the city, state, National Guard, police, active Army, and FBI. While these organizations understand the problem and are alert to it, much work lies ahead.

The implications are clear. American military and political plans must now, more than ever before, be based upon meeting a new kind of internal violence. . . .

Such planning must include training troops for urban insurrection. For the National Guard this means a complete change of direction in training as something of first priority. For the active Army, such training has serious overtones to the extent that it must train for the concrete jungle as well as for the other kind. Further, it means that Army units must be oriented and trained to know the cement-and-asphalt jungle of *every* American city. It means that maneuvers and exercises, heretofore carried out about the countryside, in the future can be conducted in large cities. Possibly the sight of such maneuvers in several cities could prove a deterrent to urban insurrection. Today's trend implies that very soon American troops will be maneuvering in metropolitan areas to an extent more than ever before imagined. Here they will be required to learn about and memorize details of many metropolitan communities, their buildings, streets, alleyways, rooftops, and sewers, just as once they learned the use of terrain features of open country. This is the only way to solve the intelligence, social, economic, and political problems associated with serious Third Front warfare which could bear the unfortunate label of "Made in the U.S.A."

TOM HAYDEN

The Occupation of Newark

The eruption of Newark began on the evening of July 12, 1967. It was not the most terrible riot during the long hot summer of that year — Detroit was far worse — nor was it the most surprising — New Haven, which was supposed to be a model city, confounded all of the experts. But it was terrible enough, and also surprising because of the things that men who were there found out about themselves and about their fellows. Tom Hayden, who was there, described some of the events of the week following July 12, and tried to give some understanding of them, too, in an article in the New York Review, *part of which is reprinted here. All of the instances cited in this article were documented by newspaper reports or eyewitness accounts. [*Source: *New York Review of Books, August 24, 1967.*]*

WEDNESDAY: JOHN SMITH STARTS A RIOT

As if to prove its inevitability, the Newark riot began with an ordinary police-brutality incident against a man with an ordinary name: John Smith, driver of Cab 45, in the employ of the Safety Cab Company. Early Wednesday night, Smith's cab drove around a police car double-parked on 15th Avenue. Two uniformed patrolmen stopped the cab. According to the police story given to the *Star-Ledger* of July 14, Smith was charged with "tailgating" and driving the wrong way on a one-way street. Later they discovered his license had expired. The officers charged that Smith used abusive language and

135

punched them. "They only used necessary force to subdue Smith, the policemen asserted."

This "necessary force" was described more fully by Smith at his bail hearing on July 13. "There was no resistance on my part. That was a cover story by the police. They caved in my ribs, busted a hernia, and put a hole in my head." Witnesses on the stoops saw Smith dragged, paralyzed, to the police station. Smith was conscious, however: "After I got into the precinct, six or seven other officers along with the two who arrested me kicked and stomped me in the ribs and back. They then took me to a cell and put my head over the toilet bowl. While my head was over the toilet bowl I was struck on the back of the head with a revolver. I was also being cursed while they were beating me. An arresting officer in the cell-block said, 'This baby is mine.' "

It was about 8 o'clock. Negro cab drivers circulated the report on Smith over their radios. Women and men shook their heads as they stood or sat in front of their homes. The word spread down 17th Avenue, west of the precinct, and across the avenue into Hayes Homes. Called the "projects" by everyone, Hayes Homes was erected in the wake of "slum clearance" in the mid-Fifties. Each of the six 12-story buildings holds about 1,000 people. People know them as foul prisons and police know them as "breeding grounds" for crime. As the word spread through Hayes Homes, people gathered at the windows and along the shadowy sidewalks facing the precinct.

What was unusual about John Smith's case was the fact that the police were forced to let respected civil rights leaders see his condition less than two hours after the beating. The police were trapped and nervous because they had been caught by civil rights leaders whose account could not be discredited. A neighborhood resident had called several of these leaders—including activists from CORE, the United Freedom Party, and the Newark Community Union Project—minutes after Smith was brought in.

After they had a heated argument about Smith with officers in the precinct, an inspector arrived from central police headquarters and agreed to let the group see the prisoner in his cell. "Don't listen to what he says. He's obviously upset and nervous as you might expect," the inspector told the group. The group was incensed after

136

seeing Smith's condition. They demanded that he be sent immediately to the hospital. The police complied, while others searched for witnesses, lawyers, and members of Smith's family.

It was at this point that witnesses who were in the precinct house say the police began putting on riot helmets. None of the activists felt there was going to be an explosion, and none remembers a crowd of more than a hundred in the street at this point. . . .

Just after midnight, two Molotov cocktails exploded high on the western wall of the precinct. A stream of fire curled fifty feet down the wall, flared for ten seconds, and died. The people, now numbering at least 500 on the street, let out a gasp of excitement. Fear, or at least caution, was apparent also: many people retreated into the darkness or behind cars in the Hayes parking lot.

After three years of wondering when "the riot" would come to Newark, people knew that this could be it. While city officials pointed with pride to Newark's record of peace, most of the community knew it was only a matter of time until the explosion: "And when Newark goes," according to street wisdom, "it's going to really go." Despite millions in antipoverty and job-training funds during the last three summers, the ailments which afflict every black community had become no better. According to the city officials themselves, Newark has the highest percentage of bad housing of any city in the nation, the highest maternal mortality rate, and the second highest infant mortality rate; the unemployment rate in the ghetto is higher than 15 percent. Every effort to create an organized movement for change has been discredited, absorbed, or met with implacable hostility by politicians. The city's 250,000 Negroes – a majority of the population – felt with good reason excluded from the institutions of business and government. . . .

On the front lines against the police that night were men between fifteen and twenty-five years old from the projects and the nearby avenues. They were the primary assailants and the most elusive enemy for the police. They were the force which broke open the situation in which masses of people began to participate. . . .

Fathers and mothers in the ghetto often complain that even they cannot understand the wildness of their kids. Knowing that America denies opportunity to black young men, black parents still share

137

with the whites the sense that youth is heading in a radically new, incomprehensible, and frightening direction. Refusal to obey authority — that of parents, teachers, and other adult "supervisors" — is a common charge against youngsters. Yet when the riot broke out, the generations came together. The parents understood and approved the defiance of their sons that night.

So while the young men grouped their forces, shouted, and armed themselves against the helmeted police with whatever they could find on the ground, the older generation gathered in larger and larger numbers in the rear. The Hayes projects are a useful terrain for people making war. The police station is well lit, but the projects are dark, especially the rooftops 100 yards above the street. Each room in the projects can be darkened to allow people to observe or attack from their windows. There is little light in the pathways, recreation areas, and parking lots around the bases of the tall buildings. The police thus were faced with the problems of ambush and of searching through a shadow world where everybody appears to be alike to an outsider. It was in this sanctuary that parents came together. It was here also that their sons could return to avoid the police.

Less than an hour after the bomb hit the precinct, the looting phase began. A group of twenty-five young people on 17th Avenue decided that the time was ripe to break into the stores. They ran up 17th Avenue toward Belmont as the word of their mission spread along the way. "They're going up to Harry's," a mother excitedly said. She and her friends looked quizzically at each other, then started running up to the corner. A boom and a crash signaled the opening of the new stage. Within fifteen minutes burglar alarms were ringing up and down Belmont and 17th. People poured out from the project areas into liquor and furniture stores as the young people tore them open.

The police now began patrolling on foot in small teams. It was clear that they were both outnumbered and uncertain of themselves in the streets. Police violence grew. The next day Newark Human Rights Commission Chairman Al Black reported to the mayor what the police did when "order" collapsed: a Negro policeman in civilian clothes was beaten by white policemen when he entered the precinct to report for duty; Mrs. Vera Brinson was told to "get the hell upstairs" and hit on the neck with a club in Hayes Homes; Gregory Smith said police shouted, "All you black niggers get upstairs" at project residents; two men were seized by police as they returned from work, one beaten by eight police at the precinct and the other punched and kicked by fifteen police at the entrance to his building. These people were not "criminals," Black told the mayor, but were working people.

But in the first hours the police could not control the streets in spite of nearly 100 arrests and numerous attacks on people. After a while they developed an uneasy coexistence with the crowd, the police in twos and threes taking up positions to "protect" stores which were already looted, while the people moved on to other stores. More police tried in vain to regain control of 17th Avenue and Belmont but were trapped in a pattern of frustrating advance-and-retreat.

One hope of the police may have been to keep the riot from spreading. Again, however, this was beyond their control. If they had used greater force on Belmont and 17th, the result probably would have been to spread the riot by making people move beyond the zone of fire. Furthermore, though all of Newark's 1,400 police were being mobilized, it is doubtful there were enough men to cordon off effectively a spreading mass of rioters. Therefore the question of when and how the riot would spread was in the hands of the people rather than the police. That it did not spread may indicate the lack of real organization. All around the original riot zone people were sitting on their stoops or sleeping in their homes within earshot of the window. Yet word did not spread until the following day.

Moreover, an incident involving Smith's fellow cab drivers Wednesday night tends to indicate that the spreading word by itself is not sufficient to spread the action. The cab drivers were the one group equipped to let thousands of people in the city know what had happened. Within a few hours of Smith's arrest, the black cabbies were deciding by radio to meet at the precinct and form a protest caravan to City Hall. Between 1 and 2 A.M. at least twenty cars were lined up along Belmont at the corner of 17th, creating new noise, excitement, and fury. After nearly an hour of waiting and planning, the cabs roared down to police headquarters, located behind City

139

Hall, to demand the release of Smith. They carried close to 100 passengers from the riot area with them. At headquarters they were able to secure a promise that Smith would be adequately treated and released after arraignment in the morning. At the same time the police closed off traffic on Broad Street in front of City Hall, thus helping further to alert citizens who had not been affected by the rioting or the cab-drivers' caravan. Police by this time were swinging their clubs freely, even at confused motorists, perhaps out of fear that bombs would be thrown against the City Hall building itself.

Yet the riot did not spread. By 4 A.M. most of the participants had gone home. . . . By 5 A.M. everyone had vanished from the streets, except the police.

THURSDAY: THE COMMUNITY TAKES POWER

Thursday morning's papers denied what everyone knew was true. Mayor Addonizio called the events of the previous evening an "isolated incident," not of genuine riot proportions. In their behavior, however, city officials showed that they were worried.

The mayor called in civil rights leaders, including both moderate ministers and some of his more militant opponents. Concessions were made. Addonizio decided to ask for City Council funds to allow additional police captaincies so that a qualified Negro officer, Eddie Williams, could become the first Negro captain. He requested that Human Rights Director James Threatt and Police Director Dominick Spina separately investigate Wednesday's conflict. He reassigned the two patrolmen who beat Smith to "administrative positions." He referred the Smith case to the County Prosecutor and FBI. He announced formation of a Blue Ribbon Commission, like the McCone Commission which investigated Watts, to examine this "isolated incident." The mayor was doing what militant politicians were demanding. But when someone told him point blank that the people had lost confidence in his administration, Addonizio replied, "That's politics. Sit down. You've said enough."

There was no civil rights leader, no organization capable of determining what was to come. Sensing this, some community activists refused to engage in what they felt were fruitless meetings downtown. Others tried to warn the mayor of what might happen, in

140

full knowledge that the mayor was now powerless. Others worked desperately for a solution that could be brought into the community in a bargain for peace. Many jockeyed for position, worrying about who had the mayor's ear, who might be blamed, who would be the channel for resources from the establishment to the community.

Some community activists settled on the idea of a demonstration at the precinct in the evening. At a neighborhood antipoverty center near the precinct, they ran off a leaflet which simply said : "Stop! Police Brutality!" It would be given out to motorists, calling for a demonstration at the precinct at 7:30 P.M. Some organizers of this demonstration probably thought it might channel energy away from violence. Others knew the violence was there and was not to be channeled into conventional protest, yet protest was the only avenue of expression familiar to them. So they proceeded. Police Director Spina would later claim that this activity helped to "fuel" the explosion later that night.

Regardless of what the mayor did, regardless of what civil rights leaders did, regardless of what planners of the demonstration did, the riot was going to happen. The authorities had been indifferent to the community's demand for justice; now the community was going to be indifferent to the authorities' demand for order. This was apparent to community organizers who walked around the projects Thursday afternoon talking to young people. All the organizers urged was that burning of buildings be minimized so as to spare lives. . . .

Heavy looting soon began on Springfield Avenue, three blocks from the precinct and the largest commercial street in the ghetto. By midnight there was action everywhere in the ghetto, although the mayor announced that the disturbance was being brought to an end. Partly the expansion was caused by people moving in new directions, outward from the looted areas where police were concentrated. Partly it was people in new neighborhoods following the example of people in the original area. A human network of communication was forming, with people in the streets as its main conductors.

The youth were again in the lead, breaking windows wherever the chance appeared, chanting "Black Power," moving in groups through dark streets to new commercial areas. This was more than a case of youth stepping in where parents feared to tread. This was the largest demonstration of black people ever held in Newark. At any major intersection, and there are at least ten such points in the ghetto, there were more than a thousand people on the streets at the same time. A small number entered stores and moved out with what they could carry; they would be replaced by others from the large mass of people walking, running, or standing in the streets. Further back were thousands more who watched from windows and stoops and periodically participated. Those with mixed feelings were not about to intervene against their neighbors. A small number, largely the older people, shook their heads.

People voted with their feet to expropriate property to which they felt entitled. They were tearing up the stores with the trick contracts and installment plans, the second-hand televisions going for top-quality prices, the phony scales, the inferior meat and vegetables. A common claim was: This is owed me. But few needed to argue. People who under ordinary conditions respected law because they were forced to do so now felt free to act upon the law as they thought it should be. When an unpopular store was opened up, with that mighty crash of glass or ripping sound of metal, great shouts of joy would sound. "Hey, they got Alice's." "They gave that place what it deserved." "They did? G-o-o-d!"

The riot was more effective against gouging merchants than organized protest had ever been. The year before a survey was started to check on merchants who weighted their scales. The survey collapsed because of disinterest: people needed power, not proof. This spring the welfare mothers spent a month planning and carrying out a protest against a single widely hated store. The owner finally was forced to close his business, but only after nineteen people were arrested in a demonstration. There was no effective follow-up against the other stores, though frightened merchants cleaned up their stores, offered bribes to organizers, and chipped in money to outfit a kid's baseball team. It was too late for concessions.

The Negro middle class and "respectable" working people participated heavily on Thursday night. Well-dressed couples with kids in their cars were a common sight. One woman, who said she already could afford the "junk" sold in the ghetto, decided to wait until the rioting spread to fancier sections where she could get expensive furs. Doubtless the mayor's failure to act on issues such as education caused disaffection among the black middle class. Doubtless, too, the middle class's willingness to consider rioting legitimate made it more likely that a riot would happen.

But it is doubtful that any tactics by the mayor could have divided the black middle class from the ghetto in such a way as to prevent a riot. The poor were going to riot. The middle class could join. Many did because their racial consciousness cut through middle-class values to make property destruction seem reasonable, especially when the white authorities cannot see who is looting. During the Watts riot the story was told of a black executive who regularly stopped to throw bricks before attending suburban cocktail parties and barbecues; the same attitude was present in Newark. When police systematically attacked Negro-owned stores later in the week, they were only confirming what the black middle class, reluctantly, was starting to understand: that racism ultimately makes no distinction between "proper" and "lowly" colored people.

Black unity, solidarity, spirit, the feeling of being home: by whatever name, the fact was plain. There is no question that a majority of Negroes gave support. People on the street felt free to take shelter from the police in the homes of people they did not know. What concerned Governor Hughes greatly the next morning was the "carnival atmosphere" of people looting even in daylight. What for Hughes seemed like "laughing at a funeral" was to many in the community more like the celebration of a new beginning. People felt as though for a moment they were creating a community of their own.

Economic gain was the basis of mass involvement. The stores presented the most immediate way for people to take what they felt was theirs. . . .

For the most part the rioting was controlled and focused. The "rampaging" was aimed almost exclusively at white-owned stores and not at such buildings as schools, churches, or banks. The latter institutions are oppressive but their buildings contain little that can be carried off. To this extent the riot was concrete rather than symbolic. There were no attacks by Negroes on "soul brother" stores.

There were people injured by glass on the streets where they fell, but they typically fell because police chased them, not because of stampeding in the rush for goods.

Basic feelings of racial hate were released at white people far less often than was suggested by the media. Many missiles were thrown at cars driven by whites but not often with murderous intent. Several times such cars were stopped, the occupants jeered at and terrified, and a few actual beatings occurred. However, no white passers-by or storeowners were killed and very few, if any, were shot at. No white neighborhoods were attacked, though rioting reached the borders of at least four separate white areas. Several white community workers felt able to move around on foot freely by day and even at night, especially in the company of Negroes. Driving was more difficult because all white people appeared to be outsiders motoring home. These conditions remained the same throughout the week, though the tensions between whites and blacks intensified as the stage of spirited looting was replaced by that of bitter confrontation with the troops.

Police behavior became more and more violent as the looting expanded. The size of the rebellion was far too large for 1,400 patrolmen. Their tactic seemed to be to drive at high speeds, with sirens whining, down major streets in the ghetto. Thus they were driving too fast for rock-throwers while still attempting a show of force. As a result of this maneuver a woman was run down and apparently killed on 17th Avenue. The sight and sound of the police also stirred the community into greater excitement.

As darkness fell, the number of arrests increased sharply. Police started firing blanks. According to the *Times* of July 14, police were asking by radio for "the word" to shoot, and when news came in that policemen in one car were shooting real bullets, another voice shouted over the radio: "It's about time; give them hell!" At midnight orders were given for police to use "all necessary means – including firearms – to defend themselves."

Murdering looters was now possible. A short time afterward, twenty-eight-year-old Tedock Bell walked out of his Bergen Street home to see what had happened to the nearby bar where he was employed. When the police came, his wife left in fright. But Tedock told his sister-in-law and her boyfriend not to run because they weren't doing anything. They did run, however, while he walked. He became the first victim a minute later. About 4 A.M. patrolmen Harry Romeo and David Martinez reported they saw four men emerge with bottles from a liquor store on Jones Street. They called halt, the officers told the Newark *News* – calling halt is a preliminary to shooting someone – but the looters ran. Martinez shot and killed one of them going through a fence.

More than 250 people were treated at City Hospital that night, at least 15 reportedly for gunshot wounds. Less than one-quarter of them were held for further diagnosis and treatment. The police took over the ambulances from the Negro drivers and rescue workers. Snipers were shooting at the ambulances, police said. By 2:20 A.M. Mayor Addonizio was revising his midnight estimate that the situation was under control. Announcing that things had deteriorated, he asked Governor Hughes for aid in restoring order.

By early Friday morning 425 people were in jail. In addition to 5 dead, hundreds were wounded or injured. The Newark *News* that morning expressed hope that Newark might again become a city "in which people can live and work harmoniously in a climate that will encourage, not repel, the expansion of the business and industry that provide jobs for all."

THE OCCUPATION

"An obvious open rebellion," asserted Governor Hughes after his tour of Newark at 5 A.M. Friday. From that announcement until Monday afternoon, the black community was under military occupation. More than 3,000 National Guardsmen were called up Friday morning from the surrounding white suburbs and southern Jersey towns. Five hundred white state troopers arrived at the same time. By mid-afternoon Friday they were moving in small convoys throughout the city, both clockwise and counterclockwise, circling around seven parts of the ghetto. Guardsmen were moving in jeeps or small open trucks, usually led or followed by carloads of troopers or Newark police. Bayonets were attached to the Guard's 30-caliber M-1 rifles or 30-caliber carbines, which they carried in addition to 45-caliber pistols. Personnel carriers weighing as much as eleven tons and trucks mounted with machine guns appeared here and there among the jeeps and police cars. The presence of these vehi-

145

cles was designed, according to Governor Hughes, to build the confidence of the Negro community. . . .

THE TERROR

We will never know the full story of how these troops and the police hurt the black people of Newark. But there is now sufficient evidence to establish the main features of their behavior.

Less than 2 percent of the Guardsmen and troopers were Negro. Virtually none of the 250 Negro Newark policemen took part in the violent suppression. The New Jersey National Guard, like that in other states, is a lily-white organization which seems to have the character of an exclusive "club" for middle-income businessmen from the suburbs. The New Jersey state troopers also are predominantly white, and many are from conservative South Jersey towns where the troopers act as local police. It was understandable that these men would bring into the ghetto racist attitudes that would soon support outright sadism. A captain who commanded helicopter-borne infantry told a *New York Times* reporter on July 14:

> They put us here because we're the toughest and the best. . . .
> If anybody throws things down our necks, then it's shoot to kill;
> it's either them or us, and it ain't going to be us.

On Saturday, the 15th, troopers charged up the stairs of the Hayes houses, shouting, "Get back, you black niggers!" There was shooting up each flight of stairs as they charged. Later, a trooper pumped more than thirty bullets into the body of a fallen teen-ager while shouting, "Die, bastard, die." A Guardsman asked a witness, "What do you want us to do, kill all your Negroes?" A Newark policeman chipped in, "We are going to do it anyway, so we might as well take care of these three now."

These are not isolated examples but a selection from innumerable incidents of the kind that were reported throughout the riots. From them we can draw three conclusions about the soldiers and the police.

Trigger-happiness because of fear, confusion, and exhaustion: Many of the troops were assigned to round-the-clock duty. During that duty they were under conditions of extreme tension. They were kept moving about by incidents or reports of looting, burning, and shooting. They drove at speeds of more than fifty miles per hour; they ran continually along the streets after people. They were surrounded by unfamiliar and hostile faces. There were no foxholes or other shelters from attack. The troopers and Guardsmen knew little or nothing about the terrain and often were unable to tell the direction of shooting. . . .

General and deliberate violence employed against the whole community: On Friday night 10 Negroes were killed, 100 suffered gunshot wounds, 500 were "treated" at City Hospital, and at least as many were arrested or held. By Sunday night another 10 were dead, at least 50 more had gunshot wounds, and another 500 were in jail. People were stopped indiscriminately in the streets, shoved, cursed, and beaten and shot. On Thursday, Joe Price, a veteran of the Korean War and an employee of ITT for fifteen years, was beaten on the head, arms, stomach, and legs by five Newark policemen inside the Fourth Precinct. He had protested police harassment of neighborhood teen-agers earlier in the day. Later, Jerry Berfet, walking peacefully on the sidewalk with two women, was stopped by police who told him to strip, ripped off his clothes, and forced him to run naked down the street. No charges were entered against either man. A Negro professional worker was arrested while driving on a quiet street after 10 P.M. curfew, beaten unconscious, and then forced to perform what his lawyer describes as "degrading acts" when he revived in the police station.

Troops fired wildly up streets and into buildings at real or imagined enemies. On Saturday, before darkness fell, three women were killed in their homes by police fire. Rebecca Brown, a twenty-nine-year-old nurse's aide, was cut nearly in half as she tried to rescue her two-year-old child from the window. Hattie Gainer, an elderly twenty-year resident of her neighborhood, was shot at her window in view of her three grandchildren. Eloise Spellman was shot through the neck in her Hayes apartment with three of her eleven children present.

A child in Scudder Homes lost his ear and eye to a bullet. A man was shot while fixing his car as police charged after a crowd. When another man told police he was shot in the side, the officer knocked him down and kicked him in the ribs.

The most obvious act of deliberate aggression was the police destruction of perhaps 100 Negro-owned stores Saturday and Sunday. One witness followed police down Bergen Street for fifteen blocks, watching them shoot into windows marked "Soul Brother." Another storeowner observed a systematic pattern. On his block three white-owned stores were looted Thursday night; no Negro stores were damaged. There were no other disturbances on his block until well after midnight Saturday when he received calls that troopers were shooting into the Negro-owned stores or were breaking windows with the butts of their guns. . . .

Cold-blooded murder: An evaluation of the deaths so far reported suggests that the military forces killed people for the purposes of terror and intimidation. Nearly all the dead were killed by police, troopers, and Guardsmen. The "crimes" of the victims were petty, vague, or unproven. None were accused by police of being snipers; only one so far is alleged to have been carrying a gun. Several of the dead were engaged in small-scale looting at most. The majority were observers; ten, in fact, were killed inside or just outside their homes. Many were killed in daylight. Nearly all the dead had families and jobs; only a few had previous criminal records. Seven of the dead were women, two were young boys. Of those known to be dead, five were killed Thursday night; one by a hit-and-run car, one allegedly shot by mistake by a sniper, three others by Newark police. Ten were slain on Friday night; six between Saturday afternoon and the early part of Sunday; one on Monday night. All but one or two of these were police victims.

Clearly the evidence points to a military massacre in Newark rather than to a two-sided war. This was not only the conclusion of the Negroes in the ghetto but of private Newark lawyers, professors of constitutional law, and representatives of the state American Civil Liberties Union. They charge that the police were the instrument of a criminal conspiracy "to engage in a pattern of systematic violence, terror, abuse, intimidation, and humiliation" to keep Negroes as second-class citizens. The police, according to the complaint, "seized on the initial disorders as an opportunity and pretext to perpetrate the most horrendous and widespread killing, violence, torture, and intimidation, not in response to any crime or civilian disorder but as a violent demonstration of the powerlessness of the plaintiffs and their class. . . ."

Thus it seems to many that the military, especially the Newark police, not only triggered the riot by beating a cab driver but then created a climate of opinion that supported the use of all necessary force to suppress the riot. The force used by police was not in response to snipers, looting, and burning but in retaliation against the successful uprising of Wednesday and Thursday nights. . . .

The riot made clear that if something is not done about the police immediately, the fears of white society will be transformed into reality: whites will be facing a black society which will not only harbor but welcome and employ snipers. The troops did not instill fear so much as a fighting hatred in the community. People of every age and background cursed the soldiers. Women spat at armored cars. Five-year-old kids clenched bottles in their hands. If the troops made a violent move, the primitive missiles were loosed at them. People openly talked of the riot turning into a showdown and, while many were afraid, few were willing to be pushed around by the troops. All told there were more than 3,000 people arrested, injured, or killed, thousands more witnessed these incidents. From this kind of violence which touches people personally springs a commitment to fight back. By the end of the weekend many people spoke of a willingness to die.

By Sunday the crisis was nearing a new stage. If the occupation of Friday and Saturday was going to continue, the community would have started to counterattack in a real way. "Why should we quit," one kid wanted to know, "when they got twenty-five of us and only two of them are dead?"

Perhaps some fear of this trend led Governor Hughes to pull the troops out Monday morning. Perhaps he could see what another three days of occupation and siege would bring. Perhaps, on the other hand, he had no choice. The troops were tired, riots were spreading to other cities of the state, a railroad strike was beginning, and there were all those political engagements awaiting a man with large ambitions. It may also be true that the governor knew the situation all along but knew as well that 90 percent of New Jersey is white and frightened. In this view, the governor took a tough line in support of the troops at the beginning so that withdrawal would be politically acceptable to white voters later on. As late as Sunday night, a top State Police official was concerned that his men would consider him "chicken" if a pull-out were discussed openly.

Does it matter what Richard Hughes believed? Whatever it was, the consequences are what matter finally. The average view of Negroes as "criminals" to be suppressed was reinforced throughout the suburbs of New Jersey. The Negro community learned more deeply why they should hate white people. The police remain a protected and privileged conservative political force, the only such force licensed to kill. With all this coming to pass, few people were joyous as the troops went home on Monday.

FROM RIOT TO REVOLUTION

This country is experiencing its fourth year of urban revolt. Yet the message from Newark is that America has learned almost nothing since Watts.

There is no national program for economic and social change which answers the questions black people are raising. On the national scene, youth unemployment is well over 30 percent in the ghettos, in spite of the draft and manpower and make-work programs. Congress can pass laws against guns and riots, the FBI and local officials can bring criminal conspiracy or red-baiting charges, but until this country does something revolutionary to support the needs and aspirations of its youth—black and white, as the youth themselves define them—there will be no end to social crisis. . . .

The use of force can do nothing but create a demand for greater force. The Newark riot shows that troops cannot make people surrender. The police had several advantages over the community, particularly in firepower and mechanical mobility. Their pent-up racism gave them a certain amount of energy and morale as well. But, as events in the riot showed, the troops could not apply their methods to urban conditions. The problem of precision shooting—for example, at a sniper in a building with forty windows and escape routes through rooftop, alley, and doorway—is just as difficult in the urban jungle as precision bombing is in Vietnam. There is a lack of safe cover. There is no front line and no rear, no way to cordon an area completely. A block which is quiet when the troops are present can be the scene of an outbreak the moment the troops leave.

At the same time, the morale supported by racism soon turns into anxiety. Because of racism, the troops are unfamiliar with both the people and layout of the ghetto. Patrol duty after dark becomes a frightening and exhausting experience, especially for men who want to return alive to their families and homes. A psychology of desperation leads to careless and indiscriminate violence toward the community, including reprisal killing, which inflames the people whom the troops were sent to pacify.

The situation thus contains certain built-in advantages for black people. The community is theirs. They know faces, corners, rooms, alleys. They know whom to trust and whom not to trust. They can switch in seconds from a fighting to a passive posture. It is impressive that state and local officials could not get takers for their offer of money and clemency to anyone turning in a sniper.

This is not a time for radical illusions about "revolution." Stagnancy and conservatism are essential facts of ghetto life. It is undoubtedly true that most Negroes desire the comforts and security that white people possess. There is little revolutionary consciousness or commitment to violence per se in the ghetto. Most of the people in the Newark ghetto were afraid, disorganized, and helpless when directly facing automatic weapons. But the actions of white America toward the ghetto are showing black people that they must prepare to fight back. The conditions are slowly being created for an American form of guerrilla warfare based in the slums. The riot represents a signal of this fundamental change.

To the conservative mind the riot is essentially anarchy. To the liberal mind it is an expression of helpless frustration. While the conservative is hostile and the liberal generous toward those who riot, both assume that the riot is a form of less-than-civilized behavior. The liberal will turn conservative if polite methods fail to stem disorder. Against these two fundamentally similar concepts, a third one must be asserted, the concept that a riot represents people making history.

The riot is certainly an awkward, even primitive, form of history-making. But if people are barred from using the sophisticated instruments of the established order for their ends, they will find another way. Rocks and bottles are only a beginning, but they get more attention than all the reports in Washington. To the people involved, the riot is far less lawless and far more representative than the system of arbitrary rules and prescribed channels which they confront every day. The riot is not a beautiful and romantic experience, but neither is the day-to-day slum life from which the riot springs. Riots will not go away if ignored and will not be cordoned off. They will only disappear when their energy is absorbed into a more decisive and effective form of history-making.

Men are now appearing in the ghettos who might turn the energy of the riot into a more organized and continuous revolutionary direction. Middle-class Negro intellectuals and Negroes of the ghetto are joining forces. They have found channels closed, the rules of the game stacked, and American democracy a system which excludes them. They understand that the institutions of the white community are unreliable in the absence of black community power. They recognize that national civil rights leaders will not secure the kind of change that is needed. They assume that disobedience, disorder, and even violence must be risked as the only alternative to continuing slavery.

The role of organized violence is now being carefully considered. During a riot, for instance, a conscious guerrilla can participate in pulling police away from the path of people engaged in attacking stores. He can create disorder in new areas the police think are secure. He can carry the torch, if not all the people, to white neighborhoods and downtown business districts. If necessary, he can successfully shoot to kill.

It is equally important to understand that the guerrilla can employ violence during times of apparent "peace." He can attack, in the suburbs or slums, with paint or bullets, symbols of racial oppression. He can get away with it. If he can force the oppressive power to be passive and defensive at the point where it is administered — by the caseworker, landlord, storeowner, or policeman — he can build people's confidence in their ability to demand change. Such attacks, which need not be on human life to be effective, might disrupt the administration of the ghetto to a crisis point where a new system would have to be considered.

These tactics of disorder will be defined by the authorities as criminal anarchy. But it may be that disruption will create possibilities of meaningful change. This depends on whether the leaders of ghetto struggles can be more successful in building strong organization than they have been so far. Violence can contribute to shattering the status quo, but only politics and organization can transform it.

The ghetto still needs the power to decide its destiny on such matters as urban renewal and housing, social services, policing, and taxation. Tenants still need concrete rights against landlords in public and private housing, or a new system of tenant-controlled living conditions. Welfare clients still need the power to receive a livable income without administrative abuse, or be able to replace the welfare system with one that meets their needs. Consumers still need to control the quality of merchandise and service in the stores where they shop. Citizens still need effective control over the behavior of those who police their community. Political structures belonging to the community are needed to bargain for, and maintain control over, funds from government or private sources.

In order to build a more decent community while resisting racist power, more than violence is required. People need self-government. We are at a point where democracy—the idea and practice of people controlling their lives—is a revolutionary issue in the United States.

STOKELY CARMICHAEL
Black Power

What has been called the American Negro Revolution took many forms in the twenty-two years between the end of World War II and 1967. At first a movement to obtain such reforms as desegregation of the armed forces, it quickly concentrated on school desegregation, an effort that won a legal victory with the Supreme Court decisions of 1954 and 1955. Desegregation of public accommodations, especially in the South, was the next goal, and although this too was largely achieved, the basic problem remained unsolved. During the late 1950s and early 1960s the movement was essentially nonviolent, despite occasional flareups, and its leaders were often if not always clergymen like Martin Luther King. But as the 1960s wore on the

153

slogan changed from equal civil rights to Black Power, which expressed the Negro's continuing frustration with the lack of real progress toward general social and economic equality in the country. Stokely Carmichael, at the time the national chairman of the Student Nonviolent Coordinating Committee, wrote the following article for the New York Review of Books *(September 22, 1966). Entitled "What We Want," the article tried to sum up the feelings and desires of younger Negroes throughout the country.*

One of the tragedies of the struggle against racism is that up to now there has been no national organization which could speak to the growing militancy of young black people in the urban ghetto. There has been only a civil rights movement, whose tone of voice was adapted to an audience of liberal whites. It served as a sort of buffer zone between them and angry young blacks. None of its so-called leaders could go into a rioting community and be listened to. In a sense, I blame ourselves—together with the mass media—for what has happened in Watts, Harlem, Chicago, Cleveland, Omaha. Each time the people in those cities saw Martin Luther King get slapped, they became angry; when they saw four little black girls bombed to death, they were angrier; and when nothing happened, they were steaming. We had nothing to offer that they could see, except to go out and be beaten again. We helped to build their frustration.

For too many years, black Americans marched and had their heads broken and got shot. They were saying to the country, "Look, you guys are supposed to be nice guys and we are only going to do what we are supposed to do—why do you beat us up, why don't you give us what we ask, why don't you straighten yourselves out?" After years of this, we are at almost the same point—because we demonstrated from a position of weakness. We cannot be expected any longer to march and have our heads broken in order to say to whites: come on, you're nice guys. For you are not nice guys. We have found you out.

An organization which claims to speak for the needs of a community—as does the Student Nonviolent Coordinating Committee—must speak in the tone of that community, not as somebody else's buffer zone. This is the significance of black power as a slogan. For once, black people are going to use the words they want to use—not just the words whites want to hear. And they will do this no matter how often the press tries to stop the use of the slogan by equating it with racism or separatism.

An organization which claims to be working for the needs of a community — as SNCC does — must work to provide that community with a position of strength from which to make its voice heard. This is the significance of black power beyond the slogan.

Black power can be clearly defined for those who do not attach the fears of white America to their questions about it. We should begin with the basic fact that black Americans have two problems: they are poor and they are black. All other problems arise from this two-sided reality: lack of education, the so-called apathy of black men. Any program to end racism must address itself to that double reality.

Almost from its beginning, SNCC sought to address itself to both conditions with a program aimed at winning political power for impoverished Southern blacks. We had to begin with politics because black Americans are a propertyless people in a country where property is valued above all. We had to work for power, because this country does not function by morality, love, and nonviolence, but by power. Thus we determined to win political power, with the idea of moving on from there into activity that would have economic effects. With power, the masses could *make or participate in making the decisions which govern their destinies, and thus create basic* change in their day-to-day lives.

But if political power seemed to be the key to self-determination, it was also obvious that the key had been thrown down a deep well many years earlier. Disenfranchisement, maintained by racist terror, makes it impossible to talk about organizing for political power in 1960. The right to vote had to be won, and SNCC workers devoted their energies to this from 1961 to 1965. They set up voter registration drives in the Deep South. They created pressure for the vote by holding mock elections in Mississippi in 1963 and by helping to establish the Mississippi Freedom Democratic Party (MFDP) in 1964. That struggle was eased, though not won, with the passage of the 1965 Voting Rights Act. SNCC workers could then address themselves to the question: "Who can we vote for, to have our needs met — how do we make our vote meaningful?"

SNCC had already gone to Atlantic City for recognition of the

155

Mississippi Freedom Democratic Party by the Democratic convention and been rejected; it had gone with the MFDP to Washington for recognition by Congress and been rejected. In Arkansas, SNCC helped thirty Negroes to run for School Board elections; all but one were defeated, and there was evidence of fraud and intimidation sufficient to cause their defeat. In Atlanta, Julian Bond ran for the state legislature and was elected – twice – and unseated – twice. In several states, black farmers ran in elections for agricultural committees which make crucial decisions concerning land use, loans, etc. Although they won places on a number of committees, they never gained the majorities needed to control them.

All of the efforts were attempts to win black power. Then, in Alabama, the opportunity came to see how blacks could be organized on an independent party basis. An unusual Alabama law provides that any group of citizens can nominate candidates for county office and, if they win 20 percent of the vote, may be recognized as a county political party. The same then applies on a state level. SNCC went to organize in several counties such as Lowndes, where black people – who form 80 percent of the population and have an average annual income of $943 – felt they could accomplish nothing within the framework of the Alabama Democratic Party because of its racism and because the qualifying fee for this year's elections was raised from $50 to $500 in order to prevent most Negroes from becoming candidates.

On May 3, five new county "freedom organizations" convened and nominated candidates for the offices of sheriff, tax assessor, members of the school boards. These men and women are up for election in November – if they live until then. Their ballot symbol is the black panther: a bold, beautiful animal, representing the strength and dignity of black demands today. A man needs a black panther on his side when he and his family must endure – as hundreds of Alabamians have endured – loss of job, eviction, starvation, and sometimes death, for political activity. He may also need a gun and SNCC reaffirms the right of black men everywhere to defend themselves when threatened or attacked.

As for initiating the use of violence, we hope that such programs as ours will make that unnecessary; but it is not for us to tell black communities whether they can or cannot use any particular form of action to resolve their problems. Responsibility for the use of violence by black men, whether in self-defense or initiated by them, lies with the white community.

This is the specific historical experience from which SNCC's call for "black power" emerged on the Mississippi march last July. But the concept of "black power" is not a recent or isolated phenomenon: It has grown out of the ferment of agitation and activity by different people and organizations in many black communities over the years. Our last year of work in Alabama added a new concrete possibility. In Lowndes County, for example, black power will mean that if a Negro is elected sheriff, he can end police brutality. If a black man is elected tax assessor, he can collect and channel funds for the building of better roads and schools serving black people — thus advancing the move from political power into the economic arena. In such areas as Lowndes, where black men have a majority, they will attempt to use it to exercise control. This is what they seek: control.

Where Negroes lack a majority, black power means proper representation and sharing of control. It means the creation of power bases from which black people can work to change statewide or nationwide patterns of oppression through pressure from strength — instead of weakness. Politically, black power means what it has always meant to SNCC: the coming-together of black people to elect representatives and *to force those representatives to speak to their needs*. It does not mean merely putting black faces into office. A man or woman who is black and from the slums cannot be automatically expected to speak to the needs of black people. Most of the black politicians we see around the country today are not what SNCC means by black power. The power must be that of a community, and emanate from there.

SNCC today is working in both North and South on programs of voter registration and independent political organizing. In some places, such as Alabama, Los Angeles, New York, Philadelphia, and New Jersey, independent organizing under the black panther symbol is in progress. The creation of a national "black panther party" must come about; it will take time to build, and it is much too early to predict its success. We have no infallible master plan and we make no claim to exclusive knowledge of how to end racism;

different groups will work in their own different ways. SNCC cannot spell out the full logistics of self-determination but it can address itself to the problem by helping black communities define their needs, realize their strength, and go into action along a variety of lines which they must choose for themselves. Without knowing all the answers, it can address itself to the basic problem of poverty; to the fact that in Lowndes County, eighty-six white families own 90 percent of the land. What are black people in that county going to do for jobs, where are they going to get money? There must be reallocation of land, of money.

Ultimately, the economic foundations of this country must be shaken if black people are to control their lives. The colonies of the United States – and this includes the black ghettoes within its borders, North and South – must be liberated. For a century, this nation has been like an octopus of exploitation, its tentacles stretching from Mississippi and Harlem to South America, the Middle East, southern Africa, and Vietnam; the form of exploitation varies from area to area but the essential result has been the same – a powerful few have been maintained and enriched at the expense of the poor and voiceless colored masses. This pattern must be broken. As its grip loosens here and there around the world, the hopes of black Americans become more realistic. For racism to die, a totally different America must be born.

This is what the white society does not wish to face; this is why that society prefers to talk about integration. But integration speaks not at all to the problem of poverty, only to the problem of blackness. Integration today means the man who "makes it," leaving his black brothers behind in the ghetto as fast as his new sports car will take him. It has no relevance to the Harlem wino or to the cottonpicker making $3 a day. As a lady I know in Alabama once said, "The food that Ralph Bunche eats doesn't fill my stomach."

Integration, moreover, speaks to the problem of blackness in a despicable way. As a goal, it has been based on complete acceptance of the fact that *in order to have* a decent house or education, blacks must move into a white neighborhood or send their children to a white school. This reinforces, among both black and white, the idea that "white" is automatically better and "black" is by definition inferior. This is why integration is a subterfuge for the maintenance of white supremacy. It allows the nation to focus on a handful of Southern children who get into white schools, at great price, and to ignore the 94 percent who are left behind in unimproved all-black schools.

Such situations will not change until black people have power— to control their own school boards, in this case. Then Negroes become equal in a way that means something, and integration ceases to be a one-way street. Then integration doesn't mean draining skills and energies from the ghetto into white neighborhoods; then it can mean white people moving from Beverly Hills into Watts, white people joining the Lowndes County Freedom Organization. Then integration becomes relevant.

Last April, before the furor over black power, Christopher Jencks wrote in a *New Republic* article on white Mississippi's manipulation of the antipoverty program:

> The war on poverty has been predicated on the notion that there is such a thing as *a community* which can be defined geographically and mobilized for a collective effort to help the poor. This theory has no relationship to reality in the Deep South. In every Mississippi county there are *two* communities. Despite all the pious platitudes of the moderates on both sides, these two communities habitually see their interests in terms of conflict rather than cooperation. Only when the Negro community can muster enough political, economic, and professional strength to compete on somewhat equal terms, will Negroes believe in the possibility of true cooperation and whites accept its necessity. En route to integration, the Negro community needs to develop greater independence—a chance to run its own affairs and not cave in whenever "the man" barks. . . . Or so it seems to me, and to most of the knowledgeable people with whom I talked in Mississippi. To OEO, this judgment may sound like black nationalism. . . .

Mr. Jencks, a white reporter, perceived the reason why America's antipoverty program has been a sick farce in both North and South. In the South, it is clearly racism which prevents the poor from running their own programs; in the North, it more often seems to be politicking and bureaucracy. But the results are not so different:

159

In the North, non-whites make up 42 percent of all families in metropolitan "poverty areas" and only 6 percent of families in areas classified as not poor. SNCC has been working with local residents in Arkansas, Alabama, and Mississippi to achieve control by the poor of the program and its funds; it has also been working with groups in the North, and the struggle is no less difficult. Behind it all is a federal government which cares far more about winning the war on the Vietnamese than the war on poverty; which has put the poverty program in the hands of self-serving politicians and bureaucrats rather than the poor themselves; which is unwilling to curb the misuse of white power but quick to condemn black power.

To most whites, black power seems to mean that the Mau Mau are coming to the suburbs at night. The Mau Mau are coming, and whites must stop them. Articles appear about plots to "get Whitey," creating an atmosphere in which "law and order must be maintained." Once again, responsibility is shifted from the oppressor to the oppressed. Other whites chide, "Don't forget—you're only 10 percent of the population; if you get too smart, we'll wipe you out." If they are liberals, they complain, "What about me?—don't you want my help any more?" These are people supposedly concerned about black Americans, but today they think first of themselves, of their feelings of rejection. Or they admonish, "You can't get anywhere without coalitions," when there is in fact no group at present with whom to form a coalition in which blacks will not be absorbed and betrayed. Or they accuse us of "polarizing the races" by our calls for black unity, when the true responsibility for polarization lies with whites who will not accept their responsibility as the majority power for making the democratic process work.

White America will not face the problem of color, the reality of it. The well-intended say: "We're all human, everybody is really decent, we must forget color." But color cannot be "forgotten" until its weight is recognized and dealt with. White America will not acknowledge that the ways in which this country sees itself are contradicted by being black—and always have been. Whereas most of the people who settled this country came here for freedom or for economic opportunity, blacks were brought here to be slaves.

When the Lowndes County Freedom Organization chose the black panther as its symbol, it was christened by the press "the Black Panther Party"—but the Alabama Democratic Party, whose symbol is a rooster, has never been called the White Cock Party. No one ever talked about "white power" because power in this country *is* white. All this adds up to more than merely identifying a group phenomenon by some catchy name or adjective. The furor over that black panther reveals the problems that white America has with color and sex; the furor over "black power" reveals how deep racism runs and the great fear which is attached to it.

Whites will not see that I, for example, as a person oppressed because of my blackness, have common cause with other blacks who are oppressed because of blackness. This is not to say that there are no white people who see things as I do, but that it is black people I must speak to first. It must be the oppressed to whom SNCC addresses itself primarily, not to friends from the oppressing group. From birth, black people are told a set of lies about themselves. We are told that we are lazy—yet I drive through the Delta area of Mississippi and watch black people picking cotton in the hot sun for fourteen hours. We are told, "If you work hard, you'll succeed"—but if that were true, black people would own this country. We are oppressed because we are black—not because we are ignorant, not because we are lazy, not because we're stupid (and got good rhythm), but because we're black.

I remember that when I was a boy, I used to go to see Tarzan movies on Saturday. White Tarzan used to beat up the black natives. I would sit there yelling, "Kill the beasts, kill the savages, kill 'em!" I was saying: Kill *me*. It was as if a Jewish boy watched Nazis taking Jews off to concentration camps and cheered them on. Today, I want the chief to beat hell out of Tarzan and send him back to Europe. But it takes time to become free of the lies and their shaming effect on black minds. It takes time to reject the most important lie: That black people inherently can't do the same things white people can do, unless white people help them.

The need for psychological equality is the reason why SNCC today believes that blacks must organize in the black community. Only black people can convey the revolutionary idea that black people are able to do things themselves. Only they can help create in the community an aroused and continuing black consciousness that will provide the basis for political strength. In the past, white allies have furthered white supremacy without the whites involved realizing it—or wanting it, I think. Black people must do things for themselves; they must get poverty money they will control and spend themselves; they must conduct tutorial programs themselves so that black children can identify with black people. This is one reason Africa has such importance: The reality of black men ruling their own natives gives blacks elsewhere a sense of possibility, of power, which they do not now have. This does not mean we don't welcome help or friends. But we want the right to decide whether anyone is, in fact, our friend. In the past, black Americans have been almost the only people whom everybody and his momma could jump up and call their friends. We have been tokens, symbols, objects – as I was in high school to many young whites, who liked having "a Negro friend." We want to decide who is our friend, and we will not accept someone who comes to us and says: "If you do X, Y, and Z, then I'll help you." We will not be told whom we should choose as allies. We will not be isolated from any group or nation except by our own choice. We cannot have the oppressors telling the oppressed how to rid themselves of the oppressor.

I have said that most liberal whites react to "black power" with the question, What about me?, rather than saying: Tell me what you want me to do and I'll see if I can do it. There are answers to the right question. One of the most disturbing things about almost all white supporters of the movement has been that they are afraid to go into their own communities – which is where the racism exists – and work to get rid of it. They want to run from Berkeley to tell us what to do in Mississippi; let them look instead at Berkeley. They admonish blacks to be nonviolent; let them preach nonviolence in the white community. They come to teach me Negro history; let them go to the suburbs and open up freedom schools for whites. Let them work to stop America's racist foreign policy; let them press this government to cease supporting the economy of South Africa.

There is a vital job to be done among poor whites. We hope to see, eventually, a coalition between poor blacks and poor whites. That is the only coalition which seems acceptable to us, and we see such a coalition as the major internal instrument of change in American society. SNCC has tried several times to organize poor whites; we are trying again now, with an initial training program in Tennessee. It is purely academic today to talk about bringing poor blacks and whites together, but the job of creating a poor-white power bloc must be attempted. The main responsibility for it falls upon whites. Black and white can work together in the white community where possible; it is not possible, however, to go into a poor Southern town and talk about integration. Poor whites everywhere are becoming more hostile – not less – partly because they see the nation's attention focused on black poverty and nobody coming to them. Too many young middle-class Americans, like some sort of Pepsi generation, have wanted to come alive through the black community; they've wanted to be where the action is – and the action has been in the black community.

Black people do not want to "take over" this country. They don't want to "get whitey"; they just want to get him off their backs, as the saying goes. It was, for example, the exploitation by Jewish landlords and merchants which first created black resentment toward Jews – not Judaism. The white man is irrelevant to blacks, except as an oppressive force. Blacks want to be in his place, yes, but not in order to terrorize and lynch and starve him. They want to be in his place because that is where a decent life can be had.

But our vision is not merely of a society in which all black men have enough to buy the good things of life. When we urge that black money go into black pockets, we mean the communal pocket. We want to see money go back into the community and used to benefit it. We want to see the cooperative concept applied in business and banking. We want to see black ghetto residents demand that an exploiting storekeeper sell them, at minimal cost, a building or a shop that they will own and improve cooperatively; they can back their demand with a rent strike, or a boycott, and a community so unified behind them that no one else will move into the building or buy at the store.

The society we seek to build among black people, then, is not a capitalist one. It is a society in which the spirit of community and humanistic love prevail. The word "love" is suspect; black expectations of what it might produce have been betrayed too often. But those were expectations of a response from the white community, which failed us. The love we seek to encourage is within the black community, the only American community where men call each other "brother" when they meet. We can build a community of love only where we have the ability and power to do so: among blacks.

163

As for white America, perhaps it can stop crying out against "black supremacy," "black nationalism," "racism in reverse," and begin facing reality. The reality is that this nation, from top to bottom, is racist; that racism is not primarily a problem of "human relations" but of an exploitation maintained — either actively or through silence — by the society as a whole. Camus and Sartre have asked, can a man condemn himself? Can whites, particularly liberal whites, condemn themselves? Can they stop blaming us, and blame their own system? Are they capable of the shame which might become a revolutionary emotion?

We have found that they usually cannot condemn themselves, and so we have done it. But the rebuilding of this society, if at all possible, is basically the responsibility of whites — not blacks. We won't fight to save the present society, in Vietnam or anywhere else. We are just going to work, in the way *we* see fit, and on goals *we* define, not for civil rights but for all our human rights.

ROY WILKINS
Whither "Black Power"?

The growing militancy of the younger generation of Negroes, most notably the group that rallied behind the slogan "black power" in the summer of 1966, got a mixed reception in both the white and the black communities of the nation. The white press, for the most part, interpreted the movement as an appeal for armed resistance against the white establishment. Others saw it as a step backward that would undermine the slow but steady improvements that had been achieved by appealing to the conscience of white America during the previous fifty years. [Source: Crisis, August-September 1966.]

*All about us are alarums and confusions as well as great and chal-

*Excerpts from keynote address delivered by Mr. Wilkins at NAACP 57th annual convention, Los Angeles, July 5, 1966. This statement was in response to the issue raised by the use of the slogan "Black Power" by Stokely Carmichael, chairman of the Student Nonviolent Coordinating Committee during the Meredith Mississippi March early in June.

164

lenging developments. Differences of opinion are sharper. For the first time since several organizations began to function where only two had functioned before, there emerges what seems to be a difference in goals.

Heretofore there were some differences in methods and emphasis but none in ultimate goals. The end was always to be the inclusion of the American Negro, without racial discrimination, as a full-fledged equal in all phases of American citizenship.

There has now emerged, first a strident and threatening challenge to a strategy widely employed by civil rights groups, namely non-violence. One organization which has been meeting in Baltimore has passed a resolution declaring for defense of themselves by Negro citizens if they are attacked.

This position is not new as far as the NAACP is concerned. Historically, our Association has defended in court those persons who have defended themselves and their homes with firearms.

But neither have we couched a policy of manly resistance in such a way that our members and supporters felt compelled to maintain themselves in an armed state, ready to retaliate instantly and in kind whenever attacked.

We venture the observation that such a published posture could serve to stir counterplanning, counteraction and possible conflict. If carried out literally as instant retaliation, in cases adjudged by aggrieved persons to have been grossly unjust, this policy could produce—in extreme situations—lynchings, or in better-sounding phraseology, private vigilante vengeance.

Moreover, in attempting to substitute for derelict enforcement machinery, the policy entails the risk of a broader, more indiscriminate crack-down by law officers under the ready-made excuse of restoring law and order.

It seems reasonable to assume that proclaimed protective violence is as likely to encourage counterviolence as it is to discourage violent persecution.

But the more serious division in the civil rights movement is the one posed by a word formulation that implies clearly a difference in goals.

No matter how endlessly they try to explain it, the term "black power" means anti-white power. In a racially pluralistic society, the concept, the formation and the exercise of an ethnically tagged power means opposition to other ethnic powers, just as the term "white supremacy" means subjection of all non-white peoples. In the black-white relationship, it has to mean that every other ethnic power is the rival and the antagonist of "black power." It has to mean "going it alone." It has to mean separatism.

Now, separatism, whether on the rarefied debate level of "black power" or on the wishful level of a secessionist Freedom City in Watts, offers a disadvantaged minority little except a chance to shrivel and die.

The only possible dividend of "black power" is embodied in its offer to millions of frustrated and deprived and persecuted black people of a solace, a tremendous psychological lift, quite apart from its political and economic implications.

Ideologically it dictates "up with black and down with white" in precisely the same manner that South Africa reverses that slogan.

It is a reverse Mississippi, a reverse Hitler, a reverse Ku Klux Klan.

If these were evil in our judgment, what virtue can we claim for black over white? If, as some proponents claim, this concept instills pride of race, cannot this pride be taught without preaching hatred or supremacy based on race?

Though it be clarified and clarified again, "black power" in the quick, uncritical and highly emotional adoption it has received from segments of a beleaguered people can mean in the end only black death. Even if, through some miracle, it should be enthroned briefly, the human spirit, which knows no color or geography or time, would die a little, leaving for wiser and stronger and more compassionate men the painful beating back to the upper trail.

We of the NAACP will have none of this. We have fought it too long. It is the ranging of race against race on the irrelevant basis of skin color. It is the father of hatred and the mother of violence.

It is the wicked fanaticism which has swelled our tears, broken our bodies, squeezed our hearts and taken the blood of our black and white loved ones. It shall not now poison our forward march.

We seek, therefore, as we have sought these many years, for the inclusion of Negro Americans in the nation's life, not their exclusion. This is our land, as much as it is any American's — every square foot of every city and town and village. The task of winning our share is not the easy one of disengagement and flight, but the hard one of work, of short as well as long jumps, of disappointments and of sweet success.

JAMES S. COLEMAN *et al.*

Equal Opportunity in Education

When the Supreme Court in its landmark decision in 1954 called for the integration of the nation's public schools, on the grounds that segregated schools were inherently unequal, it seemed to some commentators that the problem of unequal educational opportunity in the United States might be solved — not immediately, of course, but within a reasonable period of time. Desegregation did proceed, if not at the speed desired by some, at least fairly quickly in some parts of the country; and there were sections where improvement was noted. But as time went on it began to be realized that the problem went deeper than the mere segregation of schools, and that differences in the early home environment were probably far more important. Such at least was the conclusion, admittedly controversial, of James S. Coleman of Johns Hopkins University, who in 1966 published a book based on studies done by him and by a panel of educators for the U.S. Office of Education of the Department of Health, Education, and Welfare. Portions of the book's Summary Report are reprinted here. [Source: Equality of Educational Opportunity, *Washington, 1966, pp. 3-34.]*

SEGREGATION IN THE PUBLIC SCHOOLS

The great majority of American children attend schools that are largely segregated; that is, where almost all of their fellow students are of the same racial background as they are. Among minority groups, Negroes are by far the most segregated. Taking all groups, however, white children are most segregated. Almost 80 percent of all white pupils in 1st grade and 12th grade attend schools that are from 90 to 100 percent white. And 97 percent at grade 1 and 99 percent at grade 12 attend schools that are 50 percent or more white.

For Negro pupils, segregation is more nearly complete in the

167

South (as it is for whites also), but it is extensive also in all the other regions where the Negro population is concentrated: the urban North, Midwest, and West.

More than 65 percent of all Negro pupils in the 1st grade attend schools that are between 90 and 100 percent Negro. And 87 percent at grade 1 and 66 percent at grade 12 attend schools that are 50 percent or more Negro. In the South most students attend schools that are 100 percent white or Negro.

The same pattern of segregation holds, though not quite so strongly, for the teachers of Negro and white students. For the nation as a whole, the average Negro elementary pupil attends a school in which 65 percent of the teachers are Negro; the average white elementary pupil attends a school in which 97 percent of the teachers are white. White teachers are more predominant at the secondary level, where the corresponding figures are 59 and 97 percent. The racial matching of teachers is most pronounced in the South, where by tradition it has been complete. On a nationwide basis, in cases where the races of pupils and teachers are not matched, the trend is all in one direction: white teachers teach Negro children but Negro teachers seldom teach white children; just as, in the schools, integration consists primarily of a minority of Negro pupils in predominantly white schools but almost never of a few whites in largely Negro schools.

In its desegregation decision of 1954, the Supreme Court held that separate schools for Negro and white children are inherently unequal. This survey finds that, when measured by that yardstick, American public education remains largely unequal in most regions of the country, including all those where Negroes form any significant proportion of the population. Obviously, however, that is not the only yardstick. The next section of the summary describes other characteristics by means of which equality of educational opportunity may be appraised.

THE SCHOOLS AND THEIR CHARACTERISTICS
The school environment of a child consists of many elements, ranging from the desk he sits at to the child who sits next to him, and including the teacher who stands at the front of his class. A

statistical survey can give only fragmentary evidence of this environment. . . .

Statistics, too, must deal with one thing at a time, and cumulative effects tend to be lost in them. Having a teacher without a college degree indicates an element of disadvantage, but in the concrete situation, a child may be taught by a teacher who is not only without a degree but who has grown up and received his schooling in the local community, who has never been out of the state, who has a 10th-grade vocabulary, and who shares the local community's attitudes.

One must also be aware of the relative importance of a certain kind of thing to a certain kind of person. Just as a loaf of bread means more to a starving man than to a sated one, so one very fine textbook or, better, one very able teacher, may mean far more to a deprived child than to one who already has several of both.

Finally, it should be borne in mind that in cases where Negroes in the South receive unequal treatment, the significance in terms of actual numbers of individuals involved is very great, since 54 percent of the Negro population of school-going age, or approximately 3.2 million children, live in that region.

All of the findings reported in this section of the summary are based on responses to questionnaires filled out by public-school teachers, principals, district school superintendents, and pupils. The data were gathered in September and October of 1965 from 4,000 public schools. All teachers, principals, and district superintendents in these schools participated, as did all pupils in the 3rd, 6th, 9th, and 12th grades. First-grade pupils in half the schools participated. More than 645,000 pupils in all were involved in the survey. . . .

Data for Negro and white children are classified by whether the schools are in metropolitan areas or not. The definition of a metropolitan area is the one commonly used by government agencies: a city of over 50,000 inhabitants including its suburbs. All other schools in small cities, towns, or rural areas are referred to as nonmetropolitan schools. . . . For metropolitan schools there are usually five regions defined as follows:

Northeast – Connecticut, Maine, Massachusetts, New Hampshire, Rhode Island, Vermont, Delaware, Maryland, New Jersey, New York, Pennsylvania, District of Columbia. (Using 1960 census data, this region contains about 16 percent of all Negro children in the nation and 20 percent of all white children age 5 to 19.)

Midwest—Illinois, Indiana, Michigan, Ohio, Wisconsin, Iowa, Kansas, Minnesota, Missouri, Nebraska, North Dakota, South Dakota (containing 16 percent of Negro and 19 percent of white children age 5 to 19).

South—Alabama, Arkansas, Florida, Georgia, Kentucky, Louisiana, Mississippi, North Carolina, South Carolina, Tennessee, Virginia, West Virginia (containing 27 percent of Negro and 14 percent of white children age 5 to 19).

Southwest—Arizona, New Mexico, Oklahoma, Texas (containing 4 percent of Negro and 3 percent of white children age 5 to 19).

West—Alaska, California, Colorado, Hawaii, Idaho, Montana, Nevada, Oregon, Utah, Washington, Wyoming (containing 4 percent of Negro and 11 percent of white children age 5 to 19).

The nonmetropolitan schools are usually classified into only three regions:

South—As above (containing 27 percent of Negro and 14 percent of white children age 5 to 19).

Southwest—As above (containing 4 percent of Negro and 2 percent of white children age 5 to 19).

North and West—All states not in the South and Southwest (containing 2 percent of Negro and 17 percent of white children age 5 to 19). . . .

Facilities. For the nation as a whole, white children attend elementary schools with a smaller average number of pupils per room (29) than do any of the minorities (which range from 30 to 33). . . . In some regions the nationwide pattern is reversed: in the nonmetropolitan North and West and Southwest, for example, there is a smaller average number of pupils per room for Negroes than for whites. . . . Secondary-school whites have a smaller average number of pupils per room than minorities, except Indians.

Looking at the regional breakdown, however, one finds much more striking differences than the national average would suggest: In the metropolitan Midwest, for example, the average Negro has 54 pupils per room—probably reflecting considerable frequency of double sessions – compared with 33 per room for whites. Nationally, at the high-school level, the average white has 1 teacher for every 22 students and the average Negro has 1 for every 26 students. . . .

Nationally, Negro pupils have fewer of some of the facilities that seem most related to academic achievement: They have less access to physics, chemistry, and language laboratories; there are fewer books per pupil in their libraries; their textbooks are less often in sufficient supply. To the extent that physical facilities are important to learning, such items appear to be more relevant than some others, such as cafeterias, in which minority groups are at an advantage.

Usually greater than the majority-minority differences, however, are the regional differences. . . . Ninety-five percent of Negro and 80 percent of white high-school students in the metropolitan Far West attend schools with language laboratories, compared with 48 and 72 percent, respectively, in the metropolitan South, in spite of the fact that a higher percentage of Southern schools are less than 20 years old.

Finally, it must always be remembered that these statistics reveal only majority-minority average differences and regional average differences; they do not show the extreme differences that would be found by comparing one school with another.

Programs. Just as minority groups tend to have less access to physical facilities that seem to be related to academic achievement, so too they have less access to curricular and extracurricular programs that would seem to have such a relationship.

Secondary-school Negro students are less likely to attend schools that are regionally accredited; this is particularly pronounced in the South. Negro and Puerto Rican pupils have less access to college preparatory curriculums and to accelerated curriculums; Puerto Ricans have less access to vocational curriculums as well. Less intelligence testing is done in the schools attended by Negroes and Puerto Ricans. Finally, white students in general have more access to a more fully developed program of extracurricular activities, in particular those which might be related to academic matters (debate teams, for example, and student newspapers).

Again, regional differences are striking. For example, 100 percent of Negro high-school students and 97 percent of whites in the metropolitan Far West attend schools having a remedial reading teacher (this does not mean, of course, that every student uses the services of that teacher, but simply that he has access to them) compared with 46 percent and 65 percent, respectively, in the metropolitan South—and 4 percent and 9 percent in the nonmetropolitan Southwest. . . .

ACHIEVEMENT IN THE PUBLIC SCHOOLS

The schools bear many responsibilities. Among the most important is the teaching of certain intellectual skills, such as reading, writing, calculating, and problem solving. One way of assessing the educational opportunity offered by the schools is to measure how well they perform this task. Standard achievement tests are available to measure these skills, and several such tests were administered in this survey to pupils at grades 1, 3, 6, 9, and 12.

These tests do not measure intelligence, nor attitudes, nor qualities of character. Furthermore, they are not, nor are they intended to be, "culture free." Quite the reverse: they are culture bound. What they measure are the skills which are among the most important in our society for getting a good job and moving up to a better one, and for full participation in an increasingly technical world. Consequently, a pupil's test results at the end of public school provide a good measure of the range of opportunities open to him as he finishes school—a wide range of choice of jobs or colleges if these skills are very high; a very narrow range that includes only the most menial jobs if these skills are very low. . . .

With some exceptions—notably Oriental-Americans—the average minority pupil scores distinctly lower on these tests at every level than the average white pupil. The minority pupils' scores are as much as one standard deviation below the majority pupils' scores in the 1st grade. At the 12th grade, results of tests in the same verbal and nonverbal skills show that, in every case, the minority scores are farther below the majority than are the 1st-graders. For some groups, the relative decline is negligible; for others, it is large.

Furthermore, a constant difference in standard deviations over the various grades represents an increasing difference in grade level gap. For example, Negroes in the metropolitan Northeast are about 1.1 standard deviations below whites in the same region at grades 6, 9, and 12. But at grade 6 this represents 1.6 years behind; at grade 9, 2.4 years; and at grade 12, 3.3 years. Thus, by this measure, the deficiency in achievement is progressively greater for the minority pupils at progressively higher grade levels.

For most minority groups, then, and most particularly the Negro, schools provide little opportunity for them to overcome this initial deficiency; in fact they fall farther behind the white majority in the development of several skills which are critical to making a living and participating fully in modern society. Whatever may be the combination of nonschool factors—poverty, community attitudes, low educational level of parents—which put minority children at a disadvantage in verbal and nonverbal skills when they enter the first grade, the fact is the schools have not overcome it. . . .

RELATION OF ACHIEVEMENT TO SCHOOL CHARACTERISTICS

If 100 students within a school take a certain test, there is likely to be great variation in their scores. One student may score 97 percent, another 13; several may score 78 percent. This represents variability in achievement within the particular school.

It is possible, however, to compute the average of the scores made by the students within that school and to compare it with the average score, or achievement, of pupils within another school, or many other schools. These comparisons then represent variations between schools.

When one sees that the average score on a verbal achievement test in school X is 55 and in school Y is 72, the natural question to ask is: What accounts for the difference?

There are many factors that may be associated with the difference. This analysis concentrates on one cluster of those factors. It attempts to describe what relationship the school's characteristics themselves (libraries, for example, and teachers and laboratories and so on) seem to have to the achievement of majority and minority groups (separately for each group on a nationwide basis, and also for Negro and white pupils in the North and South).

The first finding is that the schools are remarkably similar in the way they relate to the achievement of their pupils when the socioeconomic background of the students is taken into account. It is known that socioeconomic factors bear a strong relation to academic achievement. When these factors are statistically controlled, however, it appears that differences between schools account for only a small fraction of differences in pupil achievement.

The schools do differ, however, in their relation to the various racial and ethnic groups. The average white student's achievement seems to be less affected by the strength or weakness of his school's facilities, curriculums, and teachers than is the average minority pupil's. To put it another way, the achievement of minority pupils depends more on the schools they attend than does the achievement of majority pupils. Thus, 20 percent of the achievement of Negroes in the South is associated with the particular schools they go to, whereas only 10 percent of the achievement of whites in the South is. Except for Oriental-Americans, this general result is found for all minorities.

The inference might then be made that improving the school of a minority pupil may increase his achievement more than would improving the school of a white child increase his. Similarly, the average minority pupil's achievement may suffer more in a school of low quality than might the average white pupil's. In short, whites and, to a lesser extent, Oriental-Americans are less affected one way or the other by the quality of their schools than are minority pupils. This indicates that it is for the most disadvantaged children that improvements in school quality will make the most difference in achievement.

All of these results suggest the next question: What are the school characteristics that are most related to achievement? In other words, what factors in the school seem to be most important in affecting achievement?

It appears that variations in the facilities and curriculums of the schools account for relatively little variation in pupil achievement insofar as this is measured by standard tests. Again, it is for majority whites that the variations make the least difference; for minorities, they make somewhat more difference. Among the facilities that show some relationship to achievement are several for which minority pupils' schools are less well equipped relative to whites. For example, the existence of science laboratories showed a small but consistent relationship to achievement, and . . . minorities, especially Negroes, are in schools with fewer of these laboratories.

The quality of teachers shows a stronger relationship to pupil achievement. Furthermore, it is progressively greater at higher grades, indicating a cumulative impact of the qualities of teachers in a school on the pupil's achievements. Again, teacher quality seems more important to minority achievement than to that of the majority.

It should be noted that many characteristics of teachers were not measured in this survey; therefore, the results are not at all conclusive regarding the specific characteristics of teachers that are most important. Among those measured in the survey, however, those that bear the highest relationship to pupil achievement are first, the teacher's score on the verbal skills test, and then his educational background — both his own level of education and that of his parents. On both of these measures, the level of teachers of minority students, especially Negroes, is lower.

Finally, it appears that a pupil's achievement is strongly related to the educational backgrounds and aspirations of the other students in the school. Only crude measures of these variables were used (principally the proportion of pupils with encyclopedias in the home and the proportion planning to go to college). Analysis indicates, however, that children from a given family background, when put in schools of different social composition, will achieve at quite different levels. This effect is again less for white pupils than for any minority group other than Orientals. Thus, if a white pupil from a home that is strongly and effectively supportive of education is put in a school where most pupils do not come from such homes, his achievement will be little different than if he were in a school composed of others like himself. But if a minority pupil from a home without much educational strength is put with schoolmates with strong educational backgrounds, his achievement is likely to increase.

This general result, taken together with the earlier examinations of school differences, has important implications for equality of educational opportunity. . . . The principal way in which the school environments of Negroes and whites differ is in the composition of their student bodies, and it turns out that the composition of the student bodies has a strong relationship to the achievement of Negro and other minority pupils.

This analysis has concentrated on the educational opportunities offered by the schools in terms of their student body composition, facilities, curriculums, and teachers. This emphasis, while entirely appropriate as a response to the legislation calling for the survey, nevertheless neglects important factors in the variability between individual pupils within the same school; this variability is roughly four times as large as the variability between schools. For example, a pupil attitude factor, which appears to have a stronger relationship to achievement than do all the "school" factors together, is the extent to which an individual feels that he has some control over his own destiny. . . . Minority pupils, except for Orientals, have far less conviction than whites that they can affect their own environments and futures. When they do, however, their achievement is higher than that of whites who lack that conviction.

Furthermore, while this characteristic shows little relationship to most school factors, it is related, for Negroes, to the proportion of whites in the schools. Those Negroes in schools with a higher proportion of whites have a greater sense of control. This finding suggests that the direction such an attitude takes may be associated with the pupil's school experience as well as his experience in the larger community.

OTHER SURVEYS AND STUDIES

Relation of integration to achievement. An education in integrated schools can be expected to have major effects on attitudes toward members of other racial groups. At its best, it can develop attitudes appropriate to the integrated society these students will live in; at its worst, it can create hostile camps of Negroes and whites in the same school. Thus, there is more to "school integration" than merely putting Negroes and whites in the same building, and there may be more important consequences of integration than its effects on achievement.

Yet the analysis of school factors described earlier suggests that, in the long run, integration should be expected to have a positive effect on Negro achievement as well. An analysis was carried out to seek such effects on achievement which might appear in the short run. This analysis of the test performance of Negro children in integrated schools indicates positive effects of integration, though rather small ones. . . .

[A] table . . . was constructed to observe whether there is any tendency for Negro pupils who have spent more years in integrated schools to exhibit higher average achievement. Those pupils who first entered integrated schools in the early grades record consistently higher scores than the other groups, although the differences are again small. No account is taken in these tabulations of the fact that the various groups of pupils may have come from different backgrounds. . . . Thus, although the differences are small, and although the degree of integration within the school is not known, there is evident, even in the short run, an effect of school integration on the reading and mathematics achievement of Negro pupils. . . .

Case studies of school integration. As part of the survey, two sets of case studies of school integration were commissioned. These case studies examine the progress of integration in individual cities and towns, and illustrate problems that have arisen not only in these communities but in many others as well. . . .

In the main report, excerpts from these case studies are presented to illustrate certain recurrent problems. A paragraph which introduces [some] of these excerpts is given below, showing the kinds of problems covered. . . .

Compliance in a small community. — Many large metropolitan areas, North and South, are moving toward resegregation despite attempts by school boards and city administrations to reverse the trend. Racial housing concentration in large cities has reinforced neighborhood school patterns of racial isolation, while, at the same time, many white families have moved to the suburbs and other families have taken their children out of the public-school system, enrolling them instead in private and parochial schools. Small towns and medium-sized areas, North and South, on the other hand, are to some extent desegregating their schools.

In the Deep South, where there has been total school segregation for generations, there are signs of compliance within a number of school systems. The emphasis on open enrollment and freedom-of-choice plans, however, has tended to lead to token enrollment of Negroes in previously white schools. In school systems integrated at some grade levels but not at others, the choice of high-school grades rather than elementary grades has tended further to cut down on the number of Negroes choosing to transfer because of the reluctance to take extra risks close to graduation. . . .

177

A voluntary transfer plan for racial balance in elementary schools. — The public schools are more rigidly segregated at the elementary level than in the higher grades. In the large cities, elementary schools have customarily made assignments in terms of neighborhood boundaries. Housing segregation has, therefore, tended to build a segregated elementary-school system in most cities in the North and, increasingly, in the South as well, where *de facto* segregation is replacing *de jure* segregation.

Various communities have been struggling to find ways to achieve greater racial balance while retaining the neighborhood school. Bussing, pairing, redistricting, consolidating, and many other strategies have been tried. Many have failed; others have achieved at least partial success. In New Haven, Conn., considerable vigor has been applied to the problem: Whereas pairing was tried at the junior-high level, introducing compulsory integration, a voluntary transfer plan was implemented at the elementary level. Relief of overcrowding was given as the central intent of the transfer plan, but greater racial balance was achieved, since it was the Negro schools that were overcrowded. With the provision of new school buildings, however, this indirect stimulus to desegregation will not be present. In New Haven the transfer plan was more effective than in many other communities because of commitment of school leadership, active solicitation of transfers by door-to-door visits, provision of transportation for those transferring, teacher cooperation, heterogeneous grouping in the classrooms, and other factors.

The original plan provided that a student could apply to any one of a cluster of several elementary schools within a designated "cluster district," and the application would be approved on the basis of availability of space, effect on racial balance and certain unspecified educational factors; that students "presently enrolled" at a particular school would be given priority; and that transportation would be provided where necessary.

Desegregation by redistricting at the junior high school level. — The junior high schools, customarily grades 7 to 9, have been the focus of considerable effort and tension in desegregation plans in many communities. With most areas clinging to the neighborhood school at the elementary level with resultant patterns of racial concentration, and with high schools already more integrated because of their lesser reliance upon neighborhood boundaries and their prior consolidation to achieve maximum resources, junior high schools have been a natural place to start desegregation plans. Like the elementary schools, they have in the past been assigned students on the basis of geography; but, on the other hand, they tend to represent some degree of consolidation in that children from several elementary schools feed one junior high school. Further, parental pressures have been less severe for the maintenance of rigid neighborhood boundaries than at the elementary level.

Pairing of two junior high schools to achieve greater racial balance has been tried in a number of communities. Redistricting or redrawing the boundaries of areas that feed the schools has been tried in other areas. In Berkeley, Calif., after considerable community tension and struggle, a plan was put into effect that desegregated all three junior high schools (one had been desegregated previously). All the 9th graders were sent to a single school, previously Negro, and the 7th and 8th graders were assigned to the other two schools. The new 9th-grade school was given a new name to signal its new identity in the eyes of the community. . . .

A plan for racial balance at the high-school level. — In a number of communities, students are assigned to high schools on the basis of area of residence and hence racial imbalance is continued. In Pasadena, Calif., a plan was initiated to redress this imbalance by opening places in the schools to allow the transfer of Negroes to the predominantly white school. A measure of success was achieved but only after much resistance. Of interest particularly in this situation was the legal opinion that attempts to achieve racial balance were violations of the Constitution and that race could not be considered as a factor in school districting. Apparently previous racial concentration, aided by districting, had not been so regarded, yet attempts at desegregation were. The School Board found its task made more difficult by such legal maneuvering. . . .

Relation of a university to school desegregation. — Education is a continuum — from kindergarten through college — and, increasingly, public-school desegregation plans are having an impact on colleges in the same area, particularly those colleges which are city or state supported. Free tuition, as in the New York City colleges, has no meaning for members of minority groups who have dropped out of school in high school and little meaning for those whose level of achievement is too low to permit work at the college level. A number of colleges, through summer tutorials and selective admittance of students whose grades would otherwise exclude them, are trying to redress this indirect form of racial imbalance.

3. The Civil Rights Movement

1961-1965

NATHAN GLAZER

The Peoples of the U.S.A.

"America for Americans," "the 100% American," "the hyphenated American," "the Melting Pot" — all of these are terms or slogans that have marked the history of immigration and ethnic assimilation in the United States. The problems of immigration have been largely solved, owing to the modern restrictions on immigrants (if in fact they can really be said to have solved the problems), but the problems of assimilation remain, particularly those of the "unwilling immigrants" — the Negroes — who a century after emancipation have still not been absorbed fully into the mainstream of American life. [Source: Nation, 100th Anniversary Issue, September 20, 1965: "The Peoples of America."]

The history of ethnicity and ethnic self consciousness in this country has moved in waves; we are now in a trough between two crests, and the challenge is to describe the shape and form of the next crest. That there will be another crest it is hardly possible to doubt. Since the end of European mass immigration to this country forty years ago we have waited for the subsidence of ethnic self-consciousness, and often announced it, and it has returned again and again. But each time it has returned in so different a form that one could well argue it was not the same thing returning at all, that what we saw was not the breakthrough of the consciousness of common origin and community among the groups that made America, but rather that ethnicity was being used as a cover for some other more significant force, which was borrowing another identity.

During the early years of the Depression, ethnicity withdrew as a theme in American life. Both those who had urged the "Americanization" of the immigrant and the creation of "cultural pluralism" now had more important concerns. Immigration was matched by a counter-emigration back to the countries of origins; one episode of American history it seemed had come to an end. Then, with the rise of Hitler, the ethnic texture of American life began to reassert itself. First Jews; then Germans; then Czechs, Poles, Italians, and even the "old Americans," remembering their origins in England, all were spurred to action and organization by Hitler and the great war that he began. Samuel Lubell has traced how the support for Franklin D. Roosevelt in the great cities shifted from class to ethnicity as the international conflict developed and various groups responded to, or against, Roosevelt, as he displayed his sentiments and allegiances.

In 1945 this great crest began to withdraw. True, there was the continuing impact on ethnic groups of the confrontation with Russia and communism, but with the passage of time this began to lose its ethnic coloration. Catholics in general were more anti-Communist than others, Poles still more so, Jews much less so. But the international conflict was so sharply colored by ideology rather than national antagonism, that with the passage of time it no longer served to set group against group (as it had in the Hitler years). Soviet opposition to Israel and Soviet anti-Semitism; the rise of a measure of cautious Polish independence; de-Stalinization in Russia—all these developments softened the sharp conflicts which had created a powerful resonance among immigrants and their children in this country.

The Eisenhower period marked thus a new trough, and it was possible to conclude that the workings of the melting pot had been retarded only slightly by the neolithic tribal ferocity of Hitler and the counterreactions he evoked. But now a new wave began to gather force, a wave that had nothing to do with international affairs. Will Herberg interpreted the increased religious activity of the postwar years as a half-embarrassed means of maintaining group identity in a democratic society which did not look with favor on the long-continued maintenance of sharply distinguished ethnic groups. The "triple melting pot" theory of Ruby Jo Reeves Kennedy, along with her data on intermarriage, suggested that old ethnic lines were being replaced by new religious lines.

The chameleon-like force of ancestral connection, one could argue, was being transmuted into the forms of religion. Those who were concerned for religion could of course take no comfort in this analysis, even if the religious denominations benefited from higher collections and new buildings. If our major religions are replacing ethnic groups, one could not yet herald the creation of a homogeneous and undivided American group consciousness in America, but at least our divisions no longer paralleled those of old Europe—

something which had deeply troubled our leaders from Washington to Woodrow Wilson – but the more acceptable divisions of religion, which ostensibly had an older and more respectable lineage and justification. Thus, if Herberg could still discern the forces of ethnic identity at work in the new clothes of religious denominationalism, at least they no longer expressed themselves openly.

But once again an unabashed ethnicity reasserted itself in the campaign of John F. Kennedy and his brief presidency. In his Cabinet, for the first time, there sat a Jew of East European origin, an Italian-American, a Polish-American. If the Jews were no longer being appointed primarily to represent a group, there was no question that this was the explanation for the appointment of an Italian-American and a Polish-American. The Catholic President was reminded by everyone that he was an Irish President. He was the first President to be elected from an immigrant group that had suffered discrimination and prejudice, and that still remembered it – and those of us from later immigrant groups, who had experienced the lordly position of the Irish in the cities of the East, discovered only with some surprise that the Irish did remember their days as a degraded minority. Those who stemmed from the new immigration now realized that the Irish shared very much the same feelings of resentment at past treatment, of gratification in present accomplishment and recognition.

But the old Americans too responded to the realization that they had an Irish President, as well as a Democratic, Catholic, and intellectual President. Certainly it is hard to explain otherwise the mutual antagonism that rapidly sprang up between the new administration and such a large part of the big business establishment, the seat of the old Americans, the "WASP" power. The administration's policies were not antagonistic to big business. There was of course the President's violent response to the steel price rise, but was not that, too, a reflection – at least in part – of old ethnic images and conflicts? No one who spoke to anyone close to those events could doubt it.

I would suggest a gentle recession, if not a trough, in the period since President Kennedy's assassination. Two events to my mind suggest the retreat of an open and congratulatory ethnic self-assertiveness, and they are related. One is the new concern with the poor, which complementarily marks all the nonpoor as members of the same group, with the same social task laid upon them; and the second is the steady radicalization of the civil rights movement and Negro opinion, and this increasingly places all the whites in the same category, without distinction. And once again a symbolic political event marks the recession of ethnic self-consciousness: the accession of President Johnson, who, like President Eisenhower, comes from a part of America that was relatively unaffected by European immigration.

I have marked recurrent crests and troughs of ethnic self-consciousness by political events, but the political events have of course paralleled social events. The crisis of the Depression erased for the moment ethnic memories and allegiances. The agony of the European peoples reawakened it. Prosperity and the rapid rise of the new immigrant groups to upper working-class and middle-class status again reduced their sense of difference. The security that came with long-sustained prosperity made it possible for the descendants of despised immigrants to again take pleasure in their origins and their differences. One of the less observed effects of affluence is that it leads people to their real or hopefully reconstructed origins. In Europe and among Americans who look to the European upper classes, this may mean acquiring crests, forebears, and antiques. Among the American descendants of European peasants and artisans, it meant, in a surprising number of cases, a new interest in the culture of the old country. But in the most recent period, the rise of the joint problems of poverty and the assimilation of the Negro raises a new set of questions. For the moment, ethnic self-assertiveness is in eclipse and even in bad odor. And the eclipse is directly related to the new problems.

Michael Harrington put the matter quite directly when he said in a recent speech that the accumulated wisdom of the great European immigrant groups in this country has become irrelevant, for it will not help the current poor and it will not help the Negroes. In varying degrees, we are hearing the same from Louis Lomax, from James Baldwin, from Nat Hentoff, and from other supporters and defenders of Negro militancy. Inevitably the next wave of ethnic self-consciousness must reflect one of the most remarkable and least expected consequences of the Negro revolution — the growing estrangement between European ethnic groups and the Negroes.

Its beginnings were studied by Samuel Lubell in the early post-war period, and we have seen the estrangement develop to the point where the fear of the white backlash—and this meant generally the backlash from recent white immigrant groups in the cities—became one of the major issues of the Goldwater-Johnson campaign. The separation, first the barest of lines, has deepened through conflicts over the adoption and administration of fair employment laws, fair housing laws, measures to combat *de facto* school segregation. The patterns under which and through which the European ethnic groups have lived—the trade unions and branches of industry dominated by one or a few ethnic groups, the ethnically concentrated neighborhood with its distinctive schools and churches and organizations—all have come under increasing attack. And thus the distinctive social patterns of the North and West, which the immigrant and the ethnic groups helped create, are now being slowly but surely turned into a Southern-like confrontation of white and black. The varied, more balanced, and more creative ethnic conflicts of the North are now in danger of being transformed into the monolithic confrontation of the South.

In the South, Northern variety never developed. One great division dominated and smothered all others, the division between black and white. In this area, the European immigrant of the later 19th and early 20th century never penetrated. All he had to offer generally was unskilled labor, and in the South the unskilled labor was the work of Negroes. The white immigrant laborer refused to enter an area in which the laborer was degraded, not only by his work but by a caste system, where wages were low and racial conflict hindered trade-union development and social legislation. The immigrant worked in the parts of the country where work had greater respect and was better rewarded. If he entered the South, it was more often as a merchant than as a worker.

But in the Northern cities, where almost half the Negroes now live, it was not inevitable that the same line of division should be imported from the South. The entry of the Negro into the Northern cities in great numbers during and after World War I and again during and after World War II raised a critical question: Was he the last of the great immigrant groups? Would his experience parallel that of the Irish and the Poles and the Jews who had arrived as exploited and unskilled workers and had moved upward, at varying speeds, into middle-class occupations, the professions, business? How would those who were themselves children and grandchildren of recent immigrant waves view him? How would he view himself and his prospects? Against whom would he measure his circumstances? And would the inevitable conflicts between the poorer and the more prosperous resemble the conflicts between Yankees and Irish, Irish and Italians—or would they take the form of the far more deadly and longer established conflict between black and white? I feel the answers are still not given. They will be shaped both by the established ethnic groups and the Negro migrant. But I fear the answer from both sides will be . . . yes, the Negro is different.

It is impossible for the history of ethnic self-consciousness to escape from the impact of Negro urban migration, for all the waves of immigration have affected the self-consciousness of waves that came before. The old Americans reacted to the first great waves of immigrants of the '40s and '50s of the 19th century with an exaggerated sense of their own high status and aristocratic connections. The early immigrants from each group withdrew from later immigrants, but were generally forced together with them because the old Americans imposed a common identity on them. The history of ethnic self-consciousness, it is clear, has not worked itself out independently of social and economic and political events. If anything, it has been a reaction to these events: the rise of one group, the occupancy of the bottom by another, the political conflicts of Europe, the sequence of immigration in each town and city and section. All these have helped mold ethnic self-consciousness, and its reflection in social activity, in political choice, in economic history.

But on the whole this self-consciousness, whatever its stages, has been marked by optimism and hope. I have described the Kennedy mood among the more recent and more sharply defined American ethnic groups as self-congratulation. Indeed it was that, though each of the groups might have found some basis for resentment rather than pride. The Irish had reached the heights of political success, and the Jews were prosperous, but both were still in large measure excluded from the pinnacles of economic power—the great banks, insurance companies, corporations. The Italians still were remarkably poorly represented in high political posts, and had a much smaller share in every establishment – economic, political, cultural – than the Jews, who had come at the same time and were less numerous. The Poles were even poorer.

And yet such invidious comparisons – which the census made clear – were rarely made. All the new groups seem to have escaped from the difficult period of second generation self-depreciation and exaggerated Americanism. All seemed to wear ethnic connection with self-assurance. Certainly the growing prosperity of Europe, the increased trade with Europe, the wide acceptance of its consumer goods here, the large influence of European culture, all made the acceptance of one's ethnic connections easier – for by doing so, after all, one was no longer acknowledging poor relations. It was fascinating to remark upon the change in the image of the homeland among the more self conscious and better educated descendants of the immigrants. Ireland was no longer the home of potatoes and cabbage, but of Joyce and the Abbey Theatre, good Irish whiskey and Georgian architecture, horseracing and tweeds. Italy became the land of chic, while Israel and Poland, if they could not compete in the arts of affluent consumption, became now paragons of political independence and heroism. Every group fortunately found something to admire in the old (or new) country, and found it easy to acknowledge the connection that had once been obscured.

But if this characterizes the most recent mood of ethnic self-consciousness, it is now challenged by the new Negro militancy and the theory on which it is reared. The self-congratulatory expressions are strangled in the throat. For a while, in the '40s and '50s, when Jewish and Catholic groups worked effectively with Urban League and NAACP, with Negroes proud of having achieved middle-class status, the older ethnic groups and their representatives could present themselves as models and elder brothers – in community organization, group defense work, in cultural and political activity. But the radical Negro mood, and its growing reflection among intellectuals, turns all whites into exploiters, with old Americans, old immigrants, and new immigrants lumped together. The success of the ethnic groups – limited as it is for many – now becomes a reproach. Their very history, which each group has been so busy writing and reconstructing, now becomes an unspoken (and some-times spoken) criticism of the Northern Negro. Both sides see it and rush to explain themselves.

What after all is the history of the American ethnic groups but a history of group and individual adaptation to difficult circum-stances? All the histories move in the same patterns. The immi-grants arrive; they represent the poorest and least educated and most oppressed of their countries in Europe and Asia. They arrive ignorant of our language and customs, exploited and abused. They huddle together in the ghettos of the cities, beginning slowly to attend to their most immediate needs – organization for companion-ship, patterns of self-aid in crisis, churches for worship, schools to maintain the old culture. American society and government is indifferent to their needs and desires; they are allowed to do what they wish, but neither hindered nor aided.

In this amorphous setting where no limits are set to group organ-ization, they gradually form a community. Their children move through the public schools and perhaps advance themselves – if not, it may be the grandchildren who do. The children are embarrassed by the poverty and ignorance of the parents. Eventually they, or the grandchildren, learn to accept their origins as poverty and igno-rance are overcome. They move into the spheres of American life in which many or all groups meet – the larger economy, politics, social life, education. Eventually many of the institutions created by the immigrants become a hindrance rather than a necessity; some are abandoned, some are changed. American society in the meantime has made a place for and even become dependent on some of these institutions, such as old-age homes and hospitals, adoption services and churches – these survive and perhaps flourish. More and more of these institutions become identified with the religious denomina-tion, rather than the ethnic group as such.

Note one element of this history: demand on government plays a small role; response by government plays a small role. There is one great exception, the labor movement. But even the labor movement, which eventually found support in public law and government administrative structure, began its history as voluntary organiza-tion in the amorphous structure of American society and achieved its first triumphs without, or even against, government.

Negro Life, 1900-1967

LIBRARY OF CONGRESS

In 1905, ten years after Booker T. Washington made his Atlanta Exposition address, W. E. B. DuBois, above, founded the Niagara Movement to protest against the indignities Negroes had suffered since Reconstruction and to challenge the basic assumptions of Washington's teachings. DuBois agreed with Washington that education and self-help were central to black progress but disagreed with Washington's belief that Negroes should delay their drive for full equality. For DuBois, total integration into American society had to be the Negro's primary goal. In 1909 DuBois and most of his followers joined the newly formed National Association for the Advancement of Colored People. The NAACP became the Negro's most active and resourceful champion; the writings of DuBois, both in the NAACP magazine *The Crisis* (which he edited for many years) and in his own books on black history and culture, influenced several generations of young black people.

BROWN BROTHERS

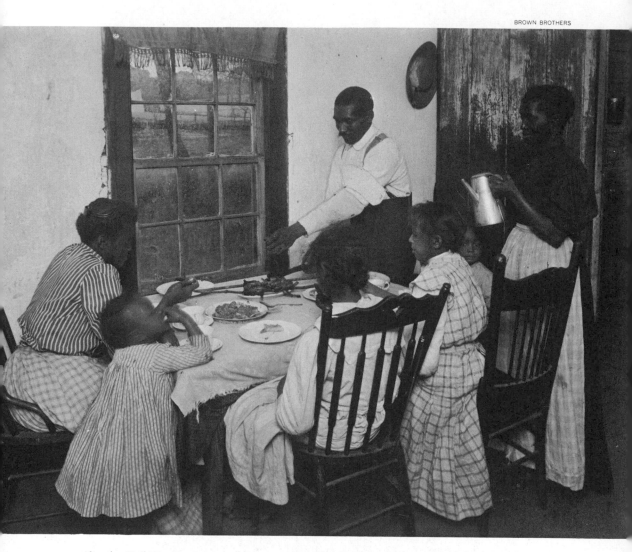

After the Civil War Negroes began to move North; but in 1900, nine out of ten still lived in the South and most of these still labored as sharecroppers. Their lot worsened as they entered the 20th century; in the century's first decade all the Southern states passed new laws designed to insure Negro political impotence and instituted poll taxes that kept most Negroes and many poor whites from voting. Jim Crow laws were strengthened and served as perpetual reminders of the black man's inferiority under the law; Southern newspapers (and some Northern ones) used news stories as well as editorial pages to paint a savage portrait of the Negro as little better than an animal; race riots and lynchings were common occurrences. Life in the North was better than it was in the South provided jobs were available. But European immigrants, who arrived on American shores in record numbers during the last years of the 19th century and the first years of the 20th, got first call on even the low-paid, unskilled jobs for which Negroes were searching. Those Negroes who did travel North and found work lived in Negro neighborhoods for the most part. Here they quickly developed their own community and became somewhat scornful of newly arrived Southern Negroes. The family above and the street at right (with its sign reading "Apartments to Let . . . For Respectable Colored Families Only") were photographed in Harlem about 1904.

BROWN BROTHERS

BROWN BROTHERS

A small insect and world events combined to turn the trickle of black migration northward into a torrent. Beginning about 1900, repeated invasions by the boll weevil, a Mexican insect, decimated the South's cotton crop. Floods and drought destroyed much of the rest. As white landlords went under, their black and white sharecroppers were left without means of support. Whether or not jobs were available in the North, Southern Negroes had to move somewhere if they were to feed their families. Meanwhile, the outbreak of World War I cut off European immigration. Beginning in 1914, Northern industry had to look elsewhere for new workers. It looked South and migration soared. By 1920, one million Negroes had gone North and the end was nowhere in sight. This crowded street fair was photographed in Harlem.

When the United States entered World War I, Negroes flocked to the colors. Some two hundred thousand served overseas. Despite the discriminations they encountered in training camps and at the front, they fought bravely; many experienced for the first time what it was like to live in a society in which they were received with friendly curiosity rather than hostility. As they fought abroad the lot of their families at home worsened. While governmental interest in Negro citizens had been minimal since Reconstruction, some integration had been instituted in the ranks of the Federal bureaucracy itself. President Woodrow Wilson ended it, decreeing segregation as his federal hiring policy.

BROWN BROTHERS

CHICAGO HISTORICAL SOCIETY

The migration of Negroes to the North brought with it the problems that have plagued urban America ever since. Whites resented Negro competition for jobs and resisted black incursions into their neighborhoods. Negro homes were bombed and race riots broke out in many cities and towns. There were 25 serious outbreaks of racial violence in the summer of 1919 alone. The worst riot, left, occurred in Chicago. It lasted 13 days and before troops, below, restored order, 38 persons were dead and 537 had been injured. Despite the violence and harassment with which they often had to deal, the Negroes who came North stayed, and wave after wave of new immigrants followed them. The tiny neighborhoods that had housed Northern Negroes before the war had now become cities within cities. Negroes started businesses (some 70,000 small businesses were owned and operated by Negroes by 1925) but success in business was hard to achieve. Throughout the economy small businesses were being replaced by major corporations, and Negroes operating with little capital often found it impossible to compete. Only those businessmen who catered to specifically Negro needs — cosmeticians, morticians, beauticians — had much chance for long-run success. Negroes also began to make their new-found political power felt. As early as 1915, a black alderman had been elected in Chicago, and in 1928 the same city sent a black Congressman to Washington.

CHICAGO HISTORICAL SOCIETY

In Harlem in the 1920s there occurred a cultural boom that has come to be called the Harlem Renaissance. Writers such as Langston Hughes, Claude McKay, Countee Cullen, and James Weldon Johnson became popular among whites as well as blacks, and white visitors trooped to Harlem to savor its nightlife and hear the music of such jazz musicians as Duke Ellington and his orchestra, right, at the Cotton Club. It seemed, for a time, that art might help bring about the racial understanding that three centuries of coexistence had failed to produce. But white fascination with Harlem soon went the way of Mah-Jongg and other fads of the twenties. However, the music of Duke Ellington and the other great black and white jazz artists of this and later periods has been called America's single most important contribution to world culture.

BROWN BROTHERS

WIDE WORLD

Life in the Northern ghettos, while materially better than it had been in the rural South, was hard, and many Negroes cast about for ways to escape its bleakness. Father Divine, shown leading a group of his followers above, and Marcus Garvey, right, offered two alternatives. Claiming to be God made flesh, Father Divine gathered his considerable following by establishing little "Heavens" in Harlem and other communities where the poor and unemployed could eat their fill at lavish feasts. His movement gained popularity because many Negroes were so discouraged by the real world that they were willing to believe in a new one, no matter how farfetched it seemed to others. The Garvey movement had a much more serious intent. Its leader was an eloquent Jamaican who believed that he had been sent to restore the world's black people to nationhood. He preached the unity of all Negroes, organized the Universal Negro Improvement Association, and made plans to take great numbers of black Americans back to Africa. His plans fell through when he was indicted for stock fraud in 1925 and was later deported. Whatever his personal frailties, his emphasis on Negro self-pride and his promotion of community with black people in other lands inspired many young Negroes and finds echoes in the recent emphasis on Black Power.

UPI COMPIX

LIBRARY OF CONGRESS

The Great Depression hit Americans of every class and color but it was especially hard on
Negroes. Sharecroppers, above, were evicted from their land and were forced to move North
where, often, no jobs were available. Northern city dwellers lost their factory jobs. Those who
held on to jobs had their wages slashed again and again. Franklin Roosevelt's New Deal programs
helped many. Although programs were segregated on the state or at least the local level, they
represented the first major evidence of governmental concern for Negroes since Reconstruction,
and the appointment of a large number of Negro specialists to federal agencies was an
unprecedented move. By the end of 1938, ten percent of America's Negroes were federal
employees. Despite inconsistencies—notably Roosevelt's failure to push for a strong anti-lynching
bill—the New Deal record was impressive enough to cause a massive shift in Negro voting
patterns. In 1932, three out of four Negroes had voted for the Republican Party of Lincoln; in 1940
eight out of ten voted for the Democratic Party of Roosevelt.

CHICAGO HISTORICAL SOCIETY

WIDE WORLD

White prejudice had kept Negroes out of labor unions and employers' use of Negroes as strikebreakers (such as the strikebreaking millinery workers at left, photographed during a 1904 strike in Chicago) had added to the determination of many unions to remain all-white. A. Philip Randolph founded the Brotherhood of Sleeping Car Porters in 1925 and succeeded in improving the conditions under which its members, almost all Negroes, worked. The Depression period saw a slow shift toward integrated unions and the rapidly growing CIO made integration a formal policy. Soon unions such as the United Mine Workers and the United Auto Workers (shown above going out on strike in Saginaw, Michigan, in 1964) were integrated in fact as well as on paper. But many unions, notably in the building trades, remain virtually all-white.

LIBRARY OF CONGRESS

World War II for the Negro was much like World War I. Black soldiers fought valiantly overseas, right, despite segregated training camps and units, while southern Negroes poured North to take new jobs in defense industries, above, and race riots took place in several cities. After the war the government increased its interest in the Negro's plight. In 1947 President Harry S. Truman's Committee on Civil Rights issued a report outlining discrimination in several areas of American life. President Truman ordered the federal government to establish fair employment practices within its own ranks and formed a special committee to force compliance with nondiscriminatory federal contracts.

LIBRARY OF CONGRESS

Negroes have gained prominence in two fields above all others: sports and entertainment. In both fields, black stars won considerable fame and wealth but had to face problems that their white counterparts never encountered. Unlike white athletes, Negroes traditionally have had to lead circumspect private lives, endure racial slurs without bristling, and steer clear of civil rights issues and political controversy. Even if they followed all these directives they often encountered discrimination off the field and awkwardness and even hostility from their own teammates. The first world-famous American Negro athlete was Jack Johnson, above, who won the heavyweight boxing title in 1908. A fine boxer and a flamboyant personality, Johnson enraged the white public by easily beating all white challengers and appearing in public with a white wife. Boxing promoters frantically searched for a "White Hope" to strip him of his crown; newsreels of his victories were withdrawn from circulation to avoid race riots, and Johnson himself was finally hounded from the country.

WIDE WORLD

Jackie Robinson, here shown stealing home, joined the Brooklyn Dodgers in 1947 to become the first black major league baseball player. By the late 1960s, about one quarter of all major leaguers were black.

WIDE WORLD

Bill Russell of the Boston Celtics became the first black coach of a professional team in any major American sport in 1967. Russell, and many other young black athletes, are no longer afraid to speak out on current issues.

Joe Louis, shown here knocking out Germany's Max Schmeling, won the heavyweight boxing title in 1937 and held it longer than any other man.

WIDE WORLD

COLUMBIA PICTURES

Show business allowed some talented Negroes to achieve fame and fortune they could not have gained in other fields. But until very recently they had to pay a heavy price for their success. Unless they were willing to play only to comparatively small Negro audiences they had to pander to the white audience's fantasy of what Negroes were like. Bert Williams, above, a gifted black comedian, was not black enough to suit his public, and had to wear blackface to make up for this deficiency. Modern black artists are increasingly able to play roles that portray a more realistic picture of the Negro world. At left is Sidney Poitier with Ruby Dee, Diana Sands, and Claudia McNeil in a scene from A Raisin in the Sun. The screenplay, drawn from her play of the same name, was written by Lorraine Hansberry.

In 1947, President Truman ordered the armed forces to desegregate, and in the Korean War black and white soldiers fought side by side in integrated units for the first time since the War of 1812. Many young Negroes found service life attractive, since promotions were generally based on merit rather than color. Negroes also fought in Vietnam, where they suffered a disproportionately high share of casualties.

Does this history have any meaning for the American Negro? This is the question that Jews and Japanese, Irish and Italians, Poles and Czechs ask themselves. Some new immigrant groups— Puerto Ricans and Mexicans—think it does have a meaning for them. They try to model their institutions on those of earlier immigrant groups. They show the same uncertainties and confusions over what to do with the culture and language they have brought with them.

The militant Negro and his white allies passionately deny the relevance or even the truth of this history. It is white history; as white history it is also the history of the exploitation of the Negro, of the creation of privilege on the basis of his unpaid and forced labor. It is not history he can accept as having any meaning for him. His fate, he insists, has been far more drastic and frightful than any other, and neither Irish famines nor Jewish pogroms make the members of these groups brothers in understanding. The hatred with which he is looked upon by whites, he believes, has nothing in common with the petty prejudices that European immigrant groups have met. And the America of today, in which he makes his great and desperate effort for full equality, he asserts, has little in common with the America of mass immigration.

A subtle intervention of government in every aspect of social life, of economy, of culture, he insists, is necessary now to create justice. Every practice must now be scrutinized anew for its impact on this totally unique and incomparable group in American life. The neighborhood school, the civil service system, the personnel procedures of our corporations, the practices of small business, the scholarship systems of our states, the composition and character of our churches, the structure of neighborhood organization, the practices of unions—all, confronted with this shibboleth, fail. The Negro has not received his due, and the essence of all of them is therefore discrimination and exclusion, and the defense of privilege. It is no wonder that ethnic self-consciousness, after its brief moment of triumph, after its legitimization in American life, now turns upon itself in confusion. After all, it is these voluntary churches, organizations, hospitals, schools, and businesses that have become the pride of ethnic groups and the seat of whatever distinctiveness they possess. It is by way of this participation that they have become part of the very fabric of American life. But the fabric is now challenged. And looked at from another perspective, the Negro perspective, the same structure that defends some measure of uniqueness by the same token defends some measure of discrimination and exclusion.

It is impossible for the ethnic groups in America, who have already moved through so many protean forms, to be unaffected by the civil rights revolution. For this raises the question of the status of the largest of American minority groups, the one most closely bound up with American history from its very beginnings. Chinese and Japanese, perhaps Puerto Ricans and Mexican-Americans can accept the patterns of development and gradual assimilation into American society that are exhibited in the history of the great European immigrant groups. For a while, some of us who studied this history and saw in its variety and flexibility some virtues for a mass, industrial society, which suppresses variety and flexibility in so many areas, hoped that the American Negro, as he entered the more open environments of Northern cities, could also move along the paths the European immigrant groups had followed.

We now wonder whether this hope was illusory. Whether it was the infection of Europeans with the virus of American racial prejudice; or the inability to confine the direct and violent conflict in the South; or the impact of slavery and Southern experience on the American Negro—it is clear, whatever the causes, that for one of the major groups in American life, the idea of pluralism, which has supported the various developments of other groups, has become a mockery. Whatever concrete definition we give to pluralism, it means a limitation of government power, a relatively free hand for private and voluntary organizations to develop their own patterns of worship, education, social life, residential concentration, and even their distinctive economic activity. All of these inevitably enhance the life of one group; from the perspective of the American Negro they are inevitably exclusive and discriminatory.

The general ideas that have justified the development of the ethnic group in America have never been too well explicated. We have tended to obscure the inevitable conflicts between individual group interest and national interest, even when they have occurred, rather than set down sharp principles to regulate the ethnic groups.

214

If an ethnic group interest clashed with a national interest, we have been quite ruthless and even extreme in overriding the group interest. Thus two world wars radically diminished the scale and assertiveness of German-American group life. But we have never fully developed what is permitted and what is not. Now a new national interest is becoming defined — the final liquidation of Negro separation, in all areas of our life: the economic, the social, the cultural, the residential.

In every area, Negro separation, regardless of its causes, is seen as unbearable by Negroes. Inevitably this must deeply mark the future development of American ethnic groups, whose continuance contributes, in some measure, to this separation. Recently in this country there has been a positive attitude to ethnic distinctiveness. Oscar Handlin and others have argued that it does not divide the nation or weaken it in war; rather it helps integrate the immigrant groups and adds a rich strand of variety to American civilization. Now a new question arises: What is its effect on the Negro?

Perhaps, ironically, the final homogenization of the American people, the creation of a common nationality replacing all other forms of national connection, will now come about because of the need to guarantee the integration of the Negro. But I believe the group character of American life is too strongly established and fits too many individual needs to be so completely suppressed. Is it not more likely that as Negro demands are in varying measure met, the Negro too will accept the virtues of our complex society, in which separation is neither forbidden nor required, but rather tolerated? Perhaps the American Negro will become another ethnic group, accepted by others and accepting himself.

MALCOLM X
Address to Mississippi Youth

Malcolm Little adopted the name Malcolm X after his conversion to the Black Muslims (the Nation of Islam) in 1952. He devoted all of his efforts to the Muslims, lending his not inconsiderable talent as a speaker to firing the spirit of protest and black nationalism that swept American Negroes after World War II. Before he left the movement in March 1964 to organize the Muslim Mosque, Inc., and later the Organization of Afro-American Unity, he had achieved a prominence second only to Elijah Muhammad. Malcolm X was assassinated in New York on February 21, 1965. The following selection is taken from an address of December 31, 1964, to thirty-seven teenagers from McComb, Mississippi, who had come to New York under the auspices of the Student Nonviolent Coordinating Committee. [Source: Malcolm X Speaks, New York, 1966, pp. 137-146.]

One of the first things I think young people, especially nowadays, should learn is how to see for yourself and listen for yourself and think for yourself. Then you can come to an intelligent decision for yourself. If you form the habit of going by what you hear others say about someone, or going by what others think about someone, instead of searching that thing out for yourself and seeing for yourself, you will be walking west when you think you're going east, and you will be walking east when you think you're going west. This generation, especially of our people, has a burden, more so than any other time in history. The most important thing that we can learn to do today is think for ourselves.

It's good to keep wide-open ears and listen to what everybody else has to say, but when you come to make a decision, you have to weigh all of what you've heard on its own, and place it where it belongs, and come to a decision for yourself; you'll never regret it. But if you form the habit of taking what someone else says about a thing without checking it out for yourself, you'll find that other people will have you hating your friends and loving your enemies. This is one of the things that our people are beginning to learn today—that it is very important to think out a situation for yourself. If you don't do it, you'll always be maneuvered into a situation where you are never fighting your actual enemies, where you will find yourself fighting your own self.

I think our people in this country are the best examples of that. Many of us want to be nonviolent and we talk very loudly, you know, about being nonviolent. Here in Harlem, where there are probably more black people concentrated than any place in the world, some talk that nonviolent talk too. But we find that they aren't nonviolent with each other. You can go out to Harlem Hospital, where there are more black patients than any hospital in the world, and see them going in there all cut up and shot up and busted up where they got violent with each other.

My experience has been that in many instances where you find Negroes talking about nonviolence, they are not nonviolent with each other, and they're not loving with each other, or forgiving with each other. Usually when they say they're nonviolent, they mean they're nonviolent with somebody else. I think you understand what I mean. They are nonviolent with the enemy. A person can come to your home, and if he's white and wants to heap some kind of brutality on you, you're nonviolent; or he can come to take your father and put a rope around his neck, and you're nonviolent. But if another Negro just stomps his foot, you'll rumble with him in a minute. Which shows you that there's an inconsistency there.

I myself would go for nonviolence if it was consistent, if everybody was going to be nonviolent all the time. I'd say, okay, let's get with it, we'll all be nonviolent. But I don't go along with any kind of nonviolence unless everybody's going to be nonviolent. If they make the Ku Klux Klan nonviolent, I'll be nonviolent. If they make the White Citizens Council nonviolent, I'll be nonviolent. But as long as you've got somebody else not being nonviolent, I don't want anybody coming to me talking any nonviolent talk. I don't think it is fair to tell our people to be nonviolent unless someone is out there making the Klan and the Citizens Council and these other groups also be nonviolent.

Now, I'm not criticizing those here who are nonviolent. I think everybody should do it the way they feel is best, and I congratulate anybody who can be nonviolent in the face of all that kind of action in that part of the world. I don't think that in 1965 you will find the upcoming generation of our people, especially those who have been

217

doing some thinking, who will go along with any form of non-violence unless nonviolence is going to be practiced all the way around.

If the leaders of the nonviolent movement can go into the white community and teach nonviolence, good. I'd go along with that. But as long as I see them teaching nonviolence only in the black community, we can't go along with that. We believe in equality, and equality means that you have to put the same thing over here that you put over there. And if black people alone are going to be the ones who are nonviolent, then it's not fair. We throw ourselves off guard. In fact, we disarm ourselves and make ourselves defenseless. . . .

The Organization of Afro-American Unity is a non-religious group of black people who believe that the problems confronting our people in this country need to be re-analyzed and a new approach devised toward trying to get a solution. Studying the problem, we recall that prior to 1939 all of our people, in the North, South, East and West, no matter how much education we had, were segregated. We were segregated in the North just as much as we were segregated in the South. Even now there's as much segregation in the North as there is in the South. There's some worse segregation right here in New York City than there is in McComb, Mississippi; but up here they're subtle and tricky and deceitful, and they make you think you've got it made when you haven't even begun to make it yet.

Prior to 1939, our people were in a very menial position or condition. Most of us were waiters and porters and bellhops and janitors and waitresses and things of that sort. It was not until war was declared with Germany, and America became involved in a man-power shortage in regards to her factories plus her army, that the black man in this country was permitted to make a few strides forward. It was never out of some kind of moral enlightenment or moral awareness on the part of Uncle Sam. Uncle Sam only let the black man take a step forward when he himself had his back to the wall.

In Michigan, where I was brought up at that time, I recall that the best jobs in the city for blacks were waiters out at the country club. In those days if you had a job waiting table in the country club, you had it made. Or if you had a job at the State House. Having a job at the State House didn't mean that you were a clerk or something of that sort; you had a shoeshine stand at the State House. Just by being there you could be around all those big-shot politicians —that made you a big-shot Negro. You were shining shoes, but you were a big-shot Negro because you were around big-shot white people and you could bend their ear and get up next to them. And ofttimes you were chosen by them to be the voice of the Negro community.

Around that time, 1939 or '40 or '41, they weren't drafting Negroes in the army or the navy. A Negro couldn't join the navy in 1940 or '41. They wouldn't take a black man in the navy except to make him a cook. He couldn't just go and join the navy, and I don't think he could just go and join the army. They weren't drafting him when the war first started. This is what they thought of you and me in those days. For one thing, they didn't trust us; they feared that if they put us in the army and trained us in how to use rifles and other things, we might shoot at some targets that they hadn't picked out. And we would have. Any thinking man knows what target to shoot at. If a man has to have someone else to choose his target, then he isn't thinking for himself—they're doing the thinking for him.

The Negro leaders in those days were the same type we have today. When the Negro leaders saw all the white fellows being drafted and taken into the army and dying on the battlefield, and no Negroes were dying because they weren't being drafted, the Negro leaders came up and said, "We've got to die too. We want to be drafted too, and we demand that you take us in there and let us die for our country too." That was what the Negro leaders did back in 1940, I remember. A. Philip Randolph was one of the leading Negroes in those days who said it, and he's one of the Big Six right now; and this is why he's one of the Big Six.

So they started drafting Negro soldiers then, and started letting Negroes get into the navy. But not until Hitler and Tojo and the foreign powers were strong enough to put pressure on this country, so that it had its back to the wall and needed us, [did] they let us work in factories. Up until that time we couldn't work in the factories; I'm talking about the North as well as the South. And when they let us work in the factories, at first they let us in only as janitors. After a year or so passed by, they let us work on machines. We became machinists, got a little more skill. If we got a little more skill, we made a little more money, which enabled us to live in a little better neighborhood. When we lived in a little better neighborhood, we went to a little better school, got a little better education and could come out and get a little better job. So the cycle was broken somewhat.

But the cycle was not broken out of some kind of sense of moral responsibility on the part of the government. No, the only time that cycle was broken even to a degree was when world pressure was brought to bear on the United States government. They didn't look at us as human beings – they just put us into their system and let us advance a little bit farther because it served their interests. They never let us advance a little bit farther because they were interested in us as human beings. Any of you who have a knowledge of history, sociology, or political science, or the economic development of this country and its race relations – go back and do some research on it and you'll have to admit that this is true.

It was during the time that Hitler and Tojo made war with this country and put pressure on it [that] Negroes in this country advanced a little bit. At the end of the war with Germany and Japan, then Joe Stalin and Communist Russia were a threat. During that period we made a little more headway. Now the point that I'm making is this: Never at any time in the history of our people in this country have we made advances or progress in any way based upon the internal good will of this country. We have made advancement in this country only when this country was under pressure from forces above and beyond its control. The internal moral consciousness of this country is bankrupt. It hasn't existed since they first brought us over here and made slaves out of us. They make it appear they have our good interests at heart, but when you study it, every time, no matter how many steps they take us forward, it's like we're standing on a – what do you call that thing? – a treadmill. The treadmill is moving backwards faster than we're able to go forward in this direction. We're not even standing still – we're going backwards.

In studying the process of this so-called progress during the past twenty years, we of the Organization of Afro-American Unity realized that the only time the black man in this country is given any kind of recognition, or even listened to, is when America is afraid of outside pressure, or when she's afraid of her image abroad. So we saw that it was necessary to expand the problem and the struggle of the black man in this country until it went above and beyond the jurisdiction of the United States. . . .

I was fortunate enough to be able to take a tour of the African continent during the summer. I went to Egypt, then to Arabia, Kuwait, Lebanon, Sudan, Ethiopia, Kenya, Tanganyika, Zanzibar, Nigeria, Ghana, Guinea, Liberia and Algeria. I found, while I was traveling on the African continent, I had already detected it in May, that someone had very shrewdly planted the seed of division on this continent to make the Africans not show genuine concern with our problem, just as they plant seeds in your and my minds so that we won't show concern with the African problem. . . .

I also found that in many of these African countries the head of state is genuinely concerned with the problem of the black man in this country; but many of them thought if they opened their mouths and voiced their concern that they would be insulted by the American Negro leaders. Because one head of state in Asia voiced his support of the civil-rights struggle [in 1963] and a couple of the Big Six had the audacity to slap his face and say they weren't interested in that kind of help — which in my opinion is asinine. So the African leaders only had to be convinced that if they took an open stand at the governmental level and showed interest in the problem of black people in this country, they wouldn't be rebuffed.

And today you'll find in the United Nations, and it's not an accident, that every time the Congo question or anything on the African continent is being debated, they couple it with what is going on, or what is happening to you and me, in Mississippi and Alabama and these other places. In my opinion, the greatest accomplishment that was made in the struggle of the black man in America in 1964 toward some kind of real progress was the successful linking together of our problem with the African problem, or making our problem a world problem. Because now, whenever anything happens to you in Mississippi, it's not just a case of somebody in Alabama getting indignant, or somebody in New York getting indignant. The same repercussions that you see all over the world when an imperialist or foreign power interferes in some section of Africa — you see

221

repercussions, you see the embassies being bombed and burned and overturned—nowadays, when something happens to black people in Mississippi, you'll see the same repercussions all over the world.

I wanted to point this out to you because it is important for you to know that when you're in Mississippi, you're not alone. As long as you think you're alone, then you take a stand as if you're a minority or as if you're outnumbered, and that kind of stand will never enable you to win a battle. You've got to know that you've got as much power on your side as that Ku Klux Klan has on its side. And when you know that you've got as much power on your side as the Klan has on its side, you'll talk the same kind of language with that Klan as the Klan is talking with you. . . .

I think in 1965, whether you like it, or I like it, or they like it, or not, you will see that there is a generation of black people becoming mature to the point where they feel that they have no more business being asked to take a peaceful approach than anybody else takes, unless everybody's going to take a peaceful approach.

So we here in the Organization of Afro-American Unity are with the struggle in Mississippi one thousand per cent. We're with the efforts to register our people in Mississippi to vote one thousand per cent. But we do not go along with anybody telling us to help non-violently. We think that if the government says that Negroes have a right to vote, and then some Negroes come out to vote, and some kind of Ku Klux Klan is going to put them in the river, and the government doesn't do anything about it, it's time for us to organize and band together and equip ourselves and qualify ourselves to protect ourselves. And once you can protect yourself, you don't have to worry about being hurt. . . .

If you don't have enough people down there to do it, we'll come down there and help you do it. Because we're tired of this old run-around that our people have been given in this country. For a long time they accused me of not getting involved in politics. They should've been glad I didn't get involved in politics, because anything I get in, I'm in it all the way. If they say we don't take part in the Mississippi struggle, we will organize brothers here in New York who know how to handle these kind of affairs, and they'll slip into Mississippi like Jesus slipped into Jerusalem.

That doesn't mean we're against white people, but we sure are against the Ku Klux Klan and the White Citizens Councils; and anything that looks like it's against us, we're against it. Excuse me for raising my voice, but this thing, you know, gets me upset. Imagine that—a country that's supposed to be a democracy, supposed to be for freedom and all of that kind of stuff when they want to draft you and put you in the army and send you to Saigon to fight for them—and then you've got to turn around and all night long discuss how you're going to just get a right to register and vote without being murdered. Why, that's the most hypocritical government since the world began! . . .

I hope you don't think I'm trying to incite you. Just look here: Look at yourselves. Some of you are teen-agers, students. How do you think I feel—and I belong to a generation ahead of you—how do you think I feel to have to tell you, "We, my generation, sat around like a knot on a wall while the whole world was fighting for its human rights—and you've got to be born into a society where you still have that same fight." What did we do, who preceded you? I'll tell you what we did: Nothing. And don't you make the same mistake we made. . . .

You get freedom by letting your enemy know that you'll do anything to get your freedom; then you'll get it. It's the only way you'll get it. When you get that kind of attitude, they'll label you as a "crazy Negro," or they'll call you a "crazy nigger"—they don't say Negro. Or they'll call you an extremist or a subversive, or seditious, or a red or a radical. But when you stay radical long enough, and get enough people to be like you, you'll get your freedom. . . .

So don't you run around here trying to make friends with somebody who's depriving you of your rights. They're not your friends, no, they're your enemies. Treat them like that and fight them, and you'll get your freedom; and after you get your freedom, your enemy will respect you. And we'll respect you. And I say that with no hate. I don't have hate in me. I have no hate at all. I don't have any hate. I've got some sense. I'm not going to let somebody who hates me tell me to love him. I'm not that wayout. And you, young as you are, and because you start thinking, you're not going to do it either. The only time you're going to get in that bag is if somebody puts you there. Somebody else, who doesn't have your welfare at heart. . . .

I want to thank all of you for taking the time to come to Harlem and especially here. I hope that you've gotten a better understanding about me. I put it to you just as plain as I know how to put it; there's no interpretation necessary. And I want you to know that we're not in any way trying to advocate any kind of indiscriminate, unintelligent action. Any kind of action that you are ever involved in that's designed to protect the lives and property of our mistreated people in this country, we're with you one thousand per cent. And if you don't feel you're qualified to do it, we have some brothers who will slip in, as I said earlier, and help train you and show you how to equip yourself and let you know how to deal with the man who deals with you. . . .

MARTIN LUTHER KING, JR.

I Have a Dream

In Washington, D.C., on August 28, 1963, more than 200,000 persons participated in a "march for jobs and freedom" at the Lincoln Memorial — one hundred years and eight months after the Emancipation Proclamation. The march was intended to prod Congress to deal at last with the issues of civil rights and poverty. The ten speakers included Eugene Carson Blake, Walter Reuther, A. Philip Randolph, Roy Wilkins, Floyd McKissick (who delivered James Farmer's address), and Whitney M. Young, Jr. But it was generally conceded that Martin Luther King, Jr., president of the Southern Christian Leadership Conference, most effectively articulated the meaning of the great demonstration in the speech reprinted below. James Reston of the New York Times *described King's speech as "a peroration that was an anguished echo from all the old American reformers, Roger Williams calling for religious liberty, Sam Adams calling for political liberty, old man Thoreau denouncing coercion, William Lloyd Garrison demanding emancipation, and Eugene V. Debs crying for economic equality — Dr. King echoed them all. . . . He was full of the symbolism of Lincoln and Gandhi, and of the cadences of the Bible." King's closing words were inscribed on his tombstone. [Source:* The SCLC Story in Words and Pictures, *Atlanta, 1964, pp. 50-51.]*

Five score years ago, a great American, in whose symbolic shadow we stand, signed the Emancipation Proclamation. This momentous decree came as a great beacon light of hope to millions of Negro slaves who had been seared in the flames of withering injustice. It came as a joyous daybreak to end the long night of captivity.

But one hundred years later, we must face the tragic fact that the Negro is still not free. One hundred years later, the life of the Negro is still sadly crippled by the manacles of segregation and the chains of discrimination. One hundred years later, the Negro lives on a lonely island of poverty in the midst of a vast ocean of material prosperity. One hundred years later, the Negro is still languished in the corners of American society and finds himself an exile in his own land. So we have come here today to dramatize an appalling condition.

In a sense we have come to our nation's Capital to cash a check. When the architects of our republic wrote the magnificent words of the Constitution and the Declaration of Independence, they were signing a promissory note to which every American was to fall heir. This note was a promise that all men would be guaranteed the unalienable rights of life, liberty, and the pursuit of happiness.

It is obvious today that America has defaulted on this promissory note insofar as her citizens of color are concerned. Instead of honoring this sacred obligation, America has given the Negro people a bad check; a check which has come back marked "Insufficient funds." But we refuse to believe that the bank of justice is bankrupt. We refuse to believe that there are insufficient funds in the great vaults of opportunity of this nation. So we have come to cash this check—a check that will give us upon demand the riches of freedom and the security of justice.

We have also come to this hallowed spot to remind America of the fierce urgency of *now*. This is no time to engage in the luxury of cooling off or to take the tranquilizing drug of gradualism. *Now* is the time to make real the promises of democracy. *Now* is the time to rise from the dark and desolate valley of segregation to the sunlit path of racial justice. *Now* is the time to open the doors of opportunity to all of God's children. *Now* is the time to lift our nation from the quicksands of racial injustice to the solid rock of brotherhood.

It would be fatal for the nation to overlook the urgency of the moment and to underestimate the determination of the Negro. This

225

sweltering summer of the Negro's legitimate discontent will not pass until there is an invigorating autumn of freedom and equality. Nineteen sixty-three is not an end, but a beginning. Those who hope that the Negro needed to blow off steam and will now be content will have a rude awakening if the nation returns to business as usual. There will be neither rest nor tranquillity in America until the Negro is granted his citizenship rights. The whirlwinds of revolt will continue to shake the foundations of our nation until the bright day of justice emerges.

But there is something that I must say to my people who stand on the warm threshold which leads into the palace of justice. In the process of gaining our rightful place we must not be guilty of wrongful deeds. Let us not seek to satisfy our thirst for freedom by drinking from the cup of bitterness and hatred. We must forever conduct our struggle on the high plane of dignity and discipline. We must not allow our creative protest to degenerate into physical violence. Again and again we must rise to the majestic heights of meeting physical force with soul force.

The marvelous new militancy which has engulfed the Negro community must not lead us to a distrust of all white people, for many of our white brothers, as evidenced by their presence here today, have come to realize that their destiny is tied up with our destiny and their freedom is inextricably bound to our freedom. We cannot walk alone.

And as we walk, we must make the pledge that we shall march ahead. We cannot turn back. There are those who are asking the devotees of civil rights, "When will you be satisfied?"

We can never be satisfied as long as the Negro is the victim of the unspeakable horrors of police brutality.

We can never be satisfied as long as our bodies, heavy with the fatigue of travel, cannot gain lodging in the motels of the highways and the hotels of the cities.

We cannot be satisfied as long as the Negro's basic mobility is from a smaller ghetto to a larger one.

We can never be satisfied as long as a Negro in Mississippi cannot vote and a Negro in New York believes he has nothing for which to vote.

No, no, we are not satisfied, and we will not be satisfied until

226

justice rolls down like waters and righteousness like a mighty stream.

I am not unmindful that some of you have come here out of great trials and tribulations. Some of you have come fresh from narrow jail cells. Some of you have come from areas where your quest for freedom left you battered by the storms of persecution and staggered by the winds of police brutality. You have been the veterans of creative suffering. Continue to work with the faith that unearned suffering is redemptive.

Go back to Mississippi, go back to Alabama, go back to South Carolina, go back to Georgia, go back to Louisiana, go back to the slums and ghettos of our Northern cities, knowing that somehow this situation can and will be changed. Let us not wallow in the valley of despair.

I say to you today, my friends, that in spite of the difficulties and frustrations of the moment I still have a dream. It is a dream deeply rooted in the American dream.

I have a dream that one day this nation will rise up and live out the true meaning of its creed: "We hold these truths to be self-evident; that all men are created equal."

I have a dream that one day on the red hills of Georgia the sons of former slaves and the sons of former slaveowners will be able to sit down together at the table of brotherhood.

I have a dream that one day even the state of Mississippi, a desert state sweltering with the heat of injustice and oppression, will be transformed into an oasis of freedom and justice.

I have a dream that my four little children will one day live in a nation where they will not be judged by the color of their skin but by the content of their character.

I have a dream today.

I have a dream that one day the state of Alabama, whose governor's lips are presently dripping with the words of interposition and nullification, will be transformed into a situation where little black boys and black girls will be able to join hands with little white boys and white girls and walk together as sisters and brothers.

I have a dream today.

I have a dream that one day every valley shall be exalted, every hill and mountain shall be made low, the rough places will be made plain, and the crooked places will be made straight, and the glory of the Lord shall be revealed, and all flesh shall see it together.

This is our hope. This is the faith with which I return to the South. With this faith we will be able to hew out of the mountain of despair a stone of hope. With this faith we will be able to transform the jangling discords of our nation into a beautiful symphony of brotherhood.

With this faith we will be able to work together, to pray together, to struggle together, to go to jail together, to stand up for freedom together, knowing that we will be free one day.

This will be the day when all of God's children will be able to sing with new meaning, "My country 'tis of thee, sweet land of liberty, of thee I sing. Land where my fathers died, land of the Pilgrims' pride, from every mountainside, let freedom ring."

And if America is to be a great nation, this must become true. So let freedom ring from the prodigious hilltops of New Hampshire. Let freedom ring from the mighty mountains of New York. Let freedom ring from the heightening Alleghenies of Pennsylvania!

Let freedom ring from the snowcapped Rockies of Colorado! Let freedom ring from the curvaceous peaks of California! But not only that; let freedom ring from Stone Mountain of Georgia! Let freedom ring from Lookout Mountain of Tennessee!

Let freedom ring from every hill and molehill of Mississippi. From every mountainside, let freedom ring.

When we let freedom ring, when we let it ring from every village and every hamlet, from every state and every city, we will be able to speed up that day when all of God's children, black men and white men, Jews and Gentiles, Protestants and Catholics, will be able to join hands and sing in the words of the old Negro spiritual, "Free at last! Free at last! Thank God Almighty, we are free at last!"

JOHN F. KENNEDY
The Negro and the American Promise

On June 11, 1963, a momentous event occurred at the University of Alabama. Two Negro residents of Alabama, who were clearly qualified for studies at the state's highest institution of learning, had been refused admittance on the grounds of their color. They had appealed this refusal to a federal court, which had demanded that they be admitted. Governor George Wallace promised to "stand in the schoolhouse door" to keep them out, but at the last moment he stepped aside as the two young Negroes, protected by federal guardsmen, entered. That night President Kennedy discussed the Alabama situation in a radio and television address to the American people, in the course of which he declared that the issue of the Negro's position in American life was no longer merely economic and political, but also moral. [Source, Congressional Record, 88 Cong., 1 Sess., pp. 10965-10966.]

This afternoon, following a series of threats and defiant statements, the presence of Alabama National Guardsmen was required on the University of Alabama to carry out the final and unequivocal order of the U.S. District Court of the Northern District of Alabama. That order called for the admission of two clearly qualified young Alabama residents who happened to have been born Negro.

That they were admitted peacefully on the campus is due in good measure to the conduct of the students of the University of Alabama, who met their responsibilities in a constructive way.

I hope that every American, regardless of where he lives, will stop and examine his conscience about this and other related incidents. This nation was founded by men of many nations and backgrounds. It was founded on the principle that all men are created equal and that the rights of every man are diminished when the rights of one man are threatened.

Today we are committed to a worldwide struggle to promote and protect the rights of all who wish to be free, and when Americans are sent to Vietnam or West Berlin, we do not ask for whites only. It ought to be possible, therefore, for American students of any color to attend any public institution they select without having to be backed up by troops.

It ought to be possible for American consumers of any color to receive equal service in places of public accommodation, such as hotels and restaurants and theaters and retail stores, without being forced to resort to demonstrations in the street; and it ought to be possible for American citizens of any color to register and to vote in a free election without interference or fear of reprisal.

It ought to be possible, in short, for every American to enjoy the privileges of being American without regard to his race or his color. In short, every American ought to have the right to be treated as he would wish to be treated, as one would wish his children to be treated. But this is not the case.

The Negro baby born in America today, regardless of the section of the nation in which he is born, has about one-half as much chance of completing high school as a white baby born in the same place on the same day, one-third as much chance of completing college, one-third as much chance of becoming a professional man, twice as much chance of becoming unemployed, about one-seventh as much chance of earning $10,000 a year, a life expectancy which is seven years shorter, and the prospects of earning only half as much.

This is not a sectional issue. Difficulties over segregation and discrimination exist in every city in every state of the Union, producing in many cities a rising tide of discontent that threatens the public safety. Nor is this a partisan issue in a time of domestic crisis. Men of goodwill and generosity should be able to unite regardless of party or politics. This is not even a legal or legislative issue alone. It is better to settle these matters in the courts than on the streets, and new laws are needed at every level, but law alone cannot make men see right.

We are confronted primarily with a moral issue. It is as old as the Scriptures and is as clear as the American Constitution.

The heart of the question is whether all Americans are to be afforded equal rights and equal opportunities, whether we are going to treat our fellow Americans as we want to be treated. If an American, because his skin is dark, cannot eat lunch in a restaurant open to the public, if he cannot send his children to the best public school available, if he cannot vote for the public officials who represent him, if, in short, he cannot enjoy the full and free life which all of us

230

want, then who among us would be content to have the color of his skin changed and stand in his place? Who among us would then be content with the counsels of patience and delay?

One hundred years of delay have passed since President Lincoln freed the slaves, yet their heirs, their grandsons, are not fully free. They are not yet freed from the bonds of injustice. They are not yet freed from social and economic oppression, and this nation, for all its hopes and all its boasts, will not be fully free until all its citizens are free.

We preach freedom around the world, and we mean it, and we cherish our freedom here at home; but are we to say to the world, and much more importantly, to each other that this is a land of the free except for the Negroes; that we have no second-class citizens except Negroes; that we have no class or caste system, no ghettoes, no master race except with respect to Negroes?

Now the time has come for this nation to fulfill its promise. The events in Birmingham and elsewhere have so increased the cries for equality that no city or state or legislative body can prudently choose to ignore them. The fires of frustration and discord are burning in every city, North and South, where legal remedies are not at hand. Redress is sought in the streets, in demonstrations, parades, and protests, which create tensions and threaten violence and threaten lives.

We face, therefore, a moral crisis as a country and as a people. It cannot be met by repressive police action. It cannot be left to increased demonstrations in the streets. It cannot be quieted by token moves or talk. It is a time to act in the Congress, in your state and local legislative body and, above all, in all of our daily lives.

It is not enough to pin the blame on others, to say this is a problem of one section of the country or another, or deplore the fact that we face. A great change is at hand, and our task, our obligation, is to make that revolution, that change, peaceful and constructive for all. Those who do nothing are inviting shame as well as violence. Those who act boldly are recognizing right as well as reality.

Next week I shall ask the Congress of the United States to act, to make a commitment it has not fully made in this century to the proposition that race has no place in American life or law. The federal judiciary has upheld that proposition in a series of forthright

231

cases. The executive branch has adopted that proposition in the conduct of its affairs, including the employment of federal personnel, the use of federal facilities, and the sale of federally financed housing.

But there are other necessary measures which only the Congress can provide, and they must be provided at this session. The old code of equity law under which we live commands for every wrong a remedy, but in too many communities, in too many parts of the country, wrongs are inflicted on Negro citizens as there are no remedies at law. Unless the Congress acts, their only remedy is in the street.

I am therefore asking the Congress to enact legislation giving all Americans the right to be served in facilities which are open to the public—hotels, restaurants, theaters, retail stores, and similar establishments. This seems to me to be an elementary right. Its denial is an arbitrary indignity that no American in 1963 should have to endure, but many do.

I have recently met with scores of business leaders urging them to take voluntary action to end this discrimination and I have been encouraged by their response; and in the last two weeks over seventy-five cities have seen progress made in desegregating these kinds of facilities. But many are unwilling to act alone, and for this reason nationwide legislation is needed if we are to move this problem from the streets to the courts.

I am also asking Congress to authorize the federal government to participate more fully in lawsuits designed to end segregation in public education. We have succeeded in persuading many districts to desegregate voluntarily. Dozens have admitted Negroes without violence. Today a Negro is attending a state-supported institution in every one of our fifty states, but the pace is very slow.

Too many Negro children entering segregated grade schools at the time of the Supreme Court's decision nine years ago will enter segregated high schools this fall, having suffered a loss which can never be restored. The lack of an adequate education denies the Negro a chance to get a decent job. The orderly implementation of the Supreme Court decision, therefore, cannot be left solely to those who may not have the economic resources to carry the legal action or who may be subject to harassment.

Other features will be also requested, including greater protection for the right to vote. But legislation, I repeat, cannot solve this problem alone. It must be solved in the homes of every American in every community across our country.

In this respect, I want to pay tribute to those citizens North and South who have been working in their communities to make life better for all. They are acting not out of a sense of legal duty but out of a sense of human decency. Like our soldiers and sailors in all parts of the world, they are meeting freedom's challenge on the firing line, and I salute them for their honor and their courage.

My fellow Americans, this is a problem which faces us all—in every city of the North as well as the South. Today there are Negroes unemployed two or three times as many compared to whites, inadequate in education, moving into the large cities, unable to find work, young people particularly out of work without hope, denied equal rights, denied the opportunity to eat at a restaurant or lunch counter or go to a movie theater, denied the right to a decent education, denied almost today the right to attend a state university even though qualified. It seems to me that these are matters which concern us all, not merely Presidents or congressmen or governors, but every citizen of the United States.

This is one country. It has become one country because all of us and all the people who came here had an equal chance to develop their talents. We cannot say to ten percent of the population that you can't have that right; that your children can't have the chance to develop whatever talents they have; that the only way that they are going to get their rights is to go into the streets and demonstrate. I think we owe them and we owe ourselves a better country than that. Therefore, I am asking for your help in making it easier for us to move ahead and to provide the kind of equality of treatment which we would want ourselves; to give a chance for every child to be educated to the limit of his talents.

As I have said before, not every child has an equal talent or an equal ability or an equal motivation, but they should have the equal right to develop their talent and their ability and their motivation to make something of themselves. We have a right to expect that the Negro community will be responsible, will uphold the law, but they have a right to expect that the law will be fair; that the Constitution

233

will be color blind, as Justice Harlan said at the turn of the century.

This is what we are talking about and this is a matter which concerns this country and what it stands for, and in meeting it I ask the support of all of our citizens.

JAMES BALDWIN

My Dungeon Shook

The 100th anniversary of the Emancipation Proclamation was ambiguously observed in the United States. Some Negroes and many whites marked the date—January 1, 1963—as of vast importance in American history, and paid homage to the men—mainly one man, Abraham Lincoln—who a century before had stated officially, and for the first time, that slavery was not only immoral but also illegal. Others were not in a celebrating mood. One of them was the noted Negro novelist James Baldwin, who may have summed up the feelings of a large number of Americans, both white and black, in the remark: "You know, and I know, that the country is celebrating one hundred years of freedom one hundred years too soon." The remark closed a letter that Baldwin wrote to his nephew and published in December 1962. The letter, slightly revised, appeared in a collection of essays published the following year. [Source: The Fire Next Time, *New York, 1963.]*

Dear James:

I have begun this letter five times and torn it up five times. I keep seeing your face, which is also the face of your father and my brother. Like him, you are tough, dark, vulnerable, moody—with a very definite tendency to sound truculent because you want no one to think you are soft. You may be like your grandfather in this, I don't know, but certainly both you and your father resemble him very much physically. Well, he is dead, he never saw you, and he had a terrible life; he was defeated long before he died because, at the bottom of his heart, he really believed what white people said about him. This is one of the reasons that he became so holy. I am sure

234

that your father has told you something about all that. Neither you nor your father exhibit any tendency towards holiness: you really *are* of another era, part of what happened when the Negro left the land and came into what the late E. Franklin Frazier called "the cities of destruction." You can only be destroyed by believing that you really are what the white world calls a *nigger*. I tell you this because I love you, and please don't you ever forget it.

I have known both of you all your lives, have carried your Daddy in my arms and on my shoulders, kissed and spanked him and watched him learn to walk. I don't know if you've known anybody from that far back; if you've loved anybody that long, first as an infant, then as a child, then as a man, you gain a strange perspective on time and human pain and effort. Other people cannot see what I see whenever I look into your father's face, for behind your father's face as it is today are all those other faces which were his. Let him laugh and I see a cellar your father does not remember and a house he does not remember and I hear in his present laughter his laughter as a child. Let him curse and I remember him falling down the cellar steps, and howling, and I remember, with pain, his tears, which my hand or your grandmother's so easily wiped away. But no one's hand can wipe away those tears he sheds invisibly today, which one hears in his laughter and in his speech and in his songs. I know what the world has done to my brother and how narrowly he has survived it. And I know, which is much worse, and this is the crime of which I accuse my country and my countrymen, and for which neither I nor time nor history will ever forgive them, that they have destroyed and are destroying hundreds of thousands of lives and do not know it and do not want to know it. One can be, indeed one must strive to become, tough and philosophical concerning destruction and death, for this is what most of mankind has been best at since we have heard of man. (But remember: *most* of mankind is not *all* of mankind.) But it is not permissible that the authors of devastation should also be innocent. It is the innocence which constitutes the crime.

Now, my dear namesake, these innocent and well-meaning people, your countrymen, have caused you to be born under conditions not very far removed from those described for us by Charles Dickens in the London of more than a hundred years ago. (I hear the chorus of the innocents screaming, "No! This is not true! How *bitter* you are!"—but I am writing this letter to *you*, to try to tell you something about how to handle *them*, for most of them do not yet really know that you exist. I *know* the conditions under which you were born, for I was there. Your countrymen were *not* there, and haven't made it yet. Your grandmother was also there, and no one has ever accused her of being bitter. I suggest that the innocents check with her. She isn't hard to find. Your countrymen don't know that *she* exists, either, though she has been working for them all their lives.)

Well, you were born, here you came, something like fourteen years ago; and though your father and mother and grandmother, looking about the streets through which they were carrying you, staring at the walls into which they brought you, had every reason to be heavyhearted, yet they were not. For here you were, Big James, named for me—you were a big baby, I was not—here you were: to be loved. To be loved, baby, hard, at once, and forever, to strengthen you against the loveless world. Remember that: I know how black it looks today, for you. It looked bad that day, too, yes, we were trembling. We have not stopped trembling yet, but if we had not loved each other none of us would have survived. And now you must survive because we love you, and for the sake of your children and your children's children.

This innocent country set you down in a ghetto in which, in fact, it intended that you should perish. Let me spell out precisely what I mean by that, for the heart of the matter is here, and the root of my dispute with my country. You were born where you were born and faced the future that you faced because you were black and *for no other reason*. The limits of your ambition were, thus, expected to be set forever. You were born into a society which spelled out with brutal clarity, and in as many ways as possible, that you were a worthless human being. You were not expected to aspire to excellence: you were expected to make peace with mediocrity. Wherever you have turned, James, in your short time on this earth, you have been told where you could go and what you could do (and *how* you could do it) and where you could live and whom you could marry. I know your countrymen do not agree with me about this, and I hear them saying, "You exaggerate." They do not know Harlem, and I do. So do you. Take no one's word for anything, including mine—but

236

trust your experience. Know whence you came. If you know whence you came, there is really no limit to where you can go. The details and symbols of your life have been deliberately constructed to make you believe what white people say about you. Please try to remember that what they believe, as well as what they do and cause you to endure, does not testify to your inferiority but to their inhumanity and fear.

Please try to be clear, dear James, through the storm which rages about your youthful head today, about the reality which lies behind the words *acceptance and integration*. There is no reason for you to try to become like white people and there is no basis whatever for their impertinent assumption that *they* must accept *you*. The really terrible thing, old buddy, is that *you* must accept *them*. And I mean that very seriously. You must accept them and accept them with love. For these innocent people have no other hope. They are, in effect, still trapped in a history which they do not understand; and until they understand it, they cannot be released from it. They have had to believe for many years, and for innumerable reasons, that black men are inferior to white men. Many of them, indeed, know better, but, as you will discover, people find it very difficult to act on what they know. To act is to be committed, and to be committed is to be in danger. In this case, the danger, in the minds of most white Americans, is the loss of their identity.

Try to imagine how you would feel if you woke up one morning to find the sun shining and all the stars aflame. You would be frightened because it is out of the order of nature. Any upheaval in the universe is terrifying because it so profoundly attacks one's sense of one's own reality. Well, the black man has functioned in the white man's world as a fixed star, as an immovable pillar: and as he moves out of his place, heaven and earth are shaken to their foundations. You, don't be afraid. I said that it was intended that you should perish in the ghetto, perish by never being allowed to go behind the white man's definitions, by never being allowed to spell your proper name. You have, and many of us have, defeated this intention; and, by a terrible law, a terrible paradox, those innocents who believed that your imprisonment made them safe are losing their grasp of reality.

But these men are your brothers—your lost, younger brothers.

And if the word *integration* means anything, this is what it means: that we, with love, shall force our brothers to see themselves as they are, to cease fleeing from reality and begin to change it. For this is your home, my friend, do not be driven from it; great men have done great things here, and will again, and we can make America what America must become. It will be hard, James, but you come from sturdy, peasant stock, men who picked cotton and dammed rivers and built railroads, and, in the teeth of the most terrifying odds, achieved an unassailable and monumental dignity. You come from a long line of great poets, some of the greatest poets since Homer. One of them said, *The very time I thought I was lost, My dungeon shook and my chains fell off.*

You know, and I know, that the country is celebrating one hundred years of freedom one hundred years too soon. We cannot be free until they are free. God bless you, James, and Godspeed.

Your uncle,
James

MARTIN LUTHER KING, JR.

Letter from Birmingham Jail

The "Negro Revolution" of the 1950s and early 1960s, which in the public mind had its beginning in the 1954 Supreme Court decision desegregating public schools, generally followed two paths: lawsuits pressed in state and federal courts, and the direct action programs of such organizations as the National Association for the Advancement of Colored People (NAACP), Congress of Racial Equality (CORE), and the Southern Christian Leadership Conference (SCLC). The Reverend Martin Luther King, Jr., who urged the tactic of passive resistance — Negroes, he said, should meet "physical force with an even stronger force, namely, soul force" — assumed the presidency of the SCLC and leadership of the new nonviolent protest movement. King and his followers chose Birmingham, Alabama, as the target of their antisegregation drive of 1963. King explained the choice: "If Birmingham could be cracked, the direction of the entire nonviolent movement in the

South could take a significant turn." While King's group was pressing a boycott that crippled business and forced Birmingham businessmen to negotiate a desegregation agreement, Attorney General Robert F. Kennedy acted to secure the immediate registration of more than 2,000 Birmingham Negroes previously denied voting rights. Federal courts upheld the right of Negroes to nonviolent protest in Birmingham and elsewhere, but not before King had been arrested and jailed. The following letter (reprinted here in part), written from his cell on April 16, 1963, contained King's answer to charges by a group of eight Birmingham clergymen that he was in their city as an "outside agitator." [Source: Christian Century, *June 12, 1963.]*

My Dear Fellow Clergymen:

While confined here in the Birmingham City Jail, I came across your recent statement calling my present activities "unwise and untimely." Seldom do I pause to answer criticism of my work and ideas. If I sought to answer all the criticisms that cross my desk, my secretaries would have little time for anything other than such correspondence in the course of the day, and I would have no time for constructive work. But since I feel that you are men of genuine goodwill and that your criticisms are sincerely set forth, I want to try to answer your statement in what I hope will be patient and reasonable terms.

I think I should indicate why I am here in Birmingham, since you have been influenced by the view which argues against "outsiders coming in." I have the honor of serving as president of the Southern Christian Leadership Conference, an organization operating in every Southern state, with headquarters in Atlanta, Georgia. We have some eighty-five affiliate organizations across the South, and one of them is the Alabama Christian Movement for Human Rights. Frequently, we share staff, educational, and financial resources with our affiliates. Several months ago the affiliate here in Birmingham asked us to be on call to engage in a nonviolent direct-action program if such were deemed necessary. We readily consented, and when the hour came we lived up to our promise. So I, along with several members of my staff, am here because I was invited here. I am here because I have organizational ties here.

But more basically, I am in Birmingham because injustice exists here. Just as the prophets of the 8th century B.C. left their villages and carried their "thus saith the Lord" far afield, and just as the apostle Paul left his village of Tarsus and carried the gospel of Jesus Christ to the far corners of the Greco-Roman world, so am I compelled to carry the gospel of freedom beyond my own hometown. Like Paul, I must constantly respond to the Macedonian call for aid.

Moreover, I am cognizant of the interrelatedness of all communities and states. I cannot sit idly by in Atlanta and not be concerned about what happens in Birmingham. Injustice anywhere is a threat to justice everywhere. We are caught in an inescapable network of mutuality, tied in a single garment of destiny. Whatever affects one directly affects all indirectly. Never again can we afford to live with the narrow, provincial "outside agitator" idea. Anyone who lives inside the United States can never be considered an outsider anywhere within its bounds.

You deplore the demonstrations taking place in Birmingham. But your statement, I am sorry to say, fails to express a similar concern for the conditions that brought about the demonstrations. I am sure that none of you would want to rest content with the superficial kind of social analysis that deals merely with effects and does not grapple with underlying causes. It is unfortunate that demonstrations are taking place in Birmingham, but it is even more unfortunate that the city's white power structure left the Negro community with no alternative. . . .

You may well ask, "Why direct action? Why sit-ins, marches, etc.? Isn't negotiation a better path?" You are quite right in calling for negotiation. Indeed, this is the very purpose of direct action. Nonviolent direct action seeks to foster such a tension that a community which has constantly refused to negotiate is forced to confront the issue. It seeks so to dramatize the issue that it can no longer be ignored. My citing the creation of tension as part of the work of the nonviolent resister may sound rather shocking. But I readily acknowledge that I am not afraid of the word "tension." I have earnestly opposed violent tension, but there is a type of constructive, nonviolent tension which is necessary for growth. Just as Socrates felt that it was necessary to create a tension in the mind so that individuals could shake off the bondage of myths and half-truths and rise to the realm of creative analysis and objective appraisal, so must we see the need for nonviolent gadflies to create the

240

kind of tension in society that will help men rise from the dark depths of prejudice and racism to the majestic heights of understanding and brotherhood.

The purpose of our direct-action program is to create a situation so crisis-packed that it will inevitably open the door to negotiation. I therefore concur with you in your call for negotiation. Too long has our beloved Southland been bogged down in a tragic effort to live in monologue rather than dialogue. . . .

We have waited for more than 340 years for our constitutional and God-given rights. The nations of Asia and Africa are moving with jetlike speed toward gaining political independence, but we still creep at horse-and-buggy pace toward gaining a cup of coffee at a lunch counter. Perhaps it is easy for those who have never felt the stinging darts of segregation to say "Wait." But when you have seen vicious mobs lynch your mothers and fathers at will and drown your sisters and brothers at whim; when you have seen hate-filled policemen curse, kick, and even kill your black brothers and sisters with impunity; when you see the vast majority of your 20 million Negro brothers smothering in an air-tight cage of poverty in the midst of an affluent society; when you suddenly find your tongue twisted as you seek to explain to your six-year-old daughter why she can't go to the public amusement park that has just been advertised on television, and see tears welling up when she is told that Funtown is closed to colored children, and see ominous clouds of inferiority beginning to form in her little mental sky, and see her beginning to distort her personality by unconsciously developing a bitterness toward white people; when you have to concoct an answer for a five-year-old son asking, "Daddy, why do white people treat colored people so mean?"; when you take a cross-country drive and find it necessary to sleep night after night in the uncomfortable corners of your automobile because no motel will accept you; when you are humiliated day in and day out by nagging signs reading "white" and "colored"; when your first name becomes "nigger," your middle name becomes "boy" (however old you are), and your last name becomes "John," and your wife and mother are never given the respected title "Mrs."; when you are harried by day and haunted by night by the fact that you are a Negro, never quite knowing what to expect next, and are plagued with inner fears and outer resent-

241

ments; when you are forever fighting a degenerating sense of "nobodiness"—then you will understand why we find it difficult to wait. There comes a time when the cup of endurance runs over, and men are no longer willing to be plunged into an abyss of injustice where they experience the bleakness of corroding despair. I hope, sirs, you can understand our legitimate and unavoidable impatience.

You express a great deal of anxiety over our willingness to break laws. This is certainly a legitimate concern. Since we so diligently urge people to obey the Supreme Court's decision of 1954 outlawing segregation in the public schools, at first glance it may seem rather paradoxical for us consciously to break laws. One may well ask, "How can you advocate breaking some laws and obeying others?" The answer lies in the fact that there are two types of laws: just and unjust. I agree with St. Augustine that "an unjust law is no law at all.". . .

Let us consider some of the ways in which a law can be unjust. A law is unjust, for example, if the majority group compels a minority group to obey the statute but does not make it binding on itself. By the same token, a law in all probability is just if the majority is itself willing to obey it. Also, a law is unjust if it is inflicted on a minority that, as a result of being denied the right to vote, had no part in enacting or devising the law. Who can say that the legislature of Alabama which set up that state's segregation laws was democratically elected? Throughout Alabama all sorts of devious methods are used to prevent Negroes from becoming registered voters, and there are some counties in which, even though Negroes constitute a majority of the population, not a single Negro is registered. Can any law enacted under such circumstances be considered democratically structured?

Sometimes a law is just on its face and unjust in its application. For instance, I have been arrested on a charge of parading without a permit. Now there is nothing wrong in having an ordinance which requires a permit for a parade. But such an ordinance becomes unjust when it is used to maintain segregation and to deny citizens the First Amendment privilege of peaceful assembly and protest.

I hope you are able to see the distinction I am trying to point out. In no sense do I advocate evading the law, as would the rabid segregationist. That would lead to anarchy. One who breaks an unjust law must do so *openly*, *lovingly*, and with a willingness to accept the penalty. I submit that an individual who breaks a law that conscience tells him is unjust and who willingly accepts the penalty of imprisonment in order to arouse the conscience of the community over its injustice is in reality expressing the highest respect for law. . . .

I must make two honest confessions to you, my Christian and Jewish brothers. First, I must confess that over the past few years I have been gravely disappointed with the white moderate. I have almost reached the regrettable conclusion that the Negro's great stumbling block in his stride toward freedom is not the White Citizen's Counciler or the Ku Klux Klaner but the white moderate who is more devoted to "order" than to justice; who prefers a negative peace which is the absence of tension to a positive peace which is the presence of justice; who constantly says "I agree with you in the goal you seek, but I cannot agree with your methods"; who paternalistically believes he can set the timetable for another man's freedom; who lives by a mythical concept of time and who constantly advises the Negro to wait for a "more convenient season." Shallow understanding from people of goodwill is more frustrating than absolute misunderstanding from people of ill will. Lukewarm acceptance is much more bewildering than outright rejection.

I had hoped that the white moderate would understand that law and order exist for the purpose of establishing justice and that when they fail in this purpose they block social progress. I had hoped that the white moderate would understand that the present tension in the South is a necessary phase of the transition from an obnoxious negative peace, in which the Negro passively accepted his unjust plight, to a substantive and positive peace, in which all men will respect the dignity and worth of human personality. Actually, we who engage in nonviolent direct action are not the creators of tension. We merely bring to the surface the hidden tension that is already alive. We bring it out in the open where it can be seen and dealt with. Like a boil that can never be cured so long as it is covered up but must be opened with all its pus-flowing ugliness to the natural medicines of air and light, injustice must be exposed, with all the tension its exposure creates, to the light of human conscience and the air of national opinion before it can be cured. . . .

You speak of our activity in Birmingham as extreme. At first I was rather disappointed that fellow clergymen would see my nonviolent efforts as those of an extremist. I began thinking about the fact that I stand in the middle of two opposing forces in the Negro community. One is a force of complacency made up of Negroes who, as a result of long years of oppression, are so completely drained of self-respect and a sense of "somebodiness" that they have adjusted to segregation, and of a few middle-class Negroes who, because of a degree of academic and economic security and because in some ways they profit by segregation, have unconsciously become insensitive to the problems of the masses. The other force is one of bitterness and hatred, and it comes perilously close to advocating violence. It is expressed in the various black nationalist groups that are springing up across the nation, the largest and best-known being Elijah Muhammad's Muslim movement. Nourished by the Negro's frustration over the continued existence of racial discrimination, this movement is made up of people who have lost faith in America, who have absolutely repudiated Christianity, and who have concluded that the white man is an incorrigible "devil."

I have tried to stand between these two forces, saying that we need emulate neither the "do-nothingism" of the complacent nor the hatred of the black nationalist. For there is the more excellent way of love and nonviolent protest. I am grateful to God that, through the influence of the Negro church, the way of nonviolence became an integral part of our struggle.

If this philosophy had not emerged, by now many streets of the South would, I am convinced, be flowing with blood. And I am further convinced that if our white brothers dismiss as "rabble-rousers" and "outside agitators" those of us who employ nonviolent direct action and if they refuse to support our nonviolent efforts, millions of Negroes will, out of frustration and despair, seek solace and security in black nationalist ideologies—a development that would inevitably lead to a frightening racial nightmare. . . .

Let me take note of my other major disappointment. Though there are some notable exceptions, I have also been disappointed with the white church and its leadership. I do not say this as one of those negative critics who can always find something wrong with the church. I say this as a minister of the gospel, who loves the church; who was nurtured in its bosom; who has been sustained by its spiritual blessings and who will remain true to it as long as the cord of life shall lengthen.

When I was suddenly catapulted into the leadership of the bus protest in Montgomery, Alabama, a few years ago, I felt we would be supported by the white church. I felt that the white ministers, priests, and rabbis of the South would be among our strongest allies. Instead, some have been outright opponents, refusing to understand the freedom movement and misrepresenting its leaders; all too many others have been more cautious than courageous and have remained silent and secure behind stained-glass windows.

In spite of my shattered dreams I came to Birmingham with the hope that the white religious leadership of this community would see the justice of our cause and with deep moral concern would serve as the channel through which our just grievances could reach the power structure. But again I have been disappointed.

I have heard numerous Southern religious leaders admonish their worshipers to comply with a desegregation decision because it is the *law*, but I have longed to hear white ministers declare, "Fol low this decree because integration is morally *right* and because the Negro is your brother." In the midst of blatant injustices inflicted upon the Negro I have watched white churchmen stand on the sideline and mouth pious irrelevancies and sanctimonious trivialities. In the midst of a mighty struggle to rid our nation of racial and economic injustice I have heard many ministers say, "Those are social issues with which the gospel has no real concern," and I have watched many churches commit themselves to a completely other-worldly religion which makes a strange, unbiblical distinction between body and soul, between the sacred and the secular.

We are moving toward the close of the twentieth century with a religious community largely adjusted to the status quo—a taillight behind other community agencies rather than a headlight leading men to higher levels of justice. . . .

But the judgment of God is upon the church as never before. If today's church does not recapture the sacrificial spirit of the early church, it will lose its authenticity, forfeit the loyalty of millions,

245

and be dismissed as an irrelevant social club with no meaning for the twentieth century. Every day I meet young people whose disappointment with the church has turned into outright disgust.

Perhaps I have once again been too optimistic. Is organized religion too inextricably bound to the status quo to save our nation and the world? Perhaps I must turn my faith to the inner spiritual church, the church within the church, as the true *ecclesia* and the hope of the world. But again I am thankful to God that some noble souls from the ranks of organized religion have broken loose from the paralyzing chains of conformity and joined us as active partners in the struggle for freedom. They have left their secure congregations and walked the streets of Albany, Georgia, with us. They have gone down the highways of the South on torturous rides for freedom. Yes, they have gone to jail with us. Some have been kicked out of their churches, have lost the support of their bishops and fellow ministers. But they have acted in the faith that right defeated is stronger than evil triumphant. Their witness has been the spiritual salt that has preserved the true meaning of the gospel in these troubled times. They have carved a tunnel of hope through the dark mountain of disappointment.

I hope the church as a whole will meet the challenge of this decisive hour. But even if the church does not come to the aid of justice, I have no despair about the future. I have no fear about the outcome of our struggle in Birmingham, even if our motives are at present misunderstood. We will reach the goal of freedom in Birmingham and all over the nation, because the goal of America is freedom. . . .

Before closing I feel impelled to mention one other point in your statement that has troubled me profoundly. You warmly commended the Birmingham police force for keeping "order" and "preventing violence." I doubt that you would have so warmly commended the police force if you had seen its angry dogs sinking their teeth into six unarmed, nonviolent Negroes. I doubt that you would so quickly commend the policemen if you were to observe their ugly and inhuman treatment of Negroes here in the City Jail; if you were to watch them push and curse old Negro women and young Negro girls; if you were to see them slap and kick old Negro men and young boys; if you were to observe them, as they did on two occasions, refuse to give us food because we wanted to sing our grace together. I cannot join you in your praise of the Birmingham Police Department.

It is true that the police have exercised discipline in handling the demonstrators. In this sense they have conducted themselves rather "nonviolently" in public. But for what purpose? To preserve the evil system of segregation. Over the past few years I have consistently preached that nonviolence demands that the means we use must be as pure as the ends we seek. I have tried to make clear that it is wrong to use immoral means to attain moral ends. But now I must affirm that it is just as wrong, or perhaps even more so, to use moral means to preserve immoral ends. Perhaps Mr. Connor and his policemen have been rather nonviolent in public, as was Chief Pritchett in Albany, Georgia, but they have used the moral means of nonviolence to maintain the immoral end of racial injustice. As T. S. Eliot has said, there is no greater treason than to do the right deed for the wrong reason.

I wish you had commended the Negro sit-inners and demonstrators of Birmingham for their sublime courage, their willingness to suffer and their amazing discipline in the midst of great provocation. One day the South will recognize its real heroes. . . . One day the South will know that when these disinherited children of God sat down at lunch counters they were in reality standing up for what is best in the American dream and for the most sacred values in our Judeo-Christian heritage, thereby bringing our nation back to those great wells of democracy which were dug deep by the founding fathers in their formulation of the Constitution and the Declaration of Independence.

Songs of the Civil Rights Movement

From time immemorial men and women engaged in a common cause have sung together. This is likely to be all the more true of rebels and revolutionaries, who, lacking the physical force of those in authority, must discover emotional and moral forces within themselves. It was true, at any

247

rate, of the Negro civil rights movement in the United States, at least until 1965 or 1966. The songs sung by civil rights marchers were in many cases very old ones. "Oh Freedom" was a Negro marching song in the Civil War; "Which Side Are You On?" is a labor song that dates from the early 1930s in Harlan County, Kentucky; "We Shall Not Be Moved" is one of the most widely known labor songs in both the United States and Canada, and also dates from the 1930s; "We Shall Overcome," perhaps the most famous of all modern civil rights songs, is at least a half century old and may be a good deal older. (The other four songs reprinted here, on the other hand, may be quite recent in origin.) But even though the tunes were old, and some of the words meaningful in other traditions of economic and social protest, all of the songs, old and new, gained new currency and new power when they were sung by white men and black men alike, in North and South, in Birmingham and Selma, Alabama, in Watts, and in Chicago. Watts, which saw the movement take another turn, may have been the last place, and 1965 the last year, in which they were sung with full effect. [Source: We Shall Overcome!, compiled by Guy and Candie Carawan, New York, 1963.]

Oh Freedom

Oh Freedom, Oh Freedom,
Oh Freedom over me, over me —

> *Chorus:*
> And before I'll be a slave
> I'll be buried in my grave
> And go home to my Lord and be free.

No segregation, no segregation,
No segregation over me, over me —

No more weeping, no more weeping,
No more weeping over me, over me —

No burning churches, no burning churches,
No burning churches over me, over me —

No more Jim Crow, no more Jim Crow,
No more Jim Crow over me, over me —

No more Barnett, no more Barnett,
No more Barnett over me, over me —

Which Side Are You On?

Come all you freedom lovers and listen while I tell
Of how the freedom riders came to Jackson to dwell.

> *Chorus:*
> Oh which side are you on, boys,
> Which side are you on? (Tell me)
> Which side are you on, boys,
> Which side are you on?

My daddy was a freedom fighter and I'm a freedom son —
I'll stick right with this struggle until the battle's won.

Don't "Tom" for "Uncle Charlie," don't listen to his lies,
'Cause black folks haven't got a chance until they organize.

They say in Hinds County, no neutrals have they met —
You're either for the Freedom Ride or you "Tom" for Ross Barnett.

Oh, people, can you stand it, oh tell me how you can?
Will you be an Uncle Tom or will you be a man?

Cap'n Ray'll holler "move on!" but the Freedom Riders won't budge,
They'll stand there in the terminals and even before the judge.

"Which Side Are You On?" By Florence Reece and James Farmer, Copyright 1947, 1963 by Stormking Music, Inc., All Rights Reserved. Used by Permission.

We Shall Not Be Moved

> We are fighting for our freedom,
>   We shall not be moved;
> We are fighting for our freedom,
>   We shall not be moved —

> *Chorus:*
> Just like a tree
> Planted by the water,
>   We shall not be moved.

> We are black and white together, etc.

> We will stand and fight together, etc.

Keep Your Eyes on the Prize

Paul and Silas, bound in jail,
Had no money for to go their bail.

Chorus:
Keep your eyes on the prize,
Hold on, hold on,
Hold on, hold on —
Keep your eyes on the prize,
  Hold on, hold on.

Paul and Silas begin to shout,
The jail door opened and they walked out.

Freedom's name is mighty sweet —
Soon one of these days we're going to meet.

Got my hand on the Gospel plow,
I wouldn't take nothing for my journey now.

The only chain that a man can stand
Is that chain of hand in hand.

The only thing that we did wrong —
Stayed in the wilderness too long.

But the one thing we did right
Was the day we started to fight.

We're gonna board that big Greyhound,
Carryin' love from town to town.

We're gonna ride for civil rights,
We're gonna ride, both black and white.

We've met jail and violence too,
But God's love has seen us through.

Haven't been to Heaven but I've been told
Streets up there are paved with gold.

Woke Up This Morning with My Mind Stayed on Freedom

Woke up this morning with my mind stayed on freedom,
Woke up this morning with my mind stayed on freedom,
Woke up this morning with my mind stayed on freedom,
  Hallelu, hallelu, hallelu, hallelu, hallelujah.

Ain't no harm to keep your mind stayed on freedom, etc.

Walkin' and talkin' with my mind stayed on freedom, etc.

Singin' and prayin' with my mind stayed on freedom, etc.

Doin' the twist with my mind stayed on freedom, etc.

Ain't Gonna Let Nobody Turn Me Round

Ain't gonna let nobody, Lordy, turn me round,
  Turn me round, turn me round.
Ain't gonna let nobody, Lordy, turn me round.

  Chorus:
  I'm gonna keep on a-walkin', Lord,
  Keep on a-talkin', Lord,
  Marching up to freedom land.

Ain't gonna let Nervous Nelly turn me round, etc.

Ain't gonna let Chief Pritchett turn me round, etc.

Ain't gonna let Mayor Daley turn me round, etc.

Ain't gonna let segregation turn me round, etc.

Ain't gonna let no jailhouse turn me round, etc.

Ain't gonna let no injunction turn me round, etc.

This Little Light of Mine

This little light of mine, I'm gonna let it shine;
This little light of mine, I'm gonna let it shine;
This little light of mine, I'm gonna let it shine;
  Let it shine, let it shine, let it shine.

The light that shines is the light of love,
Lights the darkness from above.
It shines on me and it shines on you,
And shows what the power of love can do.
I'm gonna shine my light both far and near,
I'm gonna shine my light both bright and clear.
Where there's a dark corner in this land,
I'm gonna let my little light shine.

We've got the light of freedom, we're gonna let it shine;
We've got the light of freedom, we're gonna let it shine;
We've got the light of freedom, we're gonna let it shine;
   Let it shine, let it shine, let it shine.

Deep down in the South, we're gonna let it shine, etc.

Down in Birmingham, we're gonna let it shine, etc.

All over the nation, we're gonna let it shine, etc.

Everywhere I go, I'm gonna let it shine, etc.

Tell Chief Pritchett, we're gonna let it shine, etc.

All in the jailhouse, we're gonna let it shine, etc.

On Monday he gave me the gift of love;
Tuesday peace came from above;
Wednesday he told me to have more faith;
Thursday he gave me a little more grace;
Friday he told me just to watch and pray;
Saturday he told me just what to say;
Sunday he gave me the power divine—
To let my little light shine.

We Shall Overcome

We shall overcome,
   we shall overcome,
We shall overcome some day.
Oh, deep in my heart, I do believe,
We shall overcome some day.

We are not afraid,
    we are not afraid,
We are not afraid today.
Oh, deep in my heart, I do believe,
We shall overcome some day.

We are not alone,
    we are not alone,
We are not alone today.
Oh, deep in my heart, I do believe,
We shall overcome some day.

The truth will make us free,
    the truth will make us free,
The truth will make us free some day.
Oh, deep in my heart, I do believe,
We shall overcome some day.

We'll walk hand in hand,
    we'll walk hand in hand,
We'll walk hand in hand some day.
Oh, deep in my heart, I do believe,
We shall overcome some day.

The Lord will see us through,
    the Lord will see us through,
The Lord will see us through today.
Oh, deep in my heart, I do believe,
We shall overcome some day.

New Words and Music arrangement by Zilphia Horton, Frank Hamilton, Guy Carawan and Pete Seeger TRO © Copyright 1960 and 1963 LUDLOW MUSIC, INC., New York, N.Y.   USED BY PERMISSION

Royalties derived from this composition are being contributed to the Martin Luther King, Jr., Fund under the trusteeship of the writers.

LOUIS E. LOMAX
The Black Muslims

With the exception of the "Garvey Movement," which thrived in New York's Harlem briefly after World War I, the only black separatist group to attract a widespread following in America has been the Nation of Islam or Black Muslims. The Muslim voice, like that of Garvey, is one that calls Negroes to blackness by reversing the moral values of the white man, who (despite the assumption of white supremacy that this implies) is portrayed as a powerful evil genius, never resting in his persecution of the blacks. The following assessment is by a Negro historian and journalist. [Source: The Negro Revolt, *New York, 1962, pp. 178-192.]*

The extreme form of the Negro's revolt against his plight can be seen in the rise of the Honorable Elijah Muhammad, whose followers are known as the Nation of Islam or the Black Muslims.[1] . . .

The driving force in the Black Muslim movement — they now claim a membership of over a quarter of a million[2] — is one Elijah Muhammad, a sixty-year-old American Negro who was born Elijah Poole and spent his early life as a Baptist minister. Muhammad is a strikingly unimpressive man; he is small, five feet five, and speaks with a disturbing lisp. It is difficult to believe that he is the moving spirit behind a religion that is now being taught in fifty schools across the nation. Yet when Muhammad speaks the audience sits entranced for from four to five hours while he delivers a most amazing doctrine. And it is during the mass rallies where Mr. Muhammad speaks that the Muslims can best be studied.

Their withdrawal from America is almost complete. They speak of themselves as a "nation," indicating that they are not of the American body politic; they do not vote nor do they participate in political affairs. The Muslim women keep their heads covered at all times; they wear the long, flowing, white skirts one associates with Islam. They have their own stores, supermarkets, barbershops,

[1]The term "Black Muslim" was coined by Dr. Eric Lincoln while he was preparing his Ph.D. dissertation on the followers of Muhammad. They do not use the term when speaking of themselves. They call themselves "Muslims." However, they do not object to the term employed by Lincoln.

[2]Experts on the Black Muslims say the membership does not exceed 100,000.

254

department stores and fish markets. . . .

It is clear, then, that we are witnessing the first homegrown American Negro religion. In essence, Muhammad is saying this: God and black are one, therefore all blacks are divine; the opposite of black is evil, therefore all white men are evil. Then he extends his argument: The world's black men are divine, therefore unified. The weakest link in the black brotherhood is the so-called American Negro, who is all mixed up with the white man. The return of black men to power, then, is waiting upon the American Negro to come out from among the white men and be separated—not segregated. To accomplish this Muhammad demands "some states" where the Negro can set up his own nation. (A group of us offered Muhammad Mississippi; he turned it down.)

Strangely enough Muhammad's demand for a "separate state" gets symbolic support from many non-Muslims because of incidents like the James Meredith encounter with Mississippi lawlessness. Many Negroes feel—and as a direct result of the Meredith case—that white people will never really yield, that we will spend the remainder of our lives waging a major war over a morsel. This results in a strange kind of spiritual withdrawal from the American community, a deepening faith that since we have little hope of being "of" the general American mainstream there is little or no reason why we should be "in" it, to complete the Biblical analogy. This is particularly true among the Negro masses—and they are those who come to hear Muhammad speak—who have never had a real "we" feeling about America.

But Muhammad's demands for a separate state, like his Islamic trappings, are not to be taken too seriously. Most people are convinced that he doesn't really mean this; and we are convinced that most of his followers are not culturally able to execute the alliance with traditional Islam that the spokesmen for the movement would have one believe. These—the separate state and the Islamic trappings—are not the arresting things. There are matters raised by Muhammad, however, that demand, and have received, serious attention from sober Negroes:

First, Muhammad's indictment of Christianity has forced thoughtful Negro preachers into an almost impossible position. I have talked this over with scores of Negro clergymen, and, almost to a man, they agree that Muhammad has deeply shaken the Negro

Christian community. Muhammad's recital of how the Christian faith has failed the Negro—"By their fruits ye shall know them"—has sunk deeper into the hearts of the Negro masses than Negro clergymen will admit publicly. But, and as a direct result of what Muhammad has said, Negro clergymen are scurrying around for new Sunday school picture cards, religious literature that pictures God and Christ, if not black, at least resembling a Negro. I know of one Negro minister, a Harvard graduate at that, who has delivered several sermons on the question of Christ's physical appearance. "And his hair was like lamb's wool." This, the minister says, is the only physical description of Jesus. Then he tells his middle-class Negro congregation that his, the minister's hair, looks more like lamb's wool than do Norman Vincent Peale's forelocks.

And although they are bitter ideological enemies, there is only a thin line between Muhammad and Martin Luther King. King, of course, will have none of Muhammad's blanket indictment of the white man; nor will King abide black supremacy notions. But both King and Muhammad are saying that the purpose of a religion is to explain life for the people who adopt or create it and that the function of a gospel is to speak to the frustrations of a people. Muhammad's gospel as a whole will not be accepted by the Negro. But—and this is the important thing—no gospel that fails to answer Muhammad's criticism of Christianity will be accepted either.

In the process of indicting Christianity and criticizing Negro leaders who seek "integration," Muhammad, largely through the spellbinding work of Malcolm X, has caused thousands of the Negro masses to become race-conscious in a way they never were before. It is the rise of Muhammad that has caused Jackie Robinson to realize that Negro leadership organizations are not reaching the Negro masses. William Berry, executive secretary of the Chicago Urban League, readily confesses: "Hell, these Muslims make more sense to the Negro on the street than I do!"

It is quite a pageant to see hundreds of Negro women, formerly Baptists, Methodists and what have you, marching into Washington's Uline Arena, draped in white, their heads covered, to hear Elijah speak. Their withdrawal is fairly complete. They have no more faith in the white man or in the American dream. They don't condemn the white man for they feel he is incapable of doing good. Their chant, like that of the early Jew, is, "How can we sing the Lord's song in a strange land?"

And police brutality, particularly in New York, has helped the Black Muslim movement. Two years ago, several policemen, all of them white, shot their way into a Muslim home on Long Island. They were under the mistaken impression that a fugitive was hiding there. The policemen terrorized one man, several children and two pregnant women. The Muslims retaliated with milk bottles, sticks and stones. Of course, they were all arrested for assaulting policemen. But an all-white jury set them free. Then there is the case of Johnson Hinton, a Muslim who happened to be on a Harlem street when a fight broke out. White policemen waded in swinging their clubs. Hinton fell to the ground, his head split open. He was hospitalized and five hundred Muslim men threw a cordon around the hospital and all but started a race riot. A steel plate was put in Hinton's head, and he recovered. He was acquitted of any wrongdoing. Then came the lawsuit. The jury awarded Hinton $75,000; then, rather than go through endless appeals, the City settled for $70,000.

It is no accident that the Black Muslims do a land-office recruiting job in the nation's prisons. These jails are jammed with Negroes who, even though guilty, have known the bitter taste of police brutality and short-shrift justice. To them, the Muslims present a deadly argument and the prisoners have responded by the hundreds. Just recently the Black Muslims went to court and won the right to practice their faith inside New York State prisons; in California prisons the Muslims presented such a challenge that state officials had to make special arrangements to accommodate them and their faith.

And it is just here, in their work with Negro criminals, that the Muslims have won the respect of Negro and white social workers. Their rehabilitation program is nothing short of miraculous. They start out by convincing the ex-convict that he fell into crime because he was ashamed of being black, that the white man has so psychologically conditioned him that he was unable to respect himself. Then they convince the one-time prisoner that being black is a blessing, not a curse, and that in keeping with that blessing he, the ex-convict, must clean himself up and live a life of decency and respect. As a result:

You never see a Muslim without a clean shirt and tie and coat.

You never see a Muslim drink.

You never see a Muslim smoke.

You never see a Muslim dance.

You never see a Muslim use dope.

You never see a Muslim woman with a non-Muslim man.

You never see a Muslim man with a woman other than his wife.

You never see a Muslim without some means of income.

You never see a Muslim who will not stop and come to the aid of any black woman he sees in trouble.

You seldom see a Muslim lapse back into crime. (A close friend of mine is a lawyer with Muslim clients and he tells me that he has known of only four Muslims who have returned to crime in the past five years. This is remarkable when one remembers that some six hundred convicts in prison join the Black Muslims each year. The Muslim leaders arrange parole for their converts and take them in hand. Parole officers and police have told me that the Black Muslims are the best rehabilitation agency at work among Negro criminals today.)

The crucial issue is that these criminals are rehabilitated along with the other members of the group (most of the Muslims are not ex-convicts) in a faith that denies and condemns everything American. They do it by simply reciting the facts about life for the black man in America. And it is this recital that caused James Baldwin to remark that others among us have the faith but the Muslims have the facts.

Because they have the facts, and none of us can dispute them, the Black Muslims have forced every Negro spokesman in America to assume a position more extreme than that he would have assumed had the Muslims not been among us. Not that the position is false; rather that Negro spokesmen, for all their fist-pounding, are cautious fellows. But once Malcolm X makes his speech there is neither room nor reason for this kind of caution, and the Negro spokesman who speaks less of the truth than Malcolm speaks simply cannot get a hearing among his own people.

258

The Black Muslims, like the sit-ins and the freedom rides, are part of the Negro revolt. They are not aimed in the same direction, but they stem from the same unrest: a rejection of segregation and all that it carries with it and a firm belief that the current Negro leadership organizations are not employing the proper methods to end that evil.

The Black Muslims are now accepted. Nobody bothers them much any more; they are part of the Negro community, their leaders sit on committees when community matters are being discussed. No sane man, black or white, dares plan a mass program in Harlem without including Malcolm X. For if it comes to a showdown, Malcolm can muster more people than Adam Powell, A. Philip Randolph, Martin Luther King and Roy Wilkins all put together.

The Black Muslims represent an extreme reaction to the problem of being a Negro in America today. Instead of working to improve conditions within the framework of American society, as do other Negro leadership organizations, the Black Muslims react by turning their backs on that society entirely. Their one positive aspect is that they work to make Negroes proud of being Negro.

As of now I do not feel the Black Muslims present a real threat to American society—they let off most of their steam harmlessly in their meetings and conventions, and the rituals and trappings of the faith take up much of their attention. But the Black Muslims do present a threat for the future. Should the white supremacists seem to be gaining the upper hand, if little or no progress seems to be made by the nonviolent means of CORE and the SCLC or the legalistic means of the NAACP, the Black Muslims may grow from a curiosity on the American scene into a potent and dangerous force.

259

MICHAEL HARRINGTON

Poverty in an Affluent Society

*Discussions of the plight of the poor in affluent America seemed to become
ever more common as the very affluence of the nation increased. Michael
Harrington's* The Other America *(1962) was one of the most widely read
books on the subject during the 1960s. Harrington rejected with bitter
eloquence the arguments of those who cited the encouraging economic
statistics and pointed instead to that still large proportion of Americans who
did not share in the unprecedented wealth that so many enjoyed. Parts of two
chapters of the book appear here. The first dealt with what Harrington called
the "economic underworld" of the large cities of the nation. The second dealt
with the special problem of the Negro, who, Harrington said, is "black
because he is poor," and not the other way around. [Source:* The Other
America, *New York, 1962, pp. 19-20, 71-81.]*

In New York City, some of my friends call 80 Warren Street "the
slave market."

It is a big building in downtown Manhattan. Its corridors have
the littered, trampled air of a courthouse. They are lined with em-
ployment-agency offices. Some of these places list good-paying and
highly skilled jobs. But many of them provide the work force for the
economic underworld in the big city: the dishwashers and day
workers, the fly-by-night jobs.

Early every morning, there is a great press of human beings in 80
Warren Street. It is made up of Puerto Ricans and Negroes, alcoholics, drifters, and disturbed people. Some of them will pay a flat
fee (usually around 10 percent) for a day's work. They pay $0.50 for
a $5.00 job and they are given the address of a luncheonette. If all
goes well, they will make their wage. If not, they have a legal right
to come back and get their half-dollar. But many of them don't know
that, for they are people that are not familiar with laws and rights.

But perhaps the most depressing time at 80 Warren Street is in
the afternoon. The jobs have all been handed out, yet the people still
mill around. Some of them sit on benches in the larger offices. There
is no real point to their waiting, yet they have nothing else to do. For
some, it is probably a point of pride to be here, a feeling that they are

260

somehow still looking for a job even if they know that there is no chance to get one until early in the morning.

Most of the people at 80 Warren Street were born poor. (The alcoholics are an exception.) They are incompetent as far as American society is concerned, lacking the education and the skills to get decent work. If they find steady employment, it will be in a sweatshop or a kitchen.

In a Chicago factory, another group of people are working. A year or so ago, they were in a union shop making good wages, with sick leave, pension rights, and vacations. Now they are making artificial Christmas trees at less than half the pay they had been receiving. They have no contract rights, and the foreman is absolute monarch. Permission is required if a worker wants to go to the bathroom. A few are fired every day for insubordination.

These are people who have become poor. They possess skills, and they once moved upward with the rest of the society. But now their jobs have been destroyed, and their skills have been rendered useless. In the process, they have been pushed down toward the poverty from whence they came. This particular group is Negro, and the chances of ever breaking through, of returning to the old conditions, are very slim. Yet their plight is not exclusively racial, for it is shared by all the semiskilled and unskilled workers who are the victims of technological unemployment in the mass-production industries. They are involved in an interracial misery.

These people are the rejects of the affluent society. They never had the right skills in the first place, or they lost them when the rest of the economy advanced. They are the ones who make up a huge portion of the culture of poverty in the cities of America. They are to be counted in the millions. . . .

If all the discriminatory laws in the United States were immediately repealed, race would still remain as one of the most pressing moral and political problems in the nation. Negroes and other minorities are not simply the victims of a series of iniquitous statutes. The American economy, the American society, the American unconscious are all racist. If all the laws were framed to provide equal opportunity, a majority of the Negroes would not be able to take full advantage of the change. There would still be a vast, silent, and automatic system directed against men and women of color.

261

To belong to a racial minority is to be poor, but poor in a special way. The fear, the lack of self-confidence, the haunting, these have been described. But they, in turn, are the expressions of the most institutionalized poverty in the United States, the most vicious of the vicious circles. In a sense, the Negro is classically the "other" American, degraded and frustrated at every turn and not just because of laws.

There are sympathetic and concerned people who do not understand how deeply America has integrated racism into its structure. Given time, they argue, the Negroes will rise in the society like the Irish, the Jews, the Italians, and all the rest. But this notion misses two decisive facts: that the Negro is colored, and no other group in the United States has ever faced such a problem, and that the Negro of today is an internal migrant who will face racism wherever he goes, who cannot leave his oppression behind as if it were a czar or a potato famine. To be equal, the Negro requires something much more profound than a way "into" the society; he needs a transformation of some of the basic institutions of the society.

The Negro is poor because he is black; that is obvious enough. But, perhaps more importantly, the Negro is black because he is poor. The laws against color can be removed, but that will leave the poverty that is the historic and institutionalized consequence of color. As long as this is the case, being born a Negro will continue to be the most profound disability that the United States imposes upon a citizen.

Perhaps the quickest way to point up the racism of the American economy is to recall a strange case of jubilation.

Late in 1960 the Department of Labor issued a study, "The Economic Situation of Negroes in the United States." It noted that in 1939, nonwhite workers earned, on the average, 41 percent as much as whites, and that by 1958 their wages had climbed to 58 percent of that of whites. Not a little elation greeted this announcement. Some of the editorialists cited these statistics as indicating that slow and steady progress was being made. (At this rate, the Negro would reach parity with the white some time well after the year 2000.)

To begin with, the figures were somewhat more optimistic than the reality. Part of the Negro gain reflected the shift of rural Negroes to cities and Southern Negroes to the North. In both cases, the people involved increased their incomes by going into a more prosperous section of the country. But within each area their relative position remained the same: at the bottom. Then, the statistics take a depression year (1939) as a base for comparison, and contrast it to a year of recession (1958). This tended to exaggerate the advance because Negroes in 1939 were particularly victimized.

Another important aspect of the problem was obscured by the sweeping comparisons most editorialists made between the 1939 and 1958 figures. Even the Department of Labor statistics themselves indicate that the major gain was made during World War II (the increase from 1939 to 1947 was from 41.4 percent to 54.3 of the white wage). In the postwar period the rate of advance slowed to a walk. Moreover, most of the optimism was based upon figures for Negro men. When the women are included, and when one takes a median family income from the Current Population Reports, Negroes rose from 51 percent of white family income in 1947 to 57 percent in 1952 — and then declined back to the 1947 level by 1959.

But even without these qualifications, the fact is stark enough: the United States found cause for celebration in the announcement that Negro workers had reached 58 percent of the wage level of their white co-workers. This situation is deeply imbedded in the very structure of American society.

Negroes in the United States are concentrated in the worst, dirtiest, lowest-paying jobs. A third continue to live in the rural South, most of them merely subsisting within a culture of poverty and a society of open terror. A third live in Southern cities and a third in Northern cities, and these have bettered their lot compared to the sharecroppers. But they are still the last hired and the first fired, and they are particularly vulnerable to recessions.

Thus, according to the Department of Labor in 1960, 4 percent of Negro employees were "professional, technical, and kindred workers" (compared to 11.3 percent for the whites); 2.7 percent were "managers, officials, and proprietors" (the white figure is 14.6 percent). In short, at the top of the economic structure there were 6.7 percent of the Negroes — and 25.9 percent of the whites. And this, in itself, represented considerable *gains* over the past two decades.

Going down the occupational scale, Negroes are primarily grouped in the bottom jobs. In 1960, 20 percent of the whites had high-skill industrial jobs, while the Negro share of this classification was 9 percent. Semiskilled mass production workers and laborers constituted around 48 percent of the Negro male population (and 25.3 percent of the white males). Negro women are the victims of a double discrimination. According to a New York State study, Negro female income as a percentage of white actually declined between 1949 and 1954 (and, in 1960, over a third of Negro women were still employed as domestics).

In part, this miserable structure of the Negro work force is an inheritance of the past. It reflects what happens to a people who have been systematically oppressed and denied access to skill and opportunity. If this completely defined the problem, there would be a basis for optimism. One could assume that the Negro would leave behind the mess of pottage bequeathed him by white America and move into a better future. But that is not the case. For the present position of the Negro in the economy has been institutionalized. Unless something basic is done, it will reproduce itself for years to come.

Take, as an example, the problem of automation. This has caused "structural" unemployment through the American work force, that is, the permanent destruction of jobs rather than cyclical layoffs. When this happens, the blow falls disproportionately upon the Negro. As the last significant group to enter the factory, the Negroes have low seniority (if they are lucky enough to be in union occupations), and they are laid off first. As one of the least skilled groups in the work force, they will have the hardest time getting another job. The "older" Negro (over forty) may well be condemned to job instability for the rest of his life.

All of this is immediate and automatic. It is done without the intervention of a single racist, yet it is a profound part of racism in the United States.

However, more is involved than the inevitable working of an impersonal system. The Negro lives in the other America of poverty for many reasons, and one of them is conscious racism reinforcing institutional patterns of the economy. In 1960, according to the report of Herbert Hill, Labor Secretary of the National Association for the Advancement of Colored People, Negroes made up only 1.69 percent of the total number of apprentices in the economy. The exact figure offered by Hill has been disputed; the shocking fact which he describes is agreed upon by everyone. This means that Negroes are denied access precisely to those jobs that are not low-paying and vulnerable to recession.

The main cause of this problem is the attitude of management, which fundamentally determines hiring policy. But in the case of apprenticeship programs, the labor movement and the Federal and state agencies involved also bear part of the responsibility. In the AFL-CIO, it is the politically conservative unions from the building trades who are the real stumbling block; the mass-production unions of the CIO have some bad areas, but on the whole they pioneered in bringing Negroes into the plants and integrating local organizations.

With the companies, one of the real difficulties in dealing with this structure of racism is that it is invisible. Here is a huge social fact, yet no one will accept responsibility for it. When questioned as to why there are no Negroes in sales, or in the office, the personnel man will say that he himself has nothing against Negroes. The problem, he will claim, is with subordinates who would revolt if Negroes were brought into their department, and with superiors who impose the policy. This response is standard up and down the line. The subordinates and the superiors make the same assertion.

Indeed, one of the difficulties in fighting against racist practices in the American economy is the popularity of a liberal rhetoric. Practically no one, outside of convinced white supremacists in the South, will admit to discriminatory policies. So it is that the Northern Negro has, in one sense, a more personally frustrating situation than his Southern brother. In Dixie, Jim Crow is personified, an actual living person who speaks in the accents of open racism. In the rest of the country, everybody is against discrimination for the record, and Jim Crow is a vast impersonal system that keeps the Negro down.

In the past few years, some Negro groups have been using the boycott to force companies to abandon racist hiring practices. This may well be an extraordinarily momentous development, for it is a step out of the other America, and equality will come only when the Negro is no longer poor.

But, as one goes up the occupational ladder, the resistance to

265

hiring Negroes becomes more intense. The office, for example, is a bastion of racism in American society. To some of the people involved, white-collar work is regarded as more personal, and even social, than factory work. So the integration of work appears like the integration of the neighborhood or the home. And a wall of prejudice is erected to keep the Negroes out of advancement.

Perhaps the most shocking statistic in all this is the one that describes what happens when a Negro does acquire skill and training. North, East, South, and West the pattern is the same: the more education a Negro has, the more economic discrimination he faces. Herman Miller, one of the best-known authorities on income statistics, has computed that the white Southern college graduate receives 1.85 times the compensation of his Negro counterpart, and in the North the white edge is 1.59.

What is involved in these figures is a factor that sharply distinguishes racial minorities from the old immigrant groups. When the Irish, the Jews, or the Italians produced a doctor, it was possible for him to begin to develop a practice that would bring him into the great society. There was prejudice, but he was increasingly judged on his skill. As time went on, the professionals from the immigrant groups adapted themselves to the language and dress of the rest of America. They ceased to be visible, and there was a wide scope for their talents.

This is not true of the Negro. The doctor or the lawyer will find it extremely difficult to set up practice in a white neighborhood. By far and large, they will be confined to the ghetto, and since their fellow Negroes are poor they will not receive so much money as their white colleagues. The Negro academic often finds himself trapped in a segregated educational system in which Negro colleges are short on salaries, equipment, libraries, and so on. Their very professional advancement is truncated because of it.

For the mass in the racial ghetto the situation is even more extreme. As a result of the segregation of neighborhoods, it is possible for a city like New York to have a public policy in favor of integration, and yet to maintain a system of effective segregation. In the mid-fifties, for example, the New York public-school system took a look at itself, dividing schools into Group X, with a high concentration of Negroes or Puerto Ricans, and Group Y where Negroes and

Puerto Ricans were less than 10 percent of the student body. They found that the X schools were older and less adequate, had more probationary and substitute teachers, more classes for retarded pupils, and fewer for bright children. This situation had developed with the framework of a public, legal commitment to integrated education. (Some steps have been taken to remedy the problem, but they are only a beginning.)

In the other America each group suffers from a psychological depression as well as from simple material want. And given the long history and the tremendous institutionalized power of racism, this is particularly and terribly true of the Negro.

Some commentators have argued that Negroes have a lower level of aspiration, of ambition, than whites. In this theory, the Jim Crow economy produces a mood of resignation and acceptance. But in a study of the New York State Commission Against Discrimination an even more serious situation was described: one in which Negro children had more aspiration than whites from the same income level, but less opportunity to fulfill their ambition.

In this study, Aaron Antonovsky and Melvin Lerner described the result as a "pathological condition . . . in our society." The Negro child, coming from a family in which the father has a miserable job, is forced to reject the life of his parents, and to put forth new goals for himself. In the case of the immigrant young some generations ago, this experience of breaking with the Old Country tradition and identifying with the great society of America was a decisive moment in moving upward. But the Negro does not find society as open as the immigrant did. He has the hope and the desire, but not the possibility. The consequence is heartbreaking frustration.

Indeed, Antonovsky suggests that the image of Jackie Robinson or Ralph Bunche is a threat to the young Negro. These heroes are exceptional and talented men. Yet, in a time of ferment among Negroes, they tend to become norms and models for the young people. Once again, there is a tragic gap between the ideal and the possible. A sense of disillusion, of failure, is added to the indignity of poverty.

A more speculative description of the Negro psychology has been written by Norman Mailer. For Mailer, the concept of "coolness" is a defense reaction against a hostile world. Threatened by the Man, denied access to the society, the Negro, in Mailer's image, stays loose: he anticipates disillusion; he turns cynicism into a style.

But perhaps the final degradation the Negro must face is the image the white man has of him. White America keeps the Negro down. It forces him into a slum; it keeps him in the dirtiest and lowest-paying jobs. Having imposed this indignity, the white man theorizes about it. He does not see it as the tragic work of his own hands, as a social product. Rather, the racial ghetto reflects the "natural" character of the Negro: lazy, shiftless, irresponsible, and so on. So prejudice becomes self-justifying. It creates miserable conditions and then cites them as a rationale for inaction and complacency.

One could continue describing the psychological and spiritual consequences of discrimination almost endlessly. Yet, whatever the accurate theory may be, it is beyond dispute that one of the main components of poverty for the Negro is a maiming of personality. This is true generally for the poor; it is doubly and triply true for the race poor. . . .

If, as is quite possible, America refuses to deal with the social evils that persist in the sixties, it will at the same time have turned its back on the racial minorities. There will be speeches on equality; there will be gains as the nation moves toward a constitutional definition of itself as egalitarian. The Negro will watch all this from a world of double poverty. He will continue to know himself as a member of a race-class condemned by heredity to be poor. There will be occasional celebrations – perhaps the next one will be called in twenty years or so when it is announced that Negroes have reached 70 percent of the white wage level. But that other America which is the ghetto will still stand.

There is a bitter picket-line chant that one sometimes hears when a store is being boycotted in the North:

> If you're white, you're right,
> If you're black, stay back.

It is an accurate sociological statement of the plight of the Negro in American society.

JAMES FARMER
I Will Keep My Soul

The Montgomery bus boycott that began in December 1955 marked the beginning of what has been called the direct action attack on segregation. This kind of protest was used again in February 1960 when four Negro college freshmen "sat-in" at a Woolworth lunch counter in Greensboro, North Carolina. Unlike Montgomery, where Rosa Parks's refusal to move to the rear of the bus was spontaneous, and Greensboro, where the students acted on their own initiative, the 1961 Freedom Rides were planned in advance. Their chief organizer was James Farmer, who became national director of the Congress of Racial Equality (CORE) in February 1961. Three other groups, including the Southern Christian Leadership Conference (SCLC), the Student Nonviolent Coordinating Committee (SNCC), and the Nashville Student Movement, as well as hundreds of other persons, black and white, joined the original thirteen CORE riders. The Freedom Rides resulted in an order by the Interstate Commerce Commission banning segregation in interstate terminal facilities that became effective on November 1, 1961. [Source: Progressive, November 1961.]

On May 4 of this year, I left Washington, D.C., with twelve other persons on a risky journey into the South. Seven of us were Negro and six were white. Riding in two regularly scheduled buses, one Greyhound, the other Trailways, traveling beneath overcast skies, our little band—the original Freedom Riders—was filled with expectations of storms almost certain to come before the journey was ended.

Now, six months later, as all the world knows, the fire-gutted shell of one bus lies in an Alabama junk yard, and some of the people who almost died with it are still suffering prolonged illnesses. A dozen Freedom Riders nearly gave up their lives under the fierce hammering of fists, clubs, and iron pipes in the hands of hysterical mobs. Many of the victims will carry permanent scars. One of them lies in a Detroit hospital critically ill from a cerebral hemorrhage, a direct result of the beating he took. Others have lost their jobs or have been expelled from school because of their participation in the rides. More than 350 men and women have been jailed in a half dozen states for doing what the Supreme Court of the United States had already said they had a right to do. The Interstate Commerce Commission has now issued an historic ruling in behalf of interstate bus integration which may indeed mean that the suffering of the past six months has not been in vain.

Why did we ride? What is the meaning of it all? Has the whole thing been a stunt, a gimmick engineered by irresponsible publicity seekers? Has America's prestige been damaged in the eyes of the world by the events that grew out of the Freedom Rides? These are questions frequently asked, and I think the answer should not be required to wait upon the verdict of history.

In 1946 the Supreme Court ruled in the Irene Morgan decision that segregation of interstate passengers in seating on buses was an unconstitutional burden upon commerce. A Freedom Ride later that year, called the "Journey of Reconciliation," cosponsored by the Congress of Racial Equality and the Fellowship of Reconciliation, demonstrated that segregated seating was still enforced on buses in the upper Southern states, and that anyone who challenged this segregation was subject to arrest and threatened violence. Through the years since that time reports have come into the office of the Congress of Racial Equality (CORE) of continuing segregation in seating on buses, especially in the deep South.

In 1960 the Supreme Court issued a ruling, in the Boynton case, banning segregation in the terminal facilities used by interstate passengers. Yet, in the months that followed reports continued to pour into our office indicating that the South was defying the Supreme Court's edict, just as some of the Southern states have defied the Court's school desegregation rulings. It was to close this gap between the interpretation and the implementation of the law that the Freedom Riders rode.

Who were the Freedom Riders? By what right did we seek to "meddle in the South's business"? Ever since the election of Rutherford B. Hayes to the Presidency in 1876, and the bargain with the South which it entailed, the Southern states have maintained that what they do with the Negro is their own business, and "outsiders" have no right to interfere. The Freedom Riders rejected this essentially states' right doctrine of race relations. None of us, in the

North or in the South, can afford the moral luxury of unconcern about injustice. Further, the states' rights doctrine is just as outmoded on the domestic scene as Nineteenth Century isolationism is on the international. Today, how can we think of outsiders keeping hands off injustice in Alabama, when outsiders all over the world can be threatened with destruction by events in a far away place like Laos? How would the dead of Korea view Mississippi's claim that only Mississippians have a right to concern themselves with injustice in that state?

So we came from all over the country, from both races and of all ages, to test compliance with the law, to exercise the right of all Americans to use all transportation facilities with the dignity of equality, to shake Americans out of their apathy on this issue and expose the real character of segregation to the pitiless scrutiny of a nation's conscience.

Outsiders? As Americans, from whatever state, all of us are Mississippians and Minnesotans, Carolinians and Californians, Alabamans and Arizonans. No American can afford to ignore the burning bus and the bloody heads of the mob's victims. Who can fail to be stirred by the new convicts for conscience, black and white, who walked with pride into Southern jails, especially in Mississippi, surrendering their own personal freedom in the struggle for a greater freedom for everyone?

Jail at best is neither a romantic nor a pleasant place, and Mississippi jails are no exception. The first twenty-seven Freedom Riders to arrive in Jackson saw the inside of two different jails and two different prisons—the Jackson City Jail, the Hinds County Jail, the Hinds County Prison Farm, and the State Penitentiary at Parchman. Jails are not a new experience for many of the Riders, but the Freedom Riders were definitely a new experience for Mississippi jails. For the first time, penal authorities in the citadel of segregation had a glimpse of the new Negro and the emancipated white. I do not think these jailers will ever be quite the same again after their experience. Nor will the other prisoners, black and white, be the same again, after having seen in the flesh men and women who do not believe segregation to be in the very nature of things, and who are willing to defy it.

Prison authorities frequently said, and really seemed to believe, that other Negro prisoners like things the way they are and have no sympathy with us, and that it was for our own protection that we were isolated from them. However, whenever the guards were not present, the Negro trustees went out of their way to show their sympathy by word and deed. "Keep up the good work," one said. "I admire you guys and what you are doing," said another. "I wish I could do the same thing, but I have to do what these people tell me to do." They smuggled newspapers in to us, delivered notes and messages between our cell block and that of the girl Freedom Riders, and passed on rumors which they had heard in the jail or in the community.

One night at the county jail, a voice called up from the cell block beneath us, where other Negro prisoners were housed. "Upstairs!", the anonymous prisoner shouted. We replied, "Downstairs!" "Upstairs!", replied the voice. "Sing your freedom song." And the Freedom Riders sang. We sang old folk songs and gospel songs to which new words had been written, telling of the Freedom Ride and its purpose. We sang new words to old labor songs, too. One stanza rang out: "They say in Hinds County no neutrals have they met. You're either for the Freedom Ride or you 'tom' for Ross Barnett." Then the downstairs prisoners, whom the jailers had said were our enemies, sang for us. The girl Freedom Riders, in another wing of the jail, joined in the Freedom Ride songs, and for the first time in history, the Hinds County jail rocked with singing of songs of freedom and brotherhood.

One evening at the county jail, after a rumor of our imminent transfer to the state penitentiary had reached us, the jailer came quietly to our Freedom Riders cell block. He called me, and we stood there with the bars between us, chatting. He did most of the talking. He told me about his family, his wife, and four or five children – the good records they had made in schools, including Ole Miss. He told me of his son's prowess in sports and of the children's marriages and his grandchildren. He told me, too, of his dislike of violence, and of his children's upbringing in that regard. The jailer stood there talking for more than an hour, in the first conversation we had had with him. This, I am sure, was his way of saying goodbye, and of telling us that he respects the Freedom Riders, and that whatever unpleasantness we might meet at the state penitentiary would be something of which he did not approve.

Mississippians, born into segregation, are human too. The Freedom Riders' aim is not only to stop the practice of segregation, but somehow to reach the common humanity of our fellowmen and bring it to the surface where they can act on it themselves. This is a basic motive behind the Freedom Rides, and nonviolence is the key to its realization.

It is not only that Southerners and other Americans have been shaken in their unjust racial practices, or out of their lethargy. Now, as a result of the Freedom Rides, the world at large, and especially the developing nations of Africa and Asia, have been offered the opportunity of viewing a new, more constructive approach to America's racial dilemma. If the world looks now it will see that many dedicated and conscientious Americans of both races, rather than sweeping the dirt of discrimination under the rug, are striving, at any cost, to remove the dirt from their house. If Africans witnessed our national shame in the necessity for the Freedom Rides, they saw our nation's hope and promise in the fact that there were so many Americans willing to risk their freedom and even their lives to erase that shame.

The world and America saw also the Freedom Rider's challenge to the traditions and fears which have immobilized so many Negroes in Dixie. In terminals in the South, and on the buses, many Negro passengers took the Freedom Riders' cue and dared to sit and ride "first class." This was another purpose of the Rides themselves: to break down the voluntary submission of Negroes to racial injustice, a submission created by generations of suppression with the rope and with fire and with economic reprisal. As I entered the white waiting room in one terminal in the South, a Negro woman passenger from the same bus caught my eye and anxiously beckoned me to follow her into the dingy but safe colored section. Moments later, when she saw me served at the lunch counter in the white section, she joined me for a cup of coffee.

In Jackson, Mississippi, forty-one Negro citizens of that community joined the Freedom Riders, ending up in their hometown jails. Now out on appeal bond, they report many threats of reprisals.

But there is a new spirit among Negroes in Jackson. People are learning that in a nonviolent war like ours, as in any other war, there must be suffering. Jobs will be lost, mortgages will be foreclosed, loans will be denied, persons will be hurt, and some may die. This new spirit was expressed well by one Freedom Rider in the Mississippi state penitentiary at Parchman. The guards threatened repeatedly, as a reprisal for our insistence upon dignity, to take away our mattresses. "Come and get my mattress," he shouted. "I will keep my soul."

4. The Supreme Court and the Schools

1954-1960

WILLIAM D. WORKMAN, JR.
The Case Against Forced Integration

The Supreme Court's school integration decisions in 1954 and 1955 were met by well-organized opposition, not only in the South but also in some Northern cities. By 1962, less than one-half of one percent of Southern Negroes attended previously all-white schools, and almost nothing really effective had been done about the de facto segregation in the North. Negroes were understandably impatient, and they began to charge the judicial process with being slow, cumbersome, and expensive; but at the same time segregationists intensified their attacks on the programs, such as big-city bussing, for enforced integration. William D. Workman, Jr., argued the South's position in a book from which an excerpt is reprinted here. [Source: The Case for the South, *New York, 1960, pp. 285-302.]*

It is a fair and practical question to ask now whether anything con-structive can be salvaged out of all the unpleasantness which has stemmed from the fight over racial integration. The answer might well be "Yes," a qualified "Yes."

The prospect of improving race relations in the face of intense resistance to integration is admittedly difficult under present pres-sures and hostilities, yet there are changes which can and should be made, not only for the improved welfare of Negro Southerners, but also for the justification of many arguments used by white South-erners against forced integration.

In any attempt to approach this delicately balanced situation, the advocate of change or relaxation immediately runs head on into a major division of opinion. There are those who contend that any concession whatever will tend to weaken the South's position, to crack the dike of resistance, and to make for an ultimate flooding as the dam breaks. On the other hand, there are those of equal sincerity who argue that SOME abridgments of the adamant segregation pattern MUST be made if the South is to successfully defend its main line of resistance, *i.e.,* the schools. Despite these contrary posi-tions, there is some hope of improved race relations by virtue of the fact that these two groups BOTH oppose racial integration in the schools. It may be that in joint resistance against a common foe they might find a basis for agreement on certain changes which might ease the situation, improving the lot of the Negro without damaging the lot of the white man.

For one thing, there should be some relaxation of both the legal and the social barriers which obstruct voluntary association of whites and Negroes. Much of the Southern argument against the Supreme Court decision has been based on the interpretation (whether correct or incorrect is beside the point) that enforcement of the decision would deny to the Southern man a freedom of choice as to where his child should attend school. Along with that has gone an extension of the same line of reasoning and its application into other fields—housing, churches, and so on. The essence of the white man's argument has been this: The individual should be protected in his right of freedom of association, and correspondingly, of freedom to AVOID unwanted association.

But by the same token, if the Southern segregationist wants to be free in his determination of associates, so should the Southern integrationist be free in HIS determination of associates provided, of course, that such associations are mutually acceptable, and provided further that the circumstances and conditions of integrated associations are not such as to endanger the public peace.

Much of the legislation enacted in the Southern states in both the immediate and the distant past has been aimed basically at preserving domestic tranquility as well as racial integrity. This is especially true in the fields of education and recreation, where indiscriminate mingling of the races is bound to bring discord and strife. Whatever the future may bring, and whatever may be the judgment of non-Southerners, the governmental agencies of the South are acting wisely when they seek to prevent mass mingling of the races in schools, pools, and parks. And distressing though it may be, the closing of such institutions in many cases would be the sensible alternative to the emotional, social, and physical upheaval which would follow on the heels of forced race mixing.

But where there is willingness to mix, and where such mixing would not jeopardize the public peace nor infringe upon the rights of others NOT to mix, some concessions are in order. Neither the written law of the political agency nor the unwritten law of the social community should stand in the way of whites and Negroes foregathering to confer, to discuss, or even to dine together with each other's consent and cooperation. The fact that such biracial activities might be distasteful to a large percentage of Southern whites should not be allowed to stand in the way of the integrationists' exercise of the right of peaceable assembly.

If an area of biracial activity can be carved out of the no-man's-land which now separates two races by law in most Southern communities, there seems no cause for undue alarm. If the South is to protect the right of some (most) white people to move within segregated circles, then in all fairness it should permit other white people to move within integrated circles if that be their wish. For many years to come, the impetus of such movement will have to be from the whites to the Negroes, but the Southern argument against compulsory integration should apply with equal validity against compulsory segregation of those inclined, however mistakenly, toward racial commingling, so long as the rights of all are protected with respect to preference of association.

The white Southerner can contribute importantly to the easing of the segregation tenseness, and to the ultimate adjustment of the racial problem itself, by the simple expedient—the word is used deliberately of extending to the Negro Southerner a larger and more adequate share of personal dignity and decency. This can be done with loss to neither, and with gain to both. Courtesy requires only intent and effort, and the application of those two in even small doses would repay the expenditure a thousandfold.

Many a Negro reduces his racial complaint to this basic emotion: "I just want to be treated like a man." There are those, of course, who want much more than that, who want special privilege, who wish to inject themselves into a white society which is not willing to accept them, who wish to break down every racial barrier that can be found, preferably by force—but these do not reflect the broader and more basic desire of the Southern Negro, which is simply to be accorded a better opportunity to make for himself whatever place he can in his community.

This will necessarily mean a revision of attitude on the part of those whites who say, with altogether too much condescension, "I've got nothing against the Negro, so long as he stays in his place." The fact of the matter is that the Negro is entitled to make his own place, and it ill behooves the white man to do other than help his black neighbor along.

This, too, is important: That a mere change of attitude on the part of white Southerners will aid materially in easing racial tensions. A change of attitude does not entail any change of conviction, or lessening belief in the desirability of racial segregation in the schools, and wherever else it may be needed in the particular community. A change in attitude means only that a white man can help himself, his neighborhood, and his Negro associates by simply substituting an attitude of cooperation for the old pattern of condescension.

Along with this must go a measure of insistence that the Negro play his part in what could be a new and improved level of communication. If the Negro genuinely desires to be treated with greater dignity, then his own conduct must be such as to warrant it. He cannot expect to receive dignity along with indulgence. The burden of performance rests finally upon him. He cannot continue in his improvident ways, squandering his relatively small earnings on drink, trinkets, and carousing, forsaking his family when the mood strikes him, "forgetting" legal and moral obligations – and still look for the sort of treatment reserved for more worthy persons.

Many a white man is convinced that the Negro does not have it in him to break off his old habits, to buckle down to the demanding task of becoming a more laudable citizen, to raise his standard of personal conduct to an acceptable level. But the fair-minded white will show himself willing to meet the Negro fully halfway toward the higher level of communication.

In doing so, the white Southerner himself may gain a fairer and clearer picture of Negro capabilities. There is a Southwide tendency among white people to attribute to ALL Negroes those characteristics of the Negroes with whom they habitually come into contact. Since those contacts are for the most part with Negroes in menial or very subordinate positions, there is little awareness among whites that there are Negroes whose capacities and conduct are such as to warrant better treatment from their white neighbors.

As a corollary of improved communication between the two races, with accompanying better appreciation of each other's merits, there should be the offering of greater opportunity to the Negro to participate in both the planning and the execution of programs aimed at community development. It does not require any great amount of imagination on the part of a fair-minded white man to appreciate the resentment which naturally arises among manifestly capable and decent Negroes when they are denied all opportunity to take part in the formulation of policies and decisions which will bear directly upon them. The solidly American slogan of "no taxation without representation" has a bearing here, and Negroes would be something less than Americans if they did not feel the basic unfairness of complete exclusion from the area of community betterment on the grounds of color alone. . . .

In the field of race relations, the white Southerner's major shortcoming in recent years has been by way of omission rather than commission. When the Negro complains of having been denied even the outward trappings of dignity and decent treatment, he is justified in very large measure. It is to the discredit of the white man that he has provided no place in the Southern order of things for the colored man who, by his own efforts, has brought himself up to the level of decency and achievement demanded by white society.

Old habits and old associations die hard, and few Southerners outside the ministry and, to a lesser degree, the world of education have seen fit to bring the Negro into their counsels in ANY capacity. Understandably, the capable Negro who KNOWS his own capacity has become resentful of whites who will accord him no recognition of achievement nor any degree of participation in community development, be it segregated or nonsegregated.

In all justice, however, it must be recorded that here and there about the South, degrees of recognition and participation were being accorded Negroes in slow but growing measure. A documentation of the biracial enterprises being conducted throughout the South in the years immediately preceding the Supreme Court decision presents a surprisingly long list of joint efforts. Yet the list fell far short of what could have been, and what should have been, an effective coordination between the races in every community of the region. Now, unhappily, the list has been cut to shreds by the revival of distrust and animosity engendered by the Supreme Court decision and the subsequent attempts to force integration on areas not prepared to accept it. . . .

281

One of the blind spots in the make-up of the average white Southerner is his ignorance of the attitudes and workings, and in large measure of the very existence, of a middle class Negro group. Yet these Negroes presumably have much the same outlook on life as that held by the white middle class: a preoccupation with education, for themselves and their children; an adherence to strict (or professedly strict) codes of morality; and a consuming desire to be accepted as desirable elements of the community. Because of these feelings, which are judged desirable by members of the white middle class, it comes as a shameful thing to these Negroes who, upon actually attaining such middle-class status, nevertheless are treated as being inferior to the lower-class whites who make no pretense of subscribing to the same standards of values.

Unfortunately, at this stage of the game, these able and cultured Negroes are not strong enough in either numbers or influence to set the tone of the Negro community, whether it be located North or South. Consequently, any such community of appreciable size is much more likely to reflect the habits, attitudes, and values of the lower class. And since the lower Negro classes lean noticeably toward licentiousness, there is no strong pressure of community opinion to guide individual Negroes into an acceptable mode of conduct.

It may well be that, figuratively speaking, the Negro in the South now is passing from a prolonged period of civic adolescence into his maturity. The extended length of that growing period has been due both to the paternalistic attitude of the Southern white and to the childish attitude of many a Southern Negro. Just as parents frequently are somewhat bewildered and irritated by the behavior of their own children as they move from childhood into the trying days of adolescence, so have white Southerners been puzzled by the growing restiveness and resentment of Negro Southerners. So also have many white Southerners been unwilling to recognize the fact that the Negro may be "growing up."

One of the chief rallying cries of the NAACP and its fellow travelers is that of "first-class citizenship" for the Negroes of America. The catch phrase is appealing and has been used effectively to enlist the support of well meaning persons whose heartstrings are pulled by the caterwauling which constantly arises from the professional champions of the Negro. Without in any way condoning the undeniable instances in which Negroes have been denied some of their rights, not only in the South but in the North and elsewhere about the nation, let's take a look at the reverse side of the coin and see whether the Negroes have themselves earned a categorical reputation as "first-class citizens." In the process, we might learn whether there is not a tendency among Negroes to confuse citizenship with social privilege. Citizenship is a conditional, not an absolute, right. It comes unasked as a blessing to those fortunate enough to be born in the United States, and to certain others under varying conditions, so there is no real credit attached to BECOMING or BEING an American citizen. It generally stems from the accident of birth. But even so, the right of citizenship can be forfeited, or abridged, by misconduct in any of a number of ways, and therein may lie some basis for distinction between "first-class" and "second-class" citizens.

First-class citizenship demands more than the simple payment of taxes and the rendering of obligatory military or civil service as the need arises. It demands a fulfillment of society's unwritten as well as its written responsibilities. It involves a civic consciousness which contributes to community welfare, a code of personal and family conduct which meets the standards of decency and self-respect, and a willingness to participate in as well as partake of the benefits of the social organization.

On the other hand, the citizen may lose his status, or at least his right to vote or hold office, if he is convicted of any of a number of disqualifying crimes. The list varies from state to state, but to list some which appear in many jurisdictions, there are such offenses as "burglary, arson, obtaining money or goods under false pretenses, perjury, forgery, robbery, bribery, adultery, bigamy, wife-beating, housebreaking, receiving stolen goods, breach of trust with fraudulent intent, fornication, sodomy, incest, assault with intent to ravish, miscegenation, larceny, or crimes against the election law." (S[outh] C[arolina] Constitution)

Conviction of any of those crimes automatically places an individual in the role of a "second-class citizen" regardless of race, but there are other offenses which rightfully establish offenders as something less than "first-class" citizens. And here again, as in a great number of the crimes cited above, the Negro offends out of all proportion to his numbers and far beyond the limits of provocation. Unfortunately, he has been *permitted* to do so not only through the laxity of his own standards, but by the indulgence of white persons in positions of authority. In far too many instances, white officials have tolerated intraracial crime and immorality among the Negroes out of a sense of humoring those whose pattern of life differs in such a large measure from that of white persons.

The time is at hand when such indulgence should stop short, for the good of both races. Prolonged tolerance of immorality and criminality among Negroes tends to perpetuate their inadequate social patterns and to threaten the patterns of white neighbors.

Consequently, if Negroes by and of themselves launch an all-out campaign against their own shortcomings, they can contribute to several desirable goals at one and the same time: They can materially improve the community standing of their racial group by reducing the incidence of venereal disease, illegitimacy, sexual promiscuity, indolence, and so on; they can demonstrate to themselves, and to the world at large, that they have both the capacity and the will to raise their own standards; they can enlist the support of other groups in campaigns manifestly designed for community betterment; and –this is important– they can virtually disarm their critics who employ the stereotype device against them. A stereotype label is bound to lose effectiveness in the face of statistical proof that it is factually wrong, and many of the charges brought categorically against Negro conduct are subject to statistical appraisal.

All of this presupposes that the Negro can meet the challenge, and to that extent, the suggestion accepts at face value the assertions of the NAACP and of the modern-day sociologists and anthropologists who insist that the Negro race, as a race, is not inferior to the white. Here, then, is an opportunity for them to prove the truth of that contention, and to prove it in a manner which can be understood and appreciated by the layman. They can do so by an unflagging insistence that their race measure up to community standards. This means that there is a burden of performance and respectability imposed upon the Negro if he is to qualify as a first-class citizen in fact as well as in legal standing.

But if the challenge of self-improvement confronts the Negroes

284

themselves, there is much which can be done by the white Southerners who hold the political and economic reins of the region.

For one thing, there is a dire need for improved housing facilities for Negroes. Even the most cursory study of the Negro shift in population bears out the obvious but virtually ignored fact that Negroes are moving in great numbers from the country to the city. This is no new development, and it shows no signs of either moderating or ceasing in the near future. Furthermore, it is a massive sort of flow which cannot be readily stemmed or controlled by appeals to reason or by the raising of obstacles. The impact of these incoming Negroes is being felt in city after city throughout the South as well as in the North, and there is need for both planning and action to adjust to their influx.

Since few Negro communities in metropolitan areas now have decent or adequate sections for residence, the continuing immigration of newcomers has the effect of piling up more and more residents into areas of already high population density. With this comes added problems of public health, morality, crime, and general conduct, to say nothing of the added demands for educational, social, welfare, and medical services.

Adequate planning and preparation by both white and Negro businessmen, real estate agents, community organizations, and city officials would make possible an orderly expansion of Negro residents into new areas, and might even make for gradual rather than sudden and hostile displacement of white families. One of the main complaints of white occupants and property owners in a given area threatened by Negro invasion is the abrupt and seemingly inevitable falling of property values once the neighborhood becomes "mixed." That in itself is due in no small part to the fact that the internal pressure in the "containers" of Negro population builds up to such a point that any breakout becomes anything from a spurt to a torrent, rather than a regulated flow. The need for housing is so great that, once access is obtained to other accommodations, there is a veritable deluge of Negroes into such newly available quarters. A further complication is the fact that these new or once-white quarters frequently demand a higher rental or purchase price than the average Negro family can meet. Consequently, additional families or wage earners are crowded into

285

the housing units in order to provide a greater rent-paying potential per square foot of occupancy. All of this combines to hasten the conversion of the recently acquired housing into veritable slums, which depress property values throughout the entire neighborhood.

It seems that cooperation of the type suggested above might meet this situation through the establishment of rigid zoning ordinances which would limit the occupancy of individual housing units, require the maintenance of adequate standards, and in general insure the maintenance of the area on a respectable basis for residential use.

White landlords all too frequently show interest only in draining a heavier financial return from their investment and accordingly fail to maintain their holdings in decent repair. But if these white property owners can be accused of being niggardly, their tenants in too many instances can be accused of being "niggerly," to use a word at once offensive and descriptive. The proper maintenance of housing requires joint effort by both owner and occupant, and that state of affairs very seldom prevails in the field of Negro housing. The landlords complain of Negro irresponsibility in matters of both finance and household care, while Negroes complain of indifference and callousness on the part of the white owners. Here is an area in which much work is to be done by way of persuasion and regulation on the parts of municipal leaders, whether political or not. Intelligent use can be made here of existing Negro civic groups, and others can be brought into the field to heighten the feelings of self-respect and pride of appearance which make for pleasant and healthful residential areas.

City planning, although anathema by its very title to many a rugged individualist, nevertheless can play an important role in helping communities anticipate and solve such housing problems before they reach the acute stage. One major need in this field is to plan for spatial expansion of Negro housing areas so as to serve the dual purpose of providing living space for Negroes without forcing them into white residential areas.

Today, thousands upon thousands of Negroes in the "piled-up" slums and ghettos of the North are finding that their freedom is indeed a serious thing. They find few of the helping hands, white or black, to which they could turn in their former rural settings. They are exposed to all the meanness, the grubbing, the grasping, and the greed of congested urban life, and they frequently wallow in their own helplessness and ineptitude. For them, competent guidance, advice, and instruction could mean the difference between existing and living. Whether the helping hands should be black or white, or both, and whether they should be provided by the local, the state, or the federal governments, or jointly by them all, these are questions to be answered only after more study—but tax monies expended wisely in this sort of urban demonstration work could well be bread cast upon the waters. . . .

Short of utter amalgamation of the races, a thing utterly unacceptable to white Southerners, there is no *solution* to the problem of race relations; there can only be a continual adjustment and readjustment of relationships. The sense of race, no less than those of religion or of nationality, is so deeply embedded in man's nature — both conscious and unconscious — that it cannot be eradicated in the foreseeable future, if indeed it *should* be eradicated. Some persons, whose impulses can be regulated or whose incentives can be manipulated, may rise above, or descend below, race consciousness, but the masses are not likely ever to shed their recognition of race.

Whatever may be the future of race relations in America, this much seems evident: That neither satisfaction nor peace can come from any coercive mingling of the white and black races against the will of either, and that little hope can be entertained for any assimilation of one in the other. There remains, then, only the prospect of accommodating their differences in a pattern of peaceful coexistence based upon a friendly tolerance and helpful understanding. It is the recognition of racial distinctions, not their denial, which will lessen the tensions and enhance their adjustment.

There is serious need now for a thorough reassessment of the entire picture of race relations—North and South—and for what the phrase makers might call another "agonizing reappraisal" of the costs and the consequences of the nation's forced march toward integration. The time is ripe for both sides—for all sides—of the several controversies to inventory their successes and their failures. Fresh decisions need to be made in the light of matters as they stand now, and as they seem likely to develop in the near future.

These are some of the questions to be answered before the making of new decisions, or the reaffirmation of old ones, if that be the course taken:

1. Are the people of the East, the West, and the North willing to persist in driving a divisive wedge between themselves and those of the South through endorsement of anti-Southern legislation which inevitably will perpetuate sectionalism?

2. Is the Supreme Court of the United States so convinced of the wisdom of its school integration decision that it will continue to insist upon the sociological upheaval of communities which are being transformed from peaceful neighborhoods into writhing centers of racial conflict?

3. Is the National Association for the Advancement of Colored People so determined to compel race-mixing that it cares not for the regeneration of bitter race hatred, which had been diminishing steadily for years, but which now is being planted in the hearts and minds of white youngsters and which will be a scourge to the NAACP and to the Negro for years to come, not only in the South but everywhere?

4. Are the two national political parties so base in their competition for partisan advantage that they are willing to offer up the white South as a sacrifice to the unreasoning demands of minority blocs in the North, and thereby to drive white Southerners into a third political party?

5. Is the national government prepared to display to the world at large an inability to treat fairly with the inhabitants of one-quarter of the nation, and a willingness to coerce with military might those citizens whose only fault is their insistence on preserving their racial integrity and the remaining vestiges of the local self-government presumably guaranteed to them by the Constitution of the United States?

6. Is organized labor willing to write off the South as a target for future unionization by continued agitation for "civil rights" and other class legislation?

7. Are the churches of America so confident that integration is the only Christian answer to the eternal question of race relations that they will risk driving into other denominations and other associations those equally sincere Christians who have received no divine admonition to mix the races?

288

8. Are the Negroes of the land so devoid of self-respect and pride that they stand ready to admit that their children cannot develop and improve except in the presence of the white race?

9. Are the teachers of America prepared to abandon the precept that learning is enhanced where students share similar values and backgrounds, and to embark upon the instructional ordeal of teaching discordant groups of dissimilar children?

10. Are the parents throughout the South, or throughout the nation for that matter, ready to surrender all hope of transmitting their own cultural heritage to their children, and to accept an agglutinated cultural compound distinctive only in its lack of all distinction?

11. Are the people of America so obsessed with determination to force integration upon an unwilling South that they will support their federal government in the use of bayonet-studded force to overcome resistance? . . .

"If the two races are to meet upon terms of social equality, it must be the result of natural affinities, a mutual appreciation of each other's merits, and a voluntary consent of individuals."

KENNETH ALLSOP

Black, White, and the Blues

Negroes streamed northward from the economically blighted towns and rural areas of the South in ever increasing numbers after World War II, seeking not only economic opportunity but also political freedom. They came to Washington, and New York, and Cleveland, and Detroit, and other Northern cities (and also to Los Angeles in the West), but perhaps especially to Chicago, the metropolis at the top of the Mississippi Valley that had been a magnet for immigrants for over a century. With them came Southern "poor whites" from the exhausted lands of Kentucky and Tennessee and the no longer efficient factories of West Virginia, and together they began to create what could almost be called a sub-culture in Chicago, one that the city had never known, or not known for a long time. The morals of this sub-culture may have been "bad" and its habits "un-American," but its music was superb—a fact pointed to with admiration by the Englishman Kenneth Allsop, who wrote the following "Letter from Chicago" for publication in an English magazine in 1960. The piece is reprinted here in part. [Source: Encounter, April 1960.]

On Michigan Avenue, on Chicago's South Side, a young Kentuckian wearing long Presley sideburns and a black leather jacket, and carrying a half-empty bottle of muscatel, boarded a late-night bus. He lurched down the aisle, fell into a seat and peered opaquely around. His wine-muzzy eyes lit on a Negro opposite, and a mild sort of illumination spread across his face. "Hey, you there!" he called, and an uneasy twitch of apprehensive attention galvanized all the passengers, white and colored. But no race incident was about to erupt. The Kentuckian took a pull from the bottle and leaning forward, said to the Negro emotionally: "You and me, boy, we're together. We're surrounded."

It would be heartwarming to be able to report that the Negro stepped across the aisle and that black and white hands gripped in brotherliness, whereas in fact the Negro stared straight ahead in glassy embarrassment in the hope of discouraging the drunk's confidences. He did, for the youth slumped into a muttering doze, and everyone's gaze drifted back to the bleak, neonglaring drabness beyond the window, where lay the city fiefs of racial and economic segregation.

Yet this random pulse of melodrama unexpectedly made real for me one small, strange aspect of the social turmoil that is still today as desperate a problem as it has ever been in Chicago's brief and violent history.

Immigration, the process of blood transfusion from all the world's nations that has given America both its vitality and its overheated, accelerated metabolism, has in this decade entered a new phase in Chicago. Between 1910 and 1920 the Negro population of Chicago doubled as a result of the demand for Southern labor to replace the influx of European immigrants stemmed by World War I. In the Depression years of the Thirties, the population growth of the city, including that of the Negro, ground to a halt, but in the postwar years Northern industries again tapped the South for their supplies.

What consequently happened is described by a local demographer (Professor Philip M. Hauser, of the University of Chicago) as a

290

"population explosion," a "rapidity of growth, a change in population composition, and a mushrooming of physical problems practically unique in human history." And one bizarre element in this present sociological ferment is the creation—probably extremely tenuous and temporary, but still an actuality for the moment—of a bond of sympathy between poor white and poor black from the rural South, lost and lonely in the metropolitan asphalt jungle, thrust into unfamiliarly frightening and ferocious conditions, a feeling of unity that so far all the federal integration legislation has failed to achieve in Little Rock and the Dixie hinterland.

Any day and every day the scene is the same at Chicago's railroad terminal—the uncertain surge forward through the gates of entry of the newest batch of arrivals, family groups with string-lashed suitcases and bulging bundles. The Negroes are fieldhands and levee laborers from the Mississippi Valley here to try their urban luck, whose wage rates have been $3 a day (not subsistence level in the United States) and who in recent years have heard reiteratively two alluring and challenging things in letters from friends and relatives who had earlier gone North: that $2.50 an hour can be earned in Illinois factories and that "If you can't make it in Chicago, you can't make it anywhere." It is a matter of fine degree, but the white invaders tend to be less literate and less skilled than the Negroes. Lumped together by Chicagoans—and there's a good deal of contempt in the term—as "hillbillies," but also variously known as backwoodsmen, Appalachians, poor white trash, mountain hicks, and red-necks, they are pouring in, in pursuit of jobs and the much-advertised American Good Life, from the declining coal-pit and scratch-farm regions of Missouri, Mississippi, Kentucky, Arkansas, Alabama, and Tennessee.

The Southern migrants are arriving in Chicago at the rate of 2,000 a week. There are estimated to be 65,000 hillbillies resident, but the number is hard to check for they crowd houses as subtenants, are disinclined to send their children to school, and do not register as voters. The Negroes are swelling a black population which already numbers 800,000—21 percent of the city's total—and which is thickening and expanding Chicago's black core. At a quickening rate the established white-collar class is shifting outward to the suburbs, evacuating what a generation ago were prosperous res-

291

idential districts and which are now fast becoming decaying ghettos. Nor are all the newcomers finding the jobs they expected: 75 percent of those on county welfare aid are Negroes.

Chicago is an illusory city. To drive into it by car through the great complex of eight-lane freeways that swing airily across cloverleaf junctions and coiling flyovers, and then down on to the surpassingly beautiful Lake Shore Drive, is to infer that little can ail a metropolis of such radiant magnificence. For mile upon mile the rainbow cars ooze with their big-engine casualness along those lakefront tree-arcaded boulevards, on one side the white sails of that now obligatory household accessory, the small boat, flecking Michigan's blue waters; on the other the glinting, soaring sierras of skyscraper apartment houses and office buildings, a lovely and splendid cliff range of towering white stone, glass, and metal. They made me think of white teeth that shine in a skull. At almost any point in those resplendent frontage miles you have to divert only a few blocks to be in the city's squalid interior, a complex of interminable, ugly, shabby streets which for long sections slide into some of the worst festering slums to be found anywhere, including Glasgow and the Middle East.

A truer sense of what you are entering is gained if you reach Chicago by train, as on this occasion I did from New York. As you approach the industrial fringes the rails fray out wider and wider into a vast skein, the convergence of 19 trunk lines, a 1,750-square-mile sorting center for 221,000 miles of national rail arteries that end and start here, and where 45,000 goods cars are loaded and unloaded every day. Presumably you already know that you are 1,745 miles from the West Coast and 713 miles from the East Coast, but what suddenly drives home that this is the very belly of the Middle West, the central transit point of this enormous land, and so the arrival point for job seekers from everywhere, is the sight of the banked processions of freight trucks that pass you and which are passed.

For me, the insignia on their sides were a distillation of all the romance and wonder of American history, the symbols of distance and lunging frontiers and restless adventurousness. CHESAPEAKE & OHIO, PENNSYLVANIA, B & O, SANTA FE, OVERLAND ROUTE, MID-AMERICA, ROCK ISLAND, THE CHIEF, FLORIDA EAST COAST, ARMOUR STOCK EXPRESS, SOUTHERN PACIFIC, MOBILE AND OHIO, THE ROUTE

OF THE HIAWATHA, TEXAS AND PACIFIC, WABASH, LOUISVILLE AND NASHVILLE, EVERYWHERE WEST—BURLINGTON ROUTE . . . the rumbling litany gave me a private satisfaction, for it seemed to ring with the authentic clangor of folk history, to be the essential stuff of that aspect of the American legend that is made up of such ingredients as Big Bill Haywood's itinerant union organizers—the "Wobblies" of the IWW—New Deal construction camps, the big exoduses of the *Grapes of Wrath* period, the bums produced by the big strikes and lockouts of the 1890s and the Depression hoboes riding the rods and the boxcars across the continent, the mythological John Henry, Casey Jones, and Paul Bunyan, the "fast Western" piano style of the Carolina turpentine camps, blues-minstrels like Blind Lemon Jefferson and Leadbelly, the breakout of jazz from the Mississippi Valley in the Twenties, radical guitarists like Woody Guthrie, the period of the Dust Bowl and the migratory harvest workers and loggers . . . all the movement and mixture under economic pressures, all the fluid patterns which are only just beginning to congeal into a recognizable American image.

Chicago, geographically a corradial center for so much of this flux, is still far from congealed. To talk of minorities, meaning the racial and foreign-stock inhabitants, is misleading. It is native-born Chicagoans who are the minority. In the city's 3.7 million population—6.5 million within the standard "metropolitan area"—only 40 percent are what might be called for want of a better ethnic label Anglo-Saxon American. Of the rest 15 percent are foreign-born (Polish, German, Italian, Russian, Scandinavian, and Irish in order of numbers), 24 percent second-generation foreign, and 21 percent Negro. Conditions of living are not so neatly packaged as those figures. The colored "quarter" is no longer clearly demarcated. The poverty-tide of the colored and foreign immigrants has broken through at many points into the "respectable" areas of the city and washes hungrily around eroding middle-class islands. The University of Chicago, down on the South Side at Hyde Park, is encircled now by Negro tenements. Adjacent to the Newberry Library on the Near North Side is a public school which has among its pupils Japanese, Negroes, Puerto Ricans, Greeks, Gypsies, Spaniards, Germans, Poles, Mexicans, and Chinese. Many of the Southern new arrivals are colonizing freshly invaded districts on the West Side.

293

The reason for this "population explosion" is what might be called with equal justification an "industrial explosion." It is certainly true, but impossible for the mind to grasp, that just 126 years ago this present metropolis was a village of 350 people and a few onion fields reclaimed from swamp at the junction of a river and a lake, and whose Indian name meant "the smell of skunks." In 1837, when the population had climbed to 4,179, it was incorporated as a city. Eleven years later Chicago was connected with canals and railroads, and its development as a grain and meat center began. Its population shot up. By 1860 — only twenty-three years later — it had reached 100,000; by 1910, 2 million; by 1930, 3 million. The latest spurt upward has been brought about by the opening of 5,000 new factories since 1939, by the increase of retail trade from $2 billion to $8 billion in sixteen years, by a still expanding steel industry that employs half a million men, and by an annual handling of 72 million tons of waterborne cargo — a figure which will be vastly expanded by the completion of the St. Lawrence Seaway, connecting the city direct with the Atlantic, and which, it has cautiously been predicted, will result in a fresh "economic breakthrough" and push the population up to 7 million in the next five years.

The peculiar paradox is that Chicago's mood is not in harmony with this bounding momentum of prosperity and material progress. Today this does not seem the swaggering frontier town, brassy with arrogant self-confidence and bursting vitality, that has been its reputation. A banker, one of the richest and most influential political figures in Illinois, said to me: "We're not so cocky as we once were." This is also the town whose mayor, Big Bill Thompson, threatened in 1927 to "bust the snoot" of the King of England if he showed up there, which last year turned out in millions to cheer the Queen of England. There is less pride today in the city's lurid past, the long "open town" history of unhindered prostitution, gambling, and drinking, and there is a general sensitive resentment toward inquiries about the fourteen years of Prohibition, when the corrupt alliance between crime and politics was expressed in law flouting of a blatancy and violence unparalleled in any other American community.

This new sobriety may be due to a number of factors. Perhaps to the knowledge that the racketeer, behind his contemporary facade of legitimate business, still has a powerful grip upon the administration and upon civic life – a prominent lawyer whose activities are mostly in the catering field alleged to me that "there isn't a night club or restaurant in Chicago that isn't paying protection to the hoods," and a writer, who has lived in Chicago all his life, said: "This city is as full of complicity as it ever was. The whole city's under the table. Nobody makes it legitimately." Perhaps the change is also due to the nagging knowledge that, despite that lakefront skyline of glittering pinnacles, despite piecemeal slum clearance and rehousing projects, internally the second city of the United States is a sleazy mess – decaying, declared a recent report, "not structure by structure, but by whole neighborhoods and communities at a time." Perhaps, furthermore, it is due to the racial tensions that appear to paralyze effective improvements in so many spheres.

It is no doubt logical in the light of the present situation that the anxieties of so many white Chicagoans are morbidly fixed upon the swelling voting strength of the Negroes. A Civil Rights Commission survey admits that "the Negro population in Chicago is probably as segregated as in any large city of the United States and, perhaps, more so than in most," but the point is how much longer will the Negro stay – and, those who are honest say, can he be kept – in what the survey calls "discernible enclaves"? It is estimated that if the intake continues at its present rate, by 1975 Negroes will form one-third of the population – "I figure," one businessman said to me gloomily, "that we have about twenty years left before we get our first black mayor, and then things will get really tough for the rest of us." . . .

Although "black supremacy" is an idea that is juggled about with widely different emotions by many white and colored Chicagoans, its practical application appeared to me to be far distant from realization. For what are immediately striking are the schisms that run jaggedly through the black community of Chicago. To the established Negro resident, who has possibly had a college education and pulled himself up by his bootstraps to at least a replica of the *Saturday Evening Post* cover way-of-life – good income, good house, good cars, good deep freeze, good stereo system – the rough, unsophisticated arrivals from the South are an embarrassment and a drag. As much as he can he dissociates himself from the new set-

295

tlers, who, he feels, have more affinity with the equally poor and illiterate hillbillies, Puerto Ricans, Gypsies, and Navajo, Hopi, Sioux, and Mandan Indians who in some numbers are trying to turn themselves into urban workers and are cramming together in the La Salle Street and Clark Street areas.

A young Negro recording company executive said to me: "There are internal race problems here. Because the hillbillies are dirty and lawless and dangerous when drunk, every white Chicagoan isn't identified with them. But when the Southern Negroes misbehave, we get blamed for what they do. You see, I've got the same badge of my face."

There is another, less serious but to me equally regrettable, consequence of these divisions of sympathy and understanding, which can be seen to be economically horizontal as well as racially vertical. That is the obliviousness that exists among the educated Chicagoans of both colors of a subculture renaissance that is burgeoning in the sidestreet bars and cafes deep in the slum belts. There is a new, late flowering of folk music. By this I don't mean the kind of smooth folksy cabaret dispensed at the smart Gate of Horn night club by such professionals as Josh White and the Kingston Trio, but authentic, rough, rural stuff well below the line of potential commercialization. This has two distinct forms. In the hillbilly clubs and saloons west of Broadway near Belmont Street, where Confederate flags are hung over the bar, the entertainment is a local brand of country-and-western imported from the Kentucky highlands. . . . In the Negro bars in the area of Cottage Grove Avenue and Halsted Street the blues are being sung and played with a volume and variety to be found nowhere else in the United States, not even in the Mississippi Valley where the blues were born. . . .

There are scores of places—sawdust dives into which a white man won't get admission unless escorted by a Negro known there—where blues in the old manner, crude, funky and sad, are to be heard any time after midnight. The stars in this underground and strictly zoned entertainments industry are people like Muddy Waters, Memphis Slim, Little Walter, Jimmy Reed, and Howling Wolf; but there are a hundred others, mostly immigrant Southerners, middle-aged and more, who work for the Post Office or drive delivery vans during the day, who after midnight play the blues on a guitar or mouth organ, and shout variations on such perennial themes as:

You been sweet to me and you ain't never run aroun'
Said you been sweet to your daddy and never run aroun'
But will you still be my baby when this lousy deal goes down? . . . .

The blues are a plaint, a protest music that grew out of suffering, indignity, and rotten living conditions. There is still good cause for the blues to be sung in modern Chicago. When the blues die and are heard no more, it will probably be a melancholy day for such folk-song hunters as I; but then Chicago will be a healthier city.

JOHN HOWARD GRIFFIN

The Hate Stare

The following narrative about a bus ride into Mississippi was written by a white man who underwent medical treatment to darken his skin color, enabling him to cross the color line in the deep South. John Howard Griffin spent a little over a month traveling through Louisiana, Mississippi, Alabama, and Georgia in late 1959. His experience as a "tenth-class citizen" speaks for itself. [Source: Black Like Me, New York, 1961, pp. 17–63.]

After a week of wearying rejection, the newness had worn off. My first vague, favorable impression that it was not as bad as I had thought it would be came from courtesies of the whites toward the Negro in New Orleans. But this was superficial. All the courtesies in the world do not cover up the one vital and massive discourtesy — that the Negro is treated not even as a second-class citizen, but as a tenth-class one. His day-to-day living is a reminder of his inferior status. He does not become calloused to these things — the polite rebuffs when he seeks better employment; hearing himself referred to as nigger, coon, jigaboo; having to bypass available rest-room facilities or eating facilities to find one specified for him. Each new reminder strikes at the raw spot, deepens the wound. I do not speak here only from my personal reaction, but from seeing it happen to others, and from seeing their reactions.

The Negro's only salvation from complete despair lies in his belief, the old belief of his forefathers, that these things are not direct-ed against him personally, but against his race, his pigmentation. His mother or aunt or teacher long ago carefully prepared him, ex-plaining that he as an individual can live in dignity, even though he as a Negro cannot. "They don't do it to you because you're Johnny— they don't even know you. They do it against your Negro-ness."

But at the time of the rebuff, even when the rebuff is impersonal, such as holding his bladder until he can find a "Colored" sign, the Negro cannot rationalize. He feels it personally and it burns him. It gives him a view of the white man that the white can never under-stand; for if the Negro is part of the black mass, the white is always the individual, and he will sincerely deny that he is "like that," he has always tried to be fair and kind to the Negro. Such men are offended to find Negroes suspicious of them, never realizing that the Negro cannot understand how—since as individuals they are decent and "good" to the colored—the whites as a group can still contrive to arrange life so that it destroys the Negro's sense of per-sonal value, degrades his human dignity, deadens the fibers of his being.

Existence becomes a grinding effort, guided by belly-hunger and the almost desperate need to divert awareness from the squalors to the pleasures, to lose oneself in sex or drink or dope or gut-religion or gluttony or the incoherence of falsity; and in some instances in the higher pleasures of music, art, literature, though these usually deepen perceptions rather than dull them, and can be unbearable; they present a world that is ordered, sane, disciplined to felicity, and the contrast of that world to theirs increases the pain of theirs.

When I went out that morning the face of the Negro populace was glum and angry.

At the shoe stand, Sterling did not give his usual cordial greeting. His eyes looked yellower than usual.

"You heard?" he asked.

"No . . . I haven't heard anything . . ."

He told me the Mississippi jury refused to indict in the Parker lynch case. The news had spread over the quarter like a wave of acid. Everyone talked of it. Not since I was in Europe, when the Russo-German Pact of 1939 was signed, had I seen news spread such bitterness and despair.

298

Sterling handed me this morning's issue of *The Louisiana Weekly*, a Negro newspaper. The editorial page condemned the jury's actions.

> If there was any doubt as to how "Southern Justice" operates in the State of Mississippi, it was completely dispelled . . . when the Pearl River County Grand Jury failed to return any indictments or even consider the massive information compiled by the FBI in the sensational Mack Parker kidnap-lynch murder case. . . . The axiom that a man is innocent until proved guilty by a court of law has been flagrantly ignored once again in the State of Mississippi. The fact that an accused man was deprived of a fair trial, kidnapped and murdered by a lynch mob from a Mississippi jail apparently had no effect on the thinking of the Grand Jury. The silent treatment merely gave approval of the mob taking the law into its hands. Mississippi has long had a reputation of failing to punish white men accused of criminal acts against Negroes. This is Mississippi's peculiar way of making Negroes "happy and contented" with the democratic processes and of showing the world how well they care for the Negro in respecting his rights as an American citizen.

The point that crushed most was that the FBI had supplied a dossier of evidence identifying the lynchers, and the Pearl River County Grand Jury had decided not to look inside it. . . .

No one outside of the Negro community could imagine the profound effect this action had in killing the Negro's hope and breaking his morale.

I decided it was time to go into that state so dreaded by Negroes. . . .

My money was running low so I decided to cash some travelers checks before leaving. The banks were closed, since it was past noon on Saturday, but I felt I would have no difficulty with travelers checks in any of the larger stores, especially those on Dryades where I had traded and was known as a customer.

I took the bus to Dryades and walked down it, stopping at the dime store where I'd made most of my purchases. The young white girl came forward to wait on me.

299

"I need to cash a travelers check," I said smiling.

"We don't cash any checks of any kind," she said firmly.

"But a travelers check is perfectly safe," I said.

"We just don't cash checks," she said and turned away.

"Look you know me. You've waited on me. I need some money."

"You should have gone to the bank."

"I didn't know I needed the money until after the banks closed," I said.

I knew I was making a pest of myself, but I could scarcely believe this nice young lady could be so unsympathetic, so insolent when she discovered I did not come in to buy something.

"I'll be glad to buy a few things," I said.

She called up to the bookkeeping department on an open mezzanine. "Hey! Do we cash travelers ch – –"

"No! the white woman shouted back.

"Thank you for your kindness," I said and walked out.

I went into one store after the other along Dryades and Rampart Streets. In every store their smiles turned to grimaces when they saw I meant not to buy but to cash a check. It was not their refusal – I could understand that; it was the bad manners they displayed. I began to feel desperate and resentful. They would have cashed a travelers check without hesitation for a white man. Each time they refused me, they implied clearly that I had probably come by these checks dishonestly and they wanted nothing to do with them or me.

Finally, after I gave up hope and decided I must remain in New Orleans without funds until the banks opened on Monday, I walked toward town. Small gold-lettering on the window of a store caught my attention: CATHOLIC BOOK STORE. Knowing the Catholic stand on racism, I wondered if this shop might cash a Negro's check. With some hesitation, I opened the door and entered. I was prepared to be disappointed.

"Would you cash a twenty-dollar travelers check for me?" I asked the proprietress.

"Of course," she said without hesitation, as though nothing could be more natural. She did not even study me.

I was so grateful I bought a number of paperback books – works of Maritain, Aquinas and Christopher Dawson. With these in my jacket, I hurried toward the Greyhound bus station.

300

In the bus station lobby, I looked for signs indicating a colored waiting room, but saw none. I walked up to the ticket counter. When the lady ticket-seller saw me, her otherwise attractive face turned sour, violently so. This look was so unexpected and so unprovoked I was taken aback.

"What do you want?" she snapped.

Taking care to pitch my voice to politeness, I asked about the next bus to Hattiesburg.

She answered rudely and glared at me with such loathing I knew I was receiving what the Negroes call "the hate stare." It was my first experience with it. It is far more than the look of disapproval one occasionally gets. This was so exaggeratedly hateful I would have been amused if I had not been so surprised.

I framed the words in my mind: "Pardon me, but have I done something to offend you?" But I realized I had done nothing — my color offended her.

"I'd like a one-way ticket to Hattiesburg, please," I said and placed a ten-dollar bill on the counter.

"I can't change that big a bill," she said abruptly and turned away, as though the matter were closed. I remained at the window, feeling strangely abandoned but not knowing what else to do. In a while she flew back at me, her face flushed, and fairly shouted: "I *told* you — I can't change that big a bill."

"Surely," I said stiffly, "in the entire Greyhound system there must be some means of changing a ten-dollar bill. Perhaps the manager —"

She jerked the bill furiously from my hand and stepped away from the window. In a moment she reappeared to hurl my change and the ticket on the counter with such force most of it fell on the floor at my feet. I was truly dumfounded by this deep fury that possessed her whenever she looked at me. Her performance was so venomous, I felt sorry for her. It must have shown in my expression, for her face congested to high pink. She undoubtedly considered it a supreme insolence for a Negro to dare to feel sorry for her.

I stooped to pick up my change and ticket from the floor. I wondered how she would feel if she learned that the Negro before whom she had behaved in such an unladylike manner was habitually a white man.

301

With almost an hour before bus departure, I turned away and looked for a place to sit. The large, handsome room was almost empty. No other Negro was there, and I dared not take a seat unless I saw some other Negro also seated.

Once again a "hate stare" drew my attention like a magnet. It came from a middle-aged, heavy-set, well-dressed white man. He sat a few yards away, fixing his eyes on me. Nothing can describe the withering horror of this. You feel lost, sick at heart before such unmasked hatred, not so much because it threatens you as because it shows humans in such an inhuman light. You see a kind of insanity, something so obscene the very obscenity of it (rather than its threat) terrifies you. It was so new I could not take my eyes from the man's face. I felt like saying: "What in God's name are you doing to yourself?". . .

They called the bus. We filed out into the high-roofed garage and stood in line, the Negroes to the rear, the whites to the front. Buses idled their motors, filling the air with a stifling odor of exhaust fumes. An army officer hurried to get at the rear of the white line. I stepped back to let him get in front. He refused and went to the end of the colored portion of the line. Every Negro craned his head to look at the phenomenon. I have learned that men in uniform, particularly officers, rarely descend to show discrimination, perhaps because of the integration of the armed forces. . . .

At Slidell we changed into another Greyhound bus with a new driver—a middle-aged man, large-bellied with a heavy, jowled face filigreed with tiny red blood vessels near the surface of his cheeks.

A stockily built young Negro, who introduced himself as Bill Williams, asked if I minded having him sit beside me. . . .

"People come down here and say Mississippi is the worst place in the world," Bill said. "But we can't all live in the North."

"Of course not. And it looks like beautiful country," I said, glancing out at giant pine trees.

Seeing that I was friendly, he offered advice. "If you're not used to things in Mississippi, you'll have to watch yourself pretty close till you catch on," he said.

The others, hearing, nodded agreement.

I told him I did not know what to watch out for.

"Well, you know you don't want to even look at a white woman.

In fact, you look down at the ground or the other way."

A large, pleasant Negro woman smiled at me across the aisle. "They're awful touchy on that here. You may not even know you're looking in a white woman's direction, but they'll try to make something out of it," she said.

"If you pass by a picture show, and they've got women on the posters outside, don't look at them either."

"Is it that bad?"

He assured me it was. Another man said: "Somebody's sure to say, 'Hey, boy—what are you looking at that white gal like *that* for?'"

I remembered the woman on the bus in New Orleans using almost the same expression.

"And you dress pretty well," Bill continued, his heavy black face frowning in concentration. "If you walk past an alley, walk out in the middle of the street. Plenty of people here, white and colored, would knock you in the head if they thought you had money on you. If white boys holler at you, just keep walking. Don't let them stop you and start asking you questions."

I told him I appreciated his warning.

"Can you all think of anything else?" he asked the others.

"That covers it," one of them said.

I thanked him for telling me these things.

"Well, if I was to come to your part of the country, I'd want somebody to tell me," Bill said.

He told me he was a truck driver, working out of Hattiesburg. He had taken a load to New Orleans, where he had left his truck for repairs and caught the bus back to Hattiesburg. He asked if I had made arrangements for a place to stay. I told him no. He said the best thing would be for me to contact a certain important person who would put me in touch with someone reliable who would find me a decent and safe place.

It was late dusk when the bus pulled into some little town for a stop. "We get about ten minutes here," Bill said. "Let's get off and stretch our legs. They've got a men's room here if you need to go."

The driver stood up and faced the passengers. "Ten-minute rest stop," he announced.

The whites rose and ambled off. Bill and I led the Negroes toward the door. As soon as he saw us, the driver blocked our way. Bill slipped under his arm and walked toward the dim-lit shed building.

"Hey, boy, where you going?" The driver shouted to Bill while he stretched his arms across the opening to prevent my stepping down. "Hey, you, boy, I'm talking to you." Bill's footsteps crunched unhurriedly across the gravel.

I stood on the bottom step waiting. The driver turned back to me.

"Where do you think you're going?" he asked, his heavy cheeks quivering with each word.

"I'd like to go to the rest room." I smiled and moved to step down.

He tightened his grip on the door facings and shouldered in close to block me. "Does your ticket say for you to get off here?" he asked.

"No sir, but the others—"

"Then you get your ass back in your seat and don't you move till we get to Hattiesburg," he commanded.

"You mean I can't go to the—"

"I mean get your ass back there like I told you," he said, his voice rising. "I can't be bothered rounding up all you people when we get ready to go."

"You announced a rest stop. The whites all got off," I said, unable to believe he really meant to deprive us of restroom privileges.

He stood on his toes and put his face up close to mine. His nose flared. Footlights caught silver glints from the hairs that curled out of his nostrils. He spoke slowly, threateningly: "Are you arguing with me?"

"No sir . . ." I sighed.

"Then you do like I say."

We turned like a small herd of cattle and drifted back to our seats. The others grumbled about how unfair it was. The large woman was apologetic, as though it embarrassed her for a stranger to see Mississippi's dirty linen.

"There's no call for him to act like that," she said. "They usually let us off."

I sat in the monochrome gloom of dusk, scarcely believing that in this year of freedom any man could deprive another of anything so basic as the need to quench thirst or use the rest room. There was nothing of the feel of America here. It was rather some strange country suspended in ugliness. Tension hung in the air, a continual threat, even though you could not put your finger on it.

304

"Well," I heard a man behind me say softly but firmly, "if I can't go in there, then I'm going in here. I'm not going to sit here and bust."

I glanced back and saw it was the same poorly dressed man who had so outraged Christophe. He walked in a half crouch to a place behind the last seat, where he urinated loudly on the floor. Indistinguishable sounds of approval rose around me – quiet laughter, clearing throats, whispers.

"Let's all do it," a man said.

"Yeah, flood this bus and end all this damned foolishness."

Bitterness dissolved in our delight to give the bus driver and the bus as good as they deserved.

The move was on, but it was quelled by another voice: "No, let's don't. It'll just give them something else to hold against us." an older man said. A woman agreed. All of us could see the picture. The whites would start claiming that we were unfit, that Negroes did not even know enough to go to the rest room – they just did it in the back of the bus; never mentioning, of course, that the driver would not let us off.

The driver's bullish voice attracted our attention.

"Didn't you hear me call you?" he asked as Bill climbed the steps.

"I sure didn't," Bill said pleasantly.

"You deaf?"

"No sir."

"You mean to stand there and say you didn't hear me call you?"

"Oh, were you calling me?" Bill asked innocently. "I heard you yelling 'Boy,' but that's not my name, so I didn't know you meant me."

Bill returned and sat beside me, surrounded by the approval of his people. In the immense tug-of-war, such an act of defiance turned him into a hero.

As we drove more deeply into Mississippi, I noted that the Negro comforted and sought the comfort from his own. Whereas in New Orleans he paid little attention to his brother, in Mississippi everyone who boarded the bus at the various little towns had a smile and a greeting for everyone else. We felt strongly the need to establish friendship as a buffer against the invisible threat. Like shipwrecked

305

people, we huddled together in a warmth and courtesy that was pure and pathetic.

E. FRANKLIN FRAZIER

Behind the Masks

The following selection is taken from the final chapter and from the summary conclusion of Black Bourgeoisie, *a sociological study that was first published in France in 1955 and two years later in the United States. The book quickly aroused controversy and adverse criticism from both whites and Negroes. The study was limited to the black middle class, who, Frazier claimed, represent a fusion of the peasant and the gentleman and whose ancestry was the mixed-blood aristocracy that was free before the Civil War. It was precisely this group of blacks who were most shocked by the book and who felt that Frazier, himself a Negro, had betrayed the Negro community. Whites criticized the study on the grounds that it applied equally well to middle-class whites.*

Since the black bourgeoisie live largely in a world of make-believe, the masks which they wear to play their sorry roles conceal the feelings of inferiority and of insecurity and the frustrations that haunt their inner lives. Despite their attempt to escape from real identification with the masses of Negroes, they can not escape the mark of oppression any more than their less favored kinsmen. In attempting to escape identification with the black masses, they have developed a self-hatred that reveals itself in their deprecation of the physical and social characteristics of Negroes. Likewise, their feelings of inferiority and insecurity are revealed in their pathological struggle for status within the isolated Negro world and craving for recognition in the white world. Their escape into a world of make-believe with its sham "society" leaves them with a feeling of emptiness and futility which causes them to constantly seek an escape in new delusions. . . .

Their feeling of inferiority is revealed in their fear of competition with whites. There is first a fear of competition with whites for jobs.

Notwithstanding the fact that middle-class Negroes are the most vociferous in demanding the right to compete on equal terms with whites, many of them still fear such competition. They prefer the security afforded by their monopoly of certain occupations within the segregated Negro community. For example, middle-class Negroes demand that the two Negro medical schools be reserved for Negro students and that a quota be set for white students, though Negro students are admitted to "white" medical schools. Since the Supreme Court of the United States has ruled against segregated public schools, many Negro teachers, even those who are well-prepared, fear that they can not compete with whites for teaching positions. Although this fear stems principally from a feeling of inferiority which is experienced generally by Negroes, it has other causes.

The majority of the black bourgeoisie fear competition with whites partly because such competition would mean that whites were taking them seriously, and consequently they would have to assume a more serious and responsible attitude towards their work. Middle-class Negroes, who are notorious for their inefficiency in the management of various Negro institutions, excuse their inefficiency on the grounds that Negroes are a "young race" and, therefore, will require time to attain the efficiency of the white man. The writer has heard a Negro college president, who has constantly demanded that Negroes have equality in American life, declare before white people in extenuation of the shortcomings of his own administration, that Negroes were a "child race" and that they had "to crawl before they could walk." Such declarations, while flattering to the whites, are revealing in that they manifest the black bourgeoisie's contempt for the Negro masses, while excusing its own deficiencies by attributing them to the latter. Yet it is clear that the black worker who must gain a living in a white man's mill or factory and in competition with white workers can not offer any such excuse for his inefficiency.

The fear of competition with whites is probably responsible for the black bourgeoisie's fear of competence and first-rate performance within its own ranks. When a Negro is competent and insists upon first-rate work it appears to this class that he is trying to be a white man, or that he is insisting that Negroes measure up to white standards. This is especially true where the approval of whites is taken as a mark of competence and first-rate performance. In such cases the black bourgeoisie reveal their ambivalent attitudes toward the white world. They slavishly accept the estimate which almost any white man places upon a Negro or his work, but at the same time they fear and reject white standards. For example, when a group of Negro doctors were being shown the modern equipment and techniques of a white clinic, one of them remarked to a Negro professor in a medical school, "This is the white man's medicine. I never bother with it and still I make $30,000 a year." Negroes who adopt the standards of the white world create among the black bourgeoisie a feeling of insecurity and often become the object of both the envy and hatred of this class.

Among the women of the black bourgeoisie there is an intense fear of the competition of white women for Negro men. They often attempt to rationalize their fear by saying that the Negro man always occupies an inferior position in relation to the white woman or that he marries much below his "social" status. They come nearer to the source of their fear when they confess that there are not many eligible Negro men and that these few should marry Negro women. That such rationalizations conceal deep-seated feelings of insecurity is revealed by the fact that generally they have no objection to the marriage of white men to Negro women, especially if the white man is reputed to be wealthy. In fact, they take pride in the fact and attribute these marriages to the "peculiar" charms of Negro women. In fact, the middle-class Negro woman's fear of the competition of white women is based often upon the fact that she senses her own inadequacies and shortcomings. Her position in Negro "society" and in the larger Negro community is often due to some adventitious factor, such as a light complexion or a meager education, which has pushed her to the top of the social pyramid. The middle-class white woman not only has a white skin and straight hair, but she is generally more sophisticated and interesting because she has read more widely and has a larger view of the world. The middle-class Negro woman may make fun of the "plainness" of her white competitor and the latter's lack of "wealth" and interest in "society"; nevertheless she still feels insecure when white women appear as even potential competitors.

Both men and women among the black bourgeoisie have a feeling of insecurity because of their constant fear of the loss of status. Since they have no status in the larger American society, the intense struggle for status among middle-class Negroes is, as we have seen, an attempt to compensate for the contempt and low esteem of the whites. Great value is, therefore, placed upon all kinds of status symbols. Academic degrees, both real and honorary, are sought in order to secure status. Usually the symbols are of a material nature implying wealth and conspicuous consumption. Sometimes Negro doctors do not attend what are supposedly scientific meetings because they do not have a Cadillac or some other expensive automobile. School teachers wear mink coats and maintain homes beyond their income for fear that they may lose status. The extravagance in "social" life generally is due to an effort not to lose status. But in attempting to overcome their fear of loss of status they are often beset by new feelings of insecurity. In spite of their pretended wealth, they are aware that their incomes are insignificant and that they must struggle to maintain their mortgaged homes and the show of "wealth" in lavish "social" affairs. Moreover, they are beset by a feeling of insecurity because of their struggles to maintain a show of wealth through illegal means. From time to time "wealthy" Negro doctors are arrested for selling narcotics and performing abortions. The life of many a "wealthy" Negro doctor is shortened by the struggle to provide diamonds, minks, and an expensive home for his wife.

There is much frustration among the black bourgeoisie despite their privileged position within the segregated Negro world. Their "wealth" and "social" position can not erase the fact that they are generally segregated and rejected by the white world. Their incomes and occupations may enable them to escape the cruder manifestations of racial prejudice, but they can not insulate themselves against the more subtle forms of racial discrimination. These discriminations cause frustrations in Negro men because they are not allowed to play the "masculine role" as defined by American culture. They can not assert themselves or exercise power as white men do. When they protest against racial discrimination there is always the threat that they will be punished by the white world. In spite of the movement toward the wider integration of the Negro into the general stream of American life, middle-class Negroes are still threatened with the loss of positions and earning power if they insist upon their rights. After the Supreme Court of the United States ruled that segregation in public education was illegal, Negro teachers in some parts of the South were dismissed because they would not sign statements supporting racial segregation in education.

As one of the results of not being able to play the "masculine role," middle-class Negro males have tended to cultivate their "personalities" which enable them to exercise considerable influence among whites and achieve distinction in the Negro world. Among Negroes they have been noted for their glamour. In this respect they resemble women who use their "personalities" to compensate for their inferior status in relation to men. This fact would seem to support the observation of an American sociologist that the Negro was "the lady among the races," if he had restricted his observation to middle-class males among American Negroes.

In the South the middle-class Negro male is not only prevented from playing a masculine role, but generally he must let Negro women assume leadership in any show of militancy. This reacts upon his status in the home where the tradition of female dominance, which is widely established among Negroes, has tended to assign a subordinate role to the male. In fact, in middle-class families, especially if the husband has risen in social status through his own efforts and married a member of an "old" family or a "society" woman, the husband is likely to play a pitiful role. The greatest compliment that can be paid such a husband is that he "worships his wife," which means that he is her slave and supports all her extravagances and vanities. But, of course, many husbands in such positions escape from their frustrations by having extra-marital sex relations. Yet the conservative and conventional middle-class husband presents a pathetic picture. He often sits at home alone, impotent physically and socially, and complains that his wife has gone crazy about poker and "society" and constantly demands money for gambling and expenditures which he can not afford. Sometimes he enjoys the sympathy of a son or daugher who has not become a "socialite." Such children often say that they had a happy family life until "mamma took to poker."

Preoccupation with poker on the part of the middle-class woman is often an attempt to escape from a frustrated life. Her frustration

310

may be bound up with her unsatisfactory sexual life. She may be married to a "glamorous" male who neglects her for other women. For among the black bourgeoisie, the glamour of the male is often associated with his sexual activities. The frustration of many Negro women has a sexual origin. Even those who have sought an escape from frustration in sexual promiscuity may, because of satiety or deep psychological reasons, become obsessed with poker in order to escape from their frustrations. One "society" woman, in justification of her obsession with poker remarked that it had taken the place of her former preoccupation with sex. Another said that to win at poker was similar to a sexual orgasm.

The frustration of the majority of the women among the black bourgeoisie is probably due to the idle or ineffectual lives which they lead. Those who do not work devote their time to the frivolities of Negro "society." When they devote their time to "charity" or worth-while causes, it is generally a form of play or striving for "social" recognition. They are constantly forming clubs which ostensibly have a serious purpose, but in reality are formed in order to consolidate their position in "society" or to provide additional occasions for playing poker. The idle, overfed women among the black bourgeoisie are generally, to use their language, "dripping with diamonds." They are forever dieting and reducing only to put on more weight (which is usually the result of the food that they consume at their club meetings). Even the women among the black bourgeoisie who work exhibit the same frustrations. Generally, they have no real interest in their work and only engage in it in order to be able to provide the conspicuous consumption demanded by "society." As we have indicated, the women as well as the men among the black bourgeoisie read very little and have no interest in music, art or the theater. They are constantly restless and do not know how to relax. They are generally dull people and only become animated when "social" matters are discussed, especially poker games. They are afraid to be alone and constantly seek to be surrounded by their friends, who enable them to escape from their boredom.

The frustrated lives of the black bourgeoisie are reflected in the attitudes of parents towards their children. Middle-class Negro families as a whole have few children, while among the families that constitute Negro "society" there are many childless couples. One finds today, as an American observed over forty years ago, that "where the children are few, they are usually spoiled" in middle-class Negro families. There is often not only a deep devotion to their one or two children, but a subservience to them. It is not uncommon for the only son to be called and treated as the "boss" in the family. Parents cater to the transient wishes of their children and often rationalize their behavior towards them on the grounds that children should not be "inhibited." They spend large sums of money on their children for toys and especially for clothes. They provide their children with automobiles when they go to college. All of this is done in order that the children may maintain the status of the parents and be eligible to enter the "social" set in Negro colleges. When they send their children to northern "white" colleges they often spend more time in preparing them for what they imagine will be their "social" life than in preparing them for the academic requirements of these institutions.

In their fierce devotion to their children, which generally results in spoiling them, middle-class Negro parents are seemingly striving at times to establish a human relationship that will compensate for their own frustrations in the realm of human relationships. Devotion to their children often becomes the one human tie that is sincere and free from the competition and artificiality of the make-believe world in which they live. Sometimes they may project upon their children their own frustrated professional ambitions. But usually, even when they send their children to northern "white" universities as a part of their "social" striving within the Negro community, they seem to hope that their children will have an acceptance in the white world which has been denied them. . . .

One of the chief frustrations of the middle-class Negro is that he can not escape identification with the Negro race and consequently is subject to the contempt of whites. Despite his "wealth" in which he has placed so much faith as a solvent of racial discrimination, he is still subject to daily insults and is excluded from participation in white American society. Middle-class Negroes do not express their resentment against discrimination and insults in violent outbreaks, as lower-class Negroes often do. They constantly repress their hostility toward whites and seek to soothe their hurt self-esteem in all kinds of rationalizations. They may boast of their wealth and culture as compared with the condition of the poor whites. Most often they will resort to any kind of subterfuge in order to avoid contact with whites. For example, in the South they often pay their bills by mail rather than risk unpleasant contacts with representatives of white firms. The daily repression of resentment and the constant resort to means of avoiding contacts with whites do not relieve them of their hostility toward whites. Even middle-class Negroes who gain a reputation for exhibiting "objectivity" and a "statesmanlike" attitude on racial discrimination harbor deep-seated hostilities toward whites. A Negro college president who has been considered such an inter-racial "statesman" once confessed to the writer that some day he was going to "break loose" and tell white people what he really thought. However, it is unlikely that a middle-class Negro of his standing will ever "break loose." Middle-class Negroes generally express their aggressions against whites by other means, such as deceiving whites and utilizing them for their own advantage.

Because middle-class Negroes are unable to indulge in aggressions against whites as such, they will sometimes make other minority groups the object of their hostilities. For example, they may show hostility against Italians, who are also subject to discrimination. But more often middle-class Negroes, especially those who are engaged in a mad scramble to accumulate money, will direct their hostilities against Jews. They are constantly expressing their anti-semitism within Negro circles, while pretending publicly to be free from prejudice. They blame the Jew for the poverty of Negroes and for their own failures and inefficiencies in their business undertakings. In expressing their hostility towards Jews, they are attempting at the same time to identify with the white American majority.

The repressed hostilities of middle-class Negroes to whites are not only directed towards other minority groups but inward toward themselves. This results in self-hatred, which may appear from their behavior to be directed towards the Negro masses but which in reality is directed against themselves. While pretending to be proud of being a Negro, they ridicule Negroid physical characteristics and seek to modify or efface them as much as possible. Within their own groups they constantly proclaim that "niggers" make them sick.

313

The very use of the term "nigger," which they claim to resent, indicates that they want to disassociate themselves from the Negro masses. They talk condescendingly of Africans and of African culture, often even objecting to African sculpture in their homes. They are insulted if they are identified with Africans. They refuse to join organizations that are interested in Africa. If they are of mixed ancestry, they may boast of the fact that they have Indian ancestry. When making compliments concerning the beauty of Negroes of mixed ancestry, they generally say, for example, "She is beautiful; she looks like an Indian." On the other hand, if a black woman has European features, they will remark condescendingly, "Although she is black, you must admit that she is good looking." Some middle-class Negroes of mixed ancestry like to wear Hindu costumes — while they laugh at the idea of wearing an African costume. When middle-class Negroes travel, they studiously avoid association with other Negroes, especially if they themselves have received the slightest recognition by whites. Even when they can not "pass" for white they fear that they will lose this recognition if they are identified as Negroes. Therefore, nothing pleases them more than to be mistaken for a Puerto Rican, Philippino, Egyptian or Arab or any ethnic group other than Negro.

The self-hatred of middle-class Negroes is often revealed in the keen competition which exists among them for status and recognition. This keen competition is the result of the frustrations which they experience in attempting to obtain acceptance and recognition by whites. Middle-class Negroes are constantly criticizing and belittling Negroes who achieve some recognition or who acquire a status above them. They prefer to submit to the authority of whites than to be subordinate to other Negroes. For example, Negro scholars generally refuse to seek the advice and criticism of competent Negro scholars and prefer to turn to white scholars for such co-operation. In fact, it is difficult for middle-class Negroes to co-operate in any field of endeavor. This failure in social relations is, as indicated in an important study, because "in every Negro he encounters his own self-contempt." It is as if he said, "You are only a Negro like myself; so why should you be in a position above me?"

This self-hatred often results in guilt feelings on the part of the

314

Negro who succeeds in elevating himself above his fellows. He feels unconsciously that in rising above other Negroes he is committing an act of aggression which will result in hatred and revenge on their part. The act of aggression may be imagined, but very often it is real. This is the case when middle-class Negroes oppose the economic and social welfare of Negroes because of their own interests. In some American cities, it has been the black bourgeoisie and not the whites who have opposed the building of low-cost public housing for Negro workers. In one city two wealthy Negro doctors, who have successfully opposed public housing projects for Negro workers, own some of the worst slums in the United States. While their wives, who wear mink coats, "drip with diamonds" and are written up in the "society" columns of Negro newspapers, ride in Cadillacs, their Negro tenants sleep on the dirt floors of hovels unfit for human habitation. The guilt feelings of the middle-class Negro are not always unconscious. For example, take the case of the Negro leader who proclaimed over the radio in a national broadcast that the Negro did not want social equity. He was conscious of his guilt feelings and his self-hatred in playing such a role, for he sent word privately to the writer that he never hated so much to do anything in his life, but that it was necessary because of his position as head of a state college which was under white supervision. The self-hatred of the middle-class Negro arises, then, not only from the fact that he does not want to be a Negro but also because of his sorry role in American society. . . .

The black bourgeoisie in the United States is an essentially American phenomenon. Its emergence and its rise to importance within the Negro community are closely tied up with economic and social changes in the American community. Its behavior as well as its mentality is a reflection of American modes of behavior and American values. What may appear as distortions of American patterns of behavior and thought are due to the fact that the Negro lives on the margin of American society. The very existence of a separate Negro community with its own institutions within the heart of the American society is indicative of its quasipathological character, especially since the persistence of this separate community has been due to racial discrimination and oppression.

As the result of this fact, the black bourgeoisie is unique in a

315

number of respects: First, it lacks a basis in the American economic system. Among colonial peoples and among other racial minorities, the bourgeoisie usually comes into existence as the result of its role in the economic organization of these societies. But the black bourgeoisie in the United States has subsisted off the crumbs of philanthropy, the salaries of public servants, and what could be squeezed from the meager earnings of Negro workers. Hence "Negro business" which has no significance in the American economy, has become a social myth embodying the aspirations of this class. Then, because of the position of the Negro in American life, it has been impossible for the black bourgeoisie to play the traditional role of this class among minorities. The attempt on the part of the Communist Party to assign to the black bourgeoisie the traditional role of this class, in what the Party defined as the struggle of the "Negro people" for "national liberation," only tended to emphasize the unreality of the position of the black bourgeoisie. Moreover, the black bourgeoisie have shown no interest in the "liberation" of Negroes except as it affected their own status or acceptance by the white community. They viewed with scorn the Garvey Movement with its nationalistic aims. They showed practically no interest in the Negro Renaissance. They wanted to forget the Negro's past, and they have attempted to conform to the behavior and values of the white community in the most minute details. Therefore they have often become, as has been observed, "exaggerated" Americans.

Because of its struggle to gain acceptance by whites, the black bourgeoisie has failed to play the role of a responsible elite in the Negro community. Many individuals among the first generation of educated Negroes, who were the products of missionary education, had a sense of responsibility toward the Negro masses and identified themselves with the struggles of the masses to overcome the handicaps of ignorance and poverty. Their influence over the masses was limited, to be sure—not, however, because of any lack of devotion on their part, but because of the control exercised by the white community. Nevertheless, they occupied a dignified position within the Negro community and were respected. As teachers of Negroes, they generally exhibited the same sincere interest in education and genuine culture as their missionary teachers. Therefore they did not regard teaching merely as a source of income.

316

On the other hand, today many Negro teachers refuse identification with the Negro masses and look upon teaching primarily as a source of income. In many cases they have nothing but contempt for their Negro pupils. Moreover, they have no real interest in education and genuine culture and spend their leisure in frivolities and in activities designed to win a place in Negro "society."

When the opportunity has been present, the black bourgeoisie has exploited the Negro masses as ruthlessly as have whites. As the intellectual leaders in the Negro community, they have never dared think beyond a narrow, opportunistic philosophy that provided a rationalization for their own advantages. Although the black bourgeoisie exercise considerable influence on the values of Negroes, they do not occupy a dignified position in the Negro community. The masses regard the black bourgeoisie as simply those who have been "lucky in getting money" which enables them to engage in conspicuous consumption. When this class pretends to represent the best manners or morals of the Negro, the masses regard such claims as hypocrisy.

The single factor that has dominated the mental outlook of the black bourgeoisie has been its obsession with the struggle for status. The struggle for status has expressed itself mainly in the emphasis upon "social" life or "society." The concern of the Negro for "social" life and "society" has been partly responsible for the failure of educated Negroes to make important contributions within the fields of science or art. Educated Negroes have been constantly subjected to the pressures of the black bourgeoisie to conform to its values. Because of this pressure some gifted Negroes have abandoned altogether their artistic and scientific aspirations, while others have chosen to play the role of phony intellectuals and cater to the ignorance and vanities of the black bourgeoisie in order to secure "social" acceptance. Since middle-class Negroes have never been permitted to play a serious role in American life, "social" life has offered an area of competition in which the serious affairs of life were not involved. Middle-class Negroes who have made real contributions in science and art have had to escape from the influence of the "social" life of the black bourgeoisie. In fact, the spirit of play or lack of serious effort has permeated every aspect of the life of the Negro community. It has, therefore, tended to encourage immatur-

317

ity and childishness on the part of middle-class Negroes whose lives are generally devoted to trivialities.

The emphasis upon "social" life or "society" is one of the main props of the world of make-believe into which the black bourgeoisie has sought an escape from its inferiority and frustrations in American society. This world of make-believe, to be sure, is a reflection of the values of American society, but it lacks the economic basis that would give it roots in the world of reality. In escaping into a world of make-believe, middle-class Negroes have rejected both identification with the Negro and his traditional culture. Through delusions of wealth and power they have sought identification with the white America which continues to reject them. But these delusions leave them frustrated because they are unable to escape from the emptiness and futility of their existence. Gertrude Stein would have been nearer the truth if she had said of the black bourgeoisie what she said of Negroes in general, that they "were not suffering from persecution, they were suffering from nothingness," not because, as she explained, the African has "a very ancient but a very narrow culture." The black bourgeoisie suffers from "nothingness" because when Negroes attain middle-class status, their lives generally lose both content and significance.

DWIGHT D. EISENHOWER
The Little Rock School Crisis

Following the Supreme Court's decisions of 1954 and 1955 calling for integration of schools, Southern opposition solidified into massive resistance. During a few months in 1956, five states adopted forty-two segregation measures: for example, Georgia made it a felony for school officials to spend tax monies on integrated schools, Mississippi declared it illegal for any organization to begin desegregation proceedings in state courts, and Virginia closed down the public schools in some counties rather than integrate. In Arkansas, in late summer of 1957, Governor Orval Faubus ordered the state guard to prevent Negro children from attending white schools. A federal judge

ordered the troops withdrawn, but mobs of whites refused to allow Negro
students to enter a high school in Little Rock. On September 24 President
Eisenhower took over command of the Arkansas Guard and ordered it and
federal marshals into Little Rock to restore order. His address of the same
day to the American people is reprinted here. [Source, Public Papers of
the Presidents of the United States: Dwight D. Eisenhower, Containing the
Public Messages, Speeches, and Statements of the President, January 1
to December 31, 1957, *Washington, 1958, pp. 689-694.]*

For a few minutes this evening I want to speak to you about the serious situation that has arisen in Little Rock. To make this talk I have come to the President's office in the White House. I could have spoken from Rhode Island, where I have been staying recently; but I felt that, in speaking from the house of Lincoln, of Jackson, and of Wilson, my words would better convey both the sadness I feel in the action I was compelled today to take and the firmness with which I intend to pursue this course until the orders of the federal court at Little Rock can be executed without unlawful interference.

In that city, under the leadership of demagogic extremists, disorderly mobs have deliberately prevented the carrying out of proper orders from a federal court. Local authorities have not eliminated that violent opposition, and, under the law, I yesterday issued a proclamation calling upon the mob to disperse. This morning the mob again gathered in front of the Central High School of Little Rock, obviously for the purpose of again preventing the carrying out of the court's order relating to the admission of Negro children to that school.

Whenever normal agencies prove inadequate to the task and it becomes necessary for the executive branch of the federal government to use its powers and authority to uphold federal courts, the President's responsibility is inescapable. In accordance with that responsibility, I have today issued an executive order directing the use of troops under federal authority to aid in the execution of federal law at Little Rock, Arkansas. This became necessary when my proclamation of yesterday was not observed, and the obstruction of justice still continues.

It is important that the reasons for my action be understood by all our citizens.

319

As you know, the Supreme Court of the United States has decided that separate public educational facilities for the races are inherently unequal, and, therefore, compulsory school segregation laws are unconstitutional. Our personal opinions about the decision have no bearing on the matter of enforcement, the responsibility and authority of the Supreme Court to interpret the Constitution are very clear. Local federal courts were instructed by the Supreme Court to issue such orders and decrees as might be necessary to achieve admission to public schools without regard to race – and with all deliberate speed.

During the past several years, many communities in our Southern states have instituted public-school plans for gradual progress in the enrollment and attendance of school children of all races in order to bring themselves into compliance with the law of the land. They thus demonstrated to the world that we are a nation in which laws, not men, are supreme. I regret to say that this truth – the cornerstone of our liberties – was not observed in this instance.

It was my hope that this localized situation would be brought under control by city and state authorities. If the use of local police powers had been sufficient, our traditional method of leaving the problems in those hands would have been pursued. But when large gatherings of obstructionists made it impossible for the decrees of the court to be carried out, both the law and the national interest demanded that the President take action.

Here is the sequence of events in the development of the Little Rock school case.

In May of 1955, the Little Rock School Board approved a moderate plan for the gradual desegregation of the public schools in that city. It provided that a start toward integration would be made at the present term in high school, and that the plan would be in full operation by 1963. Here I might say that, in a number of communities in Arkansas, integration in the schools has already started and without violence of any kind. Now, this Little Rock plan was challenged in the courts by some who believed that the period of time as proposed in the plan was too long.

The United States court at Little Rock, which has supervisory responsibility under the law for the plan of desegregation in the public schools, dismissed the challenge, thus approving a gradual rather than an abrupt change from the existing system. The court found that the School Board had acted in good faith in planning for a public-school system free from racial discrimination. Since that time, the court has, on three separate occasions, issued orders directing that the plan be carried out. All persons were instructed to refrain from interfering with the efforts of the School Board to comply with the law.

Proper and sensible observance of the law then demanded the respectful obedience which the nation has a right to expect from all its people. This, unfortunately, has not been the case at Little Rock. Certain misguided persons, many of them imported into Little Rock by agitators, have insisted upon defying the law and have sought to bring it into disrepute. The orders of the court have thus been frustrated.

The very basis of our individual rights and freedoms rests upon the certainty that the President and the executive branch of government will support and insure the carrying out of the decisions of the federal courts, even, when necessary, with all the means at the President's command. Unless the President did so, anarchy would result. There would be no security for any except that which each one of us could provide for himself. The interest of the nation in the proper fulfillment of the law's requirements cannot yield to opposition and demonstrations by some few persons. Mob rule cannot be allowed to override the decisions of our courts.

Now let me make it very clear that federal troops are not being used to relieve local and state authorities of their primary duty to preserve the peace and order of the community. Nor are the troops there for the purpose of taking over the responsibility of the School Board and the other responsible local officials in running Central High School. The running of our school system and the maintenance of peace and order in each of our states are strictly local affairs, and the federal government does not interfere except in a very few special cases and when requested by one of the several states. In the present case, the troops are there pursuant to law, solely for the purpose of preventing interference with the orders of the court.

The proper use of the powers of the executive branch to enforce the orders of a federal court is limited to extraordinary and compelling circumstances. Manifestly, such an extreme situation has been created in Little Rock. This challenge must be met and with such measures as will preserve to the people as a whole their lawfully protected rights in a climate permitting their free and fair exercise.

The overwhelming majority of our people in every section of the country are united in their respect for observance of the law—even in those cases where they may disagree with that law. They deplore the call of extremists to violence.

The decision of the Supreme Court concerning school integration, of course, affects the South more seriously than it does other sections of the country. In that region I have many warm friends, some of them in the city of Little Rock. I have deemed it a great personal privilege to spend in our Southland tours of duty while in the military service and enjoyable recreational periods since that time. So, from intimate personal knowledge, I know that the overwhelming majority of the people in the South—including those of Arkansas and of Little Rock—are of goodwill, united in their efforts to preserve and respect the law even when they disagree with it. They do not sympathize with mob rule. They, like the rest of our nation, have proved in two great wars their readiness to sacrifice for America.

A foundation of our American way of life is our national respect for law. In the South, as elsewhere, citizens are keenly aware of the tremendous disservice that has been done to the people of Arkansas in the eyes of the nation, and that has been done to the nation in the eyes of the world.

At a time when we face grave situations abroad because of the hatred that Communism bears toward a system of government based on human rights, it would be difficult to exaggerate the harm that is being done to the prestige and influence, and indeed to the safety, of our nation and the world. Our enemies are gloating over this incident and using it everywhere to misrepresent our whole nation. We are portrayed as a violator of those standards of conduct which the peoples of the world united to proclaim in the Charter of the United Nations. There they affirmed "faith in fundamental human rights" and "in the dignity and worth of the human person" and they did so "without distinction as to race, sex, language or religion."

And so, with deep confidence, I call upon the citizens of the state of Arkansas to assist in bringing to an immediate end all interference with the law and its processes. If resistance to the federal court orders ceases at once, the further presence of federal troops will be unnecessary, and the city of Little Rock will return to its normal habits of peace and order, and a blot upon the fair name and high honor of our nation in the world will be removed.

Thus will be restored the image of America and of all its parts as one nation, indivisible, with liberty and justice for all.

HERBERT RAVENEL SASS
Mixed Schools and Mixed Blood

Official Southern objections to the Supreme Court's demand that schools be integrated were usually based on constitutional principles, but for many Southerners the question was not political or ideological but social and, at bottom, racial. Often this was not stated explicitly, but occasionally a Southern writer would describe the feelings of his section in terms that seemed to ring true. The article by Herbert Ravenel Sass, published in the Atlantic Monthly in November 1956 and reprinted here in part, is an example of this kind of Southern comment. Brutally frank, Sass argued with clarity and force the Southern position on school integration and asserted that the South would never accept the intermingling of the races in its schools.

What may well be the most important physical fact in the story of the United States is one which is seldom emphasized in our history books. It is the fact that throughout the three and a half centuries of our existence we have kept our several races biologically distinct and separate. Though we have encouraged the mixing of many different strains in what has been called the American "melting pot," we have confined this mixing to the white peoples of European ancestry, excluding from our "melting pot" all other races. The result is that the United States today is overwhelmingly a pure white nation, with a smaller but considerable Negro population in which there is some white blood, and a much smaller American Indian population.

The fact that the United States is overwhelmingly pure white is not only important; it is also the most distinctive fact about this country when considered in relation to the rest of the New World. Except Canada, Argentina, and Uruguay, none of the approximately twenty-five other countries of this hemisphere has kept its races pure. Instead (though each contains some pure-blooded individuals) all these countries are products of an amalgamation of races— American Indian and white or American Indian, Negro, and white. In general the pure-blooded white nations have outstripped the far more numerous American mixed-blood nations in most of the achievements which constitute progress as commonly defined.

These facts are well known. But now there lurks in ambush, as it were, another fact: we have suddenly begun to move toward abandonment of our 350-year-old system of keeping our races pure and are preparing to adopt instead a method of racial amalgamation similar to that which has created the mixed-blood nations of this hemisphere; except that the amalgamation being prepared for this country is not Indian and white but Negro and white. It is the deep conviction of nearly all white Southerners in the states which have large Negro populations that the mingling or integration of white and Negro children in the South's primary schools would open the gates to miscegenation and widespread racial amalgamation.

This belief is at the heart of our race problem, and until it is realized that this is the South's basic and compelling motive, there can be no understanding of the South's attitude.

It must be realized too that the Negroes of the U.S.A. are today by far the most fortunate members of their race to be found anywhere on earth. Instead of being the hapless victim of unprecedented oppression, it is nearer the truth that the Negro in the United States is by and large the product of friendliness and helpfulness unequaled in any comparable instance in all history. Nowhere else in the world, at any time of which there is record, has a helpless, backward people of another color been so swiftly uplifted and so greatly benefited by a dominant race.

What America, including the South, has done for the Negro is the truth which should be trumpeted abroad in rebuttal of the Communist propaganda. In failing to utilize this truth we have deliberately put aside a powerful affirmative weapon of enormous potential value to the free world and have allowed ourselves to be thrown on the defensive and placed in an attitude of apologizing for our conduct in a matter where actually our record is one of which we can be very proud.

We have permitted the subject of race relations in the United States to be used not as it should be used, as a weapon for America, but as a weapon for the narrow designs of the new aggressive Negro leadership in the United States. It cannot be so used without damage to this country, and that damage is beyond computation. Instead of winning for America the plaudits and trust of the colored peoples of Asia and Africa in recognition of what we have done for our colored people, our pro-Negro propagandists have seen to it that the United States appears as an international Simon Legree—or rather a Dr. Jekyll and Mr. Hyde with the South in the villainous role.

The South has had a bad time with words. Nearly a century ago the word "slavery," even more than the thing itself, did the South irreparable damage. In a strange but real way the misused word "democracy" has injured the South; its most distinctive—and surely its greatest—period has been called undemocratic, meaning illiberal and reactionary, because it resisted the onward sweep of a centralizing governmental trend alien to our federal republic and destructive of the very "cornerstone of liberty," local self-government. Today the word "segregation" and, perhaps even more harmful, the word "prejudice" blacken the South's character before the world and make doubly difficult our effort to preserve not merely our own way of life but certain basic principles upon which our country was founded.

Words are of such transcendent importance today that the South should long ago have protested against these two. They are now too firmly imbedded in the dialectic of our race problem to be got rid of. But that very fact renders all the more necessary a careful scrutiny of them. Let us first consider the word "segregation."

Segregation is sometimes carelessly listed as a synonym of separation, but it is not a true synonym and the difference between the two words is important.

Segregation, from the Latin *segregatus* (set apart from the flock), implies isolation; separation carries no such implication. Segregation is what we have done to the American Indian—whose grievous wrongs few reformers and still fewer politicians ever bother their heads about. By use of force and against his will we have segregated him, isolated him, on certain small reservations which had and still have somewhat the character of concentration camps.

The South has not done that to the Negro. On the contrary, it has shared its countryside and its cities with him in amity and understanding, not perfect by any means, and careful of established folk custom, but far exceeding in human friendliness anything of the kind to be found in the North. Not segregation of the Negro race as the Indian is segregated on his reservations—and as the Negro is segregated in the urban Harlems of the North—but simply *separation* of the white and Negro races in certain phases of activity is what the South has always had and feels that it must somehow preserve even though the time-honored, successful, and completely moral "separate but equal" principle no longer has legal sanction.

Until the Supreme Court decision forbidding compulsory racial separation in the public schools, the South was moving steadily toward abandonment or relaxation of the compulsory separation rule in several important fields. This is no longer true. Progress in racial relations has been stopped short by the ill-advised insistence of the Northern-directed Negro leadership upon the one concession which above all the white South will not and cannot make—public school integration.

Another word which is doing grave damage to the South today is "prejudice" meaning race prejudice—a causeless hostility often amounting to hatred which white Southerners are alleged to feel in regard to the Negro. Here again the South, forgetful of the lessons of its past, has failed to challenge effectively an inaccurate and injurious word. Not prejudice but preference is the word that truth requires.

Between prejudice and preference there is vast difference. Prejudice is a preconceived unfavorable judgment or feeling without sound basis. Preference is a natural reaction to facts and conditions observed or experienced, and through the action of heredity generation after generation it becomes instinctive. Like separateness, it exists throughout the animal kingdom. Though the difference between two races of an animal species may be so slight that only a specialist can differentiate between them, the individuals of one

326

race prefer as a rule to associate with other individuals of that race.

One can cite numerous examples among birds and mammals. In the human species the history of our own country provides the most striking example of race preference. The white men and women, chiefly of British, German, Dutch, and Scandinavian stocks, who colonized and occupied what is now the United States were strongly imbued with race preference. They did not follow the example of the Spanish and Portuguese (in whom for historical reasons the instinct of race preference was much weaker) who in colonizing South and Central America amalgamated with the Indians found in possession of the land and in some cases with the Negroes brought over as slaves. Instead, the founders of the future United States maintained their practice of non-amalgamation rigorously, with only slight racial blendings along the fringes of each group.

Hence it is nonsense to say that racial discrimination, the necessary consequence of race preference, is "un-American." Actually it is perhaps the most distinctively American thing there is, the reason why the American people—meaning the people of the United States—are what they are. Today when racial discrimination of any kind or degree is instantly denounced as both sinful and stupid, few stop to reflect that this nation is built solidly upon it.

The truth is, of course, that there are many different kinds and degrees of racial discrimination. Some of them are bad—outdated relics of an earlier time when conditions were unlike those of today, and these should be, and were being, abolished until the unprecedented decree of the Supreme Court in the school cases halted all progress. But not all kinds of racial discrimination are evil—unless we are prepared to affirm that our forefathers blundered in "keeping the breed pure."

Thus it is clear that discrimination too is a misused word as commonly employed in the realm of racial relations. It does not necessarily imply either stupidity or sin. It is not a synonym for injustice, and it is very far from being, as many seem to think, a synonym for hatred. The Southern white man has always exercised discrimination in regard to the Negro but—except for a tiny and untypical minority of the white population—he has never hated the Negro. I have lived a fairly long life in a part of the South—the South Carolina Low-country—where there are many thousands of Negroes, and

327

since early boyhood I have known many of them well, in some cases for years, in town and country. I know how I feel about them and how the white people of this old plantation region, the high and the low, the rich and the poor, the large landowner and the white mechanic, feel about them.

I am sure that among white Carolinians there is, as yet, almost no hatred of the Negro, nor is there anything that can accurately be called race prejudice. What does exist, strongly and ineradicably, is race preference. In other words, we white Southerners prefer our own race and wish to keep it as it is.

This preference should not and in fact cannot be eliminated. It is much bigger than we are, a far greater thing than our racial dilemma. It is — and here is another basic fact of great significance — an essential element in Nature's huge and complex mechanism. It is one of the reasons why evolution, ever diversifying, ever discriminating, ever separating race from race, species from species, has been able to operate in an ascending course so that what began aeons ago as something resembling an amoeba has now become Man. In preferring its own race and in striving to prevent the destruction of that race by amalgamation with another race, the white South is not flouting Nature but is in harmony with her.

If the Negro also prefers his own race and wishes to preserve its identity, then he is misrepresented by his new aggressive leadership which, whether or not this is its deliberate aim, is moving toward a totally different result. Let us see why that is so.

The crux of the race problem in the South, as I have said, is the nearly universal belief of the Southern white people that only by maintaining a certain degree of separateness of the races can the racial integrity of the white South be safeguarded. Unfortunately the opinion has prevailed outside the South that only a few Southerners hold this conviction — a handful of demagogic politicians and their most ignorant followers — and that "enlightened" white Southerners recognize the alleged danger of racial amalgamation as a trumped-up thing having no real substance.

Nothing could be farther from the truth. Because the aggressive Northern-Negro leadership continues to drive onward, the white South (except perhaps that part which is now more Western than Southern and in which Negroes are few) is today as united in its conviction that its racial integrity must be protected as it was when the same conviction drove its people – the slaveholder and the non-slaveholder, the high and the low, the educated and the ignorant – to defend the outworn institution of Negro slavery because there seemed to be no other way to preserve the social and political control needed to prevent the Africanization of the South by a combination of fanatical Northern reformers and millions of enfranchised Negroes. The South escaped that fate because after a decade of disastrous experiment the intelligent people of the victorious North realized that the racial program of their social crusaders was unsound, or at least impracticable, and gave up trying to enforce it.

Now in a surging revival of that "Reconstruction" crusade – a revival which is part dedicated idealism, part understandable racial ambition, part political expediency national and international – the same social program is again to be imposed upon the South. There are new conditions which help powerfully to promote it: the Hitlerite excesses in the name of race which have brought all race distinctions into popular disrepute; the notion that the white man, by divesting himself of race consciousness, may appease the peoples of Asia and Africa and wean them away from Communism.

In addition, a fantastic perversion of scientific authority has been publicized in support of the new crusade. Though everywhere else in Nature (as well as in all our plant breeding and animal breeding) race and heredity are recognized as of primary importance, we are told that in the human species race is of no importance and racial differences are due not to heredity but to environment. Science has proved, so we are told, that all races are equal and, in essentials, identical.

Science has most certainly not proved that all races are equal, much less identical; and, as the courageous geneticist, Dr. W. C. George of the University of North Carolina, has recently pointed out, there is overwhelming likelihood that the biological consequences of white and Negro integration in the south would be harmful. It would not be long before these biological consequences became visible. But there is good hope that we shall never see them, because any attempt to force a program of racial integration upon the South would be met with stubborn, determined, and universal opposition, probably taking the form of passive resistance of a

329

hundred kinds. Though secession is not conceivable, persistence in an attempt to compel the South to mingle its white and Negro children in its public schools would split the United States in two as disastrously as in the sixties and perhaps with an even more lamentable aftermath of bitterness.

For the elementary public school is the most critical of those areas of activity where the South must and will at all costs maintain separateness of the races. The South must do this because, although it is a nearly universal instinct, race preference is not active in the very young. Race preference (which the propagandists miscall race prejudice or hate) is one of those instincts which develop gradually as the mind develops and which, if taken in hand early enough, can be prevented from developing at all.

Hence if the small children of the two races in approximately equal numbers – as would be the case in a great many of the South's schools – were brought together intimately and constantly and grew up in close association in integrated schools under teachers necessarily committed to the gospel of racial integration, there would be many in whom race preference would not develop. This would not be, as superficial thinkers might suppose, a good thing, the happy solution of the race problem in America. It might be a solution of a sort, but not one that the American people would desire. It would inevitably result, beginning with the least desirable elements of both races, in a great increase of racial amalgamation, the very process which throughout our history we have most sternly rejected. For although to most persons today the idea of mixed mating is disagreeable or even repugnant, this would not be true of the new generations brought up in mixed schools with the desirability of racial integration as a basic premise. Among those new generations mixed matings would become commonplace, and a greatly enlarged mixed-blood population would result.

That is the compelling reason, though by no means the only reason, why the South will resist, with all its resources of mind and body, the mixing of the races in its public schools. It is a reason which, when its validity is generally recognized, will quickly enlist millions of non-Southerners in support of the South's position. The people of the North and West do not favor the transformation of the

United States into a nation composed in considerable part of mixed bloods any more than the people of the South do. Northern support of school integration in the South is due to the failure to realize its inevitable biological effect in regions of large Negro population. If Northerners did realize this, their enthusiasm for mixed schools in the South would evaporate at once.

Declaration of Southern Congressmen on Integration of Schools

Southern objections to the Supreme Court's unanimous decisions calling in 1954 and 1955 for desegregation of schools were many and vehement. On March 12, 1956, a group of 101 congressmen, almost all of them from Southern states, denounced the ruling in a manifesto that was presented to Congress. Considering the Court's desegregation orders to be in violation of the Constitution, the authors of the manifesto urged their states to disobey them and vowed to oppose actions to implement the orders "by all lawful means." The manifesto, called a "Declaration of Constitutional Principles," is reprinted here. [Source: Congressional Record, 84 Cong., 2 Sess., pp. 4515-4516.]

The unwarranted decision of the Supreme Court in the public-school cases is now bearing the fruit always produced when men substitute naked power for established law.

The founding fathers gave us a Constitution of checks and balances because they realized the inescapable lesson of history that no man or group of men can be safely entrusted with unlimited power. They framed this Constitution with its provisions for change by amendment in order to secure the fundamentals of government against the dangers of temporary popular passion or the personal predilections of public officeholders.

We regard the decision of the Supreme Court in the school cases as a clear abuse of judicial power. It climaxes a trend in the federal judiciary undertaking to legislate, in derogation of the authority of Congress, and to encroach upon the reserved rights of the states and the people.

The original Constitution does not mention education. Neither does the Fourteenth Amendment nor any other amendment. The debates preceding the submission of the Fourteenth Amendment clearly show that there was no intent that it should affect the systems of education maintained by the states. The very Congress which proposed the amendment subsequently provided for segregated schools in the District of Columbia.

When the amendment was adopted, in 1868, there were thirty-seven states of the Union. Every one of the twenty-six states that had any substantial racial differences among its people either approved the operation of segregated schools already in existence or subsequently established such schools by action of the same law-making body which considered the Fourteenth Amendment.

As admitted by the Supreme Court in the public-school case (*Brown* v. *Board of Education*), the doctrine of separate but equal schools "apparently originated in *Roberts* v. *City of Boston* . . . (1849), upholding school segregation against attack as being violative of a state constitutional guarantee of equality." This constitutional doctrine began in the North – not in the South – and it was followed not only in Massachusetts but in Connecticut, New York, Illinois, Indiana, Michigan, Minnesota, New Jersey, Ohio, Pennsylvania, and other Northern states, until they, exercising their rights as states through the constitutional processes of local self-government, changed their school systems.

In the case of *Plessy* v. *Ferguson*, in 1896, the Supreme Court expressly declared that under the Fourteenth Amendment no person was denied any of his rights if the states provided separate-but-equal public facilities. This decision has been followed in many other cases. It is notable that the Supreme Court, speaking through Chief Justice Taft, a former President of the United States, unanimously declared, in 1927, in *Lum* v. *Rice*, that the "separate-but-equal" principle is "within the discretion of the state in regulating its public schools and does not conflict with the Fourteenth Amendment."

This interpretation, restated time and again, became a part of

332

the life of the people of many of the states and confirmed their habits, customs, traditions, and way of life. It is founded on elemental humanity and common sense, for parents should not be deprived by government of the right to direct the lives and education of their own children.

Though there has been no constitutional amendment or act of Congress changing this established legal principle almost a century old, the Supreme Court of the United States, with no legal basis for such action, undertook to exercise their naked judicial power and substituted their personal political and social ideas for the established law of the land. This unwarranted exercise of power by the Court, contrary to the Constitution, is creating chaos and confusion in the states principally affected. It is destroying the amicable relations between the white and Negro races that have been created through ninety years of patient effort by the good people of both races. It has planted hatred and suspicion where there has been heretofore friendship and understanding.

Without regard to the consent of the governed, outside agitators are threatening immediate and revolutionary changes in our public-school systems. If done, this is certain to destroy the system of public education in some of the states.

With the gravest concern for the explosive and dangerous condition created by this decision and inflamed by outside meddlers:

We reaffirm our reliance on the Constitution as the fundamental law of the land.

We decry the Supreme Court's encroachments on rights reserved to the states and to the people, contrary to established law and to the Constitution.

We commend the motives of those states which have declared the intention to resist forced integration by any lawful means.

We appeal to the states and people who are not directly affected by these decisions to consider the constitutional principles involved against the time when they, too, on issues vital to them, may be the victims of judicial encroachment.

Even though we constitute a minority in the present Congress, we have full faith that a majority of the American people believe in the dual system of government which has enabled us to achieve our greatness and will in time demand that the reserved rights of the

333

state and of the people be made secure against judicial usurpation.

We pledge ourselves to use all lawful means to bring about a reversal of this decision, which is contrary to the Constitution, and to prevent the use of force in its implementation.

In this trying period, as we all seek to right this wrong, we appeal to our people not to be provoked by the agitators and troublemakers invading our states and to scrupulously refrain from disorders and lawless acts.

EARL WARREN

Brown et al. v. *Board of Education of Topeka et al.*

The outset of the Negro or civil rights movement of the 1950s and 1960s may be said to have occurred on May 17, 1954, when the Supreme Court handed down its decision in Brown v. Board of Education of Topeka. *The decision, written by Chief Justice Warren for a unanimous Court, directly reversed the famous ruling in* Plessy v. Ferguson *(1896). In the earlier case the Court had upheld a Louisiana law requiring separate railroad facilities, on the grounds that if equality of accommodations existed Negroes had no recourse under the equal protection of the laws clause of the Fourteenth Amendment. The 1954 ruling held, on the contrary, that even if educational opportunities for Negroes were equal, Blacks were nevertheless discriminated against under the same clause of the same amendment. [Source: 347 U.S. 483.]*

These cases come to us from the states of Kansas, South Carolina, Virginia, and Delaware. They are premised on different facts and different local conditions, but a common legal question justifies their consideration together in this consolidated opinion.[1]

1. In the Kansas case, *Brown* v. *Board of Education*, the plaintiffs are Negro children of elementary-school age residing in Topeka. They brought this action in the United States District Court for the District of Kansas to enjoin enforcement of a Kansas statute which permits, but does not require, cities of more than 15,000 population to maintain separate school facilities for Negro and white students. Kan. Gen. Stat. Sec. 72-1724 (1949). Pursuant to that authority, the Topeka Board of Education elected to establish segregated elementary schools. Other public schools in the community, however, are operated on a nonsegregated basis. The three-judge District

In each of the cases, minors of the Negro race, through their legal representatives, seek the aid of the courts in obtaining admission to the public schools of their community on a nonsegregated basis. In each instance, they had been denied admission to schools attended by white children under laws requiring or permitting segregation according to race. This segregation was alleged to deprive

Court convened under 28 U.S.C. Sec. 2281 and 2284, found that segregation in public education has a detrimental effect upon Negro children, but denied relief on the ground that the Negro and white schools were substantially equal with respect to buildings, transportation, curricula, and educational qualifications of teachers. 98 F. Supp. 797. The case is here on direct appeal under 28 U.S.C. Sec. 1253.

In the South Carolina case, *Briggs* v. *Elliott*, the plaintiffs are Negro children of both elementary and high school age residing in Clarendon County. They brought this action in the United States District Court for the Eastern District of South Carolina to enjoin enforcement of provisions in the state constitution and statutory code which require the segregation of Negroes and whites in public schools. S.C. Const., Art. XI, Sec. 7; S.C. Code Sec. 5377 (1942). The three-judge District Court, convened under 28 U.S.C. Sec. 2281 and 2284, denied the requested relief. The court found that the Negro schools were inferior to the white schools and ordered the defendants to begin immediately to equalize the facilities. But the court sustained the validity of the contested provisions and denied the plaintiffs admission to the white schools during the equalization program. 98 F. Supp. 529. This Court vacated the District Court's judgment and remanded the case for the purpose of obtaining the court's views on a report filed by the defendants concerning the progress made in the equalization program. 342 U.S. 350. On remand, the District Court found that substantial equality had been achieved except for buildings and that the defendants were proceeding to rectify this inequality as well. 103 F. Supp. 920. The case is again here on direct appeal under 28 U.S.C. Sec. 1253.

In the Virginia case, *Davis* v. *County School Board*, the plaintiffs are Negro children of high-school age residing in Prince Edward County. They brought this action in the United States District Court for the Eastern District of Virginia to enjoin enforcement of provisions in the state constitution and statutory code which require the segregation of Negroes and whites in public schools. Va. Const., Sec. 140; Va. Code Sec. 22-221 (1950). The three-judge District Court, convened under 28 U.S.C. Sec. 2281 and 2284, denied the requested relief. The court found the Negro school inferior in physical plant, curricula, and transportation, and ordered the defendants forthwith to provide substantially equal curricula and transportation and to "proceed with all reasonable diligence and dispatch to remove" the inequality in physical plant. But, as in the South Carolina case, the court sustained the validity of the contested provisions and denied the plaintiffs admission to the white schools during the equalization program. 103 F. Supp. 337. The case is here on direct appeal under 28 U.S.C. Sec. 1253. In the Delaware case, *Gebhart* v. *Belton*, the plaintiffs are Negro children of both elementary and high-school age residing in New Castle County. They brought this action in the Delaware Court of Chancery to enjoin enforcement of provisions in the state constitution and statutory code which require the segregation of Negroes and whites in public schools. Del. Const., Art. X, Sec. 2; Del. Rev. Code Sec. 2631 (1935). The chancellor gave judgment for the plaintiffs and ordered their immediate the plaintiffs of the equal protection of the laws under the Fourteenth Amendment. In each of the cases other than the Delaware case, a three-judge federal District Court denied relief to the plaintiffs on the so-called "separate but equal" doctrine announced by this Court in *Plessy* v. *Ferguson*, 163 U.S. 537. Under that doctrine, equality of treatment is accorded when the races are provided substantially equal facilities, even though these facilities be separate. In the Delaware case, the Supreme Court of Delaware adhered to that doctrine, but ordered that the plaintiffs be admitted to the white schools because of their superiority to the Negro schools.

The plaintiffs contend that segregated public schools are not "equal" and cannot be made "equal," and that hence they are deprived of the equal protection of the laws. Because of the obvious importance of the question presented, the Court took jurisdiction.[2] Argument was heard in the 1952 Term, and reargument was heard this Term on certain questions propounded by the court.[3]

Reargument was largely devoted to the circumstances surrounding the adoption of the Fourteenth Amendment in 1868. It covered exhaustively consideration of the amendment in Congress, ratification by the states, then-existing practices in racial segregation, and the views of proponents and opponents of the amendment. This discussion and our own investigation convince us that, although these sources cast some light, it is not enough to resolve the problem with which we are faced. At best, they are inconclusive. The most avid proponents of the postwar amendments undoubtedly

admission to schools previously attended only by white children on the ground that the Negro schools were inferior with respect to teacher training, pupil-teacher ratio, extracurricular activities, physical plant, and time and distance involved in travel. 87 A. 2d 862. The chancellor also found that segregation itself results in an inferior education for Negro children (see note 10, *infra*), but did not rest his decision on that ground. *Id.*, at 865. The chancellor's decree was affirmed by the Supreme Court of Delaware, which intimated, however, that the defendants might be able to obtain a modification of the decree after equalization of the Negro and white schools had been accomplished. 91 A. 2nd 137, 152. The defendants, contending only that the Delaware courts had erred in ordering the immediate admission of the Negro plaintiffs to the white schools, applied to this Court for certiorari. The writ was granted, 344 U.S. 891. The plaintiffs, who were successful below, did not submit a cross-petition.

2. 344 U.S. 1, 141, 891.

3. 345 U.S. 972. The attorney general of the United States participated both Terms as *amicus curiae*.

intended them to remove all legal distinctions among "all persons born or naturalized in the United States." Their opponents, just as certainly, were antagonistic to both the letter and the spirit of the amendments and wished them to have the most limited effect. What others in Congress and the state legislatures had in mind cannot be determined with any degree of certainty.

An additional reason for the inconclusive nature of the amendment's history, with respect to segregated schools, is the status of public education at that time.[4] In the South, the movement toward free common schools, supported by general taxation, had not yet taken hold. Education of white children was largely in the hands of private groups. Education of Negroes was almost nonexistent, and practically all of the race were illiterate. In fact, any education of Negroes was forbidden by law in some states. Today, in contrast, many Negroes have achieved outstanding success in the arts and sciences as well as the business and professional world. It is true that public-school education at the time of the amendment had advanced further in the North, but the effect of the amendment on Northern states was generally ignored in the congressional debates.

Even in the North, the conditions of public education did not approximate those existing today. The curriculum was usually rudimentary; ungraded schools were common in rural areas; the school

4. For a general study of the development of public education prior to the amendment, see Butts and Cremin, *A History of Education in American Culture* (1953), Pts. I, II; Cubberley, *Public Education in the United States* (1934 ed.), cc. II-XII. School practices current at the time of the adoption of the Fourteenth Amendment are described in Butts and Cremin, *supra*, at 269-275; Cubberley, *supra*, at 288-339, 408-431; Knight, *Public Education in the South* (1922), cc. VIII, IX. See also H. Ex. Doc. No. 315, 41st Cong., 2nd Sess. (1871). Although the demand for free public schools followed substantially the same pattern in both the North and the South, the development in the South did not begin to gain momentum until about 1850, some twenty years after that in the North. The reasons for the somewhat slower development in the South (*e.g.*, the rural character of the South and the different regional attitudes toward state assistance) are well explained in Cubberley, *supra*, at 408-423. In the country as a whole, but particularly in the South, the war virtually stopped all progress in public education. *Id.*, at 427-428. The low status of Negro education in all sections of the country, both before and immediately after the war, is described in Beale, *A History of Freedom of Teaching in American Schools* (1941), 112-132, 175-195. Compulsory school-attendance laws were not generally adopted until after the ratification of the Fourteenth Amendment, and it was not until 1918 that such laws were in force in all the states. Cubberley, *supra*, at 563-565.

term was but three months a year in many states; and compulsory school attendance was virtually unknown. As a consequence, it is not surprising that there should be so little in the history of the Fourteenth Amendment relating to its intended effect on public education.

In the first cases in this Court construing the Fourteenth Amendment, decided shortly after its adoption, the Court interpreted it as proscribing all state-imposed discriminations against the Negro race.[5] The doctrine of "separate but equal" did not make its appearance in this Court until 1896 in the case of *Plessy* v. *Ferguson, supra,* involving not education but transportation.[6] American courts have since labored with the doctrine for over half a century.

In this Court there have been six cases involving the "separate but equal" doctrine in the field of public education.[7] In *Cumming* v. *County Board of Education,* 175 U. S. 528, and *Gong Lum* v. *Rice,* 275 U. S. 78, the validity of the doctrine itself was not challenged.[8]

5. *Slaughter-House Cases,* 16 Wall. 36, 67-72 (1873); *Strauder* v. *West Virginia,* 100 U. S. 303, 307-308 (1880): "It ordains that no state shall deprive any person of life, liberty, or property, without due process of law, or deny to any person within its jurisdiction the equal protection of the laws. What is this but declaring that the law in the states shall be the same for the black as for the white; that all persons, whether colored or white, shall stand equal before the laws of the states, and, in regard to the colored race, for whose protection the amendment was primarily designed, that no discrimination shall be made against them by law because of their color? The words of the amendment, it is true, are prohibitory, but they contain a necessary implication of a positive immunity, or right, most valuable to the colored race – the right to exemption from unfriendly legislation against them distinctively as colored – exemption from legal discriminations, implying inferiority in civil society, lessening the security of their enjoyment of the rights which others enjoy, and discriminations which are steps toward reducing them to the condition of a subject race." See also *Virginia* v. *Rives,* 100 U. S. 313, 318 (1880); *Ex parte Virginia,* 100 U. S. 339, 344-345 (1880).

6. The doctrine apparently originated in *Roberts* v. *City of Boston,* 59 Mass. 198, 206 (1850), upholding school segregation against attack as being violative of a state constitutional guarantee of equality. Segregation in Boston public schools was eliminated in 1855. Mass. Acts 1855, c. 256. But elsewhere in the North, segregation in public education has persisted in some communities until recent years. It is apparent that such segregation has long been a nationwide problem, not merely one of sectional concern.

7. See also *Berea College* v. *Kentucky,* 211 U.S. 45 (1908).

8. In the *Cumming* case, Negro taxpayers sought an injunction requiring the defendant school board to discontinue the operation of a high school for white child-

In more recent cases, all on the graduate-school level, inequality was found in that specific benefits enjoyed by white students were denied to Negro students of the same educational qualifications. *Missouri ex rel. Gaines* v. *Canada*, 305 U. S. 337; *Sipuel* v. *Oklahoma*, 332 U. S. 631; *Sweatt* v. *Painter*, 339 U. S. 629; *McLaurin* v. *Oklahoma State Regents*, 339 U. S. 637. In none of these cases was it necessary to reexamine the doctrine to grant relief to the Negro plaintiff. And in *Sweatt* v. *Painter, supra*, the Court expressly reserved decision on the question whether *Plessy* v. *Ferguson* should be held inapplicable to public education.

In the instant cases, that question is directly presented. Here, unlike *Sweatt* v. *Painter*, there are findings below that the Negro and white schools involved have been equalized, or are being equalized, with respect to buildings, curricula, qualifications and salaries of teachers, and other "tangible" factors.[9] Our decision, therefore, cannot turn on merely a comparison of these tangible factors in the Negro and white schools involved in each of the cases. We must look instead to the effect of segregation itself on public education.

In approaching this problem, we cannot turn the clock back to 1868 when the amendment was adopted, or even to 1896 when *Plessy* v. *Ferguson* was written. We must consider public education in the light of its full development and its present place in American life throughout the nation. Only in this way can it be determined if segregation in public schools deprives these plaintiffs of the equal protection of the laws.

Today, education is perhaps the most important function of state and local governments. Compulsory school-attendance laws and

ren until the board resumed operation of a high school for Negro children. Similarly, in the *Gong Lum* case, the plaintiff, a child of Chinese descent, contended only that state authorities had misapplied the doctrine by classifying him with Negro children and requiring him to attend a Negro school.

9. In the Kansas case, the court below found substantial equality as to all such factors. 98 F. Supp. 797, 798. In the South Carolina case, the court below found that the defendants were proceeding "promptly and in good faith to comply with the court's decree." 103 F. Supp. 920, 921. In the Virginia case, the court below noted that the equalization program was already "afoot and progressing" (103 F. Supp. 337, 341); since then, we have been advised, in the Virginia attorney general's brief on reargument, that the program has now been completed. In the Delaware case, the court below similarly noted that the state's equalization program was well under way. 91 A. 2d 137, 149.

the great expenditures for education both demonstrate our recognition of the importance of education to our democratic society. It is required in the performance of our most basic public responsibilities, even service in the armed forces. It is the very foundation of good citizenship. Today it is a principal instrument in awakening the child to cultural values, in preparing him for later professional training, and in helping him to adjust normally to his environment. In these days, it is doubtful that any child may reasonably be expected to succeed in life if he is denied the opportunity of an education. Such an opportunity, where the state has undertaken to provide it, is a right which must be made available to all on equal terms.

We come then to the question presented: Does segregation of children in public schools solely on the basis of race, even though the physical facilities and other "tangible" factors may be equal, deprive the children of the minority group of equal educational opportunities? We believe that it does.

In *Sweatt v. Painter, supra*, in finding that a segregated law school for Negroes could not provide them equal educational opportunities, this Court relied in large part on "those qualities which are incapable of objective measurement but which make for greatness in a law school." In *McLaurin* v. *Oklahoma State Regents, supra*, the Court, in requiring that a Negro admitted to a white graduate school be treated like all other students, again resorted to intangible considerations: " . . . his ability to study, to engage in discussions and exchange views with other students, and, in general, to learn his profession." Such considerations apply with added force to children in grade and high schools. To separate them from others of similar age and qualifications solely because of their race generates a feeling of inferiority as to their status in the community that may affect their hearts and minds in a way unlikely ever to be undone. The effect of this separation on their educational opportunities was well stated by a finding in the Kansas case by a court which nevertheless felt compelled to rule against the Negro plaintiffs:

> Segregation of white and colored children in public schools has a detrimental effect upon the colored children. The impact is greater when it has the sanction of the law; for the policy of separating the races is usually interpreted as denoting the infe-

The Nonviolent Movement

GEORGE W. GARDNER

In 1954 the U.S. Supreme Court decreed that segregated schools were unconstitutional and, a year later, ordered such schools to desegregate "with all deliberate speed." This decision and the controversy and violence that soon surrounded it seemed to serve as a call to arms for young Negroes all over the nation to join the struggle for equality in unprecedented numbers. Armed only with fierce determination and the non-violent teachings of Dr. Martin Luther King, Jr., as their battle plan, young blacks (and many young whites) offered themselves without resistance to brutal policemen. The Civil Rights Acts of 1960 and 1963 and the Voting Rights Act of 1965 were in some measure the result of sacrifices made by such young people as these, photographed at the 1963 March on Washington, who were determined that all Americans should enjoy the same rights.

HENRI CARTIER-BRESSON—MAGNUM

The nonviolent movement's first goal was an end to the Jim Crow
system in the South. While racism permeated the country, it was
most blatant and brutal in the states of the old Confederacy. Here,
custom and law served as constant reminders to Negro men and
women that they were to remain second-class citizens in
perpetuity.

In September 1957 the governor of Arkansas ordered the National
Guard to block Negro students from attending Central High
School in Little Rock. This was in direct defiance of the 1954
Supreme Court school decision. After considerable hesitation,
President Dwight D. Eisenhower federalized the National Guard
and ordered it to escort the new students to their classes. The
troops were visible proof that the Federal government could be
mobilized to protect citizens' rights when state and local
governments seemed unwilling; and shrieked abuse at the Negro
students and their uniformed guardians proved that school
integration would not easily be achieved. Its pace has been slow,
both in the South and in the North.

UPI COMPIX

BURT GLINN—MAGNUM

WIDE WORLD

On December 1, 1955, a Negro seamstress, Miss Rosa Parks, right, refused to give up her seat and move to the back of a Montgomery, Alabama, bus when ordered to do so by its driver. For this offense, which violated a local ordinance, she was arrested and fingerprinted. A group of black ministers, led by the young Dr. Martin Luther King, Jr., organized a boycott of the city bus lines in protest. Despite bombings, police harassment, legal action by the city, and great inconvenience for many Negroes who had to walk miles to work, the Negro community held out for a year until a Federal court ordered the local law overthrown. In triumph, Dr. King and his followers, left, boarded city buses once again. Non-violence had scored its first victory and produced its most eloquent leader in Dr. King.

EVE ARNOLD—MAGNUM

F. ROCKSTROH—PIX FROM PUBLIX

Beginning in 1960, Negro college students began to protest against segregated public facilities by "sitting-in" (taking seats at white lunch counters and restaurants and asking to be served). The movement, soon supported and partially organized by the Congress of Racial Equality (CORE), quickly spread across the South and into border and some Northern states as well. Despite beatings and thousands of arrests, black and white students flocked to the cause. At the left a sit-in trainee is taught to ignore taunts and physical abuse; above, a student waits to be served at a Birmingham, Alabama, lunch counter.

HENRI CARTIER-BRESSON—MAGNUM

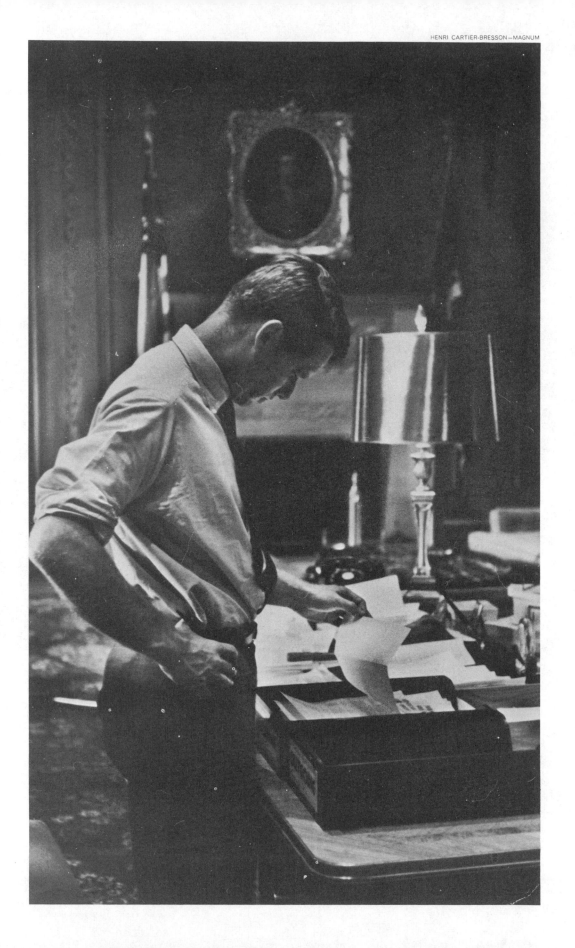

In 1961 the sit-in tactic was extended to interstate travel. Buses of "Freedom Riders" rode through the South to test the Interstate Commerce Commission's 1955 ruling that interstate travel and all the facilities that catered to it had to be open to all. The ruling had been widely ignored and when demonstrators tried to use white restaurants, rest rooms, and waiting rooms in bus, train, and airport terminals, they were often attacked or arrested. In Anniston, Alabama, a bus was burned by an angry crowd. After repeated attempts to persuade local officials to protect the "Freedom Riders" had failed, U.S. Attorney-General Robert F. Kennedy, left, ordered federal marshals to secure peace in Montgomery. They were later replaced by National Guardsmen, shown below, and instituted successful federal suits against separate airport facilities in Montgomery and New Orleans.

BRUCE DAVIDSON—MAGNUM

FRANK ROCKSTROH—PIX FROM PUBLIX

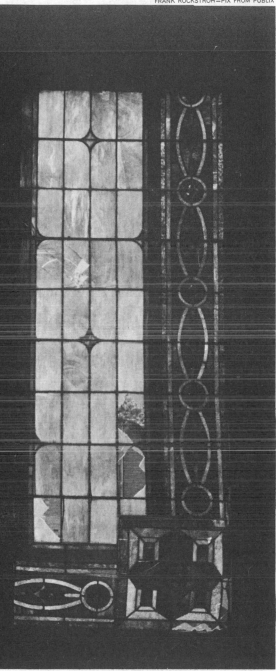

Non-violent progress was not smooth. Beatings, bombings, burning and murder were frequent reminders of the depth of white resistance to black advancement. The exact number of Negro and white victims of the struggle may never be known, but among them was Medgar Evers, the NAACP field director for Mississippi who was murdered on his own doorstep in Jackson. Three young civil rights workers — James Chaney, Andrew Goodman, and Michael Schwerner — were allegedly killed by Klansmen in Neshoba county, Mississippi. Jimmie Lee Jackson, a Negro demonstrator, Mrs. Viola Liuzzo, a Detroit housewife, and Rev. James Reeb, a Boston minister, were all murdered during their participation in the 1965 Selma campaign. This stained-glass window in the 16th Street Baptist church of Birmingham was shattered by a bomb that killed four Negro girls attending Sunday School in the basement; civil rights meetings were thought to have been held in the church. The men who planted this bomb, as well as those who committed most of the other crimes listed here, were never convicted.

Southern police were often savage in their treatment of demonstrators. Their brutality did much to anger the North, embarrass the nation, and force the federal government to act. Indeed, some of the credit for the 1964 Civil Rights Act must go to Eugene "Bull" Connor, the Birmingham police chief who used powerful fire hoses, electric cattle prods, and police dogs to break up demonstrations in his city.

CHARLES MOORE FROM BLACK STAR

BRUCE DAVIDSON—MAGNUM

WIDE WORLD

The achievements of the non-violent movement were real and important. The legal underpinnings were knocked out from under Jim Crow laws. Public facilities could no longer legally be labeled "For Whites Only." Black students began to attend previously all-white state universities, including the University of Mississippi at Oxford, above, where federal marshals and troops entered James Meredith, an air-force veteran, in 1962. Voter registration drives, led by the Student Nonviolent Coordinating Committee, produced new Negro voters, such as the elderly lady at right, registering for the first time in Selma, Alabama, and helped inspire increased black participation in politics throughout the South. Above all, the movement helped nurture a generation of young Negroes unwilling to wait any longer to be full citizens of the United States.

A.F.P. FROM PICTORIAL PARADE

Perhaps the most dramatic single event of the civil rights movement was the 1963 March on Washington. More than 200,000 black and white Americans gathered on the Washington mall to hear Dr. King speak, and to urge Congress to enact a Civil Rights bill. Millions watched on television. The President warmly greeted the march leaders. Many congressmen attended. It seemed clear that the Southern Jim Crow system, at least in its legalized form, was crumbling. After that the movement began to look northward.

riority of the Negro group. A sense of inferiority affects the motivation of a child to learn. Segregation with the sanction of law, therefore, has a tendency to [retard] the educational and mental development of Negro children and to deprive them of some of the benefits they would receive in a racial[ly] integrated school system.[10]

Whatever may have been the extent of psychological knowledge at the time of *Plessy v. Ferguson*, this finding is amply supported by modern authority.[11] Any language in *Plessy v. Ferguson* contrary to this finding is rejected.

We conclude that in the field of public education the doctrine of "separate but equal" has no place. Separate educational facilities are inherently unequal. Therefore, we hold that the plaintiffs and others similarly situated for whom the actions have been brought are, by reason of the segregation complained of, deprived of the equal protection of the laws guaranteed by the Fourteenth Amendment. This disposition makes unnecessary any discussion whether such segregation also violates the due process clause of the Fourteenth Amendment.[12]

Because these are class actions, because of the wide applicability of this decision, and because of the great variety of local conditions, the formulation of decrees in these cases presents problems of considerable complexity. On reargument, the consideration of appropriate relief was necessarily subordinated to the primary ques-

10. A similar finding was made in the Delaware case: "I conclude from the testimony that, in our Delaware society, state-imposed segregation in education itself results in the Negro children, as a class, receiving educational opportunities which are substantially inferior to those available to white children otherwise similarly situated." 87 A. 2d 862, 865.

11. K. B. Clark, *Effect of Prejudice and Discrimination on Personality Development* (Midcentury White House Conference on Children and Youth, 1950); Witmer and Kotinsky, *Personality in the Making* (1952), c. VI; Deutscher and Chein, "The Psychological Effects of Enforced Segregation: A Survey of Social Science Opinion," 26 *J. Psychol.* 259 (1948); Chein, "What are the Psychological effects of Segregation Under Conditions of Equal Facilities?" 3 *Int. J. Opinion and Attitude Res.* 229 (1949); Brameld, *Educational Costs, in Discrimination and National Welfare* (MacIver, ed., 1949), 44-48; Frazier, *The Negro in the United States* (1949), 674-681. And see generally Myrdal, *An American Dilemma* (1944).

12. See *Bolling* v. *Sharpe, post.* p. 497, concerning the due process clause of the Fifth Amendment.

tion—the constitutionality of segregation in public education. We have now announced that such segregation is a denial of the equal protection of the laws. In order that we may have the full assistance of the parties in formulating decrees, the cases will be restored to the docket, and the parties are requested to present further argument on Questions 4 and 5 previously propounded by the Court for the reargument this Term.[13] The attorney general of the United States is again invited to participate. The attorneys general of the states requiring or permitting segregation in public education will also be permitted to appear as *amici curiae* upon request to do so by Sept. 15, 1954, and submission of briefs by Oct. 1, 1954.[14]

13. "4. Assuming it is decided that segregation in public schools violates the Fourteenth Amendment

"(*a*) would a decree necessarily follow providing that, within the limits set by normal geographic school districting, Negro children should forthwith be admitted to schools of their choice, or

"(*b*) may this Court, in the exercise of its equity powers, permit an effective gradual adjustment to be brought about from existing segregated systems to a system not based on color distinctions?

"5. On the assumption on which questions 4 (*a*) and (*b*) are based, and assuming further that this Court will exercise its equity powers to the end described in question 4 (*b*),

"(*a*) should this Court formulate detailed decrees in these cases;

"(*b*) if so, what specific issues should the decrees reach;

"(*c*) should this Court appoint a special master to hear evidence with a view to recommending specific terms for such decrees;

"(*d*) should this Court remand to the courts of first instance with directions to frame decrees in these cases, and if so what general directions should the decrees of this Court include and what procedures should the courts of first instance follow in arriving at the specific terms of more detailed decrees?"

14. See Rule 42, Revised Rules of this Court (effective July 1, 1954).

5. Discrimination in War and Peace

1941-1953

LANGSTON HUGHES

Bop

Langston Hughes was the author of half a dozen books of poems, a novel, a collection of short stories, one or two plays, and an autobiography, but it is likely that his most enduring creation was Simple, the Negro protagonist of several books in which Hughes expressed his deep understanding of his race and of its relation to, and role in, the white man's world. In the vignettes that make up the Simple books, Hughes commented, in a humorous style that was only occasionally sardonic, on the paradoxes of the Negro's life in the land of the free. An example of Simple at his best is the short disquisition reprinted here, which first appeared in Simple Takes a Wife *(1953). [Source:* The Best of Simple, *New York, 1961.]*

Somebody upstairs in Simple's house had the combination turned up loud with an old Dizzy Gillespie record spinning like mad filling the Sabbath with Bop as I passed.

"Set down here on the stoop with me and listen to the music," said Simple.

"I've heard your landlady doesn't like tenants sitting on her stoop," I said.

"Pay it no mind," said Simple. "Ool-ya-koo," he sang. "Hey Ba-Ba-Re-Bop! Be-Bop! Mop!"

"All that nonsense singing reminds me of Cab Calloway back in the old *scat* days," I said, "around 1930 when he was chanting, 'Hi-de-*hie*-de-ho! Hee-de-*hee*-de hee!'"

"Not at all," said Simple, "absolutely not at all."

"Re-Bop certainly sounds like scat to me," I insisted.

"No," said Simple, "Daddy-o, you are wrong. Besides, it was not *Re*-Bop. It is *Be*-Bop."

"What's the difference," I asked, "between *Re* and *Be?*"

"A lot," said Simple. "Re-Bop was an imitation like most of the white boys play. Be-Bop is the real thing like the colored boys play."

"You bring race into everything," I said, "even music."

"It is in everything," said Simple.

"Anyway, Be-Bop is passé, gone, finished."

"It may be gone, but its riffs remain behind," said Simple. "Be-

Bop music was certainly colored folks' music—which is why white folks found it so hard to imitate. But there are some few white boys that latched onto it right well. And no wonder, because they sat and listened to Dizzy, Thelonius, Tad Dameron, Charlie Parker, also Mary Lou, all night long every time they got a chance, and bought their records by the dozens to copy their riffs. The ones that sing tried to make up new Be-Bop words, but them white folks don't know what they are singing about, even yet."

"It all sounds like pure nonsense syllables to me."

"Nonsense, nothing!" cried Simple. "Bop makes plenty of sense."

"What kind of sense?"

"You must not know where Bop comes from," said Simple, astonished at my ignorance.

"I do not know," I said. "Where?"

"From the police," said Simple.

"What do you mean, from the police?"

"From the police beating Negroes' heads," said Simple. "Every time a cop hits a Negro with his billy club, that old club says, 'BOP! BOP! . . . BE-BOP! . . . MOP! . . . BOP!'

"That Negro hollers, 'Ooool-ya-koo! Ou-o-o!'

"Old Cop just keeps on, 'MOP! MOP! . . . BE-BOP! . . . MOP!' That's where Be-Bop came from, beaten right out of some Negro's head into them horns and saxophones and piano keys that plays it. Do you call that nonsense?"

"If it's true, I do not," I said.

"That's why so many white folks don't dig Bop," said Simple. "White folks do not get their heads beat *just for being white*. But me—a cop is liable to grab me almost any time and beat my head—*just* for being colored.

"In some parts of this American country as soon as the polices see me, they say, 'Boy, what are you doing in this neighborhood?'

"I say, 'Coming from work, sir.'

"They say, 'Where do you work?'

"Then I have to go into my whole pedigree because I am a black man in a white neighborhood. And if my answers do not satisfy them, BOP! MOP! . . . BE-BOP! . . . MOP! If they do not hit me, they have already hurt my soul. *A dark man shall see dark days*. Bop

362

comes out of them dark days. That's why real Bop is mad, wild, frantic, crazy—and not to be dug unless you've seen dark days, too. Folks who ain't suffered much cannot play Bop, neither appreciate it. They think Bop is nonsense—like you. They think it's just crazy crazy. They do not know Bop is also MAD crazy, SAD crazy, FRANTIC WILD CRAZY—beat out of somebody's head! That's what Bop is. Them young colored kids who started it, they know what Bop is."

"Your explanation depresses me," I said.

"Your nonsense depresses me," said Simple.

HARRY S. TRUMAN
Civil Rights Message

President Truman devoted considerable attention to the problem of civil rights for Negroes and other persecuted minorities. Following the Committee on Civil Rights report of 1947, Truman recommended congressional action to implement the committee's recommendations. On February 2, 1948, the President presented to Congress his first major civil rights program. Though Congress remained on the whole unresponsive, the program was influential in emphasizing the urgency of civil rights and in laying out the guidelines for later legislation. The President's message is reprinted here in part. [Source: 80 Congress, 2 Session, House Document No. 516.]

Today the American people enjoy more freedom and opportunity than ever before. Never in our history has there been better reason to hope for the complete realization of the ideals of liberty and equality.

We shall not, however, finally achieve the ideals for which this nation was founded so long as any American suffers discrimination as a result of his race, or religion, or color, or the land of origin of his forefathers.

Unfortunately there still are examples—flagrant examples—of discrimination which are utterly contrary to our ideals. Not all groups of our population are free from the fear of violence. Not all groups are free to live and work where they please or to improve their conditions of life by their own efforts. Not all groups enjoy the full privileges of citizenship and participation in the government under which they live.

We cannot be satisfied until all our people have equal opportunities for jobs, for homes, for education, for health, and for political expression, and until all our people have equal protection under the law.

One year ago I appointed a committee of fifteen distinguished Americans and asked them to appraise the condition of our civil rights and to recommend appropriate action by federal, state, and local governments. The committee's appraisal has resulted in a frank and revealing report. This report emphasizes that our basic human freedoms are better cared for and more vigilantly defended than ever before, but it also makes clear that there is a serious gap between our ideals and some of our practices. This gap must be closed.

This will take the strong efforts of each of us individually, and all of us acting together through voluntary organizations and our governments.

The protection of civil rights begins with the mutual respect for the rights of others, which all of us should practise in our daily lives. Through organization in every community — in all parts of the country — we must continue to develop practical, workable arrangements for achieving greater tolerance and brotherhood.

The protection of civil rights is the duty of every government which derives its powers from the consent of the people. This is equally true of local, state, and national governments. There is much that the states can and should do at this time to extend their protection of civil rights. Wherever the law-enforcement measures of state and local governments are inadequate to discharge this primary function of government, these measures should be strengthened and improved.

The federal government has a clear duty to see that constitutional guarantees of individual liberties and of equal protection under the laws are not denied or abridged anywhere in our Union. That duty is shared by all three branches of the government, but it can be fulfilled only if the Congress enacts modern, comprehensive civil

364

rights laws, adequate to the needs of the day, and demonstrating our continuing faith in the free way of life.

I recommend, therefore, that the Congress enact legislation at this session directed toward the following specific objectives:

1. Establishing a permanent Commission on Civil Rights, a Joint Congressional Committee on Civil Rights, and a Civil Rights Division in the Department of Justice.

2. Strengthening existing civil rights statutes.

3. Providing federal protection against lynching.

4. Protecting more adequately the right to vote.

5. Establishing a Fair Employment Practice Commission to prevent unfair discrimination in employment.

6. Prohibiting discrimination in interstate transportation facilities.

7. Providing home rule and suffrage in presidential elections for the residents of the District of Columbia.

8. Providing statehood for Hawaii and Alaska and a greater measure of self-government for our island possessions.

9. Equalizing the opportunities for residents of the United States to become naturalized citizens.

10. Settling the evacuation claims of Japanese-Americans. . . .

The legislation I have recommended for enactment by the Congress at the present session is a minimum program if the federal government is to fulfill its obligation of insuring the constitutional guarantees of individual liberties and of equal protection under the law.

Under the authority of existing law the executive branch is taking every possible action to improve the enforcement of the civil rights statutes and to eliminate discrimination in federal employment, in providing federal services and facilities, and in the armed forces.

I have already referred to the establishment of the Civil Rights Division of the Department of Justice. The Federal Bureau of Investigation will work closely with this new division in the investigation of federal civil rights cases. Specialized training is being given to the Bureau's agents so that they may render more effective service in this difficult field of law enforcement.

It is the settled policy of the United States government that there shall be no discrimination in federal employment or in providing federal services and facilities. Steady progress has been made toward this objective in recent years. I shall shortly issue an executive order containing a comprehensive restatement of the federal nondiscrimination policy, together with appropriate measures to ensure compliance.

During the recent war and in the years since its close, we have made much progress toward equality of opportunity in our armed services without regard to race, color, religion, or national origin. I have instructed the secretary of defense to take steps to have the remaining instances of discrimination in the armed services eliminated as rapidly as possible. The personnel policies and practices of all the services in this regard will be made consistent.

I have instructed the secretary of the army to investigate the status of civil rights in the Panama Canal Zone with a view to eliminating such discrimination as may exist there. If legislation is necessary, I shall make appropriate recommendations to the Congress. . . .

The position of the United States in the world today makes it especially urgent that we adopt these measures to secure for all our people their essential rights.

The peoples of the world are faced with the choice of freedom or enslavement, a choice between a form of government which harnesses the state in the service of the individual and a form of government which chains the individual to the needs of the state.

We in the United States are working in company with other nations who share our desire for enduring world peace and who believe with us that, above all else, men must be free. We are striving to build a world family of nations—a world where men may live under governments of their own choosing and under laws of their own making.

As part of that endeavor, the Commission on Human Rights of the United Nations is now engaged in preparing an international bill of human rights by which the nations of the world may bind themselves by international covenant to give effect to basic human rights and fundamental freedoms. We have played a leading role in this undertaking designed to create a world order of law and justice fully protective of the rights and the dignity of the individual.

To be effective in these efforts, we must protect our civil rights so that by providing all our people with the maximum enjoyment of personal freedom and personal opportunity we shall be a stronger nation—stronger in our leadership, stronger in our moral position, stronger in the deeper satisfactions of a united citizenry.

We know that our democracy is not perfect. But we do know that it offers a fuller, freer, happier life to our people than any totalitarian nation has ever offered.

If we wish to inspire the peoples of the world whose freedom is in jeopardy, if we wish to restore hope to those who have already lost their civil liberties, if we wish to fulfill the promise that is ours, we must correct the remaining imperfections in our practice of democracy.

We know the way. We need only the will.

HARRY S. TRUMAN

Desegregation of the Armed Forces

Even after World War II the armed forces were still racially segregated. But the notable accomplishments of Negro soldiers in the war, as well as the sense of equality they had enjoyed while off-duty in Europe, led many Negroes to protest against this discrimination. A. Philip Randolph and other Negro leaders began to make plans for a mass civil disobedience campaign against the draft unless Negro demands for integration were met. On July 26, 1948, President Truman issued the following executive order establishing a committee to report on racial conditions in the armed forces and recommend ways to promote integration. The committee's report, Freedom to Serve, *published in May 1950, was in large measure implemented during the Korean War. [Source:* Code of Federal Regulations, Title 3 — The President, 1943-1948 Compilation, *Washington, 1957, p. 772.]*

Establishing the President's Committee on Equality of Treatment and Opportunity in the Armed Services

Whereas it is essential that there be maintained in the armed services of the United States the highest standards of democracy, with equality of treatment and opportunity for all those who serve in our country's defense:

Now, Therefore, by virtue of the authority vested in me as President of the United States by the Constitution and the statutes of the United States, and as Commander in Chief of the armed services, it is hereby ordered as follows:

1. It is hereby declared to be the policy of the President that there shall be equality of treatment and opportunity for all persons in the armed services without regard to race, color, religion, or national origin. This policy shall be put into effect as rapidly as possible, having due regard to the time required to effectuate any necessary changes without impairing efficiency or morale.

2. There shall be created in the national military establishment an advisory committee to be known as the President's Committee on Equality of Treatment and Opportunity in the Armed Services, which shall be composed of seven members to be designated by the President.

3. The committee is authorized on behalf of the President to examine into the rules, procedures, and practices of the armed services in order to determine in what respect such rules, procedures and practices may be altered or improved with a view to carrying out the policy of this order. The committee shall confer and advise with the secretary of defense, the secretary of the Army, the secretary of the Navy, and the secretary of the Air Force, and shall make such recommendations to the President and to said secretaries as in the judgment of the committee will effectuate the policy hereof.

4. All executive departments and agencies of the federal government are authorized and directed to cooperate with the committee in its work, and to furnish the committee such information or the services of such persons as the committee may require in the performance of its duties.

5. When requested by the committee to do so, persons in the armed services or in any of the executive departments and agencies of the federal government shall testify before the committee and shall make available for the use of the committee such documents and other information as the committee may require.

6. The committee shall continue to exist until such time as the President shall terminate its existence by executive order.

Racial Discrimination in Washington, D.C.

In 1946 President Truman established an advisory Committee on Civil Rights to recommend "more adequate and effective means and procedures for the protection of the civil rights of the people of the United States." A year later the Committee published To Secure These Rights, *one of the first comprehensive surveys of civil rights in America. The report, drafted by a professor of political science at Dartmouth College, resulted in little legislation, but it succeeded in dramatizing the civil rights problem. The following selection from the report deals with civil rights in Washington, D.C. [Source:* To Secure These Rights, *New York, 1947: "Civil Rights in the Nation's Capital."]*

Throughout the country, our practice lags behind the American tradition of freedom and equality. A single community — the nation's capital — illustrates dramatically the shortcomings in our record and the need for change. The District of Columbia should symbolize to our own citizens and to the people of all countries our great tradition of civil liberty. Instead, it is a graphic illustration of a failure of democracy. As the seat of our federal government under the authority of Congress, the failure of the District is a failure of all of the people.

For Negro Americans, Washington is not just the nation's capital. It is the point at which all public transportation into the South becomes "Jim Crow." If he stops in Washington, a Negro may dine like other men in the Union Station, but as soon as he steps out into the capital, he leaves such democratic practices behind. With very few exceptions, he is refused service at downtown restaurants, he may not attend a downtown movie or play, and he has to go into the poorer section of the city to find a night's lodging. The Negro who decides to settle in the District must often find a home in an overcrowded, substandard area. He must often take a job below the level of his ability. He must send his children to the inferior public schools set aside for Negroes and entrust his family's health to medical agencies which give inferior service. In addition, he must endure the countless daily humiliations that the system of segregation imposes upon the one-third of Washington that is Negro.

The origin of the pattern of discrimination in Washington is partly explained by its location in a border area where many Southern customs prevail. Certain political and local pressure groups and the administrative decisions of municipal officials contribute to its persistence. Attempts to guarantee equal rights on a segregated basis have failed. In recent years the "separate and unequal" pattern has been extended to areas where it had not previously existed. Except where the federal government has made a few independent advances, as in federal employment and the use of federal recreational facilities, racial segregation is rigid. It extends to ludicrous extremes. Inconsistencies are evident: Constitution Hall, owned by the Daughters of the American Revolution, seats concert audiences without distinctions of color, but allows no Negroes on its stage to give regular commercial concerts. On the other hand, the commercial legitimate theater has had Negro actors on its stage, but stubbornly refuses to admit Negro patrons.

Discrimination in education. — The core of Washington's segregated society is its dual system of public education. It operates under congressional legislation which assumes the fact of segregation but nowhere makes it mandatory. The Board of Education and a white superintendent of schools administer two wholly separate school systems. The desire of Congress to insure equal facilities is implemented by a requirement that appropriations be allocated to white and Negro education in proportion to the numbers of children of school age. But this has not been successful. Negro schools are inferior to white schools in almost every respect. The white school buildings have a capacity which is 27 percent greater than actual enrollment. In the colored schools, enrollment exceeds building capacity by 8 percent. Classes in the Negro schools are considerably larger and the teaching load of the Negro teachers considerably heavier. Less than 1 percent of all white school children, but over 15 percent of colored children, receive only part-time instruction. Similar inequalities exist in school buildings, equipment, textbook supplies, kindergarten classes, athletic and recreational facilities.

The District superintendent of schools recently answered charges of inequality in school facilities with the statement that, "Absolute equality of educational opportunity is impossible. Reasonable equality . . . is the goal." The conditions described above eloquently document the extent to which even "reasonable equality" is impossible in a segregated school system.

Official freezing of the segregated school system is complete. The Board of Education frowns on visits by whites to Negro schools and by Negroes to white schools. Intercultural education programs are stillborn because they are considered a threat to the prevailing pattern. Interracial athletic and forensic competition is forbidden. Two cases illustrate the lengths to which the District's officialdom goes to prevent interracial contact. During the war, the Office of Price Administration asked permission to use a school building at night for in-service training of its clerks. The request was denied solely because the class would have included both white and colored employees. In the other case, a white girl was ordered to withdraw from a Negro vocational school where she had enrolled for a course not offered by any other public school in Washington.

Private universities in the District have followed the lead of the public schools. Two of the large universities and most of the smaller schools admit no colored students. American University admits them to its School of Social Science and Public Affairs, but not to the College of Arts and Sciences. Catholic University, on the other hand, presents an outstanding example of successful interracial education. In the last few years, Negroes have been admitted, and there is no color distinction in classes. Last year a Negro was elected a class officer. The presence of Howard University in Washington alleviates somewhat the problem of higher education for the District's Negroes. While Howard University is primarily a Negro institution, it also admits white students.

Discrimination in housing. — In the past, many of Washington's Negroes and whites have lived close together in many parts of the city, and where mixed neighborhoods still exist, incidents of racial friction are rare. Now, however, Negroes are increasingly being forced into a few overcrowded slums.

Programs for the development of highways, parks, and public buildings have often played an unfortunate role in rooting out Negro neighborhoods. There has been a commendable desire to beautify the city of Washington. But there has been little concern for the fate of persons displaced by beautification projects.

The superior economic position of whites also contributes to the shrinkage of Negro neighborhoods. In areas like Georgetown and the old fort sites, white residents and realtors have been buying up Negro properties and converting them to choice residential use. Only occasionally does this process work in reverse: in deteriorating areas, white owners can sometimes get higher prices from Negroes, who have little from which to choose, than they can from white buyers.

The chief weapon in the effort to keep Negroes from moving out of overcrowded quarters into white neighborhoods is the restrictive covenant. New building sites and many older areas are now covenanted. Some covenants exclude all nonmembers of the Caucasian race; others bar only Negroes, or Negroes and members of "Semitic races." Even where covenants do not prevail, the powerful local real estate fraternity protects white areas from "invasion." The all-white Washington Real Estate Board has a "code of ethics" which prohibits its members from selling land in predominantly white areas to Negroes, and the realtors are supported in this practice by nonmember dealers, banks, and loan companies. Two of the city's newspapers will not accept ads offering property in white areas for sale to Negroes. Because the policy of the National Capital Housing Authority is to follow the "community pattern," all public housing projects are completely segregated and housing for Negroes is built only in established Negro neighborhoods. The Authority has spent most of its funds for permanent housing to build homes for Negroes, but its appropriations have been limited.

Housing conditions are poor for Washington residents in general, but, largely because of the pressures just described, they are much worse for Negroes. According to a recent Board of Trade report on city planning, 70 percent of the inhabitants of the city's three worst slum areas are Negroes. The largest single slum in the District houses about 7 percent of the white and 30 percent of the Negro population. In 1940, one-eighth of the white dwellings in Washington and 40 percent of those occupied by Negroes were substandard; 15 percent of white-occupied and 38 percent of Negro-occupied dwellings had more than one person per room.

Discrimination in employment. — More than one-third of the jobs in Washington are with the federal government. Therefore, discriminatory practices of government agencies, which have already been discussed, are important to District Negroes. The District government itself has only a small proportion of Negro employees, and most of these are confined to unskilled and menial jobs. Partial exceptions to this are the Metropolitan Police, the segregated Fire Service, and the school system with its segregated staff. A ranking District official during the war told an interviewer: "Negroes in the District of Columbia have no right to ask for jobs on the basis of merit," the rationalization being that whites own most of the property and pay the bulk of municipal taxes.

Negroes are confined to the lowest paid and least skilled jobs in private employment. In 1940, three-fourths of all Negro workers in Washington were domestics, service workers, or laborers, while only one-eighth of the white workers held jobs of that type. At the other end of the scale, only one-eighth of all Negro workers were clerks, salesmen, managers, proprietors, or professionals, while two-thirds of the white workers were in jobs of this kind. There are similar striking racial differences in average income and length of work-week.

A few examples will illustrate the part discrimination has played in causing these differences. During the war, Washington's public transportation system bogged down badly for lack of qualified streetcar and bus operators. The Capital Transit Company advertised for workers hundreds of miles away and even recruited government employees on a part-time basis. In spite of this, the company would not employ qualified Negroes as operators. In build ing construction, one of Washington's largest industries, the various building trade unions discriminate against colored craftsmen. They are either excluded completely, allowed to work only on projects to be occupied by Negroes, admitted only as helpers to white journeymen, or not allowed to become apprentices. The numerous large white hotels employ Negroes only in such capacities as chambermaids, busboys, waiters, and coal stokers. There are no colored salespeople in the large department stores. In laundries and cleaning plants where wages are low and hours long, most of the workers are colored, but supervisors are white; where whites and Negroes perform the same work, there is a wage differential of from 20 to 30 percent. The District Bar Association and the Medical Society are for whites only.

Discrimination in health services. – The greatest inequalities are

373

evident in Washington's concern for the health of its residents. Freedmen's Hospital, federally supported and affiliated with Howard University, is for Negroes only, and three-fourths of the beds in the municipal Gallinger Hospital are usually occupied by Negroes in segregated wards. Four of the twelve private hospitals in the city do not admit Negro inpatients, and the rest accept only a few in segregated wards. It is peculiarly shocking to find church hospitals practising discrimination. Far fewer hospital beds in proportion to population are available to Negroes than to whites. Sickness rates are higher among Negroes than whites, which aggravates this situation. All but the smallest clinics are segregated. Group Health Association, however, does not discriminate either in membership or services.

No Negro physician is allowed to practise in Gallinger Hospital, although it is publicly supported and the majority of its patients are colored. Nor are they allowed in St. Elizabeth's, a federal institution, or any of the private hospitals. Only Freedmen's is open to them, and then only for the care of assigned ward patients. Thus the Negro physician cannot follow his own patients into the hospital. Negro medical students are similarly discriminated against in the provision of training facilities.

Public and private agency welfare services are available to both colored and white residents, but institutional care is provided only on a segregated basis, and the institutions for Negroes are far inferior in both number and quality to those for whites. Here, again, the lower economic position of Negroes and their consequent need for care aggravates the problem.

Discrimination in recreational services. — In the field of public recreation, compulsory segregation has increased over the past twenty-five years. Various public authorities have closed to one race or the other numerous facilities where whites and Negroes once played together harmoniously. In 1942, the District of Columbia Board of Recreation was set up to centralize the control of public recreation facilities. Congress eliminated from the locally sponsored bill a provision that would have required the new board to continue segregation. But it took no positive stand on the issue, and the board has adopted regulations which enforce segregation in all the parks and playgrounds under its control.

Under this policy, facilities in seven out of twenty-six "natural areas" in the District have been turned over to Negroes. Because the Negro areas are disproportionately concentrated in the older, crowded parts of the city, white facilities are generally superior to those allotted to Negroes. Furthermore, whites and Negroes alike who live far from facilities open to their race have easy access to none. White residents who had shared with Negroes the use of the Rose Park Tennis Courts protested in vain against being barred from them.

On the other hand, recreation facilities under the jurisdiction of the Department of the Interior are open to all races, and serious friction is nonexistent. District officials have tried repeatedly to have these facilities turned over to the Recreation Board. The transfer has not been made because the board will not agree to refrain from imposing segregation in their use.

Most private recreational groups follow the official policy of segregation, although occasional interracial competitions have been held successfully by some. The Washington branch of the Amateur Athletic Union allows no interracial contests under its auspices. For example, no Negro may enter the local Golden Gloves Tournament, although they compete in the national tournament.

Discrimination in places of public accommodation. — Public transportation is provided without separation of the races, and the spectators at most professional sporting events are unsegregated. But other public accommodations are a focal point of Negro resentment, because rigorous segregation in practice means exclusion. No downtown theater except the burlesque house admits Negroes. They may see movies only in their neighborhood houses. Some department stores and many downtown shops exclude Negro patrons by ignoring them or refusing to show the stock they request or making them wait until all white customers have been served. A Negro is seldom accepted at the downtown hotels unless special arrangements are made. Although they may dine at the Union Station, the YWCA, and the cafeterias in government office buildings, the overwhelming majority of downtown restaurants are closed to them.

The shamefulness and absurdity of Washington's treatment of Negro Americans is highlighted by the presence of many dark-skinned foreign visitors. Capital custom not only humiliates colored citizens but is a source of considerable embarrassment to these visitors. White residents, because they are the dominant group, share in both the humiliation and the embarrassment. Foreign officials are often mistaken for American Negroes and refused food, lodging, and entertainment. However, once it is established that they are not Americans, they are accommodated.

This is the situation that exists in the District of Columbia. The committee feels most deeply that it is intolerable.

Hallelujah I'm A-Travelin'

"Hallelujah I'm A-Travelin' " is said to have been composed by an unknown Negro tenant farmer in Tennessee in 1946 to express his joy at the Supreme Court's decision in the case of Morgan v. Virginia, *which banned discrimination in interstate travel. Whether or not the song was actually occasioned by the Court's action, it became popular during the ensuing period and was taken up by civil rights marchers a decade later.* [Source: This Singing Land, *compiled and edited by Irwin Silber, 1965, Amsco Music Publishing Co., Used by Permission.*]

Stand up and rejoice! A great day is here!
We are fighting Jim Crow, and the vict'ry is near!

Chorus:
Hallelujah, I'm a-travelin'
Hallelujah, ain't it fine?
Hallelujah, I'm a travelin'
Down freedom's main line!

I read in the news, the Supreme Court has said,
"Listen here, mister Jim Crow, it's time you was dead."

The judges declared in Washington town,
"You white folks must take that old Jim Crow sign down."

I'm paying my fare on the Greyhound Bus line,
I'm riding the front seat to Nashville this time.

Columbia's the gem of the ocean, they say,
We're fighting Jim Crow in Columbia today.

I hate Jim Crow and Jim Crow hates me,
And that's why I'm fighting for my liberty.

GUNNAR MYRDAL

Negro Leadership in North and South

Gunnar Myrdal, a Swedish economist and sociologist, was commissioned by the Carnegie Corporation in 1938 to investigate the conditions of the Negro in the United States. In 1944 the results of his study were published in An American Dilemma. The Negro Problem and Modern Democracy, *which has been acclaimed as one of the most thorough and perceptive analyses of the Negro in America. "Our task in this inquiry," Myrdal wrote in 1944, " is to ascertain social reality as it is. We shall seek to depict the actual life conditions of the American Negro people and their manifold relations to the larger American society . . . to discover and dissect the doctrines and ideologies, valuations, and beliefs, embedded in the minds of white and Negro Americans." The following is a portion of the chapter entitled "Compromise Leadership." [Source:* An American Dilemma, *New York, 1944, pp. 768-780.]*

THE DAILY COMPROMISE

In discussing the accommodating Negro leader . . . we assumed for the purposes of abstract analysis that the protest motive was absent. This assumption, however, has some real truth in it. . . . The accommodation motive has predominant importance in the daily life of the American Negroes. But it is true that the protest motive is ever present. In some degree it has reached practically all American Negroes. To many individuals it is a major interest. And the Negro protest is bound to rise even higher. But the influence of the protest motive is limited mainly to the propagation of certain ideas about how things *should* be. In any case, but few Negro individuals are in a position to do anything practical about it. Everyone, however, has to get on with his own life from day to day, *now and here*. Even when

377

the individual plans for future employment, for business, or for schooling, he has to reckon with the world as it is. He has to accommodate.

The Negro protest is thus mainly suppressed and turned inward. But it has effects upon Negro personality, upon the relations between the classes in the Negro community, and also upon caste relations. The whites, on their side, are accustomed to a certain amount of Negro unreliability, dishonesty, laziness, secretiveness, and even insolence and impudence. They shut their eyes to its explanation in Negro dissatisfaction and the other results of the caste system. The average white man, in the South, actually gets enjoyment out of observing and joking about Negro inefficiency and slyness.

He knows that he gets the services of Negroes for a cheap price, and so he can afford to joke about this. But, apparently, he also wants to convince himself that the Negroes are well satisfied. Now and then, however, he reveals to the observer, more or less incidentally, that he knows about and understands the Negro protest.

The Southerner keeps watching all the time for germs of unrest and dissatisfaction in the Negro community. He preserves the machinery of caste controls in a state of perpetual preparedness and applies it occasionally as an exercise or a demonstration. In this system, the Negroes *have* to accommodate individually and as a group. This is the situation in the South. . . . The Northern situation is considerably different.

THE VULNERABILITY OF THE NEGRO LEADER
In the protective Negro community much goes on which the white man does not know about. The reality of this reserve is well known to Negroes, and it is coming to effective use in the Negro church, the Negro school, and the Negro press. But the Negro leader has stepped out of the anonymity, and the eyes of influential white people are focused on him. He has to watch his moves carefully in order not to fall out with them. This would end his usefulness to the Negro community as a go-between. And it would spell his own ruin, as the whites have a close control on his income and his status.

In the South practically all Negro teachers—from the lonely teacher in a dilapidated one-room schoolhouse isolated off somewhere in a rural county, to the president of a Negro college—are appointed by white leaders and they hold their position under the threat of being dismissed if they become troublesome. The Negro church is often claimed to be the one independent Negro institution founded entirely upon the organizational efforts and the economic contributions of the Negro people themselves. But the observer finds that to an amazing extent there are ties of small mortgage loans and petty contributions from whites which restrict the freedom of the preachers. Negro professionals and Negro businessmen, operating in the tight areas behind the caste wall, are also dependent on the goodwill, the indulgence, and sometimes the assistance of whites. The same is even more true of the successful Negro landowner, who in most Southern areas meets the envy of poor whites, and so needs the protection of the substantial white people in the community. And for all local Negro leaders, it is perhaps not the economic sanction that is most important, but the sanction of physical punishment, destruction of property, and banishment.

In a sense, every ambitious and successful Negro is more dependent upon the whites than is his caste fellow in the lower class. He is more conspicuous. He has more to lose and he has more to gain. If he becomes aggressive, he is adding to all the odds he labors under, the risk of losing the goodwill and protection of the influential whites. The Southern whites have many ways of keeping this prospect constantly before his mind. He knows he has to "go slow."

IMPERSONAL MOTIVES

This should not be construed to imply that there is a crude self-seeking opportunism on the part of Negro leaders or a cynical despotism on the part of the whites. The power situation is conducive to the creation of both, and the standards of power morals are low. But even the most right-minded, ambitious Negro would be foolish not to realize that he has to keep in line if he wants to do something for his own people. Accommodation on his part can be, and often is, altruistically motivated. He can view it as a sacrifice of personal dignity and conviction which he undergoes to further, not only his own aspirations but also those of his whole group. He can point out, rightly, that reckless opposition on his part might endanger Negro welfare.

379

There is much bitterness among Southern Negro leaders because they are criticized for being "Uncle Toms," especially by Northern Negro intellectuals. They will tell the observer that it takes little courage to stay in the safety of the North and to keep on protesting against Negro sufferings in the South. "They should come down here and feel the fears, uncertainties, and utter dependence of one of us in their own bones," said one prominent Negro banker in the Upper South. And he added: "If they then continued their outbursts, we would know that they are crazy, and we would have to try to get rid of them as a public danger. But, sure, they would come along. They would be cautious and pussy-footing as we are."

On the white side, the motives are usually neither base nor crude. Often a Southern school board will try to appoint the best Negro they can get for teacher, school principal, or college president. When they look for a "cautious," "sane," "sober," "safe," "restrained," and "temperate" Negro, they have in view a person who they honestly think will be good for "racial harmony." The same is true when they help a Negro preacher whom they consider a well-intentioned person. Mortgage loans and contributions to Negro churches are most of the time not given with the conscious intent to fabricate caste controls but to help religious work among Negroes by ministers who have their respect. But they operate within the framework of the Southern white philosophy of race relations.

According to this philosophy, the whites should "look after their Negroes." Negroes should not protest but accommodate. They should not demand their rights but beg for help and assistance. Everything then works out for the good of both groups. When they dismiss a "radical" professor from a Southern Negro college or put the screws on an incautious preacher, doctor, or businessman or do not listen to his requests any longer, they act "in the best interest of the Negro group." Even whites who personally would prefer to be more broad-minded, even Northern philanthropists who would help the South, have to take into account "the public opinion among whites," what "people will stand for down here."

The selection and the behavior of Negro leaders in the South is an outcome of this fact, that practically all the economic and political powers are concentrated in the white caste while the small amount of influence, status, and wealth that there is in the Negro community is derivative and dependent. The Negro masses are well aware of this situation. They need Negro leaders who can get things from the whites. They know that a Negro leader who starts to act aggressively is not only losing his own power and often his livelihood but might endanger the welfare of the whole Negro community.

In Southern Negro communities there is apparently much suspicion against "radical," "hot-headed," and "outspoken" Negroes. Negroes do not want to be observed associating with such persons, because they might "get in trouble." A barricade will often be thrown up around them by a common consent that they are "queer." The Negro community itself will thus often, before there is any white interference, advise individual Negroes who show signs of aggression that they had better trim their sails.

THE PROTEST MOTIVE

Nevertheless, the protest motive is not without influence on Negro leadership in the South. For one thing, some protest is almost a necessary ingredient in the leadership appeal to Negroes. The furthering of race pride and racial solidarity is the means of diminishing internal strivings in the Negro community and of lining up the community into a working unity. Whites sometimes understand this, and there is, therefore, also a certain amount of "tolerated impudence" which a trusted and influential Negro leader can get away with even in the presence of whites. If the Negro community feels sure that he, nevertheless, retains the ear of whites, such a guarded outspokenness will increase his prestige. Negro leaders are often keenly aware of just how far they can go with white people—just what they can afford to say, how they should say it, and when they should say it. Often a protest will be produced under the cover of a joke, or in a similar form, so that the whites do not quite get the full meaning or, anyhow, can pretend that they have not got it. There is a whole technique for how to "tell it right in the face of the whites" without being caught. The stories about such successful protests under cover form a mythology around a Negro leader who has the admiration and allegiance of his community.

But much more generally the Negro community enjoys the demonstration of the Negro protest—as long as it does not become too

381

dangerous for racial harmony. The vicarious satisfaction taken in the victories of Negro athletes who have beaten white competitors has long been observed. The esteem in the Negro community for the "bad nigger" is another point. The "bad nigger" is one who will deliberately run the risks involved in ignoring the caste etiquette, behaving impudently and threateningly toward whites and actually commiting crimes of violence against them. Because he often creates fear in the white community, and because he sometimes acts the role of "Robin Hood" for lesser Negroes in trouble with whites, he is accorded a fearful respect by other Negroes. He certainly does not become a Negro "leader." But, particularly in the lower classes, he is a race hero and will be protected by them by means of pretended ignorance as to his doings and whereabouts.

Whenever a Negro leader can afford—without endangering his own status or the peace of the Negro community—to speak up against, or behave slightingly toward, members of the superior caste, this will increase his prestige.

THE DOUBLE ROLE

More generally, the presence of the protest motive in the Negro community tends to induce the Negro leader to take on two different appearances: one toward the whites and another toward the Negro followership. Toward the Negroes he will pretend that he has dared to say things and to take positions much in exaggeration of what actually has happened. The present author, when comparing notes from interviews in the Negro community with what the white community leaders have told him about their "good Negroes," has frequently observed this discrepancy.

A dual standard of behavior is not unnatural for a Southern Negro. It is rather to be expected of anybody in the lower layer of the Southern caste system. But the Negro leaders especially are pressed into such a pattern as they are more regularly, and in a sense professionally, in contact with whites and have a more considerable stake in the game.

> They play two roles and must wear two fronts. . . . The adjustments and adaptations of the Negro leader are apt to be more pronounced and in bolder relief than those of the com-

mon Negro for the reason that the Negro leader clearly has much more to lose. He has two worlds to please and to seek his status in.

There is a limit, though, to what an accommodating Negro leader can pretend in the Negro community of what he has been bold enough to say or do. What he says to the Negroes, if it is really startling, will most of the time be reported by servants and other stool pigeons to the whites, and might make them suspicious of him.

The Negro community gets a revenge against the whites, not only out of the Negro leaders' cautious aggressions but also out of the whites' being deceived. The satisfaction when some member of the community has succeeded in "pulling the wool" over the eyes of trusting white men is apparent. If deception is achieved, the Negroes seem to enjoy their leaders' spreading the flattery thick when approaching the whites. This is the most concealed, the almost perverted, form of the Negro protest.

NEGRO LEADERSHIP TECHNIQUES

This situation is likely to make the Negro leader sophisticated and "wise." He becomes intensely conscious of all his moves. One Southern Negro leader outlined the most effective technique to use when approaching influential white people to get them to do something for the Negro community, in the following words:

> Don't emphasize the Negro's "right" . . . don't *press* for anything . . . make him feel he's a big man, get to other white men to make him want to avoid seeming small, and you can make him jump through the barrel. You can make him a friend or a rattlesnake, depending on your approach.

Another Negro leader told us:

> I'm a respectable citizen, but when I try to get my rights I do so in a way that will not be obnoxious, and not in a radical way. I don't believe in radicalism. We *ask* for things, but never *demand*. When I'm in Rome, I burn Roman candles . . . but I don't "Uncle Tom."

A Negro editor in another Southern city explained:

383

If a Negro goes so far as to make an enemy of the white man who has the power he is foolish. You can't hit a man in the mouth and expect him to loan you money. By all means keep in with the man who hires and pays you. A man wouldn't be head of a big concern if he weren't a smart man, and a smart man will always react to facts. My approach is to the fellow on top because he is going to have to take care of me and I must work with him – he has the stick.

The successful Negro leader becomes a consummate manipulator. Getting the white man to do what he wants becomes a fine art. This is what is called "playing 'possum." The Negro leader gets satisfaction out of his performance and feels pride in his skill in flattering, beguiling, and outwitting the white man. The South is full of folklore and legend on this aspect of Negro leadership. And the stories are told among whites too, just as are stories about clever children or animals.

Every person in this game has a double standard of understanding and behavior. The white leaders know that they are supposed to be outwitted by the subservient but sly Negro leaders. In the Southern aristocratic tradition they are supposed not only to permit and to enjoy the flattery of the Negro leaders but also to let them get away with something for themselves and for their group. It is the price due the Negro leaders for their adaptive skills and for their tactful abstention from raising the Negro protest. The Negro leaders also know their double role.

The Negro community is thus, on the one hand, filled by the Negro protest and it demands to be appealed to in terms of Negro solidarity. It also wants to feel that the protest is getting over to the whites. On the other hand, the Negro community knows the caste situation, is afraid of radical leaders and troublemakers, and wants its go-betweens to be able to make some real deliveries.

MORAL CONSEQUENCES

This situation is pregnant with all sorts of double-dealing, cynicism, and low morals in the Negro community. The leaders are under constant suspicion from the Negro community that they are dishonest, venal, and self-seeking. One observing Negro citizen expressed

384

a common view when he told us: "You give a few Negroes a break, hand them a job, and all problems are solved." The complaints about "bad leadership" – "incompetent," "selfish," "treacherous," "corrupt" – were raised in every single Negro community the present author has visited. These complaints may, indeed, be said to constitute one of the unifying popular theories in the Negro world, a point upon which everybody can agree. "There are few Negro leaders," Ralph Bunche confirms, "who are not suspect immediately they attain any eminence. The racial situation has created a vicious circle in Negro reasoning on leadership, and the Negro leader is caught in it."

The Negro community in the South cannot expect – and does not want – its leaders to act out the protest the common Negroes actually feel. There is, indeed, little reason to believe that the leaders are less militant than the community seriously wants them to be. But the common Negroes do feel humiliated and frustrated. And they can afford to take it out on their leaders by defaming them for their "kowtowing," "pussyfooting," and "Uncle Tomming"; by calling them "handkerchief heads" and "hats in hand"; and particularly by suspecting them for being prepared to barter away their own honor and the interests of the group for a job or a hand-out. *The Negro hates the Negro role in American society, and the Negro leader, who acts out this role in public life, becomes the symbol of what the Negro hates.*

The Southern Negro leader – not being allowed to state and follow a clear ideological line but doomed to opportunism, having constantly to compromise with his pride and dignity, and never being allowed to speak upon the authority of the strength of an organized group behind him but appearing as an individual person trusted by the adversary group before him – does not have the sanctions ordinarily operating to preserve the honor and loyalty of a representative leader. The temptation to sell out the group and to look out for his own petty interest is great. He thus easily comes to justify the common suspicions around him by becoming a self-seeker and opportunist. The anger in the Negro community against unscrupulous leaders is often directed against the fact that they do not get more for themselves out of their unscrupulousness in sacrificing the common interest:

385

> That [leadership] which can be bought . . . is usually purchaseable for "peanut money." The scorn for the practice among Negroes, frequently expressed is often less due to the fact that Negro leaders "sell out" than because they do so so cheaply.

LEADERSHIP RIVALRY

Since power and prestige are scarce commodities in the Negro community, the struggle for leadership often becomes ruthless. Such is the situation even in those fields where there is little white interference. White influence is likely to increase bitter personal rivalry, as the leader comes to operate as a single individual, trusted by the whites but generally without any organized backing or control in the Negro community and without a cause or an issue.

For the same reasons this rivalry does not provide a check on dishonesty. It rather loosens still more the loyalty of the Negro community. It also provides the influential whites with increased possibilities to "divide and rule." And it defiles still more the atmosphere around Negro leadership. The rivalry, the envy, and the disunity in the Negro community, and the destructive effects, are felt by even the poorest Negro, who will everywhere tell the inquirer that "Negroes just can't stick together." "Lambasting our leaders is quite a popular pastime," observes James Weldon Johnson. Under those circumstances the attainment of Negro leadership also tends to "do something" to the individual Negro:

> For when a value is scarce its possession tends to inflate the possessor. The Negro leader often quickly puffs up when given power. He "struts" and puts up a big front, or puts on "airs," often indulges in exhibitionism. It is often truly said that the Negro leader "can't stand power." Actually, there is a sort of ambivalence which characterizes the attitudes of Negro leaders. The leader will pay lip-service to the concepts of democracy for he understands their significance and appeal to the Negro as a group. But in his personal views and relationship the Negro leader is ordinarily very allergic to democracy—he prefers to play the role of the aristocrat, or the dictator or tyrant. *For leadership itself is a form of escape.*

QUALIFICATIONS

It should be observed that *these detrimental effects upon public confidence and morals in the Negro community are derivative from the basic lack of democracy inherent in the Southern caste situation*, and, further, that *they become increased by the rising Negro protest as long as it is denied free outlet*. They have close parallels in all other subordinate groups.

In this situation it is understandable why so many well-equipped upper-class Negroes in the South withdraw voluntarily from attempting to play a leadership role. . . . But many cannot afford to withdraw entirely. So many of the vocations and positions which mean an economic and social career in the Negro community are under white control, directly or indirectly. And the influential whites reckon on their Negro college presidents, their Negro high-school principals, their favored Negro ministers, farmers, and businessmen to shepherd the Negro community.

This may, indeed, be a blessing to the Negro community as so many of the most devoted and capable Negro leaders in the South actually are persons who would prefer to stay away and mind their own business, if their position, and, especially, white expectations, did not draw them out as Negro leaders. It must never be forgotten—in spite of what many Negro interlocutors in their dismay and pessimism tell the interviewer to the contrary—that *there are in the South many honest and diligent Negro leaders* who unselfishly forward Negro interests by a slow, patient, but determined, plodding along against odds and difficulties. And an important aspect of the changing South is that—as the general educational level is raised, racial liberalism progresses, and federal agencies become important—*they are the Negro leaders to become increasingly trusted by the whites in power.*

Negro March on Washington

Asa Philip Randolph was one of the most active and effective twentieth-century leaders in the Negro's fight to improve his conditions in America. Prominent in the labor movement since 1925, when he organized the Brotherhood of Sleeping Car Porters, he was elected vice-president of the AFL-CIO in 1957. One of his most significant efforts in behalf of the Negro was during the campaign undertaken in 1941 to eliminate segregation in the armed forces and discrimination in employment. A march on Washington planned for July 1941 had been averted after Randolph had conferred with President Roosevelt, who then issued an executive order against discrimination in war industries. The following selection includes an article by Randolph, "Why Should We March?" published in November 1942, and the program of the organizers of the March on Washington Movement. [Source: Survey Graphic, November 1942.]

A. PHILIP RANDOLPH

Why Should We March?

Though I have found no Negroes who want to see the United Nations lose this war, I have found many who, before the war ends, want to see the stuffing knocked out of white supremacy and of empire over subject peoples. American Negroes, involved as we are in the general issues of the conflict, are confronted not with a choice but with the challenge both to win democracy for ourselves at home and to help win the war for democracy the world over.

There is no escape from the horns of this dilemma. There ought not to be escape. For if the war for democracy is not won abroad, the fight for democracy cannot be won at home. If this war cannot be won for the white peoples, it will not be won for the darker races.

Conversely, if freedom and equality are not vouchsafed the peoples of color, the war for democracy will not be won. Unless this double-barreled thesis is accepted and applied, the darker races will never wholeheartedly fight for the victory of the United Nations. That is why those familiar with the thinking of the American Negro have sensed his lack of enthusiasm, whether among the educated or uneducated, rich or poor, professional or nonprofessional, religious or secular, rural or urban, North, South, East, or West.

That is why questions are being raised by Negroes in church, labor union, and fraternal society; in poolroom, barbershop, schoolroom, hospital, hairdressing parlor; on college campus, railroad, and bus. One can hear such questions asked as these: What have Negroes to fight for? What's the difference between Hitler and that "cracker" Talmadge of Georgia? Why has a man got to be Jim-Crowed to die for democracy? If you haven't got democracy yourself, how can you carry it to somebody else?

What are the reasons for this state of mind? The answer is: discrimination, segregation, Jim Crow. Witness the Navy, the Army, the Air Corps; and also government services at Washington. In many parts of the South, Negroes in Uncle Sam's uniform are being put upon, mobbed, sometimes even shot down by civilian and military police, and, on occasion, lynched. Vested political interests in race prejudice are so deeply entrenched that to them winning the war against Hitler is secondary to preventing Negroes from winning democracy for themselves. This is worth many divisions to Hitler and Hirohito. While labor, business, and farm are subjected to ceilings and floors and not allowed to carry on as usual, these interests trade in the dangerous business of race hate as usual.

When the defense program began and billions of the taxpayers' money were appropriated for guns, ships, tanks, and bombs, Negroes presented themselves for work only to be given the cold shoulder. North as well as South, and despite their qualifications, Negroes were denied skilled employment. Not until their wrath and indignation took the form of a proposed protest march on Washington, scheduled for July 1, 1941, did things begin to move in the form of defense jobs for Negroes. The march was postponed by the timely issuance (June 25, 1941) of the famous Executive Order No. 8802 by President Roosevelt. But this order and the President's Committee on Fair Employment Practice, established thereunder, have as yet only scratched the surface by way of eliminating discriminations on account of race or color in war industry. Both management and labor unions in too many places and in too many ways are still drawing the color line.

It is to meet this situation squarely with direct action that the March on Washington Movement launched its present program of protest mass meetings. Twenty thousand were in attendance at Madison Square Garden, June 16; 16,000 in the Coliseum in Chicago, June 26; 9,000 in the City Auditorium of St. Louis, August 14.

Meetings of such magnitude were unprecedented among Negroes. The vast throngs were drawn from all walks and levels of Negro life – businessmen, teachers, laundry workers, Pullman porters, waiters, and red caps; preachers, crapshooters, and social workers; jitterbugs and Ph.D.'s. They came and sat in silence, thinking, applauding only when they considered the truth was told, when they felt strongly that something was going to be done about it.

The March on Washington Movement is essentially a movement of the people. It is all Negro and pro-Negro, but not for that reason antiwhite or anti-Semitic, or anti-Catholic, or antiforeign, or antilabor. Its major weapon is the nonviolent demonstration of Negro mass power. Negro leadership has united back of its drive for jobs and justice. "Whether Negroes should march on Washington, and if so, when?" will be the focus of a forthcoming national conference. For the plan of a protest march has not been abandoned. Its purpose would be to demonstrate that American Negroes are in deadly earnest and all out for their full rights. No power on earth can cause them today to abandon their fight to wipe out every vestige of second-class citizenship and the dual standards that plague them.

A community is democratic only when the humblest and weakest person can enjoy the highest civil, economic, and social rights that the biggest and most powerful possess. To trample on these rights of both Negroes and poor whites is such a commonplace in the South that it takes readily to antisocial, antilabor, anti-Semitic, and anti-Catholic propaganda. It was because of laxness in enforcing the Weimar Constitution in republican Germany that Nazism made headway. Oppression of the Negroes in the United States, like suppression of the Jews in Germany, may open the way for a fascist dictatorship.

By fighting for their rights now, American Negroes are helping to make America a moral and spiritual arsenal of democracy. Their fight against the poll tax, against lynch law, segregation, and Jim Crow, their fight for economic, political, and social equality, thus becomes part of the global war for freedom.

Program of the March on Washington Movement

1. We demand, in the interest of national unity, the abrogation of every law which makes a distinction in treatment between citizens

based on religion, creed, color, or national origin. This means an end to Jim Crow in education, in housing, in transportation, and in every other social, economic, and political privilege; and, especially, we demand, in the capital of the nation, an end to all segregation in public places and in public institutions.

2. We demand legislation to enforce the Fifth and Fourteenth amendments guaranteeing that no person shall be deprived of life, liberty, or property without due process of law, so that the full weight of the national government may be used for the protection of life and thereby may end the disgrace of lynching.

3. We demand the enforcement of the Fourteenth and Fifteenth amendments and the enactment of the Pepper Poll Tax Bill so that all barriers in the exercise of the suffrage are eliminated.

4. We demand the abolition of segregation and discrimination in the Army, Navy, Marine Corps, Air Corps, and all other branches of national defense.

5. We demand an end to discrimination in jobs and job training. Further, we demand that the FEPC be made a permanent administrative agency of the U.S. government and that it be given power to enforce its decisions based on its findings.

6. We demand that federal funds be withheld from any agency which practises discrimination in the use of such funds.

7. We demand colored and minority group representation on all administrative agencies so that these groups may have recognition of their democratic right to participate in formulating policies.

8. We demand representation for the colored and minority racial groups on all missions, political and technical, which will be sent to the peace conference so that the interests of all people everywhere may be fully recognized and justly provided for in the postwar settlement.

I Got My Questionnairy

World War II, like other wars in which Americans have been engaged, produced its quota of songs expressing the feelings of the participants. "I Got My Questionnairy" is a Negro Blues song that was transcribed by a collector during the war. [Source: Negro Folk Music, U.S.A., New York, 1963.]

> Well I got my questionnairy,
> And it leads me to the war.
> Well I got my questionnairy,
> And it leads me to the war.
> Well I'm leavin', pretty baby,
> Child, can't do anything at all.
>
> Uncle Sam aint no woman,
> But he sure can take your man.
> Uncle Sam aint no woman,
> But he sure can take your man.
> Boys, they got 'em in the service
> Doin' something I can't understand.

FRANKLIN D. ROOSEVELT

Discrimination in Wartime Employment

During the spring of 1941, leaders of the Negro community laid plans for a march on Washington on the 1st of July. A. Philip Randolph, president of the Brotherhood of Sleeping Car Porters and one of the most influential Negro leaders of this century, explained the reasons for the march, which in fact did not occur. "When the defense program began and billions of the taxpayers' money were appropriated for guns, ships, tanks, and bombs," Randolph later said, "Negroes presented themselves for work only to be given the cold shoulder. . . . Not until their wrath and indignation took the form of a proposed protest march on Washington . . . did things begin to move in the form of defense jobs for Negroes." The march was averted by President Roosevelt's

Executive Order No. 8802, issued June 25, which established the President's
Committee on Fair Employment Practices. [Source: U.S. Congressional
Service, 77 Congress, 1 Session, No. 8802.]

*Reaffirming policy of full participation in the defense program by all
persons, regardless of race, creed, color, or national origin, and
directing certain action in furtherance of said policy*

Whereas it is the policy of the United States to encourage full
participation in the national defense program by all citizens of the
United States, regardless of race, creed, color, or national origin, in
the firm belief that the democratic way of life within the nation can
be defended successfully only with the help and support of all
groups within its borders; and

Whereas there is evidence that available and needed workers
have been barred from employment in industries engaged in defense production solely because of considerations of race, creed,
color, or national origin to the detriment of workers' morale and of
national unity:

Now, Therefore, by virtue of the authority vested in me by the
Constitution and the statutes, and as a prerequisite to the successful conduct of our national defense production effort, I do hereby
reaffirm the policy of the United States that there shall be no discrimination in the employment of workers in defense industries or
government because of race, creed, color, or national origin; and I
do hereby declare that it is the duty of employers and of labor organizations, in furtherance of said policy and of this order, to provide for the full and equitable participation of all workers in defense
industries, without discrimination because of race, creed, color,
or national origin;

And it is hereby ordered as follows:

1. All departments and agencies of the government of the United
States concerned with vocational and training programs for defense production shall take special measures appropriate to assure
that such programs are administered without discrimination because of race, creed, color, or national origin.

2. All contracting agencies of the government of the United
States shall include in all defense contracts hereafter negotiated by
them a provision obligating the contractor not to discriminate

393

against any worker because of race, creed, color, or national origin.

3. There is established in the Office of Production Management a Committee on Fair Employment Practice, which shall consist of a chairman and four other members to be appointed by the President. The chairman and members of the committee shall serve as such without compensation but shall be entitled to actual and necessary transportation, subsistence, and other expenses incidental to performance of their duties. The committee shall receive and investigate complaints of discrimination in violation of the provisions of this order and shall take appropriate steps to redress grievances which it finds to be valid. The committee shall also recommend to the several departments and agencies of the government of the United States and to the President all measures which may be deemed by it necessary or proper to effectuate the provisions of this order.

6. The Cost of Prejudice
1928-1941

W. C. HANDY

How the Blues Came To Be

The son of a minister, W. C. Handy was born in Alabama in 1873. He was first a schoolteacher but his love of music led him to become a bandmaster. Although blind at the age of thirty, Handy nevertheless conducted his own orchestra for the next eighteen years. In 1911 he wrote and orchestrated "Memphis Blues" for the mayor of Memphis, Edward H. "Boss" Crump, which, in combination with his "St. Louis Blues" of 1914, made him the most famous jazz musician in the land and earned him the title "Father of the Blues." Ragtime was the prevalent jazz style at the time, but Handy introduced a nostalgic element, chiefly by means of the "blue" lowered seventh, that became the characteristic feature of all Blues written thereafter. "Most white people," Handy once said, "think that the Negro is always cheerful and lively, but he isn't, though he may seem that way when he is most troubled. The Negro knows the Blues as a state of mind, and that's why his music has that name." The following selection is taken from Handy's autobiography, published in 1941. [Source: Father of the Blues, Arna Bontemps, ed., New York, 1941, pp. 71-88.]

Southern Negroes sang about everything. Trains, steamboats, steam whistles, sledge hammers, fast women, mean bosses, stubborn mules all become subjects for their songs. They accompany themselves on anything from which they can extract a musical sound or rhythmical effect, anything from a harmonica to a washboard.

In this way, and from these materials, they set the mood for what we now call blues. My own fondness for this sort of thing really began in Florence, back in the days when we were not above serenading beneath the windows of our sweethearts and singing till we won a kiss in the shadows or perhaps a tumbler of good homemade wine. In the Delta, however, I suddenly saw the songs with the eye of a budding composer. The songs themselves, I now observed, consisted of simple declarations expressed usually in three lines and set to a kind of earthborn music that was familiar throughout the Southland half a century ago. Mississippi with its large plantations and small cities probably had more colored field hands than any other state. Consequently we heard many such song fragments as *Hurry Sundown, Let Tomorrow Come,* or

> Boll Weevil, where you been so long?
> Boll Weevil, where you been so long?
> You stole my cotton, now you want my corn.

Clarksdale was eighteen miles from the river, but that was no distance for roustabouts. They came in the evenings and on days when they were not loading boats. With them they brought the legendary songs of the river.

> Oh, the Kate's up the river,
>   Stack O' Lee's in the ben',
> Oh, the Kate's up the river,
>   Stack O' Lee's in the ben',
> And I ain't seen ma baby since I can't tell when. . . .

At first folk melodies like these were kept in the back rooms of my mind while the parlor was reserved for dressed-up music. Musical books continued to get much of my attention. There was still an old copy of Steiner's *First Lessons in Harmony,* purchased back in Henderson for fifty cents. While traveling with the minstrels I had bought from Lyon and Healy a copy of Moore's *Encyclopedia of Music.* For a time books became a passion. I'm afraid I came to think that everything worthwhile was to be found in books. But the blues did not come from books. Suffering and hard luck were the midwives that birthed these songs. The blues were conceived in aching hearts.

I hasten to confess that I took up with low folk forms hesitantly. I approached them with a certain fear and trembling. Like many of the other musicians who received them with cold shoulders at first, I began by raising my eyebrows and wondering if they were quite the thing. I had picked up a fair training in the music of the modern world and had assumed that the correct manner to compose was to develop simples into grandissimos and not to repeat them monotonously. As a director of many respectable, conventional bands, it was not easy for me to concede that a simple slow-drag and repeat could be rhythm itself. Neither was I ready to believe that this was just what the public wanted. But we live to learn.

398

My own enlightenment came in Cleveland, Mississippi. I was leading the orchestra in a dance program when someone sent up an odd request. Would we play some of "our native music," the note asked. This baffled me. The men in this group could not "fake" and "sell it" like minstrel men. They were all musicians who bowed strictly to the authority of printed notes. So we played for our anonymous fan an old-time Southern melody, a melody more sophisticated than native. A few moments later a second request came up. Would we object if a local colored band played a few dances?

Object! That was funny. What hornblower would object to a time-out and a smoke—on pay? We eased out gracefully as the newcomers entered. They were led by a long-legged chocolate boy and their band consisted of just three pieces, a battered guitar, a mandolin, and a worn-out bass.

The music they made was pretty well in keeping with their looks. They struck up one of those over-and-over strains that seem to have no very clear beginning and certainly no ending at all. The strumming attained a disturbing monotony, but on and on it went, a kind of stuff that has long been associated with cane rows and levee camps. Thump-thump-thump went their feet on the floor. Their eyes rolled. Their shoulders swayed. And through it all that little agonizing strain persisted. It was not really annoying or unpleasant. Perhaps "haunting" is a better word, but I commenced to wonder if anybody besides small town rounders and their running mates would go for it.

The answer was not long in coming. A rain of silver dollars began to fall around the outlandish, stomping feet. The dancers went wild. Dollars, quarters, halves—the shower grew heavier and continued so long I strained my neck to get a better look. There before the boys lay more money than my nine musicians were being paid for the entire engagement. Then I saw the beauty of primitive music. They had the stuff the people wanted. It touched the spot. Their music wanted polishing, but it contained the essence. Folks would pay money for it. The old conventional music was well and good and had its place, no denying that, but there was no virtue in being blind when you had good eyes.

That night a composer was born, an *American* composer. Those country black boys at Cleveland had taught me something that could not possibly have been gained from books, something that would, however, cause books to be written. Art, in the highbrow sense, was not in my mind. My idea of what constitutes music was changed by the sight of that silver money cascading around the splay feet of a Mississippi string band. Seven years prior to this, while playing a cornet solo, Hartman's *Mia*, on the stage in Oakland, California, I had come to the conclusion, because of what happened in this eleven minute solo, that the American people wanted movement and rhythm for their money. Then too, the Broadway hits *Yankee Grit* and *Uncle Sammy*—two steps in six-eight time that we featured in Mississippi—did not have this earthy flavor.

Once the purpose was fixed I let no grass grow under my feet. I returned to Clarksdale and began immediately to work on this type of music. Within a day or two I had orchestrated a number of local tunes, among them *The Last Shot Got Him*, *Your Clock Ain't Right*, and the distinctly Negroid *Make Me a Pallet on Your Floor*. My hunch was promptly justified, for the popularity of our orchestra increased by leaps and bounds. But there was also another consequence. Bids came to us to play in less respectable places. We took these in our stride on the grounds that music, like joy, should be unconfined. Moreover there was money to be made, and who were we to turn up our noses?

Across the tracks of the Y. & M. V. railroad in Clarksdale there was a section called the "New World." It was the local red-light district. To the New World came lush octoroons and quadroons from Louisiana, soft cream-colored fancy gals from Mississippi towns. Just beyond this section lived some of the oldest and most respectable Negro families. On their way to the Baptist or Methodist churches they were required to pass before the latticed houses of prostitution. Occasionally they caught glimpses of white men lounging with the pretty near-white "imports." By using their imaginations they could assume what went on in the dim rooms beyond.

As musicians we didn't have to guess. As musicians, too, hired to play music rather than to discuss morals, we kept our mouths shut. We knew that big shot officials winked at the New World, but that was neither here nor there to the men with the horns and the fiddles. What was important was that these rouge-tinted girls, wearing silk

stockings and short skirts, bobbing their soft hair and smoking cig-
arets in that prim era, long before these styles had gained respectability, were among the best patrons the orchestra had. They employed us for big nights, occasions when social or political figures of
importance were expected to dine and dance with their favorite cre-
ole belles. Contacts made in these shady precincts often led to jobs
in chaste great houses of the rich and well-to-do.

The shuttered houses of the New World called for appropriate
music. This led us to arrange and play tunes that had never been
written down and seldom sung outside the environment of the oldest profession. Boogie-house music, it was called. Much of it has
since been fumigated and played in the best of society, but then
Dopy McKnight thumped out the tunes on a rickety piano. We took
them up, arranged orchestrations and played them to the wild approval of the richly scented yellow gals and their company. I have
intimated that silver money had always been plentiful in the Delta;
now at last we began to come in for our share of it.

The Delta had also its share of melodrama. Engagements in the
New World plunged us into the tide. One evening a vivid octoroon,
who had been winking at our violinist, shared a drink with him. Her
ofay (white) company turned and put a pistol to the musician's tem-
ple. He promised to pull the trigger if he opened his mouth. He'd just
as soon do it immediately, he said, if the boy felt like giving any back
talk. When it was over, I recalled a saying that is almost an axiom
among Negroes of the South. The thought of it is that more black
men are killed by whites for merely conversing with colored girls of
this type than for violating, as the orators like to put it, the sanctity
of white womanhood. Ho-hum. The world is powerfully big, and a
queer place.

As a sideline in Clarksdale I did a kind of bootleg business in
Northern Negro newspapers and magazines. Not only did I supply
the colored folks of the town but also got the trade of the farmers,
the croppers, and the hands from the outlying country. They would
come to my house on their weekly visits to the city, give me the high
sign, and I would slip them their copies of the *Chicago Defender*,
the *Indianapolis Freeman* or the *Voice of the Negro*. This
may sound like a tame enough enterprise to those whose memories
are short, but oldsters of those parts will not have to be told that I

401

was venturing into risky business. Negro newspapers were not plentiful in those days, and their circulation in cities like Clarksdale was looked upon with strong disfavor by certain of the local powers. But because I was favorably known to most of the white folks as the leader of the band that gave the weekly concerts on the main street, they never suspected me of such dark business as distributing Northern literature to Negroes of the community. In fact, Clarksdale and I remained on such good terms that when there came a time to call upon the well-to-do townsfolk to help us foot the bill for new uniforms, instruments, and other equipment for the men, the needed amount was oversubscribed before the bank closed on the day when the campaign was begun.

When we blossomed forth in the glad rags, the town stuck out its chest proudly. We were theirs, they had helped dress us up and everybody was pleased with the results, including ourselves. Senator John Sharp Williams, a great favorite of the people, came to town, giving us our first opportunity to show our appreciation by welcoming him with good music and gay uniforms. The occasion, as much as it pleased us all, was of no long-range consequence, so far as I recall, but it represents another line of the work that fell to our band during those days and in the years that followed. We were frequently hired, as on this occasion, to furnish music for political rallies.

This meant that we had to absorb a "passel" of oratory of the brand served by some Southern politicians just this side of the turn of the century. We appeared with one gubernatorial candidate who regularly treated his audiences to the following titbit:

> Ladies and Gentlemen:
>
> I come before you as a candidate for the governorship of the grand old state of Mississippi. And I pledge you my sacred word of honor that if you elect me your governor, I shall not spend one dollar for nigger education.
>
> Now I want to tell you why I will not spend one dollar of the state's money for nigger education; education unfits the nigger. Let me prove it to you conclusively. I am right.
>
> When this great country of ours was torn by strife, and we followed the fortunes of the Confederacy, we left behind our mothers, our daughters, our sweethearts, and our wives; and

we left them behind with our niggers, and they guarded them like so many faithful watchdogs. Now what kind of nigger did we leave them with? It was the uneducated nigger.

Suppose we again had to go to war, would you trust them with the nigger of today? (A chorus of no's came in answer.) That's why I wouldn't spend one dollar for nigger education.

His voice quavered and a mist came to his eyes as he extended one arm while resting the other dramatically over his heart. Then as the concluding words trailed off, we struck up *Dixie*. Outside we exchanged amazed glances among ourselves and laughed. He was not elected.

Each time we played for him, I was reminded of the first time I had listened to oratory of this sort. As a schoolboy in Florence I had gone home, buried my head in a pillow and wept after listening to sentiments like these uttered from the courthouse steps by a politician of the same stripe. Later I had wandered off alone in the woods across the road from the cabin in which I was born. There, point by point, I had undertaken to answer the man of ill will. Slowly, deliberately, I had torn his arguments to bits. At the top of my voice I had hurled the lie into his teeth. The woodland took up my shouts. The words of my defiance echoed and reechoed. That pleased me. I went home and slept well, a great burden removed. In Clarksdale the members of my band nudged one another with their elbows when we were safely out of the crowd. Then we all laughed—laughed.

But playing for the political campaigns was not always the bitter pill this particular candidate made it. We were engaged for ex-Governor Earl Brewer when he made a delayed entrance into a red-hot, seven-cornered race for the governorship. Here the story was not the same. The ex-governor did not hesitate to touch on the Negro, but no tirade came from him. Instead he gave the finest tribute to Negro music that I had ever been permitted to hear. A tribute deeply felt and moving when he referred to our loyalty. He was not elected that year, but later when the time came for another campaign, he was not even opposed—elected unanimously.

Either way, however, we were undismayed. We could laugh and we could make rhythm. What better armor could you ask?

Negroes react rhythmically to everything. That's how the blues came to be. Sometimes I think that rhythm is our middle name. When the sweet good man packs his trunk and goes, that is occasion for some low moaning. When darktown puts on its new shoes and takes off the brakes, jazz steps in. If it's the New Jerusalem and the River Jordan we're studying, we make the spirituals. The rounders among us, those whose aim in life is just to become bigger rounders — well, they're the ones we can thank for the Frankie and Johnnie songs. In every case the songs came from down deep. . . .

More than once during my travels in the North and South I had passed through towns with signs saying, "Nigger don't let the sun go down on you here." And once, at least, we played in a town where the boot was on the other foot. Though Mound Bayou had no such words addressed to "peckerwoods" or "rednecks," the sentiment among its all Negro population was perhaps in some ways similar. Yet salesmen and other white visitors who found it necessary to spend the night there received all possible hospitality.

This town, thirty miles south of Clarksdale on the Y. & M.V. railroad, was founded by Isaiah T. Montgomery, former bodyguard and slave of Jeff Davis, President of the Confederacy. The occasion for our band's visit was the dedication of the Bank of Mound Bayou, and we came largely through the instigation of Charles Banks the cashier. A Clarksdale boy himself, Banks had gained his training in the same Planters Bank that now employed our Stack. We carried the band to Mound Bayou to pay our respects to this home town boy, but we stayed on to admire the new Carnegie Library and blink in amazement at colored railroad ticket agents, colored telegraph operators, and pretty brownskins at telephone switchboards.

My personal admiration for the enterprise of the Negroes of Mound Bayou was so great that later, when they held the grand opening of their oil mill, I brought a band from Memphis at my own expense just to help them do the thing up brown. Booker T. Washington was the speaker for this occasion. After the address I dined with him in the home of Mr. and Mrs. Charles Banks and began to feel that the privilege of knowing the educator was ample recompense for my small contribution to the event. Later, however, Banks and his associates insisted on sending us a check in token of their gratitude for our contribution.

A picture of Clarksdale during the years I spent there would be incomplete without the blind singers and footloose bards that were forever coming and going. Usually the fellows were destitute. Some came sauntering down the railroad tracks, others dropped from freight cars, while still others caught rides on the big road and entered town on the top of cotton bales. A favorite hangout with them was the railroad station. There, surrounded by crowds of country folks, they would pour out their hearts in song while the audience ate fish and bread, chewed sugarcane, dipped snuff while waiting for trains to carry them down the line.

They earned their living by selling their own songs – "ballets," as they called them – and I'm ready to say in their behalf that seldom did their creations lack imagination. Many a less gifted songsmith has plied his trade with passing success in Tin Pan Alley. Some of these country boys hustled on trains. Others visited churches. I remember buying such a ballet (ballad) entitled *I've Heard of a City Called Heaven*. It was printed on a slip of paper about the size of a postcard. Fifty years later, after I had published a choral arrangement of that piece, I heard the number sung with great success by the Hall Johnson Singers in *The Green Pastures*.

Mature years and a busy life have not enabled me to shake off a certain susceptibility to these dusky bards. Every time I put by enough money for a trip to Europe, I end up by purchasing a ticket to one of the more remote sections of the deep South, knowing fully in my mind that Europe and all its environs carry no such rich traditions and inspirational fertility as are embodied in this section of our America.

JONATHAN DANIELS
Can the South Rule Itself?

Jonathan Daniels, editor from 1933 to 1942 of the Raleigh (N.C.) News and Observer, *was one of the strongest Southern supporters of the New Deal. In 1936, when the federal government was investigating the impoverished condition of the South's economy and when it regarded the South as the nation's most serious economic problem, Daniels set out on a tour to see for himself. Traveling by automobile throughout the region, he accumulated numerous impressions that were incorporated in his book,* A Southerner Discovers the South *(1938). The following selection is drawn from the book's last chapter.* [*Source:* A Southerner Discovers the South, *New York, 1938: "Dixie Destination."*]

A traveler comes to destinations. Or hopes to.

I remember when I was young and Admiral Robert E. Peary and Dr. Frederick Cook were quarreling (I was a great and small partisan of Dr. Cook) that I conceived of the North Pole as such a trimmed tree trunk as the Southern Bell Telephone Company or the Carolina Power & Light Company sometimes imbedded in the sidewalk before our house. I would not have been surprised, of course, had the North Pole been a little more ornate, and a trifle more impervious to heat and cold and bug and polar bear. But it provided a definite destination for the explorer. And I think that the moment when loss of faith in Dr. Cook began to set in was when he failed to show a lantern slide of it in his illustrated lecture at the Academy of Music.

Certainly now at the end of my travels in discovery of the South I wish I had a definite destination to report—or a plan. Certainly a plan. For the South, the Philosophers at Chapel Hill tell me, will not escape without a plan or at least a planning. I agree.

All people are planners.

"I aim to plant lespedeza in that field if I ever get around to it. But it just seems natural somehow to put it in cotton."

All people are regionalists.

I discovered that when I was twelve. And I still believe that Dr. Howard W. Odum missed one of the best indices of the Southern region when he failed to determine a line on one side of which all nice children say, "No, ma'am" and "Yes, ma'am," to the teacher and on the other side of which they get laughed at for saying it by all, including teacher. Such a line, I understand, no longer exists. At any rate, when I asked my daughter about it she said, "Hunh?"

But certainly all people are planners and regionalists. The plan may not extend beyond dinner time and the region may not reach beyond the creek. Indeed, in one section of North Carolina, plan and region are combined.

"Well, I guess we'll do like the folks across the river do."

"How's that?"

"Do without."

In more ways than one that has been the regional plan of the American South, and I for one Southerner, speaking also without fear of contradiction for 25,000,000 others, am ready to find another.

This program was adopted shortly after the surrender at Appomattox and has been in force almost without interruption since. That was a grand war for the poets and the politicians, but I am beginning to wonder quite seriously whether the Civil War itself ever made any really profound difference in the life and history of the South. The war itself seems a detail almost insignificant between what went before and what came after. Mine, I suppose, was the last Southern generation reared in a combination of indignation and despair. Now, fortunately, save in a few groups devoted to a form of rebel yelling which is also a form of ancestor whooping, the Civil War as such plays little or no part in the life and thinking of the South. That means, I hope, escape from the old Do-Without Economy of the Southern States, for the chief injury inflicted upon us late Confederates by the war was the excuse which it gave us for giving up and sitting in the sun. The South was poor; the war caused it. The South was ignorant; the war made us too poor to educate. The South was slow; well, after what the damyankees did it wasn't any use to stir. The war provided a satisfying, acceptable, and even mildly exhilarating excuse for everything from Captain Seabrook's wooden leg to the quality of education dispensed at the Centennial School.

Unfortunately, like a great many simple explanations, this one did not explain. The tariff did at least as much damage in Dixie as Sherman and Grant together in making the South poor and keeping it poor. Indeed, while Grant and Sherman have gone to whatever they had coming to them, the tariff remains. The process of selling the fertility of the land along with the cotton began a long time before the Civil War and had reduced Virginia gentlemen to the unpleasant business of breeding slaves for the Deep South markets. Even now men tremble over the possible loss of cotton markets; it is a trembling like that of the old slave fearful of losing his chains. The contempt for labor which everywhere and in all times has been an inevitable item of slavery was full grown before 1860. The hookworm was in the South but not discovered. Yellow fever, typhoid, and malaria were there but not understood. Pellagra was seen as clay eating and was considered a perverse habit of the perverted po' whites. Most of the white people were desperately poor. Most of the Negroes had instinctively developed an apparently racial shiftlessness as a shrewd labor defense under slavery long before ladies and gentlemen on the Charleston housetops applauded the firing on Fort Sumter. And Reconstruction: Mississippi had defaulted on its bonds sometime in the '40s. The Rothschilds were involved, and, if Mississippi paid her debts, the Governor said, he was fearful that they might use the money to gain control of the sepulcher of Our Blessed Savior. That would never do, so Mississippi defaulted, and there was not a Negro in the Legislature that did it.

The Civil War killed men and broke hearts and caused a tremendous amount of private suffering. But war is too spectacular. All of the major faults and flaws in Southern economy were on the way to full growth before the war began. But it served as an alibi—a magnificent alibi—for them all, and for those that came after, too. In a false present, the South had begun the adoration of a fictitious past. . . .

The South's faults were many, but the South's faults were not alone. The war and Reconstruction were important as memory of them served as a screen of emotionalism behind which moved, ever praising Lee, those unemotional gentlemen from the North who knew what they wanted and how much they would have to pay for it, which was not much. This second wave of carpetbaggers was received with honors and banquets and bands. They were the agents of the new and ever greater absentee ownership of the South. They came from the North with excellent financial connections to buy up broken-down Southern railroads and other properties, and they picked up some pretty bargains and some pretty Southerners.

The town was properly impressed when Colonel Cadwallader entertained Mr. Prentiss, the Boston banker. (It continues impressed when his name is Manaccus and he is in the garment business.) The banks of those same gentlemen who bought up Southern railroads were also deeply interested in Northern railroads. It has even been suggested that while they were ever willing to make money they were also careful not to build up Southern traffic and industry at the expense of those older developed areas of the North and East through which their older lines ran. Freight rates certainly have not been shaped to aid the industrial development of the South; instead they still sit providing inland the protection which tariffs provide on coast and frontier. Some trade tacticians feel that freight rate and tariff together made a prettier pincher than that which Grant and Sherman applied on the Confederacy.

Of course, all ownership in this modern corporate civilization assumes the pattern of absentee ownership. Stockholders, South as North, are increasingly irresponsible and uncreative as individual capitalists. But the control of capital is in the North and East, and it may be significant that the only industrial development which has taken place in the South since the industrial North overcame the country culture of the South has been in the widely dispersed manufacture of textiles and in the new big industry of the cigarette. Otherwise, the South, devoted to the culture of cotton and tobacco, the prices of which are fixed in world markets, still buys from the protected factories of the North. Its new overseers, faithful to the absentee owners, beg and plead and promise for more absentee investment and control while simultaneously they cry to hysteria in condemnation of foreign agitators among nice native labor.

There is reason for both fear and elation. The new pincher movement upon the South has not been applied in recent years with the precision which Grant and Sherman exercised, or perhaps the body seized is a good deal less easily grasped than was the old half-dead Confederacy between Richmond and Atlanta. At any rate those capitalists, local and absentee, who are concerned for low wages in the South, and those who are concerned for sales in the South, do not seem to be acting in perfect unity. The most profoundly disturbing foreign agitators in the region are the salesmen of Chevrolets and radios, gaudy machine-stitched dresses, and other shining gadgets and gewgaws. Even the power companies, incited by TVA, are

409

filling the towheads and the burr-heads with glittering dreams. Not only the spindle has come South, so also has the automobile. The worker and the mill have both become mobile. As whole mills may move from Massachusetts to Mississippi, so may whole philosophies.

It is not the Communists who are coming but the advertisers. The cabins of the South are wallpapered with the pages of newspapers and magazines, and so much advertising has a practically permanent appeal. There may not come to the cabin in a year enough money to meet for a month the requirements of the persuasive suggestion that it is easy to own a Packard. But if all of those who see the walls cannot read them, all of them can desire. If they lack the money, they can wish for it. They can be dissatisfied with the old Do-Without Plan of the Southern regions of the United States. They are. And those new absentees who are coming South in a movement which New England Governors call "a threat from the South" should come warned: the South has much to offer, place and people and resources and power, but it does not honestly have docility to offer. Such as it possessed is disappearing before the building of desire. And the first problem of the South today is people. It is by no means limited to the South. Indeed, it is the newly exciting question of the possibility of democracy. In contemplation of it too many people have been looking at Italy and Spain and Russia and Germany, as well as at the old democracies of England and France. It is less disturbing to consider it over water, perhaps, but the seeing is clearer in the South. Contemplate the questions:

Are the Southern people capable of serving, governing, and saving themselves?

Or must they depend for guidance in government and to decency and adequacy in living upon an oligarchy of so-called aristocrats, a committee of experts, a ring of politicians? Upon plutocrat, demagogue, or professor?

Is democracy possible in the South? (Is it possible anywhere?)

Surely, those questions are properly raised with regard to the folk of a region in which the sharp-eyed regional planners have found natural resources in superabundance, population in abundance, but a deficiency in science, skills, technology, and organization, waste in its general economy and a richness, combined with immaturity and multiple handicaps, in its culture. The trends they discovered show hesitancy and relative regression in many aspects of culture. They found the lowest incomes and the poorest fed people in America in a region which should be a garden.

Beyond those findings, I pretend to no simple, certain answers to the questions. In the first place, of course, the Southern people will not show their capability or the lack of it in a vacuum. They must work in a realm, not only patterned by their past and their prejudices but also one definitely shaped by tariffs and freight rates fixed largely at the North for the benefit of the North. It is a region governed in important degree by absentee owners and one which has been stirred deeply more frequently by reflex response to exterior criticism than by agitators, native or foreign, at work within. It is a sensitive region, more romantic than idealistic, and one which is expiating for more sins than its own, though there are enough of them.

The answers like the questions go deep into the past. Important aspects of democracy grew in the South. Much of its philosophy was shaped at Monticello by Thomas Jefferson. But Jefferson in Virginia and John Adams in Massachusetts died on the same afternoon in 1826. And sometime thereafter, perhaps at the very time it began to become solidly Democratic, the South discarded democracy. Or perhaps more fairly stated, its democracy was destroyed

From the beginning there were Southerners, big and rich, who held to the faith that wisdom reposed only in the big and the rich and that therefore the franchise should be restricted to them. More and more democracy asserted itself against them. Requirements for voting and office were slowly but steadily scaled down. And then, after a long and passionate war, in the South the electorate was enlarged, by force from without, by thousands of Negroes and decreased by thousands of white men who had formerly borne arms as Southerners and so as Confederates and so as Rebels. The result was a condition which seemed intolerable to the most faithful Democrats. Perhaps at that time no entry of any sort by the Negroes into the rights of citizenship would have been tolerable to the South. Certainly, however, the Negroes were given no chance to be absorbed. They were hurried from slavery into a power which, in general, other men misused.

411

Any unemotional reader of history must recognize the similarity between the Ku Klux of the South and the Brown Shirts of Germany and the Black Shirts of Italy and the similarity of the conditions which created them. They provided a rank-and-file violence. But in the South they brought the Bourbons to power. And the native Bourbon has steadily served the large propertied classes, absentee or local, in the exploitation of the South. Almost without exception the rout of the carpetbaggers, the Negroes, and the scallywags carried the old planter class and a new promoter class to power also over the vast white mass of little farmers and storekeepers, mechanics and laborers. For them as for the Negroes, to too great an extent, democracy was in the years afterwards effectually denied.

But little men stir: And men to lead them. There was, for instance, Benjamin Ryan Tillman in South Carolina. And "Pitchfork Ben" was by no means the only name applied to him. Low Country aristocrats still snort to speak of him. After him there were others like him—and not like him. There will be more. They are Southern demagogues, some better and some worse, but all indicative of a Southern unwillingness to leave government entirely to the political gentlemen or the gentlemen of business—gentlemen who know exactly what they want and how much they will pay for it. It is only an alternative, when as in the case of such a man as Huey Long, he leaves as a political estate a power to plunder. Neither he nor his inheritors discovered that power. It always exists when the people are incapable of government or careless of government. And Southerners might be plundered by the very people who made them also for a time incapable of government. They were. And those who plundered them also saw signs of inferiority in the poverty that was left.

There are Southerners still who would more quickly deny the ability of the people of the South to manage the South than any people outside of it. They are the persisting and ineradicable Bourbons and Brigadiers who are devoted to a class before a region. That made them readier to serve as the agents of the new mastery. They still serve it and serving also themselves believe they serve the South. Their minds are still patterned in that master-slave concept which in sense of superiority applied not only to slaves but to white men lacking slaves. They apply it now to the cotton mill as well as to

412

the plantation. Many aristocrats in the South—and that is the name for both the Coca-Cola bottler and the member of the Society of the Cincinnati—do not believe and never have believed that the people should—if they could—govern the South. Such a faith or faithlessness leads to the unincorporated mill village and the company union. Included under it are both the kindliest paternalism and the most vicious and careless exploitation.

This lack of faith by the few great in the many small seems to me sad, but the saddest thing in the South is the fact that those at the top who do not believe in the intelligence of those at the bottom have not shown themselves capable of a leadership satisfactory to the people they assume to lead—nor, so far as I could discover, to anybody else. The market for stuffed shirts is glutted.

Finally, the people are not as disturbing as the patricians. The most encouraging thing is that the ordinary Southern whites, given fair chance and training, are showing themselves capable of performing the best types of work. This is so in the South. TVA discovered it and was surprised. Others are discovering it. And in the black and white migration to the North this generation of Southern immigrants has been able to compete with the workers already on the ground. The depression saw them shivering and jobless in every Northern city: by the thousands it sent them scurrying home again. Now they and more beside them move again. They are, of course, inadequately trained, inadequately skilled. Sometimes they are underfed. Sometimes they are sick. Sometimes they are criminal, feebleminded, perverted, insane. But they move and they will move. They march to eat. They will not be stopped. They need not be feared unless they are resisted.

But fear in the South has slandered both of them: The Southern Negro is not an incurably ignorant ape. The Southern white masses are not biologically degenerate.

Both are peoples capable of vastly more training than they possess. Both are peoples who may hang heavy on the national advance, or help to speed and sustain it. Both are peoples who could consume and produce more wealth. And they are capable of happy, productive, peaceful life, side by side. White men and black men have shared the South's too little for a long time and, though there is more than a casual connection between hunger and lynchings, they have shared it in relative quiet, decency and peace. They would be able to build a South in terms of the South's potentiality, if together they had a chance to make and share plenty.

Increasingly the ancient and venerable Do-Without Plan is deserted. But what of a new plan for the South? The materials for its shaping have grown at the University of North Carolina in a huge, wise book, *Southern Regions of the United States*. But I believe that the new Southern plan will grow more directly from itching than from statistics. The South is awaking, scratching at new desires. A plan of course should provide the way to fulfilment, and, at the moment, the South faces the prospect of plenty with more wish than way.

"Chile, yo' eyes is bigger'n yo' belly."

But the big-eyed stage is important. Once they were sleepy. Now they stir and are wide open at last. And a regional plan is a plot from seeing to getting, from needing to wanting, to possessing. Such an ordered program in the South must include expansions of facilities for public education in a region lacking skills, for public health in a region still plagued by preventable diseases, for public welfare in a country in which the private welfare of so many is so insecure. None of these are in any sense simply Southern. The children of the South—which is the land of children in America—are more and more the adults of tomorrow in other States and so they will be the criminals or the sick or the creative or the consumers or the burdens of other States soon, very soon.

Such a plan for a new, free, fed, housed, happy South must include not merely program at home for improvement but also program in the nation for the relinquishment of advantages elsewhere over the South. Perhaps those advantages are so deeply fixed as in freight rate and tariff that to change them to give the South a chance might do vast harm elsewhere, might cause much suffering in the areas which have grown rich on advantage, like that which wrings the hearts of Northerners when they see it in the South. Perhaps the South, as New England seems now fearing, may be able to escape its single-slavery to cotton and advance to a diverse industrial and agricultural development despite the imperial advantages which New England took as its loot after the Civil War.

There was some sort of bargain then, now dimly seen. The Negroes were sold down the river again after emancipation, and the price paid was a fixed economic differentiation which left the whole South in slavery to New England instead of some of the South in slavery to other Southerners. But I mean to start no new war: the South is at last escaping from the economic occupation which succeeded the military occupation. The South is at last escaping from the more destructive Reconstruction which economically continued the South as captive. And New England is afraid: the terrible danger is that it is about to lose at last the slavery from which it profited long after Lincoln in a manner of speaking set the Negroes free. Of course everybody was free in the South, free to fight among themselves for the too little that was left when tribute was paid.

Cato the Elder was no more implacable than the Brahmans of Boston who came after the Abolitionists with considerably cooler heads. The South was not plowed up and planted with salt as Carthage was. If no more generous, Bostonians (citizens of a region and an attitude and not a town) were less wasteful. They recognized that the South kept in its place (a place in the nation geographically similar to that of the Negro in the South) might be useful and profitable. It was. And as a Southerner at the end of discovery I ask now only that they recognize the poverty of the South as a part of the same civilization as Harvard and in a measure as the creation of the same people. Cato did not ride through Carthage on the train and blame its condition on the Carthaginians. That much only I ask of the Yankees.

A good deal more is necessary for the Southerners. Item one is escape from pretentiousness. The Southerner has deluded only himself. The boy who was brought into Savannah from Bryan County with malaria, pellagra, hookworm, and a pelvis pierced by his thighbone as a result of malnutrition nevertheless insisted in the hospital that he was the best alligator catcher on the coast of Georgia. Perhaps he was. Maybe still one Reb can beat ten Yankees. It is irrelevant. But planning in the South must begin at the bottom where so many of its people are. There is no handle on its top by which it can be lifted. Tyranny, like that of Huey Long's, would be swifter. Government by an oligarchy of plutocrats might possibly provide a more orderly way, though it would be concerned with profits first and people only afterwards, not recognizing that there is

415

a difference. But in the South the tyrants and the plutocrats and the poor all need teaching. One of them no more than the others. All are in the warm dark, and whether they like it or not—white man, black man, big man—they are in the dark together. None of them will ever get to day alone.

RICHARD WRIGHT
The Way Up and Out

Black Boy, *of which Chapter Thirteen is reprinted here, was Richard Wright's third book. It appeared in 1945, although parts of it were written as early as 1937, and confirmed the estimate of Wright as a major American writer that had been produced by* Uncle Tom's Children (1938) *and the even more impressive* Native Son (1940). *After the war Wright took his family to Paris, where he became a celebrated expatriate. He never returned to the United States.*

One morning I arrived early at work and went into the bank lobby where the Negro porter was mopping. I stood at a counter and picked up the Memphis *Commercial Appeal* and began my free reading of the press. I came finally to the editorial page and saw an article dealing with one H. L. Mencken. I knew by hearsay that he was the editor of the *American Mercury*, but aside from that I knew nothing about him. The article was a furious denunciation of Mencken, concluding with one, hot, short sentence: Mencken is a fool.

I wondered what on earth this Mencken had done to call down upon him the scorn of the South. The only people I had ever heard denounced in the South were Negroes, and this man was not a Negro. Then what ideas did Mencken hold that made a newspaper like the *Commercial Appeal* castigate him publicly? Undoubtedly he must be advocating ideas that the South did not like. Were there, then, people other than Negroes who criticized the South? I knew that during the Civil War the South had hated northern whites, but I had not encountered such hate during my life. Knowing no more of Mencken than I did at that moment, I felt a vague sympathy for him. Had not the South, which had assigned me the role of a non-man, cast at him its hardest words?

Now, how could I find out about this Mencken? There was a huge library near the riverfront, but I knew that Negroes were not allowed to patronize its shelves any more than they were the parks and playgrounds of the city. I had gone into the library several times to get books for the white men on the job. Which of them would now help me to get books? And how could I read them without causing concern to the white men with whom I worked? I had so far been successful in hiding my thoughts and feelings from them, but I knew that I would create hostility if I went about this business of reading in a clumsy way.

I weighed the personalities of the men on the job. There was Don, a Jew; but I distrusted him. His position was not much better than mine and I knew that he was uneasy and insecure; he had always treated me in an offhand, bantering way that barely concealed his contempt. I was afraid to ask him to help me to get books; his frantic desire to demonstrate a racial solidarity with the whites against Negroes might make him betray me.

Then how about the boss? No, he was a Baptist and I had the suspicion that he would not be quite able to comprehend why a black boy would want to read Mencken. There were other white men on the job whose attitudes showed clearly that they were Kluxers or sympathizers, and they were out of the question.

There remained only one man whose attitude did not fit into an anti-Negro category, for I had heard the white men refer to him as a "Pope lover." He was an Irish Catholic and was hated by the white Southerners. I knew that he read books, because I had got him volumes from the library several times. Since he, too, was an object of hatred, I felt that he might refuse me but would hardly betray me. I hesitated, weighing and balancing the imponderable realities.

One morning I paused before the Catholic fellow's desk.

"I want to ask you a favor," I whispered to him.

"What is it?"

"I want to read. I can't get books from the library. I wonder if you'd let me use your card?"

He looked at me suspiciously.

"My card is full most of the time," he said.

"I see," I said and waited, posing my question silently.

"You're not trying to get me into trouble, are you, boy?" he asked, staring at me.

"Oh, no, sir."

"What book do you want?"

"A book by H. L. Mencken."

"Which one?"

"I don't know. Has he written more than one?"

"He has written several."

"I didn't know that."

"What makes you want to read Mencken?"

"Oh, I just saw his name in the newspaper," I said.

"It's good of you to want to read," he said. "But you ought to read the right things."

I said nothing. Would he want to supervise my reading?

"Let me think," he said. "I'll figure out something."

I turned from him and he called me back. He stared at me quizzically.

"Richard, don't mention this to the other white men," he said.

"I understand," I said. "I won't say a word."

A few days later he called me to him.

"I've got a card in my wife's name," he said. "Here's mine."

"Thank you, sir."

"Do you think you can manage it?"

"I'll manage fine," I said.

"If they suspect you, you'll get in trouble," he said.

"I'll write the same kind of notes to the library that you wrote when you sent me for books," I told him. "I'll sign your name."

He laughed.

"Go ahead. Let me see what you get," he said.

That afternoon I addressed myself to forging a note. Now, what were the names of books written by H. L. Mencken? I did not know any of them. I finally wrote what I thought would be a foolproof note: *Dear Madam: Will you please let this nigger boy* — I used the word "nigger" to make the librarian feel that I could not possibly be the author of the note — *have some books by H. L. Mencken?* I forged the white man's name.

418

I entered the library as I had always done when on errands for whites, but I felt that I would somehow slip up and betray myself. I doffed my hat, stood a respectful distance from the desk, looked as unbookish as possible, and waited for the white patrons to be taken care of. When the desk was clear of people, I still waited. The white librarian looked at me.

"What do you want, boy?"

As though I did not possess the power of speech, I stepped forward and simply handed her the forged note, not parting my lips.

"What books by Mencken does he want?" she asked.

"I don't know, ma'am," I said, avoiding her eyes.

"Who gave you this card?"

"Mr. Falk," I said.

"Where is he?"

"He's at work, at the M— —Optical Company," I said. "I've been in here for him before."

"I remember," the woman said. "But he never wrote notes like this."

Oh, God, she's suspicious. Perhaps she would not let me have the books? If she had turned her back at that moment, I would have ducked out the door and never gone back. Then I thought of a bold idea.

"You can call him up, ma'am," I said, my heart pounding.

"You're not using these books, are you?" she asked pointedly.

"Oh, no, ma'am. I can't read."

"I don't know what he wants by Mencken," she said under her breath.

I knew now that I had won; she was thinking of other things and the race question had gone out of her mind. She went to the shelves. Once or twice she looked over her shoulder at me, as though she was still doubtful. Finally she came forward with two books in her hand.

"I'm sending him two books," she said. "But tell Mr. Falk to come in next time, or send me the names of the books he wants. I don't know what he wants to read."

I said nothing. She stamped the card and handed me the books. Not daring to glance at them, I went out of the library, fearing that the woman would call me back for further questioning. A block away from the library I opened one of the books and read a title: *A Book of Prefaces*. I was nearing my nineteenth birthday and I did not know how to pronounce the word "preface." I thumbed the pages and saw strange words and strange names. I shook my head, disappointed. I looked at the other book; it was called *Prejudices*. I knew what that word meant; I had heard it all my life. And right off I was on guard against Mencken's books. Why would a man want to call a book *Prejudices*? The word was so stained with all my memories of racial hate that I could not conceive of anybody using it for a title. Perhaps I had made a mistake about Mencken? A man who had prejudices must be wrong.

When I showed the books to Mr. Falk, he looked at me and frowned.

"That librarian might telephone you," I warned him.

"That's all right," he said. "But when you're through reading those books, I want you to tell me what you get out of them."

That night in my rented room, while letting the hot water run over my can of pork and beans in the sink, I opened *A Book of Prefaces* and began to read. I was jarred and shocked by the style, the clear, clean, sweeping sentences. Why did he write like that? And how did one write like that? I pictured the man as a raging demon, slashing with his pen, consumed with hate, denouncing everything American, extolling everything European or German, laughing at the weaknesses of people, mocking God, authority. What was this? I stood up, trying to realize what reality lay behind the meaning of the words . . . Yes, this man was fighting, fighting with words. He was using words as a weapon, using them as one would use a club. Could words be weapons? Well, yes, for here they were. Then, maybe, perhaps, I could use them as a weapon? No. It frightened me. I read on and what amazed me was not what he said, but how on earth anybody had the courage to say it.

Occasionally I glanced up to reassure myself that I was alone in the room. Who were these men about whom Mencken was talking so passionately? Who was Anatole France? Joseph Conrad? Sinclair Lewis, Sherwood Anderson, Dostoevski, George Moore, Gustave Flaubert, Maupassant, Tolstoy, Frank Harris, Mark Twain, Thomas Hardy, Arnold Bennett, Stephen Crane, Zola, Norris, Gorky, Bergson, Ibsen, Balzac, Bernard Shaw, Dumas, Poe, Thomas Mann, O. Henry, Dreiser, H. G. Wells, Gogol, T. S. Eliot, Gide, Baudelaire, Edgar Lee Masters, Stendhal, Turgenev, Huneker, Nietzsche, and

Black Power

RIZZOLI PRESS—PIX FROM PUBLIX

The Jim Crow system in the South had been an easily identifiable target for the civil rights movement. In the North, the problems of the ghetto were more subtle, more complex, and harder to pinpoint. The tactics that had partially succeeded in the South seemed inadequate to the Northern task. To a new generation of Northern Negro leaders, integration into an otherwise unchanged American society seemed almost irrelevant. The psychological scars left by centuries of dispossession could not be healed by more jobs, better schools, and open housing alone. To be black and poor in an affluent America was to feel actually inferior—or invisible—with only white models and values to work toward. The new leaders urged their people to become self-aware, to take pride in their race, and to celebrate their own Negro culture. The spokesmen of the new movement differed widely among themselves about how best to achieve these goals, but virtually all of them looked to the writings of the late Malcolm X, above, for guidance. A superb orator, he first became known as the chief spokesman for the Black Muslim sect. Later he developed a broader perspective, rejecting the Muslim's doctrinal hatred of all whites, and emphasizing self-pride. His autobiography, unfinished at the time of his murder (reputedly at the hands of the Black Muslims), has become a major source of inspiration for young black people.

GEORGE W. GARDNER

BRUCE DAVIDSON—MAGNUM

In the late 1960s, some ten million Negroes lived outside the South. Two-thirds of them lived in big city ghettos, walled in by whites determined to keep them contained. Black unemployment was twice as high as white unemployment, and the jobs available to blacks were three times as likely to be low-paying. About 40 percent of Negroes lived below the federally defined poverty level, and 40 percent of those lived in the cities. Black fathers, unable to find work to feed their families, often deserted them. Mothers were forced to work and spent little time with their children. Crime rates and narcotics addiction soared. Absentee landlords were unwilling or unable to keep up the crumbling buildings in which the ghetto dwellers were forced to live. White shop owners often exploited their customers with inflated prices and misleading installment credit contracts. Schools were rundown, overcrowded, and understaffed. Governmental programs to eliminate the ghettos were both inadequate and insensitive to the wishes of those they were supposed to aid. The bleak public housing development, above, masks the fact that this is the same old slum made vertical.

The leaders of the Southern civil rights movement chose open housing as the goal for their first major Northern campaign. To Dr. King and others, dispersal seemed a good way to start solving the ghetto problem. The white North, which had watched the Southern struggle on television, had decried mob violence and laughed at official ineptitude. But when Northern Negroes began campaigning against de facto *segregation—the paralegal, informal practices that resulted in closed neighborhoods, all-black schools of poor quality, and increasingly high unemployment in the ghettos—Northern white sympathy began to fade. Attempts to break down discrimination in the sale or rental of homes, even in areas with state and local ordinances that forbade it, met with almost no success. The jeering whites, below, poured into the streets of Gage Park, a white working-class neighborhood in Chicago, to block the 1966 open housing march led by Dr. King. Attempts to integrate Northern city schools met with equally adamant but often more genteel opposition. The marchers at right are protesting a busing plan that would have achieved limited integration in New York City by transporting some white children to black schools and some black children to white schools.*

NORRIS MCNAMARA—NANCY PALMER AGENCY

UPI COMPIX

"DETROIT FREE PRESS" FROM BLACK STAR

*In the summer of 1965 and in each succeeding summer, the
frustrations of the ghettos exploded into violence. While the worst
riots occurred in Detroit (above), Los Angeles, and Newark (right,
top and bottom), few cities with large Negro populations escaped.
Stores and tenements were looted and burned. Negro-owned
stores (identified by scrawled "Soul Brother" signs) were usually
left alone. Hardest hit were white-owned credit stores and
run-down residences owned by absentee whites who had failed
to maintain their property.*

To many big-city blacks, surrounded by crime that never seemed to diminish, white policemen were representatives of a foreign power interested only in preserving order (often with brutal force) and uninterested in protecting black citizens. When, as often happened, the police were unable to quell riots, national guardsmen and regular army troops were sent in to clear the streets. An uneasy peace was restored, but little was done to alleviate the miserable living conditions.

"WORLD TELEGRAM AND SUN"

WIDE WORLD

Official reaction to the city riots was often unimaginative. Congress cut funds for already inadequate poverty programs and passed hastily devised anti-riot legislation. When the President's Commission on Civil Disorders published a report that pinpointed white racism as the source of the nation's racial woes, the administration reacted with displeased silence. City, state, and federal governments instituted riot training programs, below, and amassed arsenals of new riot weapons. The need for training had been made clear during the riots when terrified policemen and ill-prepared troops had often been panicky and trigger-happy, but the use of new riot weapons — chemical sprays, armored personnel carriers, masonry-piercing guns, nausea gas — made black talk of white police forces as "armies of occupation" seem justified. As if to emphasize the national drift toward violence, Martin Luther King, Jr., Nobel Laureate and apostle of non-violence, was assassinated on April 4, 1968, in Memphis, Tennessee.

KEN REGAN

BURK UZZLE—MAGNUM

WIDE WORLD

Black-owned factory that manufactures baseball bats in Watts, the Los Angeles suburb that was the scene of the first major riot of the 1960s. The factory offers jobs and initiative to local youths.

Faced with governmental inaction, white intransigence, and their own increasing bitterness, many young Negroes turned to the spokesmen for Black Power, by which was meant economic and political autonomy. The slogan's militant ring and the hostile tone of its most outspoken advocates terrified many whites who somehow thought they were about to be "taken over" by blacks. The idea of community autonomy, however, is solidly rooted in American tradition. Most immigrant groups had controlled their own communities when they were confined to ghettos. To the advocates of Black Power, Negro ownership of ghetto businesses and property, and control of public services, were vital to community betterment. They believed that political and economic power within the ghetto would allow residents to grow with pride and responsibility into a true community. Black Power was still largely a slogan as the 1960s ended, but hints of its possible future as a unifying force could already be seen.

Carl Stokes was elected the first black mayor of a major city when he won a hotly contested election in Cleveland, Ohio, in 1967. Stokes, a Democrat, received almost universal black support and considerable white support as well.

WIDE WORLD

WIDE WORLD

Black artists and writers are becoming increasingly interested in the lives and culture of their own people. In 1967 actor Robert Hooks, left, and playwright Douglas Turner Ward founded the New York Negro Ensemble Company, a widely acclaimed repertoire group that trained and encouraged new Negro actors, playwrights, and backstage personnel.

F. D. DANDRIDGE—PIX FROM PUBLIX

Whether or not Black Power can change the ghetto remains to be seen. The ghetto poses many problems for the future. Will the American people respond intelligently to the needs of its black citizens? Will the drift toward violence be checked? Are the bonds that make a political community possible strong enough to save the modern city? Whatever happens it is clear that the little girl, above, peering from her Harlem tenement window, will grow up in a world very different from the one her parents knew.

scores of others? Were these men real? Did they exist or had they existed? And how did one pronounce their names?

I ran across many words whose meanings I did not know, and I either looked them up in a dictionary or, before I had a chance to do that, encountered the word in a context that made its meaning clear. But what strange world was this? I concluded the book with the conviction that I had somehow overlooked something terribly important in life. I had once tried to write, had once reveled in feeling, had let my crude imagination roam, but the impulse to dream had been slowly beaten out of me by experience. Now it surged up again and I hungered for books, new ways of looking and seeing. It was not a matter of believing or disbelieving what I read, but of feeling something new, of being affected by something that made the look of the world different.

As dawn broke I ate my pork and beans, feeling dopey, sleepy. I went to work, but the mood of the book would not die; it lingered, coloring everything I saw, heard, did. I now felt that I knew what the white men were feeling. Merely because I had read a book that had spoken of how they lived and thought, I identified myself with that book. I felt vaguely guilty. Would I, filled with bookish notions, act in a manner that would make the whites dislike me?

I forged more notes and my trips to the library became frequent. Reading grew into a passion. My first serious novel was Sinclair Lewis's *Main Street*. It made me see my boss, Mr. Gerald, and identify him as an American type. I would smile when I saw him lugging his golf bags into the office. I had always felt a vast distance separating me from the boss, and now I felt closer to him, though still distant. I felt now that I knew him, that I could feel the very limits of his narrow life. And this had happened because I had read a novel about a mythical man called George F. Babbitt.

The plots and stories in the novels did not interest me so much as the point of view revealed. I gave myself over to each novel without reserve, without trying to criticize it; it was enough for me to see and feel something different. And for me, everything was something different. Reading was like a drug, a dope. The novels created moods in which I lived for days. But I could not conquer my sense of guilt, my feeling that the white men around me knew that I was changing, that I had begun to regard them differently.

Whenever I brought a book to the job, I wrapped it in newspaper—a habit that was to persist for years in other cities and under other circumstances. But some of the white men pried into my packages when I was absent and they questioned me.

"Boy, what are you reading those books for?"

"Oh, I don't know, sir."

"That's deep stuff you're reading, boy."

"I'm just killing time, sir."

"You'll addle your brains if you don't watch out."

I read Dreiser's *Jennie Gerhardt* and *Sister Carrie* and they revived in me a vivid sense of my mother's suffering; I was overwhelmed. I grew silent, wondering about the life around me. It would have been impossible for me to have told anyone what I derived from these novels, for it was nothing less than a sense of life itself. All my life had shaped me for the realism, the naturalism of the modern novel, and I could not read enough of them.

Steeped in new moods and ideas, I bought a ream of paper and tried to write; but nothing would come, or what did come was flat beyond telling. I discovered that more than desire and feeling were necessary to write and I dropped the idea. Yet I still wondered how it was possible to know people sufficiently to write about them? Could I ever learn about life and people? To me, with my vast ignorance, my Jim Crow station in life, it seemed a task impossible of achievement. I now knew what being a Negro meant. I could endure the hunger. I had learned to live with hate. But to feel that there were feelings denied me, that the very breath of life itself was beyond my reach, that more than anything else hurt, wounded me. I had a new hunger.

In buoying me up, reading also cast me down, made me see what was possible, what I had missed. My tension returned, new, terrible, bitter, surging, almost too great to be contained. I no longer *felt* that the world about me was hostile, killing; I *knew* it. A million times I asked myself what I could do to save myself, and there were no answers. I seemed forever condemned, ringed by walls.

I did not discuss my reading with Mr. Falk, who had lent me his library card; it would have meant talking about myself and that would have been too painful. I smiled each day, fighting desperately to maintain my old behavior, to keep my disposition seemingly

434

sunny. But some of the white men discerned that I had begun to brood.

"Wake up there, boy!" Mr. Olin said one day.

"Sir!" I answered for the lack of a better word.

"You act like you've stolen something," he said.

I laughed in the way I knew he expected me to laugh, but I resolved to be more conscious of myself, to watch my every act, to guard and hide the new knowledge that was dawning within me.

If I went north, would it be possible for me to build a new life then? But how could a man build a life upon vague, unformed yearnings? I wanted to write and I did not even know the English language. I bought English grammars and found them dull. I felt that I was getting a better sense of the language from novels than from grammars. I read hard, discarding a writer as soon as I felt that I had grasped his point of view. At night the printed page stood before my eyes in sleep.

Mrs. Moss, my landlady, asked me one Sunday morning:

"Son, what is this you keep on reading?"

"Oh, nothing. Just novels."

"What you get out of 'em?"

"I'm just killing time," I said.

"I hope you know your own mind," she said in a tone which implied that she doubted if I had a mind.

I knew of no Negroes who read the books I liked and I wondered if any Negroes ever thought of them. I knew that there were Negro doctors, lawyers, newspapermen, but I never saw any of them. When I read a Negro newspaper I never caught the faintest echo of my preoccupation in its pages. I felt trapped and occasionally, for a few days, I would stop reading. But a vague hunger would come over me for books, books that opened up new avenues of feeling and seeing, and again I would forge another note to the white librarian. Again I would read and wonder as only the naïve and unlettered can read and wonder, feeling that I carried a secret, criminal burden about with me each day.

That winter my mother and brother came and we set up housekeeping, buying furniture on the installment plan, being cheated and yet knowing no way to avoid it. I began to eat warm food and to my surprise found that regular meals enabled me to read faster. I may have lived through many illnesses and survived them, never suspecting that I was ill. My brother obtained a job and we began to save toward the trip north, plotting our time, setting tentative dates for departure. I told none of the white men on the job that I was planning to go north; I knew that the moment they felt I was thinking of the North they would change toward me. It would have made them feel that I did not like the life I was living, and because my life was completely conditioned by what they said or did, it would have been tantamount to challenging them.

I could calculate my chances for life in the South as a Negro fairly clearly now.

I could fight the southern whites by organizing with other Negroes, as my grandfather had done. But I knew that I could never win that way; there were many whites and there were but few blacks. They were strong and we were weak. Outright black rebellion could never win. If I fought openly I would die and I did not want to die. News of lynchings were frequent.

I could submit and live the life of a genial slave, but that was impossible. All of my life had shaped me to live by my own feelings and thoughts. I could make up to Bess and marry her and inherit the house. But that, too, would be the life of a slave; if I did that, I would crush to death something within me, and I would hate myself as much as I knew the whites already hated those who had submitted. Neither could I ever willingly present myself to be kicked, as Shorty had done. I would rather have died than do that.

I could drain off my restlessness by fighting with Shorty and Harrison. I had seen many Negroes solve the problem of being black by transferring their hatred of themselves to others with a black skin and fighting them. I would have to be cold to do that, and I was not cold and I could never be.

I could, of course, forget what I had read, thrust the whites out of my mind, forget them; and find release from anxiety and longing in sex and alcohol. But the memory of how my father had conducted himself made that course repugnant. If I did not want others to violate my life, how could I voluntarily violate it myself?

I had no hope whatever of being a professional man. Not only had I been so conditioned that I did not desire it, but the fulfillment of such an ambition was beyond my capabilities. Well-to-do Negroes

436

lived in a world that was almost as alien to me as the world inhabited by whites.

What, then, was there? I held my life in my mind, in my consciousness each day, feeling at times that I would stumble and drop it, spill it forever. My reading had created a vast sense of distance between me and the world in which I lived and tried to make a living, and that sense of distance was increasing each day. My days and nights were one long, quiet, continuously contained dream of terror, tension, and anxiety. I wondered how long I could bear it.

ROBERT C. WEAVER
A Wage Differential Based on Race

Franklin D. Roosevelt was the most popular President, among Negroes, since Lincoln. Although he said very little publicly about Negroes, Roosevelt went out of his way to see that the numerous New Deal relief, recovery, and reform programs dealt with their special problems. Assistance came from the Federal Employment Relief Administration (FERA), the Works Projects Administration (WPA), the Tennessee Valley Authority (TVA), and in the area of public housing. However, the National Recovery Administration (NRA) came in for special criticism because its wage policies had the effect of freezing many Negroes out of jobs. Robert C. Weaver, who was to become secretary of housing and urban development in President Johnson's cabinet, was adviser on Negro affairs in the department of the interior during the New Deal. [Source: Crisis, *August 1934.]*

No issue affecting Negroes under the recovery program is of more importance than that of wage policy under the NRA. There is no other question arising out of the new deal which has excited more discussion among enlightened Negroes. Like most important controversies, this is a complicated matter. To discuss it intelligently, one must consider the philosophy of the recovery program and the implications of the Negro's position in American Life.

There are two observations which are fundamental. In the first

437

place, Southern industrial life is personal and paternalistic. The employers like to keep in touch with the workers. This paternalism is especially present in the relationship between the white employer and his Negro workers. A manufacturer of the deep South explained why he preferred Negro workers saying that he could handle them easier — they felt close to the boss and he felt close to them. On the other hand, the philosophy behind minimum wage provisions (and all social legislation) is that of an impersonal and highly developed industrial life. Thus there is a fundamental conflict between the Southern system and the labor provisions of the NRA.

The very idea of a sub-marginal minimum for Negro workers is an expression of the second important feature in the situation — the tendency to lump all Negroes together and judge them by the least desirable and the least able in the group. This tendency is, of course, the most arbitrary and pernicious feature of race prejudice.

Since the inauguration of the NRA, there has been a series of attempts to establish lower minimum rates of wages for Negro workers. First it was said that Negroes have a lower standard of living. Then, lower wages were defended on the basis of the Negro's lower efficiency. Lastly, it was pointed out that lower wages for Negroes were traditional and should be incorporated as a feature of the New Deal. However, the most telling and important argument for a lower minimum wage for Negroes was the fact that they were being displaced from industry as a result of the operation of the labor provision of the NRA.

Long before the New Deal was thought of, there was a constant displacement of Negroes by white workers. Certain cities in the South replaced their colored workers with whites; in other places organizations were initiated to foster the substitution of white for black laborers in all positions. The minimum wage regulations of the NRA accelerated this tendency. Indeed, it resulted in wholesale discharges in certain areas. More recently, the tendency has been arrested.

There are many causes for the failure of the program to be carried further. In the first place, there is reason to believe that employers resorted to the discharge of colored workers as a means of forcing the NRA to grant a racial differential. They declared that if a

438

man had to be paid as much as twelve dollars a week, they would pay a white worker that wage. Then, too, there are many instances where it is impossible to discharge a whole working force. Even modern industry with its automatic machinery requires workers of some training, and training is a time and money consuming process. Thus, where Negroes formed a large percentage of the total working force, it was often impracticable to displace them and hire a new all-white labor force.

Nevertheless, there have been many displacements of Negroes. All the available evidence seems to indicate, as one would expect, that perhaps the greater part of this substitution of white for Negro workers has occurred in small enterprizes where the Negro is often the marginal worker. In such plants, the separation of Negro workers presented no important question of organizational integrity or of training.

Out of these developments a movement for a racial differential has arisen. The motivating force for such a campaign has come from the Southern employers who have, for the most part, shifted their emphasis from standard of living and tradition to efficiency and displacement. The latter feature — the loss of job opportunities to Negroes — has been made much of in recent months. Appeals have been made to Negro leaders to endorse a lower minimum wage for Negroes on the ground that such action is necessary if Negroes are not to be forced out of industry. The colored leaders have been careful in their championing of this cause. A few have been convinced that it is the only possible way out; some have supported the policy because of local pressure in the South but most have tried to keep out of the discussion. Many are almost convinced that it is the proper choice but fear a loss of prestige among Negroes if they speak in favor of such a measure.

Briefly, the only possible argument for a racial wage differential is one based upon a *de facto* situation. Negroes have lost jobs as a result of the NRA, and a lower wage for them would counteract this tendency. It would assure Negroes of retaining their old jobs and perhaps it would lead to a few additional ones. It may be observed that this reasoning is correct as far as it goes. Certainly, a racial differential would do much to arrest and, perchance, offset the displacement of Negro workers. But there is more involved in this question than the arresting of Negro displacement. In it are the elements which combine to establish the whole industrial position of colored Americans.

The establishment of a lower minimum wage for Negroes would have far reaching effects. It would brand black workers as a less efficient and submarginal group. It would increase the ill-will and friction between white and colored workers. It would destroy much of the advance Negroes have made in the industrial North. It would destroy any possibility of ever forming a strong and effective labor movement in the nation. The ultimate effect would be to relegate Negroes into a low wage caste and place the federal stamp of approval upon their being in such a position.

It was pointed out above that the most damnable feature of racial prejudice in America is the tendency to judge all Negroes by the least able colored persons. Obviously, a racial minimum is an expression of such an attitude. Were this not true, why should Negroes be singled out for a special – and lower – rate of pay? There have been no satisfactory or convincing studies of racial efficiency. (Efforts along this line are even more crude than the measures we have which have been set up to gauge intelligence.) Indeed, it is absurd to talk about racial efficiency since Negroes, like every other group of human beings vary in their effectiveness. The efficiency of a worker depends upon his native ability, environment and specific training. These factors differ between individuals rather than between races. A racial differential on the other hand would say, in effect, that efficiency is based on race and the individual black worker – because he is a Negro – is less efficient.

Now, there is still another phase of this matter. The very attitude which dictates a racial differential would make such a provision most discriminatory against colored workers. Any minimum wage tends to become a maximum. In the case of Negro workers this tendency would be accentuated. Since all Negroes are usually considered the same regardless of their ability, a lower minimum for black labor would in fact, mean that practically all Negroes would receive wages lower than their white prototypes. Not only would this be manifestly unfair, but in certain areas it would undermine the race's industrial progress of the last twenty years. During this period, Negroes have entered the industries of the North and the

440

West as never before. They came from the South, where they were treated with mercy (as opposed to justice), and faced a situation which was new to them. Standards of efficiency were higher and they had to measure up to these new standards. Some failed but the recent data on Negro participation in Northern industry show that many succeeded. It has been a difficult process of adaptation. The fruits have been higher wages and less racial discrimination in rates of pay. To establish a differential based on race, would be, in effect, to take away the fruits of this hard-won victory.

Nor would the white worker respond favorably to the notion of a lower minimum for Negro workers. His first response in the South would be favorable because his ego would be flattered. But when the lower minimum destroyed the effectiveness of the higher minimum, the white recipient of the latter would blame the Negro. The black worker, North and South, would be regarded as the force which rendered it impossible for workers to demand a decent wage and find employment. This would occasion no end of misunderstanding and hatred between the white and black worker.

It is clear that the unity of all labor into an organized body would be impossible if there were a racial differential. The essence of collective bargaining is an impersonal and standard wage. Unionism rests upon the cooperation of all workers. A racial wage differential prevents both of these developments. It would, therefore, destroy the possibility of *a real labor movement* in this country.

The Evils of Segregation

The following exchange of views on the significance of segregation appeared in the June 1934 issue of Crisis. *Francis J. Grimké, a prominent Negro minister in Washington, D.C., was the son of Henry Grimké, a member of an aristocratic Charleston, South Carolina, family, and of slave Nancy Weston. Despite his white father, he was treated as the son of a slave; but with the assistance of his well-known Abolitionist aunt, Angelina Grimké-Weld, he went to Princeton Theological Seminary. W. E. B. Du Bois,*

who founded the NAACP in 1909 and was the editor of the Crisis, *had been
the leading Negro spokesman since the turn of the century.*

FRANCIS J. GRIMKÉ
A Challenge to Du Bois

Why Dr. DuBois has reopened the question of segregation in *The
Crisis* I am at a loss to know. Can it be possible that in the remotest
part of his brain he is beginning to think, after all, that it is a condition that ought to be accepted, a condition that we ought to stop
fussing about? If so, then his leadership among us is at an end; we
can follow no such leader. That is what I wrote after reading Dr.
DuBois' initial article in *The Crisis.*

If we have any doubt, if we are not quite clear in our own minds in
regard to it, it is well to reopen it. But if we are already convinced
that we are right, why reopen it? Do we need to be more thoroughly
convinced, more firmly persuaded than we are that we are right?
Or, will the reopening of it help to convince the white man that he
is wrong? If so, well.

Underlying the idea of race segregation is that of inferiority. It
is always a badge of inferiority, and is so intended by those who
impose it. It is one way of expressing contempt for the segregated,
on the part of those who impose the segregation. In sheer self-
respect, therefore, on the part of the segregated, it should be resented. It may be necessary for a time to endure it, but it should
never be accepted as a finality.

Segregation produces a condition that is not conducive to the
best interest of either race. It tends to build up a false or artificial
sense of superiority in the one, and is sure to create or engender in
the other, feelings of resentment, of hatred, of discontent, out of
which no good can come to either, but will continue to be a source of
friction, of irritation.

No race, with any self-respect, can accept the status of a segregated group for itself. To do so is virtually to admit its inferiority, to
be content to have limits placed upon its possibilities by another
race. The whole thing is wrong, wrong in principle, wrong in spirit.
It violates every principle of right and is contrary to the spirit of
Jesus Christ and to the noble ideal of brotherhood.

No race has a right to force upon another race the status of infe-

442

riority. And no race, however humble, however far behind in the process of development, should accept from another race such a status as its right and proper place in the Divine order of things. No limits can be placed upon the progress of a race except that which it places upon itself. Segregation is to be fought, therefore, now and always. One of the great evils of segregation is, that when a race has been segregated, when people have been taught to look down upon its members as inferiors, they are thus exposed to all kinds of brutality, to all kinds of injustice and oppression. The feeling is, they are inferior, and are not entitled therefore to the treatment that would be proper to accord to those of a superior brand. It is this sense of the inborn inferiority of the Negro, so deeply ingrained in the Southern white man, especially of the lower classes, that is responsible for much of the brutality that is manifested towards him in the South. The feeling is, "He is only a nigger." And being only a nigger anything is good enough for him, nothing is too mean or contemptible to visit upon him. This fact is very forcibly brought out in "The Tragedy of Lynching," by Arthur Raper.

Page 13, we read: "Do you think I am going to risk my life protecting a nigger?" said a county sheriff.

Page 19: "Most apologists for lynching, like the lynchers themselves, seem to assume that the Negro is irredeemably inferior by reason of his race that it is a plan of God that the Negro and his children shall forever be 'hewers of wood and drawers of water.' With this weighty emphasis upon the essential racial inferiority of the Negro, it is not surprising to find the mass of whites ready to justify any and all means to 'keep the Negro in his place.' "

Page 22: "The most fundamental way in which the church is related to mob violence is that, not infrequently, the local church leaves unchallenged the general assumption that the Negro is innately inferior and of little importance. Upon this assumption ultimately rests the justification of lynching."

The Negro, therefore, for his own sake, as well as for the sake of the white man, must resent segregation. It exposes him to all kinds of brutality, and develops in the white man, more and more, the traits of the brute. Segregation is bad for the black man. It is bad for the white man. There must be no let up therefore in the steady protest against it. As I said before, it may be necessary for a time to

443

endure it, but never should it be accepted as a finality. Mr. Monroe Trotter is right, in publishing week after week in the *Guardian*, in large letters, the ringing words "Segregation for Colored is the Real, Permanent, Damning Degradation in the U.S.A." And the thought must not be allowed to drop out of the consciousness of the race, must not be allowed to be forgotten or minimized by it. If we are content to be a segregated group, our self-respect is sadly in need of repairs. The consciousness of the fact that we are men, created in the image of God, with all the possibilities open to us that are open to other race groups, needs to be quickened, to be stimulated afresh and kept vigorously alive.

The attempt of one race to put the stamp of inferiority upon another is the most shameful spectacle of which I can conceive: and is evidence, not of superiority, of which the white man is so prone to boast, but of inferiority, and inferiority of the most contemptible kind. To seek to destroy the self-respect of a race, and to beget in others contempt for it, is as despicable a thing as poor, fallen human nature is capable of. The test of true nobility, of real greatness of soul is not to be found in that kind of conduct. And the white man will one day, let us hope, come to see the heinousness of it, and repent, and show himself to be a *man*, — a *true* man, in the highest and best sense of the term.

W. E. BURGHARDT DU BOIS
Reply to Grimké

I publish Dr. Grimke's article with great pleasure. First, because it is a strong argument; but more especially because of the great respect in which *The Crisis* and the world holds the pastor of the 15th Street Presbyterian Church of Washington, D.C. And it is right here, and because of my thinking of this church that my real difference of opinion with Dr. Grimke comes. What Negro in the United States does not know of this institution? I doubt if there is in the country or in the world a group of people who, for so many years, have stood out for their intellectual accomplishment, their moral worth, and the sheer physical beauty of the membership. I can remember yet the thrill which I had when first I sat in this church in 1890, and realized the men and the women whose work had gone to make it.

There was the memory of John F. Cook, who founded the church

444

and led the black people of the District of Columbia and gave them their organized schools. In these pews sat Lucy Moton, a great teacher; John Nalle, for forty years supervising principal of the schools; Willis Menard, once elected Congressman from Louisiana; George F. T. Cook, Dean of Howard; Dr. Furman Shadd, the well-known physician; Elizabeth Keckley, dressmaker to the wife of Abraham Lincoln; and members of the families of John R. Lynch, Senator Bruce, James Wormley and Richard T. Greener.

Indeed, the membership list of the 15th Street Presbyterian Church forms a Who's Who of colored Washington and a roll of honor of the Negro in America. Moreover, this church has had at its head for a half century a man of sound learning, deep thought, and unblemished moral character. A man whose physical comeliness, human sympathy, and unlimited ability to work, has made him an outstanding and constructive leader of the Negro race.

Why, then, in an argument on segregation, has Dr. Grimke said *nothing* of the 15th Street Presbyterian Church? This church is a result of segregation. It was founded because white Presbyterians could not listen to a pastor of Dr. Grimke's learning and character and would not sit in the same pews with the distinguished people who belonged to this church. There is no use trying to salve our logic by saying that this church represents "voluntary" segregation. It represents compulsion and compulsion of the most despicable sort. Not the compulsion of sticks and stone and fists, but that withdrawal of skirts and "brotherly" advice, and unbending and unending pressure that would make an upright human being worship in Hell rather than try to be a member of a white Presbyterian Church. And yet, the separation of this class of colored people from white people was ridiculous. And what proves it is ridiculous, is the success, the outstanding success of this church. And it is only by making our segregated institutions successful and conspicuously successful, that we are going to get into our hands a weapon which in the long run is bound to kill and discredit segregation if human reason lasts. And this is the point, and the only point, where I differ with Dr. Grimke.

Dr. Grimke is perfectly right in stressing the evil of segregation, and the assumption of inferiority upon which it is based. But on the other hand, and just as strongly and enthusiastically he should say to the world that the 15th Street Presbyterian Church is a success; that it has been the great privilege of his life to preside over such a church and to build it up, and to have the benediction of contact with the fine and beautiful and trained human beings which have passed through it. That it would be a worthy ambition for any boy to become a minister of God and have a church of this sort, and this is true whether that boy is black or white. That consequently, having segregation forced upon us, we must not simply make the best of it. We must make our segregated institutions so fine and outstanding and put so much of belief and thought and loyalty in them, that the separation upon which they are based, and the doctrine of inferiority which led to them, will be confounded and contradicted by its inherent and evident foolishness.

In fine, we can only regret that Dr. Grimke sees in the 15th Street Presbyterian Church only the insult that caused its founding, and has no word for the magnificence of the opportunity which he has had in leading and developing it.

LOREN MILLER
Uncle Tom in Hollywood

By 1930 there were over 20,000 movie houses in the United States, with a weekly audience of more than 100 million people. Movies were thus a potent social and cultural force, a fact that disturbed Hollywood, which in general tried to divest its productions of any ideological content. ("Messages," as one producer remarked, "are for Western Union.") Nevertheless, even when the movies were trying merely to reflect current states of mind, they were actually reinforcing them. This was fine when it was a question of portraying the traditional American ideals of love, justice, right, wrong, happiness, honor, and patriotism. But other "ideals" and popular beliefs were also portrayed, as this article by Loren Miller pointed out. [Source: Crisis, *November 1934.]*

A few years ago I attended a showing of Trader Horn, a Metro-Goldwyn-Mayer film, at a Negro theater. One scene depicts the "beautiful"—of course, blond—heroine in the clutches of "savage" Africans. In typical Hollywood thriller style the girl is saved just as all hope is ebbing away. At this particular showing the audience burst into wild applause when the rescue scene flashed on the screen. I looked around. Those who were applauding were ordinary Negro working people and middle class folk. Hollywood's movie makers had made the theme so commonplace and glorious that it seemed quite natural white virtue should triumph over black vice. Obviously those spectators were quite unconscious of the fact that they were giving their stamp of approval to a definite pattern of racial relationships in which they are always depicted as the lesser breed.

Unwritten, but iron clad rules in the movie industry require that films in which racial relationships are depicted show the white man as the overlord. Ordinarily Negroes get servant parts in which they are either buffoons or ubiquitous Uncle Toms. A written section of the code forbids the showing of miscegenation. Where there is racial clash as in "Birth of a Nation" the Negro is pictured as vicious and depraved. Occasional pictures such as "Hallelujah" or "Hearts in Dixie" purport to treat Negro life seriously but even there the economic roots of the Negro question are carefully avoided and the Negro is shown as a lowly, loyal and contented fellow happy in his lot.

DEPICT NEGRO TO WORLD

News reels poke fun at Negro revivals or baptisings and avoid such "dangerous" subjects as the Scottsboro case. I heard dozens of administration spokesmen pleading for pet Roosevelt legislation or unimportant special laws but I did not hear a single lawmaker plead for the anti-lynching bill during the past year.

The cumulative effect of constant picturization of this kind is tremendously effective in shaping racial attitudes. Hollywood products are seen in every nook and corner of the world. Millions of non-residents of the United States depend almost entirely on the movies for their knowledge of Negro life, as those who have been abroad can testify. Other millions of white Americans of all ages confirm their beliefs about Negroes at the neighborhood theaters while Negroes themselves fortify their inferiority complex by seeing

447

themselves always cast as the underdog to be laughed at or despised.

Although the Hollywood portrayal of Negro life is so out of focus that it is in effect rabid anti-Negro propaganda, it would be unfair to tax the movie magnates with inventing their product out of whole cloth. It is easy enough to see that the movies but reflect the traditional American outlook on the Negro question. By giving that tradition wide and effective circulation and by implying its artistic truthfulness, the movie makers are certainly doing more than their share to whip up prejudice and making the breakdown of racial chauvinism more difficult. Of course, Hollywood excuses its actions on the grounds that it is merely supplying the audiences with what they want. The argument is ingenious and plausible enough until one remembers how the movies consciously set out to mold public sentiment, as they did in the last war in the face of an overwhelming pacifist spirit among the American people. The differences in treatment of the Massie and the Scottsboro cases also illustrate the fact that the movies are deliberately used to further causes dear to the hearts of those who control them.

At the present time the movie makers are being attacked by a group of moralists in an effort to force them to make "clean" films. Negroes can expect little from this crusade because the moralists themselves define "cleanliness" in traditional terms. The Catholics, for example, list the showing of miscegenation as objectionable along with perversion and sexual intercourse. Another plumed knight of the crusade is William Randolph Hearst, an accomplished race baiter whose newspapers are distinctly unfriendly to all colored peoples. Hardly an organization enlisted in the present purity drive is opposed to Jim Crow and all that it means. The Negro will have to fend for himself. And he will learn that the opposition is formidable.

BUSINESS-POLITICAL ALLIANCE

Those who control the movies are powerful in other phases of American life. The Chase National Bank, controlled by the Rockefellers, has its hands on a half dozen studios. A manual of corporate directorates will reveal the fact that movie boards interlock with those of other basic monopolies. The political tie-up is as plain.

448

Louis B. Mayer of the Metro-Goldwyn-Mayers, is the personal friend of Herbert Hoover and a power in Republican politics. Jack Warner of Warner Brothers is commonly reputed to be the Roosevelt spokesman in Hollywood. These all powerful business men-politicians direct the destinies of the film world. The pictures they produce accord roughly yet firmly with their politico-economic outlook. Certainly, these men are farsighted enough to realize that the movies are valuable aids in preserving the status quo on which their own welfare and profits depend. An important factor in the preservation of the status quo is the continued subordination of the Negro people. White superiority has cash value to them.

What can the Negro do? The first impulse is to say that he should produce his own films. Something of that sort is attempted in the Micheaux pictures. However the run-of-mine films produced by Negro companies fail miserably because their producers simply ape the white movies. Thus, we have ridiculous productions depicting burnt cork Clark Gables and Norma Shearers living in mansions and ordering butlers about. All semblance of reality is eschewed in efforts to match the current white films. Negro pictures of the past have been as out of focus as those produced by Hollywood. Those faults could be overcome, but tremendous technical difficulties both in production and distribution would remain. The average owner of the small theater is under the thumb of the Hollywood producers and must take the pictures they offer him. Doubtless these Hollywood producers would not look kindly on competition even if capital for production could be obtained. I believe that the cost of production would be prohibitive. The best that can be hoped for in that direction, I believe, is the production of 16 millimeter films that might be shown in small halls. A "little movie" movement comparable to the "little theater" might be started.

ACTION AGAINST BOX OFFICE

The second move lies in protest. Negroes have used this weapon in the past to some degree. Past protest has taken the form of appeals to authority to ban such shows as "Birth of a Nation." Some success has been registered, but that method has its limitations. In a showdown the political and economic power of Hollywood is great enough to force permission to show any film that it may produce.

449

Again, protest of that kind can never reach the pictures in which the anti-Negro propaganda is introduced by always showing him at his worst or as an inferior, nor can it compel favorable news reel showings. Protest to be of its greatest value must be inculcated in the great mass of Negro people. They must be taught to recognize and resent anti-Negro sentiment in such a manner that their feelings can reach the box office. They must let Hollywood know that they object vigorously to being shown as buffoons, clowns or butts for jest. They must stop applauding for such imperialistic jingoism as Trader Horn.

The Negro masses will adopt a critical attitude only if organs of opinion and Negro leadership establish an adequate critique for their guidance. Criticism of the movies is in a deplorable state at the present time. Negro magazines give no attention to it at all until some monstrosity such as the "Birth of a Nation" is announced. Negro newspapers have pages devoted to the theater and the film, but those pages are jokes, or worse. Most of such a page is given over to reprinting blurbs at the request of theater owners. Not long since, I saw one of these blurbs in a Negro newspaper lauding a white woman for her success in maintaining her virtue on a South Sea Island! What space is not given over to the publicity men is reserved for pumping some Negro bit actor up to the dimensions of a star. One not acquainted with American life and reading only a Negro newspaper theatrical page could believe easily enough that some 45-second Negro bit player, depicting a servant, was the star of the film being reviewed! Such criticism is worse than useless; it is the abjectness of a beggar fawning over a penny tossed him by his lord. It is acceptance of "our place."

Nor is it easy to over-emphasize the importance of the movies as agents in shaping public opinion. It is vitally important that immediate and active steps be taken to try and effect a change in their present attitude toward the Negroes they depict. The people who can change that attitude are the theatergoers themselves. And they can and will do it if they are armed with an intelligently critical spirit. These same people could become the base for the "little movie" movement if they were taught to demand pictures that reflect their own lives and aspirations. So long as we sit acquiescent and give either passive or active support to the Hollywood bilge of the present

450

we are guilty of teaching ourselves, our own children, and millions of white, yellow and brown movie-goers the world over that the Negro is an inferior. It's time we took up arms on the Hollywood front. We might get in some telling blows just now when the movie makers are already under fire.

JAMES WELDON JOHNSON
Race Prejudice and the Negro Artist

In the atmosphere of nativism and xenophobia that followed the war, it was perhaps not surprising that the American Negro continued to be victimized by the social, political, and economic exclusion that had increasingly been his lot since the end of Reconstruction. The Negro was savagely persecuted in the 1920s and the prosperity of the period passed him by. Nonetheless, Negroes began to make their presence felt in the cultural life of the nation: in literature, drama, and the concert stage. James Weldon Johnson, poet, professor, and secretary from 1916 to 1930 of the National Association for the Advancement of Colored People, argued, in an article that is reprinted here in part, that this renaissance had softened the prejudice that many Americans felt toward Negroes. [Source: Harper's, November 1928.]

What Americans call the Negro problem is almost as old as America itself. For three centuries the Negro in this country has been tagged with an interrogation point; the question propounded, however, has not always been the same. Indeed, the question has run all the way from whether or not the Negro was a human being, down — or up — to whether or not the Negro shall be accorded full and unlimited American citizenship. Therefore, the Negro problem is not a problem in the sense of being a fixed proposition involving certain invariable factors and waiting to be worked out according to certain defined rules.

It is not a static condition; rather, it is and always has been a series of shifting interracial situations, never precisely the same in any two generations. As these situations have shifted, the methods and manners of dealing with them have constantly changed. And never has there been such a swift and vital shift as the one which is taking place at the present moment; and never was there a more revolutionary change in attitudes than the one which is now going on.

The question of the races — white and black — has occupied much of America's time and thought. Many methods for a solution of the problem have been tried — most of them tried *on* the Negro, for one of the mistakes commonly made in dealing with this matter has been the failure of white America to take into account the Negro himself and the forces he was generating and sending out. The question repeated generation after generation has been: what shall we do with the Negro? — ignoring completely the power of the Negro to do something for himself, and even something to America.

It is a new thought that the Negro has helped to shape and mold and make America. It is, perhaps, a startling thought that America would not be precisely the America it is today except for the powerful, if silent, influence the Negro has exerted upon it — both positively and negatively. It is a certainty that the nation would be shocked by a contemplation of the effects which have been wrought upon its inherent character by the negative power which the Negro has involuntarily and unwittingly wielded.

A number of approaches to the heart of the race problem have been tried: religious, educational, political, industrial, ethical, economic, sociological. Along several of these approaches considerable progress has been made. Today a newer approach is being tried, an approach which discards most of the older methods. It requires a minimum of pleas, or propaganda, or philanthropy. It depends more upon what the Negro himself does than upon what someone does for him. It is the approach along the line of intellectual and artistic achievement by Negroes and may be called the art approach to the Negro problem. This method of approaching a solution of the race question has the advantage of affording great and rapid progress with least friction and of providing a common platform upon which most people are willing to stand. The results of this method seem to carry a high degree of finality, to be the thing itself that was to be demonstrated.

I have said that this is a newer approach to the race problem; that is only in a sense true. The Negro has been using this method for a very long time; for a longer time than he has used any other method, and, perhaps, with farther-reaching effectiveness. For more than a century his great folk-art contributions have been exerting an ameliorating effect, slight and perhaps, in any one period, imperceptible, nevertheless, cumulative. In countless and diverse situations song and dance have been both a sword and a shield for the Negro. Take the spirituals: for sixty years, beginning with their introduction to the world by the Fisk Jubilee Singers, these songs have touched and stirred the hearts of people and brought about a smoothing down of the rougher edges of prejudice against the Negro. Indeed, nobody can hear Negroes sing this wonderful music in its primitive beauty without a softening of feeling toward them.

What is there, then, that is new? What is new consists largely in the changing attitude of the American people. There is a coming to light and notice of efforts that have been going on for a long while, and a public appreciation of their results. Note, for example, the change in the reaction to the spirituals. Fifty years ago white people who heard the spirituals were touched and moved with sympathy and pity for the "poor Negro." Today, the effect is not one of pity for the Negro's condition but admiration for the creative genius of the race.

All of the Negro's folk-art creations have undergone a new evaluation. His sacred music — the spirituals; his secular music — ragtime, blues, jazz, and the work songs; his folklore — the Uncle Remus plantation tales; and his dances have received a new and higher appreciation. Indeed, I dare to say that it is now more or less generally acknowledged that the only things artistic that have sprung from American soil and out of American life, and been universally recognized as distinctively American products, are the folk creations of the Negro. The one thing that may be termed artistic, by which the United States is known the world over, is its Negro-derived popular music. The folk creations of the Negro have not only received a new appreciation; they have — the spirituals excepted — been taken over and assimilated. They are no longer racial, they are national; they have become a part of our common cultural fund.

Negro secular music has been developed into American popular music; Negro dances have been made into our national art of dancing; even the plantation tales have been transformed and have come out as popular bedtime stories. The spirituals are still distinct Negro folk songs, but sooner or later our serious composers will take them as material to go into the making of the "great American music" that has so long been looked for.

But the story does not halt at this point. The Negro has done a great deal through his folk-art creations to change the national attitudes toward him; and now the efforts of the race have been reinforced and magnified by the individual Negro artist, the conscious artist. It is fortunate that the individual Negro artist has emerged; for it is more than probable that with the ending of the creative period of blues, which seems to be at hand, the whole folk creative effort of the Negro in the United States will come to a close. All the psychological and environmental forces are working to that end. At any rate, it is the individual Negro artist that is now doing most to effect a crumbling of the inner walls of race prejudice; there are outer and inner walls. The emergence of the individual artist is the result of the same phenomenon that brought about the new evaluation and appreciation of the folk-art creations. But it should be borne in mind that the conscious Aframerican artist is not an entirely new thing. What is new about him is chiefly the evaluation and public recognition of his work.

When and how did this happen? The entire change, which is marked by the shedding of a new light on the artistic and intellectual achievements of the Negro, the whole period which has become ineptly known as "the Negro renaissance," is the matter of a decade, it has all taken place within the last ten years. More forces than anyone can name have been at work to create the existing state; however, several of them may be pointed out.

What took place had no appearance of a development; it seemed more like a sudden awakening, an almost instantaneous change. There was nothing that immediately preceded it which foreshadowed what was to follow. Those who were in the midst of the movement were as much astonished as anyone else to see the transformation. Overnight, as it were, America became aware that there were Negro artists and that they had something worthwhile to offer. This awareness first manifested itself in black America, for, strange as it may seem, Negroes themselves, as a mass, had had little or no consciousness of their own individual artists.

454

Black America awoke first to the fact that it possessed poets. This awakening followed the entry of the United States into the Great War. Before this country had been in the war very long there was bitter disillusionment on the part of American Negroes—on the part both of those working at home and those fighting in France to make the world safe for democracy. The disappointment and bitterness were taken up and voiced by a group of seven or eight Negro poets. They expressed what the race felt, what the race wanted to hear. They made the group at large articulate. Some of this poetry was the poetry of despair, but most of it was the poetry of protest and rebellion. Fenton Johnson wrote of civilization:

> I am tired of work; I am tired of building up somebody else's civilization.
> Let us take a rest, M'lissy Jane.
>
> You will let the old shanty go to rot, the white people's clothes turn to dust, and the Calvary Baptist Church sink to the bottomless pit.
>
> Throw the children into the river; civilization has given us too many. It is better to die than it is to grow up and find out that you are colored.
>
> Pluck the stars out of the heavens. The stars mark our destiny. The stars marked my destiny.
> I am tired of civilization.

Joseph Cotter, a youth of twenty, inquired plaintively from the invalid's bed to which he was confined:

> Brother, come!
> And let us go unto our God.
> And when we stand before Him
> I shall say,
> "Lord, I do not hate
> I am hated.
> I scourge no one,
> I am scourged.
> I covet no lands,
> My lands are coveted.

> I mock no peoples,
> My people are mocked."
> And, brother, what shall you say?

But among this whole group the voice that was most powerful was that of Claude McKay. Here was a true poet of great skill and wide range, who turned from creating the mood of poetic beauty in the absolute, as he had so fully done in such poems as "Spring in New Hampshire," "The Harlem Dancer," and "Flame Heart," for example, and began pouring out cynicism, bitterness, and invective. For this purpose, incongruous as it may seem, he took the sonnet form as his medium. There is nothing in American literature that strikes a more portentous note than these sonnet-tragedies of Mc-Kay. Here is the sestet of his sonnet, "The Lynching":

> Day dawned, and soon the mixed crowds came to view
> The ghastly body swaying in the sun:
> The women thronged to look, but never a one
> Showed sorrow in her eyes of steely blue;
> And little lads, lynchers that were to be,
> Danced round the dreadful thing in fiendish glee.

The summer of 1919 was a terrifying period for the American Negro. There were race riots in Chicago and in Washington and in Omaha and in Phillips County, Arkansas; and in Longview, Texas; and in Knoxville, Tennessee; and in Norfolk, Virginia; and in other communities. Colored men and women, by dozens and by scores, were chased and beaten and killed in the streets. And from Claude McKay came this cry of defiant despair, sounded from the last ditch:

> If we must die—let it not be like hogs
> Hunted and penned in an inglorious spot,
>
> Oh, Kinsmen! We must meet the common foe;
> Though far outnumbered, let us still be brave,
> And for their thousand blows deal one deathblow!
> What though before us lies the open grave?
> Like men we'll face the murderous, cowardly pack,
> Pressed to the wall, dying, but—fighting back!

But not all the terror of the time could smother the poet of beauty

456

and universality in McKay. In "America," which opens with these lines:

> Although she feeds me bread of bitterness,
> And sinks into my throat her tiger's tooth,
> Stealing my breath of life, I will confess
> I love this cultured hell that tests my youth

he fused these elements of fear and bitterness and hate into verse which by every test is true poetry and a fine sonnet.

The poems of the Negro poets of the immediate post-war period were widely printed in Negro periodicals; they were committed to memory; they were recited at school exercises and public meetings; and were discussed at private gatherings. Now, Negro poets were not new; their line goes back a long way in Aframerican history. Between Phillis Wheatley, who as a girl of eight or nine was landed in Boston from an African slave ship, in 1761, and who published a volume of poems in 1773, and Paul Laurence Dunbar, who died in 1906, there were more than thirty Negroes who published volumes of verse—some of it good, most of it mediocre, and much of it bad.

The new thing was the effect produced by these poets who sprang up out of the war period. Negro poets had sounded similar notes before, but now for the first time they succeeded in setting up a reverberating response, even in their own group. But the effect was not limited to black America; several of these later poets in some subtle way affected white America. In any event, at just this time, white America began to become aware and to awaken. In the correlation of forces that brought about this result it might be pointed out that the culminating effect of the folk-art creations had gone far toward inducing a favorable state of mind. Doubtless it is also true that the new knowledge and opinions about the Negro in Africa —that he was not just a howling savage, that he had a culture, that he had produced a vital art—had directly affected opinion about the Negro in America. However it may have been, the Negro poets growing out of the war period were the forerunners of the individuals whose work is now being assayed and is receiving recognition in accordance with its worth.

And yet, contemporaneously with the work of these poets, a

significant effort was made in another field of art — an effort which might have gone much farther at the time had it not been cut off by our entry into the War, but which, nevertheless, had its effect. Early in 1917, in fact on the very day we entered the War, Mrs. Emily Hapgood produced at the Madison Square Garden Theater three plays of Negro life by Ridgley Torrence, staged by Robert Edmond Jones, and played by an all-Negro cast. This was the first time that Negro actors in drama commanded the serious attention of the critics and the general public.

Two of the players, Opal Cooper and Inez Clough, were listed by George Jean Nathan among the ten actors giving the most distinguished performances of the year. No one who heard Opal Cooper chant the dream in the *Rider of Dreams* can ever forget the thrill of it. A sensational feature of the production was the singing orchestra of Negro performers under the direction of J. Rosamond Johnson — singing orchestras in theaters have since become common. The plays moved from the Garden Theater to the Garrick, but the stress of war crushed them out.

In 1920, Charles Gilpin was enthusiastically and universally acclaimed for his acting in *The Emperor Jones*. The American stage has seldom seen such an outburst of acclamation. Mr. Gilpin was one of the ten persons voted by the Drama League as having done most for the American theater during the year. Most of the readers of these pages will remember the almost national crisis caused by his invitation to the Drama League Dinner.

And along came *Shuffle Along;* and all of New York flocked to an out-of-the-way theater in West Sixty-third Street to hear the most joyous singing and see the most exhilarating dancing to be found on any stage in the city. The dancing steps originally used by the "policeman" in *Shuffle Along* furnished new material for hundreds of dancing men. *Shuffle Along* was actually an epoch-making musical comedy. Out of *Shuffle Along* came Florence Mills, who, unfortunately, died so young but lived long enough to be acknowledged here and in Europe as one of the finest singing comediennes the stage had ever seen and an artist of positive genius.

In 1923 Roland Hayes stepped out on the American stage in a blaze of glory, making his first appearances as soloist with the Boston Symphony Orchestra, and later with the Philharmonic. Few single artists have packed such crowds into Carnegie Hall and the finest concert halls throughout the country as has Roland Hayes; and, notwithstanding the éclat with which America first received him, his reputation has continued to increase and, besides, he is rated as one of the best box-office attractions in the whole concert field. Miss Marian Anderson appeared as soloist with the Philadelphia Symphony Orchestra and in concert at the Lewisohn Stadium at New York City College. Paul Robeson and J. Rosamond Johnson and Taylor Gordon sang spirituals to large and appreciative audiences in New York and over the country, giving to those songs a fresh interpretation and a new vogue.

Paul Robeson—that most versatile of men, who has made a national reputation as athlete, singer, and actor—played in Eugene O'Neill's *All God's Chillun* and added to his reputation on the stage, and, moreover, put to the test an ancient taboo; he played the principal role opposite a white woman. This feature of the play gave rise to a more acute crisis than did Gilpin's invitation to the Drama League Dinner. Some sensational newspapers predicted race riots and other dire disasters, but nothing of the sort happened; the play went over without a boo. Robeson played the title role in a revival of *The Emperor Jones* and almost duplicated the sensation produced by Gilpin in the original presentation.

There followed on the stage Julius Bledsoe, Rose McClendon, Frank Wilson, and Abbie Mitchell, all of whom gained recognition. At the time of this writing each of these four is playing in a Broadway production. Paradoxical it may seem, but no Negro comedian gained recognition in this decade. Negro comedians have long been a recognized American institution and there are several now before the public who are well known, but their reputations were made before this period. The only new reputations made on the comedy stage were made by women, Florence Mills and Ethel Waters. In addition there are the two famous Smiths, Bessie and Clara, singers of blues and favorites of vaudeville, phonograph, and radio audiences. . . .

During the present decade the individual Negro artist had definitely emerged in three fields, in literature, in the theater, and on the concert stage; in other fields he has not won marked distinction. To point to any achievement of distinction in painting, the

459

Negro must go back of this decade, back to H. O. Tanner, who has lived in Europe for the past thirty-five years; or farther back to E. M. Bannister, who gained considerable recognition a half century ago. Nevertheless, there is the work of W. E. Scott, a mural painter, who lives in Chicago and has done a number of public buildings in the Middle West; and of Archibald J. Motley, who recently held a one-man exhibit in New York which attracted very favorable attention. The drawings of Aaron Douglas have won for him a place among American illustrators. To point to any work of acknowledged excellence in sculpture the Negro must go back of this decade to the work of two women, Edmonia Lewis and Meta Warrick Fuller, both of whom received chiefly in Europe such recognition as they gained. There are several young painters and sculptors who are winning recognition.

But the strangest lack is that with all the great native musical endowment he is conceded to possess, the Negro has not in this most propitious time produced a single outstanding composer. There are competent musicians and talented composers of songs and detached bits of music, but no original composer who, in amount and standard of work and in recognition achieved, is at all comparable with S. Coleridge-Taylor, the English Negro composer. Nor can the Negro in the United States point back of this decade to even one such artist. It is a curious fact that the American Negro through his whole history has done more highly sustained and more fully recognized work in the composition of letters than in the composition of music. It is the more curious when we consider that music is so innately a characteristic method of expression for the Negro.

What, now, is the significance of this artistic activity on the part of the Negro and of its reactions on the American people? I think it is twofold. In the first place, the Negro is making some distinctive contributions to our common cultural store. I do not claim it is possible for these individual artists to produce anything comparable to the folk-art in distinctive values, but I do believe they are bringing something fresh and vital into American art, something from the store of their own racial genius—warmth, color, movement, rhythm, and abandon; depth and swiftness of emotion and the beauty of sensuousness. I believe American art will be richer because of these elements in fuller quantity.

But what is of deeper significance to the Negro himself is the effect that this artistic activity is producing upon his condition and status as a man and citizen. I do not believe it an overstatement to say that the "race problem" is fast reaching the stage of being more a question of national mental attitudes toward the Negro than a question of his actual condition. That is to say, it is not at all the problem of a moribund people sinking into a slough of ignorance, poverty, and decay in the very midst of our civilization and despite all our efforts to save them; that would indeed be a problem. Rather is the problem coming to consist in the hesitation and refusal to open new doors of opportunity at which these people are constantly knocking. In other words, the problem for the Negro is reaching the plane where it is becoming less a matter of dealing with what he is and more a matter of dealing with what America thinks he is.

Now, the truth is that the great majority of Americans have not thought about the Negro at all, except in a vague sort of way and in the form of traditional and erroneous stereotypes. Some of these stereotyped forms of thought are quite absurd, yet they have had serious effects. Millions of Americans have had their opinions and attitudes regarding their fellow colored citizens determined by such a phrase as, "A nigger will steal," or "Niggers are lazy," or "Niggers are dirty."

But there is a common, widespread, and persistent stereotyped idea regarding the Negro, and it is that he is here only to receive; to be shaped into something new and unquestionably better. The common idea is that the Negro reached America intellectually, culturally, and morally empty, and that he is here to be filled – filled with education, filled with religion, filled with morality, filled with culture. In a word, the stereotype is that the Negro is nothing more than a beggar at the gate of the nation, waiting to be thrown the crumbs of civilization.

Through his artistic efforts the Negro is smashing this immemorial stereotype faster than he has ever done through any other method he has been able to use. He is making it realized that he is the possessor of a wealth of natural endowments and that he has long been a generous giver to America. He is impressing upon the national mind the conviction that he is an active and important force in American life; that he is a creator as well as a creature; that he has given as well as received; that he is the potential giver of larger and richer contributions.

In this way the Negro is bringing about an entirely new national conception of himself; he has placed himself in an entirely new light before the American people. I do not think it too much to say that through artistic achievement the Negro has found a means of getting at the very core of the prejudice against him by challenging the Nordic superiority complex. A great deal has been accomplished in this decade of "renaissance." Enough has been accomplished to make it seem almost amazing when we realize that there are less than twenty-five Negro artists who have more or less of national recognition; and that it is they who have chiefly done the work.

A great part of what they have accomplished has been done through the sort of publicity they have secured for the race. A generation ago the Negro was receiving lots of publicity, but nearly all of it was bad. There were front page stories with such headings as, "Negro Criminal," "Negro Brute." Today, one may see undesirable stories, but one may also read stories about Negro singers, Negro actors, Negro authors, Negro poets. The connotations of the very word "Negro" have been changed. A generation ago many Negroes were half or wholly ashamed of the term. Today, they have every reason to be proud of it.

For many years and by many methods the Negro has been overcoming the coarser prejudices against him; and when we consider how many of the subtler prejudices have crumbled, and crumbled rapidly under the process of art creation by the Negro, we are justified in taking a hopeful outlook toward the effect that the increase of recognized individual artists fivefold, tenfold, twentyfold, will have on this most perplexing and vital question before the American people.

Index of Authors

ALLSOP, KENNETH (?-   ), English author. Literary editor (1940s and '50s) of the (London) *Daily Mail*; contributor to *Encounter*; wrote *Adventure Lit Their Star* (1950), *The Angry Decade* (1958), *The Bootleggers* (1961), and *Scan* (1965).

BALDWIN, JAMES (Aug. 2, 1924-   ), author and lecturer on civil rights. Member of the national advisory board of the Congress of Racial Equality; wrote *Go Tell It on the Mountain* (1953), *Nobody Knows My Name* (1961), *Another Country* (1962), *The Fire Next Time* (1963), and *Tell Me How Long the Train's Been Gone* (1968).

BOND, JULIAN (Jan. 14, 1940-   ), public official. Elected to the Georgia Legislature in 1965, he was refused a seat because of his anti-war views. Twice re-elected, he was admitted to the legislature only after the U.S. Supreme Court declared his exclusion unconstitutional, late in 1966. His name was put in nomination for the vice-presidency at the 1968 Democratic Convention, but he withdrew because of the age requirement.

CARMICHAEL, STOKELY (Sept. 12, 1942-   ), civil rights activist. Former field secretary for the Student Nonviolent Coordinating Committee; enunciator of the "black power" slogan in the civil rights movement, co-author of *Black Power* (1968).

CHARLES, RAY (Sept. 23, 1930-   ), entertainer. Blinded by glaucoma, he attended a school for the blind in St. Augustine, Florida. There he garnered a comprehensive musical education, and at the age of 17 set out for Seattle and a show business career. His first national fame came in 1954 with a recording of "I Got a Woman." His musical style combines elements of blues, jazz, country-western, and rock. He has continued to be a successful innovative performer.

CHISHOLM, SHIRLEY ANITA (Nov. 30, 1924-   ), public official, civil rights advocate. After four years in the N.Y. Assembly, she was elected to Congress in 1968, becoming the nation's first black Congresswoman. A strong advocate of women's rights as well as civil rights for blacks, she announced her intention of seeking the 1972 Democratic presidential nomination.

COBBS, PRICE M. (Nov. 2, 1928-   ), psychiatrist. Has worked for over ten years with Negro patients; assistant professor of psychiatry at the University of California, San Francisco Medical Center; author of magazine articles.

COLEMAN, JAMES S. (May 12, 1926-   ), sociologist and educator. Assistant professor of sociology at the University of Chicago (1956-59); professor of social relations at Johns Hopkins University (1959-   ). Author of *Community Conflict* (1957); *The Adolescent Society* (1961); *Adolescents and the Schools* (1965).

DANIELS, JONATHAN W. (April 26, 1902-   ), journalist and author. Editor (1933-42, 1948-   ) of the *Raleigh* (N.C.) *News and Observer*; administrative assistant (1943-45) and press secretary (1945) to F. D. Roosevelt; wrote *A Southerner Dis-*

covers the South (1938), a biography of Harry S. Truman (1950), and *The Time Between the Wars* (1966).

DU BOIS, W. E. BURGHARDT (Feb. 23, 1868-Aug. 27, 1963), educator, editor, and author. Professor of economics and history (1897-1910) and of sociology (1932-44) at Atlanta University; a founder (1909) of the NAACP; editor (1910-32) of *Crisis;* wrote *The Souls of Black Folk* (1903) and edited *Encyclopedia of the Negro* (1933-45).

EDELSON, MARK (?-   ), writer. Freelance writer and contributor to the *National Review.*

EISENHOWER, DWIGHT D. (Oct. 14, 1890-March 28, 1969), soldier and statesman. Thirty-fourth President of the United States (1953-61); supreme Allied commander in North Africa (1942) and in the western Mediterranean (1943); commander in chief of Allied forces in Western Europe (1943-45); general of the Army (1944); member (1945) of the Allied Control Council for Germany; president (1948-53) of Columbia University; supreme commander (1951-52) of NATO forces; wrote *Crusade in Europe* (1948).

FARMER, JAMES (Jan. 12, 1920-   ), civil rights leader. Helped found (1942) the Congress of Racial Equality (CORE); its national chairman (1942-44, 1950) and national director (1961-66); leader of CORE freedom ride (1961); president (1966) of a private antipoverty agency, Center for Community-Action Education, Inc.; wrote *Freedom—When?* (1965).

FRAZIER, E. FRANKLIN (Sept. 24, 1894-May 17, 1962), sociologist. Professor of sociology at Fisk University (1929-34); professor and head of Sociology Department at Howard University (1934-59); did independent research in the West Indies on race and culture contacts (1949); wrote *The*

Negro Family in America (1932), *Negro Youth at the Crossroads* (1940), *The Negro in the U.S.* (1949), and *Black Bourgeoisie* (1957).

GIBSON, KENNETH ALLEN (May 15, 1932-   ), civil engineer and politician. Worked for Newark's housing authority; also active in several civil rights organizations. In the spring of 1970 he was elected mayor of Newark, whose population had become over 60% black and 10% Spanish-speaking. He is one of the first black men to become mayor of a large city.

GLAZER, NATHAN (Feb. 25, 1923-   ), sociologist. On editorial staff of *Commentary* magazine (1945-53); professor of sociology at the University of California at Berkeley (1963-   ); co-author of *The Lonely Crowd* (1950) and *Faces in the Crowd* (1952), author of *The Social Basis of American Communism* (1961).

GRIER, WILLIAM H. (Feb. 7, 1926-   ), psychiatrist. Has worked for over ten years with Negro patients; was assistant professor of psychiatry at Wayne (Mich.) State University; currently assistant professor of psychiatry at University of California, San Francisco Medical Center; director of the San Francisco Child Psychiatric Clinic; on the board of the San Francisco educational TV network.

GRIFFIN, JOHN HOWARD (June 16, 1920-   ), author. After musical studies, became totally blind (1946); turned to writing; regained his sight (1957); toured the South (1960) disguised as a Negro, on assignment from *Sepia* magazine; wrote *The Devil Rides Outside* (1952), *Nuni* (1956), and *Black Like Me* (1961).

GRIMKÉ, FRANCIS J. (1850-1937), clergyman and civil rights leader. After graduation (1878) from Princeton Theological Seminary, went to the Fifteenth Street Presbyterian Church;

464

Washington, D.C., where he remained as pastor until his death; lectured and wrote against segregation in the churches; opposed position taken by Booker T. Washington.

HANDY, W. C. (Nov. 16, 1873-March 28, 1958), composer. Conducted his own orchestra (1903-21); established the popularity of blues music through his "Memphis Blues" (1911) and "St. Louis Blues" (1914); published anthologies of Negro spirituals and blues and studies of Negro musicians.

HARRINGTON, MICHAEL (Feb. 24, 1928-), author. Member (from 1960) of the national executive committee of the Socialist Party; editor 1961-62) of *New America*; chairman (from 1964) of the League for Industrial Democracy; edited *Labor in a Free Society* (with Paul Jacobs, 1959) and wrote *The Other America* (1963).

HARRIS, ROY V. (Oct. 2, 1895-), lawyer and politician. Elected to Georgia House of Representatives from Jefferson County and served 1921-27. He spent one term in the state Senate in 1931, before being returned to the House where he served several more terms and was speaker for several sessions 1937-46. Long influential in state politics, he has not held elective office since 1946, although he has more recently served on the board of regents of the state university. Until February 17, 1972, he was chairman of the Georgia American Party.

HAYDEN, THOMAS (Dec. 11, 1939-), a founder of Students for a Democratic Society. Community worker at Newark, N.J.; active in antiwar and protest movements; made an "unauthorized" trip to North Vietnam in December 1965, in company with Staughton Lynd and Herbert Aptheker; co-author of *The Other Side* (1967), author of *Rebellion in Newark* (1967).

HUGHES, LANGSTON (Feb. 1, 1902-May 22, 1967), author. Wrote short stories (*The Ways of White Folks*, 1934), humorous works (*Simple Speaks His Mind*, 1950), poetry (*The Dream Keeper*, 1932; *Selected Poems*, 1959), opera libretti (*The Barrier*, 1950), lyrics for musical productions (*Street Scene*, 1946).

JACKSON, GEORGE (Sept. 23, 1941-August 21, 1971), born and raised in Chicago, but moved with family to the Watts area of Los Angeles in 1956. Frequently in trouble with the law, he was sentenced to from one year to life in prison in 1960. Self-educated while incarcerated at Paso Robles, Soledad Prison, and San Quentin, he became an articulate spokesman for militant black power. During an apparent prison-break attempt, he was slain, along with four others, at San Quentin. Author of the best-selling *Soledad Brother: The Prison Letters of George Jackson* (1970).

JACKSON, JESSE L. (Oct. 8, 1941-), Baptist clergyman and civil rights activist. While in school he became active in the sit-ins and protest marches of the civil rights movement. In 1966 he was appointed director of Chicago's Southern Christian Leadership Conference office, called Operation Breadbasket. He was ordained in 1968. Relieved of his SCLC post in 1971, he formed People United to Save Humanity (PUSH).

JOHNSON, JAMES WELDON (June 17, 1871-June 26, 1938), lawyer and poet. First Negro lawyer admitted to Florida bar (1897); U.S. consul (1906) in Venezuela and (1909-12) in Nicaragua; a founder and secretary (1916-30) of the National Association for the Advancement of Colored People; professor of creative literature (from 1930) at Fisk University; wrote *Fifty Years and Other Poems* (1917), God's Trombones (1927); edited *The Book of Ameri-*

465

can Negro Poetry (1922).

JOHNSON, THOMAS A. (Oct. 11, 1928-), correspondent for the *New York Times.*

JORDAN, VERNON E. (Aug. 15, 1935-), lawyer, fund raiser, civil rights activist. Georgia field secretary for the NAACP, he became executive director for the United Negro College Fund in 1970. In 1971, he was appointed to succeed the late Whitney Young, Jr., as executive director of the National Urban League.

KENNEDY, JOHN F. (May 29, 1917-Nov. 22, 1963), political leader and statesman. Thirty-fifth President of the United States (1961-63); U.S. representative from Massachusetts 1947-53); U.S. senator (1953-60); wrote *Why England Slept* (1940), *Profiles in Courage* (1956), *The Strategy of Peace* (1960); assassinated Nov. 22, 1963.

KING, MARTIN LUTHER, JR. (Jan. 15, 1929-April 4, 1968), Baptist clergyman and civil rights leader. President of the Southern Christian Leadership Conference; vice-president of the Baptist Teaching Union; leader of voter registration drives throughout the South and the civil rights march on Washington (1963); received Nobel Peace Prize (1964); assassinated April 4, 1968.

LOMAX, LOUIS E. (Aug. 16, 1922-), writer. After a number of years as a newspaperman (1941-58), he is now a free-lance writer and television personality; wrote *The Reluctant African* (1960) and *The Negro Revolt* (1962).

MALCOLM X (Malcolm Little) (May 19, 1925-Feb. 21, 1965), civil rights leader. Dropped out of school (1940) and was sent to prison for burglary (1946); while in prison, became a convert to the Nation of Islam (Black Muslims), eventually rising to second in command of that organiza-

tion; after two trips to African and the Middle East (1964), withdrew from the Muslims and denounced black nationalism; was assassinated Feb. 21, 1965, by members of a rival group.

MILLER, LOREN (1903-July 2, 1967), lawyer. Practised law in Los Angeles, specializing in cases involving discrimination in housing; publisher of a Negro newspaper, the *California Eagle;* served as a vice-president of the NAACP; municipal judge in Los Angeles (?1950-67).

MUHAMMAD, ELIJAH (Elijah Poole) (Oct. 10, 1897-), religious leader. Because of an alleged vision had by his mother that he would deliver the oppressed American Negroes, Elijah was set above his twelve brothers and sisters and took a position of leadership in his family; met (1931) Wali Farad (Wallace D. Fard), founder of the Nation of Islam (Black Muslims), becoming his lieutenant; when Farad mysteriously disappeared (1934), he assumed leadership of the organization; his program one of racial separation, personal reclamation, economic independence, and black unification.

MYRDAL, GUNNAR (Dec. 6, 1898-), Swedish economist and public official. Professor (1933-50) of economics and (1960-) of international economics at the University of Stockholm; legislator (1936-38, 1944-45) and cabinet minister (1945-47); director (1947-57) of UN Economic Commission for Europe; wrote *An American Dilemma: The Negro Problem and Modern Democracy* (Carnegie Endowment report, 1944); *Beyond the Welfare State* (1960); and *Challenge to Affluence* (1963).

RANDOLPH, A. PHILIP (April 15, 1889-), labor leader. Organized (1925) the Brotherhood of Sleeping Car

466

Porters; vice-president (1957-) of the executive council and member of the AFL-CIO.

RIGG, ROBERT B. (Oct. 27, 1913-), army officer. Former intelligence officer and expert in military strategy; author of *War: 1974* (1958).

ROOSEVELT, FRANKLIN D. (Jan. 30, 1882-April 12, 1945), lawyer and statesman. Thirty-second President of the United States (1933-45) and the only President to be elected to a third (and a fourth) term; assistant secretary of the Navy (1913-20) under Wilson; governor of New York (1929-33); initiated national administrative and legislative reforms known as the "New Deal"; chief architect of the United Nations.

SASS, HERBERT RAVENEL (Nov. 2, 1884-Feb. 18, 1958), naturalist and author. Contributor to the *Charleston* (S.C.) *News and Courier* and to the *Atlantic Monthly*; wrote several books on South Carolina history.

TRUMAN, HARRY S. (May 8, 1884-), political leader and statesman. Thirty-third President of the United States (1945-53); presiding judge (1926-34) of Jackson County (Mo.) Court; U.S. senator from Missouri (1935-45); Vice-President of the United States (1945) under F. D. Roosevelt; succeeded to the Presidency upon Roosevelt's death (April 12, 1945).

WARREN, EARL (March 19, 1891-), public official and jurist. Deputy district attorney (1920-25) and district attorney (1925-39) of Alameda County, Calif.; attorney general of California (1939-43); governor (1943-53); chief justice (1953-69) of the U.S. Supreme Court; chairman 1963-64) of the presidential Commission to Investigate the Assassination of John F. Kennedy.

WEAVER, ROBERT C. (Dec. 29, 1907-), economist and first Negro cabinet member. Adviser (1934-37) on Negro affairs to the Department of the Interior; special assistant (1937-40) to the administrator of the Housing Authority; held various advisory and administrative positions in government agencies and private foundations (1940-66); named secretary of the newly created Department of Housing and Urban Development on Jan. 13, 1966; wrote *The Negro Ghetto* (1948) and *The Urban Complex* (1964).

WILKINS, ROY (Aug. 30, 1901-), social welfare executive and civil rights leader. Was managing editor (1923-31) of the *Kansas City Call*; assistant secretary (1931-49), acting secretary (1949-50), administrator (1950, executive secretary (1955-64), and executive director (1965-), of the National Association for the Advancement of Colored People (NAACP).

WOODWARD, C. VANN (Nov. 13, 1908-), one of America's leading historians; professor or lecturer at numerous colleges and universities. He has also been president of the American Historical Association, the Organization of American Historians, and the Southern Historical Society. Among his many books, several deal with the South: *Origins of the New South* (1951); *The Strange Career of Jim Crow* (1955); and *The Burden of Southern History* (1960). Since 1961 he has been Sterling Professor of History at Yale University.

WORKMAN, WILLIAM D., JR. (fl. 1959), author.

WRIGHT, RICHARD (Sept. 4, 1908-Nov. 28, 1960), author. The grandson of slaves, he became a member (1932) of the Communist Party and editor (1937) of the *Daily Worker*; broke left-wing affiliations after World War II and moved to Paris to protest treatment of Negroes in the U.S.; wrote autobiographical works (*Uncle*

467

Tom's Children, 1938, *Black Boy*, 1945); political tracts (*The Color Curtain*, 1956, *White Man, Listen!*, 1957); and novels (*Native Son*, 1940, *The Outsider*, 1953, *The Long Dream*, 1958). Died in Paris.

YOUNG, WHITNEY MOORE, JR. (July 31, 1921-March 11, 1971), civil rights leader and social work administrator. First became associated with the work of the Urban League in St. Paul, Minn. After serving as dean of the School for Social Work in Atlanta 1954-1960, he was appointed executive director of the National Urban League in 1961. Author of several books including *To Be Equal* (1964). Died suddenly in Nigeria while on a tour of Africa.